More critical praise for *Managed Trading* . . .

"*Managed Trading* is worthwhile reading for anyone who is in the business of money management."

> —Jeff Yass
> Managing Director
> Susquehanna Investments

"Jack has written the definitive books on technical and fundamental analysis; now he addresses the ultimate investment strategy— a diversified portfolio of managers. A must-read for institutional investors, pension fund trustees, and money managers."

> —Blair Hull
> Managing Principal
> Hull Trading

"*Managed Trading* is a valuable contribution to the literature on managed futures. Schwager provides a lucid examination of performance evaluation procedures and portfolio considerations. I am confident that this book will be beneficial to investors and trading professionals."

> —Morton S. Baratz
> Executive Vice President and COO
> Allied Capital Asset Management, Inc.

Schwager on Futures

Managed Trading

Schwager on Futures Series

FUNDAMENTAL ANALYSIS
TECHNICAL ANALYSIS
MANAGED TRADING: MYTHS & TRUTHS
A STUDY GUIDE FOR FUNDAMENTAL ANALYSIS
A STUDY GUIDE FOR TECHNICAL ANALYSIS

Schwager on Futures

Managed Trading

Myths & Truths

Jack D. Schwager

John Wiley & Sons, Inc.

New York · Chichester · Brisbane · Toronto · Singapore

With love to my son Daniel,
whose solid character and sense of humor
are a constant source of delight,
who waited patiently, and impatiently, for this book
and its two companion volumes to be completed,
with a promise to make up for our time lost.

Copyright © 1996 by Jack D. Schwager.
Published by John Wiley & Sons, Inc.

Library of Congress Cataloging-in-Publication Data:

Schwager, Jack D., 1948-
    Managed trading: myths and truths/Jack D. Schwager.
      p. cm.
    Includes index.
    ISBN 0-471-02057-5 (cloth: alk. paper)
    1. Commodity futures. 2. Futures. 3. Financial futures.
  4. Foreign exchange futures. I. Title. II. Series.
  HG6046.S393   1996
  332.65'5—dc20   96-10256

Printed in the United States of America

10 9 8 7 6 5 4 3 2 1

Foreword

My experience on Wall Street suggests that the financial world is permeated with mythology. Respected financial executives, who would scoff at the idea of generating profits from fortune-tellers, feel that the direction of financial markets is, to a great extent, predictable. They often offer their views on future market performance unhesitatingly. Other investment professionals believe that the best way to achieve high returns is through the purchase of undervalued assets. Beyond these myths, however, are facts that present an entirely different picture. As an investor or portfolio manager, you should question these presumptions and consider approaches followed by some of the world's great traders. In doing so, you may gain insights that will influence your interpretation of events occurring in the world's evolving financial markets.

While almost everyone on Wall Street has a strong opinion on markets, the fact is that no one can predict with consistent accuracy the future direction of markets or of investment returns. People read the phrase "past performance is not necessarily indicative of future results" and assume the opposite. The future is not predictable, and I have yet to meet anyone on Wall Street or off, with or without a computer or doctorate, who accurately predict future events.

A favorite Wall Street myth is that there are investment bargains. People are always looking to buy something cheaply and sell it when it becomes "properly priced." A close look at truly talented traders would dispel this notion. Great traders know that sustained profits are made by buying something expensive. Whether it is the New York Yankees or Coca-Cola, buying and holding items highly valued is prudent. Whether it is their scarcity value, a sustainable competitive advantage in their market, or extraordinary management, there are reasons why something highly valued is likely to become more so over time.

Another relatively new financial mythology has developed around derivatives. Derivatives were developed as a mechanism to transfer risk from those seeking to avoid it to those seeking to profit from it. In today's world, though, it is difficult to differentiate between those two groups of users. When those who should be using derivatives to reduce risk seek profits and fail, often due to bargain hunting, they make great headlines. The press suggests that derivatives are highly risky and that risk should be avoided at all costs. The view that derivatives are dangerous and speculative is promulgated. The facts do not support this view, however.

When used properly, derivatives serve an important role in the well-diversified investment portfolio. Managed futures is a prudent way to utilize the benefits derivatives offer investors. Simply stated, they are a method for decreasing portfolio risk without sacrificing investment returns. When building portfolios, most institutional investors fear conventionality risk—the danger that they may not perform as well as their peers or a benchmark. Little thought has been given to a scenario where long-term returns are flat or negative. This is the investor's risk. The conventional view is as follows: If the S&P makes an inflation-adjusted return of negative 10 percent over a decade, and the manager experiences only a negative 7 percent return, the manager has been successful. Of course, the manager would not have protected the purchasing power of their clients, the investors. And that is, in fact, their job.

As we near the millennium, not only must investors contend with global market and counterparty risks, but we may also face huge systemic problems due to the unrealistic, often unduly optimistic, assumptions made by the planners of the world's largest financial institutions. Examples of faulty or, at worst, irrational funding assumptions may be at the core of many of our societies' major institutions—whether Social Security, Medicare, or the larger public and private public pension funds of the world. Consider how these institutions will meet their obligations if securities prices fail to constantly rise.

One of my primary assessments in today's global marketplace is that systemic risk in the financial markets is far higher than ever before in human history. Never before have linkages among financial markets worldwide been so strong. Never before has there been the incredible speed with which assets can be transported, transacted, and liquidated. The combination of transaction speed and the rise of "stateless" assets has broad implications for fiduciaries, especially in light of the degree of conventionality risk present in pension and other long-term portfolios. No one seems to remember that the Dow lost over 70 percent of its purchasing power between 1961 and 1982.

It is my conviction that the managed futures industry has an important role to play in protecting traditional investment portfolios. Virtually everyone in the managed futures industry knows if you take 5 percent of a stock portfolio and put that 5 percent into managed futures, you get a higher return on the overall stock portfolio and lower volatility. Those who have incorporated managed futures in their investment mix have found them to be an effective and responsible way to enhance their risk-adjusted returns. It is, therefore, simply prudent for a portfolio manager to undertake such a strategy.

The compelling case for including managed futures in an investment portfolio is one of the pivotal issues addressed by *Managed Trading: Myths & Truths*. In the exhaustively researched final chapter of this volume, Jack Schwager demonstrates that managed futures can significantly improve portfolio performance under almost any set of reasonable assumptions.

In *Managed Trading,* Schwager also explores the most important issues surrounding the use of managed futures as a viable investment vehicle. Using much of his own quantitative research in addition to summarizing the findings of prior empirical studies, he seeks to provide conclusive answers to the problems all investors face when analyzing the performance of managed futures advisors. This book is invaluable to institutional and individual investors who are contemplating the use of managed futures in their portfolios, as well as those who are already well acquainted with the benefits of such investments. Additionally, members of the managed futures community will find this book to be among the most authoritative yet written on the subject.

Although you might not expect a book of this type to be controversial, its definitive approach to answering tough questions will cause a stir. Some readers in the managed futures community may well disagree with a number of positions taken on the relevant issues, but with controversy comes greater awareness of the work that needs to be done and, ultimately, the progress that can be made in educating investors about the benefits of managed futures. Adopting standardized methodologies for performance analysis, including appropriate benchmarks, should be a primary goal of the industry. This book offers concrete recommendations with regard to these issues, although the debate over which analytical methodologies are most appropriate will probably not end here.

In Part One, readers will find useful tools and techniques for properly evaluating CTA returns. Investors are sometimes puzzled by how their performance can vary significantly from an advisor's reported performance data. This book offers a detailed analysis of the factors that determine an investor's net results.

A number of statistical measures are normally used to evaluate the returns of managed futures advisors, but few are actually meaningful. For example, the Sharpe Ratio is widely used as a method of calculating risk-adjusted returns. I feel that Jack's modified version of this statistic does a much better job of describing the risk/reward of a managed futures investment.

For those who may be wondering, Part Two asks the question, "Is Past Performance Predictive of Future Performance?" The answer, which is multifaceted, may surprise you.

In *Managed Trading,* Jack Schwager has performed an outstanding service to investors who want to understand more about the nature and benefits of returns from managed futures. Using the tools provided in this book, institutional and individual investors alike will be able to position themselves well for long-term success by supplementing their traditional portfolios with a viable investment that has characteristics like no other. In fact, it is the attribute of noncorrelation to stocks and bonds that truly makes managed futures "a prudent part of every portfolio."

JOHN W. HENRY

Westport, Connecticut
July 1996

Preface

The goal of this book is nothing short of shattering widely held, but totally erroneous, conceptions and beliefs regarding managed trading. Some of the key points demonstrated in this book include:

- Why "actual" performance results may be a misnomer.
- Why many investors in managed futures lose money even when they select a winning commodity trading advisor (CTA).
- Why the actual performance of funds and pools invariably falls far short of prospectus results.
- Why superior performing money managers in the past cannot be assumed to be more likely to realize relatively superior performance in the *future*.
- Why it is usually better to invest in CTAs when they are experiencing drawdowns as opposed to when they are on winning streaks.
- Why rebalancing—*shifting assets from winners to losers* at fixed time intervals (e.g., monthly)—tends to improve performance in the vast majority of cases.
- Why all conventional CTA indexes are misleading.
- Why diversification almost invariably improves the odds of obtaining superior performance, in return/risk terms.
- The simple explanation for the contradictory results reached by academic researchers regarding the merits of adding managed futures to standard stock/bond portfolios.

Investors are truly their own worst enemy. The natural instincts of most investors lead them to do exactly the wrong thing with uncanny persistence. Investors who understand these flaws and are aware of the fallacies in conventional assumptions regarding managed trading should have an important advantage in investment success. It is hoped that reading this book will contribute to that understanding.

JACK D. SCHWAGER

New York, New York
July 1996

Acknowledgments

In writing this book, I have been very fortunate to draw on the advice and aid of some of the industry's leading experts. First and foremost, I thank Professor Scott Irwin of Ohio State University for providing me with a stack of academic articles pertinent to the research focus of this book. Professor Irwin's encompassing knowledge of the prior research in the field saved me untold hours of research time. In addition, his own articles on managed futures were probably the most lucid I found. Finally, I thank Professor Irwin for his meticulous review of the manuscript and his many helpful suggestions.

I am grateful also to Professor Wade Brorsen for his extremely thorough review of the manuscript and his many insightful comments. Although the numerous revisions engendered by Professor Brorsen's suggestions caused my publisher much grief, they significantly improved the precision of the work.

Whereas Professors Brorsen and Irwin are among managed futures' leading theorists, John Henry is certainly one of the industry's leading practitioners. By any measure—assets managed, cumulative trading profits, length of track record—John Henry is one of the most successful CTAs. I am grateful to John for writing the Foreword, as well as for his on-target suggestions that led to the replacement of some unduly broad generalizations with more precise language.

My thanks also to Mort Baratz, one of the pioneers in championing the role of managed futures in investment portfolios. Mort offered a number of suggestions after reviewing the manuscript. All were sound and incorporated.

The insights and comments provided by Arthur Bell, Jr., regarding performance reporting issues were invaluable in verifying the accuracy of the material in Chapters 1 and 2, providing the necessary corrections, and identifying desirable clarifications. I consider Arthur to be the foremost expert on accounting issues in the managed futures industry, and I greatly appreciate his thorough review of the aforementioned chapters.

I thank Professor Franklin Edwards of Columbia University and Dr. James Park for authoring an excellent overview and evaluation of the merit of managed futures as a portfolio investment, and most particularly for the comprehensive summary table in their article, which has been reproduced in this book. This table succinctly summarized prior research on the subject so well that it spared me the need to write a chapter covering the same material.

I thank Richard Oberuc of Burlington Hall Asset Management for providing the description of the risk of ruin, which has been incorporated in this book.

Professor Thomas Schneeweis of the University of Massachusetts provided me with numerous studies conducted by his research group: Center for International Security and Derivative Markets. These studies, which covered many of the same issues discussed in this book, provided a very useful reference source, and I am appreciative of Professor Schneeweis's assistance.

I thank David McCarthy of Global Asset Management for giving me his unpublished thesis, which contained useful research and insights on the relationship between past and future performance.

The managed futures industry is serviced by a number of excellent statistical services. These services were quite helpful in providing necessary research data, as well as granting permission to reproduce selected charts and tables. Specifically, I would like to thank the following:

- Philip Aouad of Refco Information Services (see credit at the end of these acknowledgments)
- Lois Peltz of Managed Account Reports
- Sol Waksman of the Barclay Trading Group
- John Sundt of Stark Research Inc.

My thanks as well to my partner and friend, Louis Lukac, without whom I probably would never have become a CTA, and hence would never have acquired the experience and knowledge that allowed me to write this book. I also thank Louis for catching some errors in the manuscript.

Finally, I thank my wife Jo Ann, and my children Daniel, Zachary, and Samantha for their patience, grace, and understanding, which made this book possible.

The computer CTA database used in the original research studies contained in this book was provided courtesy of Refco Information Service, Inc., One World Trade Center, 200 Liberty Street, New York, N.Y. 10281 (212-693-7397). The analytical software employed—ENCORR/Analyzer and Optimizer— was provided courtesy of Ibbotson Associates, 225 North Michigan Avenue, Suite 700, Chicago, Ill. 60601 (312-616-1620).

J.D.S.

Contents

PART TWO: IS PAST PERFORMANCE PREDICTIVE OF FUTURE PERFORMANCE?

Introduction

THE SCOPE OF THE BOOK

During the past decade, managed futures have become an increasingly important alternative asset class. This book explores a range of topics related to the evaluation of managed futures as a stand-alone investment and as a component of a diversified investment portfolio.

Part One: Performance Issues

The first part of the book deals with a variety of factors related to the evaluation of the performance records of individual money managers, referred to in the industry as commodity trading advisors (CTAs). Particular attention is paid to the potential pitfalls in comparing the performance records of individual CTAs with those of other CTAs and industry indexes. This section is most relevant to those involved in CTA selection, as well as regulators who establish the rules and guidelines for performance reporting. For most other readers, a detailed comprehension of all the topics discussed in this section is unnecessary, and an understanding of the broad issues raised and the potential pitfalls in interpreting performance records will suffice.

The subject of performance evaluation is divided into five chapters:

- Chapter 1 explains why "actual" results reported in CTA disclosure documents may sometimes be a misnomer.
- Chapter 2 examines a variety of factors that could severely distort performance results, including additions and withdrawals, notional funding, extracted results, and composite tables. This chapter also explains the important distinction between hypothetical and simulated results.
- Chapter 3 provides an overview of performance measures, with a particular focus on the potential drawbacks of these statistics and the

pitfalls in their interpretation. The chapter also introduces a new performance measure—the Return Risk Ratio—that appears to more closely describe an investor's intuitive sense of return/risk than does the widely used Sharpe Ratio.

- Chapter 4 explains the importance of using identical assumptions and data definitions when comparing performance results for different CTAs.
- Chapter 5 explains why all conventional indexes of CTA performance overstate return/risk.

Part Two: Is Past Performance Predictive of Future Performance?

The assumption that past performance is a good indicator of future performance is taken for granted by many investors. It shouldn't be. The findings in Part Two will no doubt be quite surprising to many investors. This section encompasses the following subjects:

- Chapter 6 demonstrates that prospectus returns are a very poor indication of future returns and explains why this is the case.
- Chapter 7 reviews the key academic literature that addresses the question of whether past performance can predict future performance and reconciles the contradictory conclusions reached by these different studies.
- Chapter 8 contains original, up-to-date research on the same question.

Part Three: Investment and Portfolio Issues

The final part of the book focuses on a number of practical issues related to investment. Some of the investment advice offered strongly contradicts the conventional wisdom. The topics covered include:

- Chapter 9 explains the pitfalls of implementing an investment when it is doing particularly well and provides empirical proof demonstrating that entering an investment on a drawdown is usually a better strategy than entering it on an upside excursion in equity.
- Chapter 10 explains the rationale for shifting assets from better-performing CTAs in a pool to poorer-performing CTAs, and provides empirical proof for this counterintuitive proposition.

- Chapter 11 considers the question of whether diversification is beneficial.
- Chapter 12 explores the question of whether managed futures should be included in investment portfolios and provides a comprehensive empirical study that unambiguously concludes it should.

THE BASICS

Although this book is primarily aimed at participants in the managed futures industry—fund and pool operators, money managers, market regulators, existing investors, and academic researchers—much of the material and many of the key conclusions are relevant to any serious investor. In fact, it is my sincere belief that most investors could improve the performance of their overall portfolios by applying the advice in this volume. Therefore, this preliminary section addresses some of the basic questions that are pertinent to readers who have little or no experience in the field, but may be interested in acquiring the knowledge to make intelligent decisions regarding managed futures investment. Readers who already understand the basics of managed futures can skip ahead to Chapter 1.

What Are Managed Futures?

Today's futures markets encompass all of the world's major market groups: domestic interest rates (e.g., T-bonds), foreign interest rates (e.g., German bund), domestic stock indexes (e.g., S&P 500), foreign stock indexes (e.g., FTSE 100), currencies (e.g., Japanese yen), precious metals (e.g., gold), energy (e.g., crude oil), and agricultural markets (e.g., corn). Although the futures markets had their origin in agricultural commodities, this sector now accounts for less than one-fifth of total futures trading.

Managed futures are investments that seek to earn a return from trading profits in futures markets and other related markets (e.g., interbank currency, spot and forward physical commodities, interest rate instruments, futures options, and over-the-counter options). The traders who manage these investments are called commodity trading advisors (CTAs). There is a wide variety in the market sectors traded by different CTAs. Some CTAs trade a broadly diversified group of futures markets, while others may specialize in a single market or market sector. Some CTAs trade only futures, while others also trade in one or more of the aforementioned related markets. The trading styles used by CTAs also vary greatly. Some CTAs use only fundamental analysis, some only technical analysis, and some a hybrid of the two. Some CTAs base their trading decisions on fully automated computer programs, while others make discretionary trading decisions. Some CTAs seek to profit from price trends, some by anticipating trend reversals, and some by taking advantage of price disparities in related markets.

The essence of a managed futures investment is that returns are dependent on trading profits (short as well as long positions), as opposed to buy-and-hold positions. Thus the profit or loss realized in a managed futures investment will depend on the skill of the trader and the degree to which market conditions are favorable to the trading strategies employed.[1] In contrast, in a typical equity mutual fund, profit or loss will depend primarily on whether the stock market is rising and secondly on the market selection skill of the manager (i.e., the ability to buy stocks that do better than a broad index). Another way of viewing this distinction is that the success of a managed futures investment will depend on the ability of traders to correctly anticipate the direction of the markets traded,[2] whereas the success of a typical mutual fund investment will depend primarily on the price direction of the stock market being up.

There are three basic types of managed futures investments: (1) individual managed accounts, (2) private pools, and (3) public funds. This list is in descending order of the minimum size investment accepted. Although public funds allow much smaller investments than private pools or individual managed accounts (many CTAs do not accept accounts under $1 million), they also usually have higher total costs (fees plus commissions).

An individual managed account is simply a futures account in which all trading activity is directed by a CTA (in contrast to a conventional futures account in which trading decisions are made by the investor, either independently or with advice from a broker). A description of pools and funds is provided by the following excerpt taken from *Managed Futures in the Institutional Portfolio* by Charles Epstein (Wiley, 1992):

> All pools and funds are generally organized as limited partnerships in the United States and in many ways function similarly to mutual funds. Each is constructed to offer more flexibility than partnerships enjoy under the Investment Company Act of 1940. As limited partnerships, funds and pools have several distinct advantages over individually managed accounts.
>
> In a limited partnership, for example, an investor's risk is restricted to his original investment. Additionally, limited partnerships receive simplified

---

[1]The latter factor may well be the more important. Using trend-following traders as an example, low-skilled traders in markets that witness sustained trends are likley to do better than high-skilled traders in markets characterized by choppy, sideways price movement.

[2]A small minority of CTAs, however, seek to earn profits by taking advantage of pricing inefficiencies between related markets, implementing a long position in one market versus a short position in another, as opposed to making trades that are price-directional bets.

monthly reports and enjoy additional diversification that can only be achieved by pooling the capital of several investors. Limited partnerships also must pay any ongoing costs from an offering, such as audit and legal expenses.

"Fund" generally refers to a public offering registered with the Securities and Exchange Commission (SEC) in which units are publicly offered for a limited period. There is generally no subsequent offering of units once the original period has expired. Funds generally have the smallest minimum investment requirements and as such, have been largely used by individual investors. "Pools" generally refer to private limited partnerships that are subject to securities regulations affecting private placements. Pools are developed by a CPO and are offered by private placement to a limited number of nonaccredited investors and to an unlimited number of accredited investors. (An accredited investor is one who meets pre-defined suitability and income guidelines.)

The aggregate amount of trading capital in a pool is generally lower than that found in funds, but the number of limited partners in a pool is always fewer than those in funds. Because of this structure, pools often have less overhead which can reduce the partner's costs. Another benefit of pools is their ability to limit the maximum number of partners. This gives the general partner greater investment management flexibility. Pools can also accept ongoing investments from the partners once the initial subscription period has ended.

What Are the Costs in Managed Futures Investments?

Ongoing costs consist of three elements: (1) commissions, (2) management fees, and (3) profit incentive fees. In addition to these three basic charges that apply to virtually all managed futures investments, some funds may also charge an annual administrative fee or keep a portion of interest income. Funds and pools may also charge an up-front load to pay for organization costs.

Commissions are usually charged on a per-round-turn basis, but it has become increasingly common for some funds to cap commissions at an annualized fixed percentage of equity (typically, 7–10%). In the early to mid-1980s round-turn commissions were often as high as $50–$80. Round-turn commissions are now typically under $25 and often less than $15.

The management fee is a monthly charge based on an annualized percentage of total assets (typically, 1–4% per year). The profit incentive fee is usually a quarterly charge equal to a percentage of new net profits (typically, 20–30%). Combined management and profit incentive fees have also been declining. For example, nowadays a typical management and profit incentive fee combination might be 2% and 20%, compared with 6% and 15% 10 to 15 years ago. (At a net annual profit of 20% or less, each 1% management fee is equivalent to a profit incentive fee of 5% or more. In this context, fees have declined by about one-third relative to earlier levels.) The significant decline in commissions and fees witnessed since the early to mid-1980s will enhance the future attractiveness of managed futures as an investment vehicle.

Why Are Managed Futures Important to the Investor?

The importance of managed futures to investors pivots on one key fact: Over the long-term, managed futures are almost totally uncorrelated with stocks and bonds. Consequently, managed futures provide excellent diversification when added to a conventional stock/bond portfolio. It has been mathematically demonstrated that a noncorrelated asset can enhance portfolio performance if its return merely exceeds the risk-free return (i.e., T-bill rate). The addition of managed futures to a portfolio can increase the portfolio return, decrease the portfolio risk, or some combination of the two. This essential aspect of managed futures is explored in great detail in the final chapter of this book.

What Are the Sources of Information on a Managed Futures Investment?

Information about a CTA (background of principals, trading methods, fees, etc.) and performance statistics are available in a disclosure document. There are also a number of commercial services (listed in Chapter 3) that report CTA performance. Information on futures funds and pools are provided in prospectuses.

INDUSTRY GROWTH

In practical terms, managed futures represents a relatively new investment sector. Managed futures were virtually nonexistent prior to the late 1970s. Even as recently as 1985, total assets under management in all futures products were estimated to be under $2 billion. The industry grew dramatically between 1986 and 1993, with estimated assets under management mushrooming from under $2 billion to nearly $20 billion. This growth coincided with the expanding acceptance of managed futures as a reasonable component in an overall investment portfolio, reflecting the sector's competitive long-term returns vis-à-vis alternative investments and its ideal diversification properties: near-zero correlation with returns in the stock and bond markets.

During the past three years, total assets under management have stagnated near the $20 billion level. This leveling-off process was probably a consequence of excessive growth during the 1986–1992 period, as well as the industry's lackluster performance during 1992–1995—two factors that are probably not unrelated. In coming years, the managed futures industry's capacity should continue to grow steadily, albeit not at the exponential rate of the late 1980s and early 1990s, as trading volumes in individual futures markets expand and new futures markets are developed. Therefore, managed futures will remain a significant investment sector that will probably grow more prominent over time.

Part One

PERFORMANCE ISSUES

1 Why "Actual" Trading Results Are Sometimes a Misnomer

"Actual" results refer to monthly return figures derived in accordance with procedures defined by the Commodity Futures Trading Commission (CFTC). Specifically, for each month, *percent return* is defined as the net dollar profit/loss divided by the beginning month equity. The *net dollar profit/loss* is simply the gross trading profit/loss increased by interest income and reduced by commissions, management fees, and performance incentive fees.[1] The monthly percent returns in an "actual" performance table therefore represent the actual percent returns realized by investors in the past. Sounds eminently fair, doesn't it? As we shall see, however, although "actual" results often provide a realistic representation of past performance, in some instances, "actual" results can yield a grossly distorted performance picture as viewed from the perspective of a current investor.

In order to illustrate this point, Figure 1.1 compares the net asset values (NAVs)[2] of commodity trading advisor (CTA) A and CTA B.[3] If you were told that both graph lines were based on "actual" trading results, calculated in accordance with CFTC requirements, which CTA would you be likely to choose? The answer is so obviously CTA A that you know I am going to tell

---

[1]We avoid the complication of intramonth additions/withdrawals, which will be addressed separately in Chapter 2.

[2]The NAV at the end of any given month is equal to the starting NAV value (usually assumed to be 1,000, but sometimes set at 1.0 or 100) multiplied by the product of all returns expressed as factors of 1.0. For example, if the starting NAV value is 1,000 and the first three monthly returns are +4%, −2%, and +3%, the NAV at the end of the third month would equal 1,049.776 (1,000 × 1.04 × 0.98 × 1.03 = 1049.776).

[3]In the futures industry, most money managers (i.e., those registered with the CFTC) are called *commodity trading advisors* (CTAs), an unfortunately inappropriate choice of names. In this book, the industry-specific name "CTA" and the more generic term "money manager" are used interchangeably.

Figure 1.1
NAV COMPARISON: CTA A VERSUS CTA B

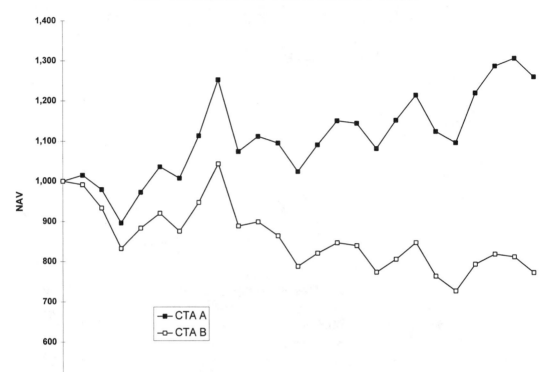

you CTA B. But why? Suppose you are now provided with the additional information that CTA A is a T-bond floor trader who has decided to trade off-the-floor, while CTA B is an off-the-floor trader who had to accept a very high commission rate structure in order to raise funds for management in his startup years. (While established CTAs will resist high commission costs because of its negative impact on their "actual" trading results, startup CTAs may sometimes have to accede to uncomfortably high commission costs as a precondition to receiving funds to manage, since it is extremely difficult to raise trading equity without a prior track record.)

You probably can now see the gist of the explanation for the paradox just presented. CTA A's commission costs will be going up dramatically as he switches from trading on the floor to trading off the floor. At the same time, CTA B, who has now established a track record, will be able to negotiate substantially lower commission costs on equity raised from brokerage firms.

This is not intended to imply that brokerage firms will routinely seek to charge excessive commissions on managed trading agreements. In fact, most reputable brokerage firms will make an effort to keep commission costs fair and competitive. However, some individual brokers or small brokerage operations (particularly non-U.S. ones) may seek to maximize their own commission income at the expense of their clients, and in our example, it is assumed that this is the type of entity that provided trading funds to CTA B in his startup years.

Can realistic commission cost assumptions alone be sufficient to offset the wide gap between CTA A and CTA B? Indeed they can. Assume that as a floor trader CTA A averaged 12,000 round-turn contract transactions per year, per $1 million managed, a perfectly reasonable estimate for a floor trader. Further assume that CTA A's commission cost was $5 per round-turn trade as a floor trader and will rise to $15 per trade when he makes the transition to being an off-the-floor trader. At the assumed 12,000 contracts per year, per $1 million traded (1,000 contracts per month), this factor would reduce his performance by 1.0 percent, per month: (–$10 × 1,000)/$1,000,000.

As for CTA B, assume that in order to raise initial funds for management without a prior track record, he had to agree to a commission structure of $95 per round turn trade. (Although this figure may sound high, I can assure you that I know of examples of even higher commission rates under such circumstances.) Assume that CTA B trades 3,600 round-turn contracts per year, per $1 million, a reasonable figure for an off-the-floor trader. If CTA B is now able to negotiate the same $15 per round-turn commission cost structure, his average profit per trade will increase by $80 per round turn. At the assumed 3,600 contracts per year, per $1 million traded (300 contracts per month), this factor would boost his performance by 2.4 percent, per month: ($80 × 300)/$1,000,000.

Table 1.1 derives the month-ending NAVs for CTA A for the given stream of gross monthly percent returns (expressed as factors of 1), reduced by CTA A's commission costs[4] and a 25 percent quarterly profit incentive fee. (It is assumed that both CTA A and CTA B receive a 0/25 compensation—0 percent management fee and 25 percent profit incentive fee. For simplicity of exposition, we assume that CTA A and CTA B are not credited with any interest rate income.) Table 1.2 derives the month-ending NAVs for CTA B, assuming that CTA B realizes the *exact same* stream of gross monthly percent returns, reduced by the same profit incentive fees, with the only difference being the commission costs ($95/round turn). The NAVs derived in Tables 1.1 and 1.2 are the NAVs that were shown in Figure 1.1.

---

[4]Commissions implied by the assumed 1,000 trades per month, per $1 million of equity, at $5 round turn are equivalent to a commission rate of 0.5 percent (0.005) of beginning month NAV ($5 × 1,000 ÷ $1,000,000 = 0.005).

Table 1.1
NAV FOR CTA A

Month	Beginning Month NAV	Gross Percent Return (Expressed as a Factor of 1)	Gross Profit/Loss	Commissions[a]	Cumulative Net Profit/Loss Since Last Incentive Charge	Quarterly Profit Incentive[b]	Ending Month NAV
Jan	1,000.00	1.02	20.00	5.00	15.00	0.00	1,015.00
Feb	1,015.00	0.97	−30.45	5.08	−20.53	0.00	979.48
Mar	979.48	0.92	−78.36	4.90	−103.78	0.00	896.22
Apr	896.22	1.09	80.66	4.48	−27.60	0.00	972.40
May	972.40	1.07	68.07	4.86	35.60	0.00	1,035.60
Jun	1,035.60	0.98	−20.71	5.18	9.71	2.43	1,007.29
Jul	1,007.29	1.11	110.80	5.04	105.76	0.00	1,113.05
Aug	1,113.05	1.13	144.70	5.57	244.90	0.00	1,252.18
Sep	1,252.18	0.88	−150.26	6.26	88.37	22.09	1,073.57
Oct	1,073.57	1.04	42.94	5.37	37.57	0.00	1,111.14
Nov	1,111.14	0.99	−11.11	5.56	20.91	0.00	1,094.47
Dec	1,094.47	0.94	−65.67	5.47	−50.23	0.00	1,023.33
Jan	1,023.33	1.07	71.63	5.12	16.28	0.00	1,089.85
Feb	1,089.85	1.06	65.39	5.45	76.23	0.00	1,149.79
Mar	1,149.79	1.02	23.00	5.75	93.47	23.37	1,143.67
Apr	1,143.67	0.95	−57.18	5.72	−62.90	0.00	1,080.77
May	1,080.77	1.07	75.65	5.40	7.35	0.00	1,151.02
Jun	1,151.02	1.08	92.08	5.76	93.67	23.42	1,213.93
Jul	1,213.93	0.93	−84.97	6.07	−91.04	0.00	1,122.88
Aug	1,122.88	0.98	−22.46	5.61	−119.12	0.00	1,094.81
Sept	1,094.81	1.12	131.38	5.47	6.79	1.70	1,219.02
Oct	1,219.02	1.06	73.14	6.10	67.05	0.00	1,286.06
Nov	1,286.06	1.02	25.72	6.43	86.34	0.00	1,305.35
Dec	1,305.35	0.98	−26.11	6.53	53.70	13.43	1,259.29

[a]Commissions are assumed to equal 0.0005 of beginning month NAV (1,000 trades per month, per $1 million, at $5 round turn).

[b]Profit incentive fee paid quarterly and assumed to equal 25 percent of cumulative net new profits since payment of last incentive fee. It should be noted, however, that in practice, although the profit incentive fee is paid quarterly, it would be accrued monthly. For clarity of exposition, this table and the other tables in this chapter do not show these intraquarter accruals. Appendix 1 at the end of this book provides a counterpart for Table 1.1, with accruals shown in accordance with CFTC accounting regulations. Analogous tables would apply in practice to the other tables shown in this chapter.

Table 1.2
NAV FOR CTA B

Month	Beginning Month NAV	Gross Percent Return (Expressed as a Factor of 1)	Gross Profit/Loss	Commissions[a]	Cumulative Net Profit/Loss Since Last Incentive Charge	Quarterly Profit Incentive[b]	Ending Month NAV
Jan	1,000.00	1.02	20.00	28.50	−8.50	0.00	991.50
Feb	991.50	0.97	−29.75	28.26	−66.50	0.00	933.50
Mar	933.50	0.92	−74.68	26.60	−167.79	0.00	832.21
Apr	832.21	1.09	74.90	23.72	−116.61	0.00	883.39
May	883.39	1.07	61.84	25.18	−79.95	0.00	920.05
Jun	920.05	0.98	−18.40	26.22	−124.57	0.00	875.43
Jul	875.43	1.11	96.30	24.95	−53.22	0.00	946.78
Aug	946.78	1.13	123.08	26.98	42.88	0.00	1,042.88
Sep	1,042.88	0.88	−125.15	29.72	−111.99	0.00	888.01
Oct	888.01	1.04	35.52	25.31	−101.78	0.00	898.22
Nov	898.22	0.99	−8.98	25.60	−136.36	0.00	863.64
Dec	863.64	0.94	−51.82	24.61	−212.79	0.00	787.21
Jan	787.21	1.07	55.10	22.44	−180.12	0.00	819.88
Feb	819.88	1.06	49.19	23.37	−154.30	0.00	845.70
Mar	845.70	1.02	16.91	24.10	−161.48	0.00	838.52
Apr	838.52	0.95	−41.93	23.90	−227.31	0.00	772.69
May	772.69	1.07	54.09	22.02	−195.24	0.00	804.76
Jun	804.76	1.08	64.38	22.94	−153.80	0.00	846.20
Jul	846.20	0.93	−59.23	24.12	−237.15	0.00	762.85
Aug	762.85	0.98	−15.26	21.74	−274.15	0.00	725.85
Sep	725.85	1.12	87.10	20.69	−207.73	0.00	792.27
Oct	792.27	1.06	47.54	22.58	−182.77	0.00	817.23
Nov	817.23	1.02	16.34	23.29	−189.72	0.00	810.28
Dec	810.28	0.98	−16.21	23.09	−229.02	0.00	770.98

[a]Commissions are assumed to equal 0.0285 of beginning month NAV (300 trades per month, per $1 million, at $95 round turn).

[b]Profit incentive fee paid quarterly and assumed to equal 25 percent of cumulative net new profits since payment of last incentive fee. These are equal to 0 in every period because no ending-quarter NAV exceeds the 1,000 starting NAV level. It should be noted, however, that in practice, although the profit incentive fee is paid quarterly, it would be accrued monthly. For clarity of exposition, this table does not show these intraquarter accruals.

Now, here is the crux of the matter. A new investor will not be aided by the fact that CTA A had very low commissions in the past, nor will he be hurt by the fact that CTA B paid exorbitant commission costs in the past, since both CTA A and CTA B will be exposed to equivalent commission costs in the future. *The new investor will be concerned about the implications of past performance, given the cost structure his investment will experience, not the cost structure experienced by past investors!*

Tables 1.3 and 1.4 show what happens to NAV values if the current cost structure is used to adjust the past performance record. As was previously discussed, CTA A will see his performance go down by 1.0 percent per month, while CTA B will see his performance rise by 2.4 percent per month. Figure 1.2 now compares the resulting adjusted NAVs. If CTA A and CTA B continue to trade *with exactly the same skill and success rate as in the past*, Figure 1.2 will represent the relevant track record for new investors. Note that in sharp contrast to the implications of Figure 1.1, when the two sets of past results are adjusted to reflect equal commission rates, as they are in Tables 1.3 and 1.4 and Figure 1.2, CTA B now appears to be the clearly superior performer.

Of course, actual comparisons between CTA track records will usually not involve as extreme a distortion as in our example. However, while the degree to which "actual" results overstated CTA A's performance and understated CTA B's performance is hardly typical, these examples are consistent with actual situations. The intention of our illustration was to show the range of distortion possible in comparisons using "actual" performance tables.

A table that adjusts past performance for the cost structure relevant to a new investor is called a *pro forma* table. It is the pro forma table that shows results that are relevant to new investors, and from the perspective of new investors, these results are far more actual than "actual" results. Ironically, CFTC regulations require "actual" results, not pro forma results. As was seen in our example, this can lead to highly misleading comparisons between CTA track records.

Actually, there is more to the story than commission cost changes. The effect of slippage—the difference between actual fills and the midpoint between bid and asked prices—can often significantly swamp commission costs. The off-the-floor trader has negative slippage in that he will usually have to buy at the higher asked price and sell at the lower bid price. Floor traders, however, have positive slippage—that is, they will typically buy at the lower bid price and sell at the higher asked price, with an off-the-floor customer on the other side of the trade. This market-making activity is in fact how many floor traders make a living.

CTA B, who was previously an off-the-floor trader, remains so, and therefore does not experience any change in his slippage costs. CTA A, however, will see the slippage factor reversed from positive to negative. This

Table 1.3
NAV FOR CTA A AT $15 ROUND-TURN COMMISSION

Month	Beginning Month NAV	Profit/Loss as a Factor of 1	Gross Profit/Loss	Commissions[a]	Cumulative Net Profit/Loss Since Last Incentive Charge	Quarterly Profit Incentive[b]	Ending Month NAV
Jan	1,000.00	1.02	20.00	15.00	5.00	0.00	1,005.00
Feb	1,005.00	0.97	−30.15	15.08	−40.23	0.00	959.78
Mar	959.78	0.92	−76.78	14.40	−131.40	0.00	868.60
Apr	868.60	1.09	78.17	13.03	−66.26	0.00	933.74
May	933.74	1.07	65.36	14.01	−14.90	0.00	985.10
Jun	985.10	0.98	−19.70	14.78	−49.38	0.00	950.62
Jul	950.62	1.11	104.57	14.26	40.93	0.00	1,040.93
Aug	1,040.93	1.13	135.32	15.61	160.63	0.00	1,160.63
Sep	1,160.63	0.88	−139.28	17.41	3.95	0.99	1,002.96
Oct	1,002.96	1.04	40.12	15.04	25.07	0.00	1,028.04
Nov	1,028.04	0.99	−10.28	15.42	−0.63	0.00	1,002.33
Dec	1,022.33	0.94	−60.14	15.04	−75.80	0.00	927.16
Jan	927.16	1.07	64.90	13.91	−24.81	0.00	978.15
Feb	978.15	1.06	58.69	14.67	19.21	0.00	1,022.17
Mar	1,022.17	1.02	20.44	15.33	24.32	6.08	1,021.20
Apr	1,021.20	0.95	−51.06	15.32	−66.38	0.00	954.82
May	954.82	1.07	66.84	14.32	−13.86	0.00	1,007.34
Jun	1,007.34	1.08	80.59	15.11	51.61	12.90	1,059.91
Jul	1,059.91	0.93	−74.19	15.90	−90.09	0.00	969.82
Aug	969.82	0.98	−19.40	14.55	−124.04	0.00	935.88
Sep	935.88	1.12	112.31	14.04	−25.77	0.00	1,034.14
Oct	1,034.14	1.06	62.05	15.51	46.54	0.00	1,080.68
Nov	1,080.68	1.02	21.61	16.21	5.40	0.00	1,086.08
Dec	1,086.08	0.98	−21.72	16.29	−38.01	0.00	1,048.07

[a]Commissions are assumed to equal 0.0015 of beginning month NAV (1,000 trades per month, per $1 million, at $15 round turn).
[b]Profit incentive fee paid quarterly and assumed to equal 25 percent of cumulative net new profits since payment of last incentive fee. It should be noted, however, that in practice, although the profit incentive fee is paid quarterly, it would be accrued monthly. For clarity of exposition, this table does not show these intraquarter accruals.

effect can be quite substantial even in highly liquid markets with very tight bid/ask spreads. For example, in the T-bond market, the bid/ask spread is often only one tick. Even at this one tick minimum, the per trade (round-turn) slippage-related cost difference between an on-the-floor and off-the-floor trader is $31.25 (the value of one tick in the T-bond market). This value

Table 1.4
NAV FOR CTA B AT $15 ROUND-TURN COMMISSION

Month	Beginning Month NAV	Gross Percent Return (Expressed as a Factor of 1)	Gross Profit/Loss	Commissions[a]	Cumulative Net Profit/Loss Since Last Incentive Charge	Quarterly Profit Incentive[b]	Ending Month NAV
Jan	1,000.00	1.02	20.00	4.50	15.50	0.00	1,015.50
Feb	1,015.50	0.97	−30.47	4.57	−19.53	0.00	980.47
Mar	980.47	0.92	−78.44	4.41	−102.38	0.00	897.62
Apr	897.62	1.09	80.79	4.04	−25.64	0.00	974.36
May	974.36	1.07	68.21	4.38	38.18	0.00	1,038.18
Jun	1,038.18	0.98	−20.76	4.67	12.75	3.19	1,009.56
Jul	1,009.56	1.11	111.05	4.54	106.51	0.00	1,116.07
Aug	1,116.07	1.13	145.09	5.02	246.58	0.00	1,256.14
Sep	1,256.14	0.88	−150.74	5.65	90.19	22.55	1,077.20
Oct	1,077.20	1.04	43.09	4.85	38.24	0.00	1,115.44
Nov	1,115.44	0.99	−11.15	5.02	22.07	0.00	1,099.27
Dec	1,099.27	0.94	−65.96	4.95	−48.84	0.00	1,028.36
Jan	1,028.36	1.07	71.99	4.63	18.52	0.00	1,095.72
Feb	1,095.72	1.06	65.74	4.93	79.33	0.00	1,156.53
Mar	1,156.53	1.02	23.13	5.20	97.26	24.32	1,150.15
Apr	1,150.15	0.95	−57.51	5.18	−62.68	0.00	1,087.46
May	1,087.46	1.07	76.12	4.89	8.55	0.00	1,158.69
Jun	1,158.69	1.08	92.70	5.21	96.03	24.01	1,222.17
Jul	1,222.17	0.93	−85.55	5.50	−91.05	0.00	1,131.11
Aug	1,131.11	0.98	−22.62	5.09	−118.76	0.00	1,103.40
Sep	1,103.40	1.12	132.41	4.97	8.68	2.17	1,228.68
Oct	1,228.68	1.06	73.72	5.53	68.19	0.00	1,296.87
Nov	1,296.87	1.02	25.94	5.84	88.29	0.00	1,316.97
Dec	1,316.97	0.98	−26.34	5.93	56.03	14.01	1,270.70

[a]Commissions are assumed to equal 0.0045 of beginning month NAV (300 trades per month, per $1 million, at $15 round turn).

[b]Profit incentive fee paid quarterly and assumed to equal 25 percent of cumulative net new profits since payment of last incentive fee. It should be noted, however, that in practice, although the profit incentive fee is paid quarterly, it would be accrued monthly. For clarity of exposition, this table does not show these intraquarter accruals.

actually represents more than double the typical round-turn commission costs paid by accounts managed by established CTAs.

Since CTA A is making the transition to being an off-the-floor trader, his average profit per trade will go down substantially, because of the shift in slippage from positive to negative. A slippage factor of $30 per round-turn trade

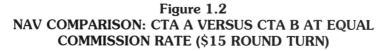

Figure 1.2
**NAV COMPARISON: CTA A VERSUS CTA B AT EQUAL
COMMISSION RATE ($15 ROUND TURN)**

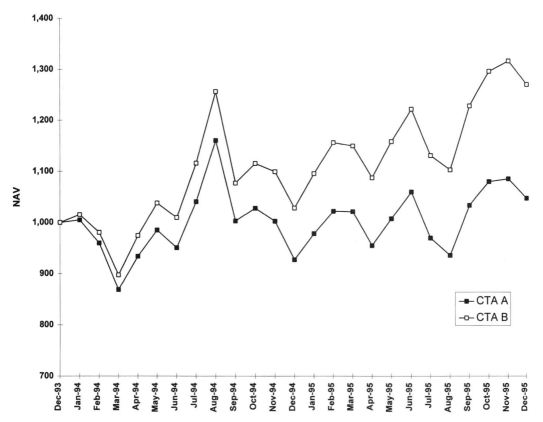

($15 per one side transaction) would seem to be a very conservative figure. Therefore, CTA A's net profit per trade would be reduced by an additional $30 per round turn due to slippage. At 1,000 trades per month, per $1 million traded, the net performance drag due to this factor would be 3.0 percent ($30,000/$1,000,000)—three times the impact of the increase in commission costs. Therefore, as a result of slippage, CTA A's performance is likely to deteriorate even further relative to CTA B than shown in the pro forma results in Figure 1.2. The slippage factor, however, cannot be accounted for by a pro forma adjustment because it is not quantifiable.

Commission and slippage changes are not the only factors that can distort performance results. Changes in management and performance incentive fees can also have a major distortive effect. For example, consider Figure 1.3, which compares the NAVs of CTA C and CTA D. Clearly, CTA C appears to have a much better performance record. In actuality, as can be ascertained in

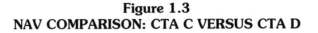

Figure 1.3
NAV COMPARISON: CTA C VERSUS CTA D

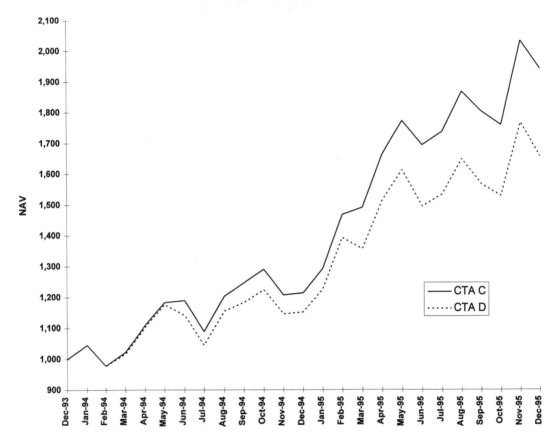

Tables 1.5 and 1.6, both sets of NAVs were constructed using the *same* set of monthly gross returns (and assuming the same commission costs). The difference between the two series is due to the fact that the results for CTA C do not include any management or incentive fees during the period shown, while the results for CTA D are reduced by a profit incentive fee of 25 percent of net new profits paid quarterly. (As before, we assume a 0 percent management fee/25 percent profit incentive fee compensation structure. For simplicity of exposition, we also assume that the CTAs are not credited with any interest rate income.)

Why would a CTA manage money without charging any fees? Once again, such a situation is fairly common for startup CTAs whose main objective is likely to be obtaining trading funds in order to establish a track record. Since it is very difficult to raise money without a track record, a startup CTA

Table 1.5
NAV FOR CTA C

Month	Beginning Month NAV	Profit/Loss as a Factor of 1	Gross Profit/Loss	Commissions[a]	Cumulative Net Profit/Loss Since Last Incentive Charge	Quarterly Profit Incentive[b]	Ending Month NAV
Jan	1,000.00	1.05	50.00	4.50	45.50	0.00	1,045.50
Feb	1,045.50	0.94	−62.73	4.70	−21.93	0.00	978.07
Mar	978.07	1.05	48.90	4.40	22.57	0.00	1,022.57
Apr	1,022.57	1.09	92.03	4.60	110.00	0.00	1,110.00
May	1,110.00	1.07	77.70	4.99	182.70	0.00	1,182.70
Jun	1,182.70	1.01	11.83	5.32	189.21	0.00	1,189.21
Jul	1,189.21	0.92	−95.14	5.35	88.72	0.00	1,088.72
Aug	1,088.72	1.11	119.76	4.90	203.58	0.00	1,203.58
Sep	1,203.58	1.04	48.14	5.42	246.31	0.00	1,246.31
Oct	1,246.31	1.04	49.85	5.61	290.55	0.00	1,290.55
Nov	1,290.55	0.94	−77.43	5.81	207.31	0.00	1,207.31
Dec	1,207.31	1.01	12.07	5.43	213.95	0.00	1,213.95
Jan	1,213.95	1.07	84.98	5.46	293.46	0.00	1,293.46
Feb	1,293.46	1.14	181.08	5.82	468.73	0.00	1,468.73
Mar	1,468.73	1.02	29.37	6.61	491.49	0.00	1,491.49
Apr	1,491.49	1.12	178.98	6.71	663.76	0.00	1,663.76
May	1,663.76	1.07	116.46	7.49	772.74	0.00	1,772.74
Jun	1,772.74	0.96	−70.91	7.98	693.85	0.00	1,693.85
Jul	1,693.85	1.03	50.82	7.62	737.04	0.00	1,737.04
Aug	1,737.04	1.08	138.96	7.82	868.19	0.00	1,868.19
Sep	1,868.19	0.97	−56.05	8.41	803.74	0.00	1,803.74
Oct	1,803.74	0.98	−36.07	8.12	759.54	0.00	1,759.54
Nov	1,759.54	1.16	281.53	7.92	1,033.15	0.00	2,033.15
Dec	2,033.15	0.96	−81.33	9.15	942.68	0.00	1,942.68

[a]Commissions are assumed to equal 0.0045 of beginning month NAV (300 trades per month, per $1 million, at $15 round turn).
[b]Profit incentive fee assumed to be equal to 0.

may very well be willing to forgo all fees as an incentive for an investor to provide trading funds. Imagine CTA C, having established a favorable track record, no longer finds it necessary to waive fees in order to attract investment funds and is now charging a 25 percent profit incentive fee on all new accounts. In this example, the "actual" track record is represented by CTA C, but the relevant track record for new investors is represented by CTA D—

Table 1.6
NAV FOR CTA D

Month	Beginning Month NAV	Gross Percent Return (Expressed as a Factor of 1)	Gross Profit/Loss	Commissions[a]	Cumulative Net Profit/Loss Since Last Incentive Charge	Quarterly Profit Incentive[b]	Ending Month NAV
Jan	1,000.00	1.05	50.00	4.50	45.50	0.00	1,045.50
Feb	1,045.50	0.94	−62.73	4.70	−21.93	0.00	978.07
Mar	978.07	1.05	48.90	4.40	22.57	5.64	1,016.93
Apr	1,016.93	1.09	91.52	4.58	86.95	0.00	1,103.87
May	1,103.87	1.07	77.27	4.97	159.25	0.00	1,176.18
Jun	1,176.18	1.01	11.76	5.29	165.72	41.43	1,141.22
Jul	1,141.22	0.92	−91.30	5.14	−96.43	0.00	1,044.78
Aug	1,044.78	1.11	114.93	4.70	13.79	0.00	1,155.01
Sep	1,155.01	1.04	46.20	5.20	54.79	13.70	1,182.31
Oct	1,182.31	1.04	47.29	5.32	41.97	0.00	1,224.28
Nov	1,224.28	0.94	−73.46	5.51	−36.99	0.00	1,145.32
Dec	1,145.32	1.01	11.45	5.15	−30.69	0.00	1,151.62
Jan	1,151.62	1.07	80.61	5.18	44.74	0.00	1,227.05
Feb	1,227.05	1.14	171.79	5.52	211.00	0.00	1,393.31
Mar	1,393.31	1.02	27.87	6.27	232.60	58.15	1,356.76
Apr	1,356.76	1.12	162.81	6.11	156.71	0.00	1,513.46
May	1,513.46	1.07	105.94	6.81	255.84	0.00	1,612.60
Jun	1,612.60	0.96	−64.50	7.26	184.08	46.02	1,494.82
Jul	1,494.82	1.03	44.84	6.73	38.12	0.00	1,532.93
Aug	1,532.93	1.08	122.63	6.90	153.85	0.00	1,648.67
Sep	1,648.67	0.97	−49.46	7.42	96.98	24.24	1,567.55
Oct	1,567.55	0.98	−31.35	7.05	−38.40	0.00	1,529.14
Nov	1,529.14	1.16	244.66	6.88	199.38	0.00	1,766.93
Dec	1,766.93	0.96	−70.68	7.95	120.75	30.19	1,658.11

[a]Commissions are assumed to equal 0.0045 of beginning month NAV (300 trades per month, per $1 million, at $15 round turn).

[b]Profit incentive fee paid quarterly and assumed to equal 25 percent of cumulative net new profits since payment of last incentive fee. It should be noted, however, that in practice, although the profit incentive fee is paid quarterly, it would be accrued monthly. For clarity of exposition, this table does not show these intraquarter accruals.

the track record CTA C would have realized if past investors were charged fees equal to those incurred by new investors. In effect, the track record for CTA D actually represents the pro forma results for CTA C. Once again, it is the pro forma results that are far more relevant to new investors than the so-called "actual" results.

CONCLUSION

The key point in this chapter is that actual results include commission costs, management fees, and profit incentive fees, items that have nothing to do with a CTA's "actual" performance. If the past levels of these various charges differ substantially from those that would be incurred by a current investor, so-called "actual" results could be misleading. In such situations, actual results can overstate true performance if past costs were lower (for example, if no profit incentive or management fees were charged), and understate performance if past costs were higher (for example, if sharply higher commissions were charged in the early portion of the track record). Investors, therefore, need to ascertain that commissions and fees during the period depicted in the track record are representative of current charges. If this is not the case, a pro forma track record that adjusts past results for current commission costs and fee charges will provide a much more meaningful representation.

Generally speaking, in the case of single-manager performance results,[5] a properly constructed pro forma table will provide a much more realistic performance picture than a table based on actual results. In fact, it would make sense for pro forma adjustments to be required (rather than merely permitted) if past commissions or fees were substantially lower than current charges, causing past performance to be overstated.[6]

---

[5]A strong distinction needs to be made between pro forma results applied to the single CTA and pro forma results for a combined group of CTAs. In the case of the individual CTA, pro forma results are used to restate past performance so that it is consistent with current commission costs and fee levels, an adjustment that this chapter has argued yields more meaningful results than so-called actual results. The situation is strikingly different, however, when pro forma results are used to show the combined performance for a group of CTAs selected for a fund. In this instance, pro forma results incorporate a strong element of hindsight (since the particular group of CTAs selected for the fund were chosen based on how good their combined performance would have been in the past) and need to be viewed very cautiously. In fact, a proposed NFA rule change, which at this writing appears likely to be adopted, would with the exception of extraordinary circumstances prohibit the use of pro forma results to depict the combined performance of a selected group of CTAs.

[6]In certain extreme cases (e. g., past track records that do not include any fees whatsoever when fees are being charged to new investors), the CFTC does require pro forma results.

2 Performance Reporting: Sources of Distortion and Special Cases

ADDITIONS AND WITHDRAWALS

Additions or withdrawals of equity do not present any problem if they occur at the end of a month. In this case, the addition or withdrawal will not have any effect on the performance of the month just ended and will not distort the following month's performance figure because it will show up in that month's beginning equity. If, however, an addition or withdrawal occurs partway into a month, it can cause a significant distortion if percent return is computed in the conventional manner (net profit/loss divided by beginning month equity), especially if the addition or withdrawal represents a substantial portion of total equity.

If additions or withdrawals occur at the start of a month (or stated equivalently, the end of the prior month), the rate of return (ROR) for the month is simply defined as the net profit/loss divided by the beginning net asset value (BNAV). In cases where there are intramonth additions/withdrawals substantial enough to cause "material"[1] differences in performance, the Commodity Futures Trading Commission (CFTC) provides four alternative methods of calculation:

1. *Time-weighting.* In the time-weighting method, the BNAV is adjusted upward by time-weighted additions and downward by time-weighted withdrawals. For additions, the time-weighting represents the percentage of the month for which funds were available, while for withdrawals the time-weighting represents the percentage of the month for which funds were unavailable. For example, if the actual BNAV was $1,000,000 and an addi-

---

[1]The CFTC defines four conditions of materiality in its advisory. (*Source: Adjustment for Additions and Withdrawals to Computations of Rate of Return in Performance Records of Commodity Pool Operators and Commodity Trading Advisors,* Commodity Futures Trading Commission, 56 F.R. 8109, February 27, 1991.)

tional $1,200,000 was deposited on the 10th of the month, and $600,000 was withdrawn on the 20th of the month, the BNAV would be adjusted upward by $800,000 (because the $1,200,000 added was available for two-thirds of the month) and downward by $200,000 (because the $600,000 withdrawn was unavailable for one-third of the month). Therefore, the adjusted BNAV would be $1,600,000, a 60 percent increase over the actual BNAV. Thus, if the net profit for the month equaled $100,000, the ROR would be 6.25 percent instead of the 10.00 percent that would have been implied using the actual BNAV.

2. *Average Daily Equity (ADE).* The average daily equity (ADE) approach calculates the monthly ROR by dividing the net profit/loss for the month by the arithmetic average of the liquidating equity on each day of the month (as opposed to dividing by the BNAV). Note that the ADE method is quite similar to time-weighting. In fact, the two methods would yield identical results if the profit/loss was equal to zero each day (i.e., if changes in daily equity were only due to additions/withdrawals). While this is obviously an unlikely event if there are any net positions, the key point is the inference that the two methods will yield very similar results if additions/withdrawals are large relative to profit/loss levels. (If additions/withdrawals range between moderately larger to smaller than profit/loss levels, the two methods will still not yield substantially disparate results, since each approach will imply only modest adjustments in the BNAV.)

3. *Compounded ROR.* In this method, the rate of return is calculated for each subperiod between additions/withdrawals (as if each such subperiod were itself an entire month). As the name implies, the compounded ROR for the entire month would be equal to the compounded return for the subperiods. For example, assume a $1,000,000 starting equity and the following subperiod returns and additions/withdrawals:

	Subperiod Starting Equity	Subperiod Percent Return	Subperiod Profit/Loss	Addition/ Withdrawal
Month start	1,000,000	+ 8.0	80,000	+ 200,000
After first addition/withdrawal	1,280,000	+12.0	153,600	+400,000
After second addition/withdrawal	1,833,600	−10.0	−183,360	−600,000
After third addition/withdrawal	1,050,240	+20.0	210,048	0
Month end	1,260,288			

In this example, the compounded ROR would be equal to $(1.08 \times 1.12 \times 0.9 \times 1.2) - 1 = 0.3064 = 30.64\%$.

The compounded ROR method will precisely reflect the return realized by accounts that did not experience any additions or withdrawals during the month, given the following set of assumptions: (1) in actual trading, the CTA adjusts the trading leverage daily to account for changes in equity, and (2) the subperiods in the compounded ROR calculation are defined as days.[2,3]

4. *Only Accounts Traded.* The only accounts traded (OAT) method calculates the monthly ROR in the conventional manner of dividing the net profit/loss by the BNAV, except that accounts that traded for only part of the month or witnessed "material" additions/withdrawals during the month would be excluded from the calculation. By excluding these accounts, *the calculated figure will reflect the ROR that would have been realized by an investor with an account that was active at the start of the month and held till the end of the month without any additions or withdrawals.* In effect, by removing the influence of intramonth additions/withdrawals, the OAT method yields an undistorted *actual* return figure.

Which of the preceding four methods is most accurate? If the intention is to show the percent return that would have been realized by an investor with an account open throughout the month, without the distortion of additions/ withdrawals, the OAT method is the only approach that will provide a precise answer.[4] However, sometimes there will not be any other similar accounts to use for the OAT calculation (for example, if all trading is done in a single account, pool, or fund). In this case, another method must obviously be employed, and the compounded ROR calculation will typically result in the smallest distortion among the alternative approaches cited.[5]

The other two methods—time-weighting and ADE—yield only approximations of actual return levels and are never precisely correct, except by rare

---

[2]The CFTC rules *require* that compounding be done *at least* as frequently as additions or withdrawals are made, but *allow* compounding to be done daily.

[3]The compounded ROR method would also yield the same return as accounts without any additions or withdrawals if the trading leverage in such accounts were adjusted to reflect current equity *at the times of the additions and withdrawals.* However, this case is of little practical consequence, since there is obviously no reason to assume that leverage in existing accounts would have been adjusted on the addition/withdrawal dates had there been no additions or withdrawals.

[4]The compounded ROR method will also yield the same return realized by accounts without additions or withdrawals in the special case in which leverage is adjusted for equity changes on a daily basis and the subperiods in the calculation are defined as days.

[5]For example, in the tabular example that was previously provided to illustrate the calculation of the compounded ROR, an account without any additions or withdrawals would have recorded a 30 percent return for the month (8% + 12% − 10% + 20%), which is fairly close to the 30.64 percent figure that was derived by the compounded ROR method. Although the two figures will not always be this close, this comparison is not atypical.

chance occurrence. Moreover, these approaches can sometimes be subject to extreme distortions. *In fact, as will be demonstrated in the next section, it is not unusual for time-weighting (and by implication the ADE method) to result in greater distortions than the unadjusted BNAV does—the very method it was intended to correct!* (Since the ADE method requires far more computation than time-weighting and both methods yield similar results, the ADE approach is used only infrequently. Consequently, we will focus solely on time-weighting; however, conclusions similar to those reached for time-weighting would apply to the ADE method as well.)

TIME-WEIGHTING: A STATISTICAL ABOMINATION

A valid return calculation should depend on the performance of the CTA, not the timing of additions and withdrawals by investors. Based on this very simple criterion, time-weighting is a disaster. *To demonstrate this point, we will use the exact illustrations of time-weighting provided by the CFTC in their own advisory.*[6]

> If actual BNAV were $100,000 and an additional $150,000 were deposited on the 10th of the month, and $90,000 was withdrawn on the 20th of the month, the $100,000 BNAV would have to be adjusted: (1) Upward by two-thirds of the $150,000, or $100,000, because the funds were available for 20 days of the month; and (2) downward by $30,000, because the funds were not available for one-third of the month. Therefore, the adjusted BNAV which should be used in computing ROR would be $170,000 or a 70 percent increase over actual BNAV.

In the same advisory, the CFTC provides the following table as an illustration of the compounded ROR method:

	Account Value	Change in Value
Start of month	$10,000	+10% ($1,000 profit)
End of first accounting period	$11,000	$4,000 (addition)
Start of second accounting period	$15,000	−20% ($3,000 loss)
End of second accounting period	$12,000	$2,000 (withdrawal)
Start of third accounting period	$10,000	+25% ($2,500 profit)
End of month	$12,500	

---

[6]*Adjustment for Additions and Withdrawals to Computations of Rate of Return in Performance Records of Commodity Pool Operators and Commodity Trading Advisors,* Commodity Futures Trading Commission, 56 F.R. 8109, February 27, 1991.

$$ROR = [(1 + 0.1)(1 - 0.2)(1 + 0.25)] = 10\%$$

In the following table, we incorporate the subperiod returns of this compounded ROR illustration in the immediately preceding time-weighting example:[7]

	Account Value	Change in Value
Start of month	$100,000	+10% ($10,000 profit)
End of first accounting period	$110,000	$150,000 (addition)
Start of second accounting period	$260,000	-20% ($52,000 loss)
End of second accounting period	$208,000	$90,000 (withdrawal)
Start of third accounting period	$118,000	+25% ($29,500 profit)
End of month	$147,500	

The net profit/loss for the entire month would be equal to the sum of the subperiod profit/loss amounts:

$$\text{Net profit/loss} = \$10,000 - \$52,000 + \$29,500 = -\$12,500$$

The ROR using the time-weighting approach would be equal to the net profit/loss divided by the adjusted BNAV:

$$\text{Time-weighting ROR} = -\$12,500 \div \$170,000 = -7.35\%$$

How close is this figure to the return that would have been realized without the distortion of additions or withdrawals? Given the same set of returns during the three subperiods (+10%, -20%, and +25%), an investor who made no additions or withdrawals would have experienced a monthly return equal to the sum of the subperiod returns: +15% (assuming leverage is not adjusted intramonth). Note that the return indicated by the time-weighting calculation is not even remotely close to this undistorted return. There is an enormous 22.35 percent difference between the two monthly return figures, and even the signs are opposite. Again, it should be stressed that this mammoth deviation is not the product of an artificial example, but is implied by the examples provided in the CFTC's own advisory!

---

[7]The time-weighting example itself did not contain any subperiod return assumptions, since it only dealt with the BNAV adjustment, which doesn't require any return information.

It is true that in the foregoing example, time-weighting at least provided a closer estimate of actual return than the unadjusted calculation:

$$\text{Unadjusted ROR} = -\$12,500 \div \$100,000 = -12.5\%$$

Nevertheless, when the actual return is +15%, a −7.35% estimate hardly provides much of an improvement over a −12.5% estimate. Moreover, time-weighting can often lead to an even more distorted estimate than the unadjusted figure. For example, the following table duplicates the previous tabular illustration, the only difference being that the withdrawal at the end of the second period is assumed to be equal to $12,000 instead of $90,000.

	Account Value	Change in Value
Start of month	$100,000	+10% ($10,000 profit)
End of first accounting period	$110,000	$150,000 (addition)
Start of second accounting period	$260,000	−20% ($52,000 loss)
End of second accounting period	$208,000	$12,000 (withdrawal)
Start of third accounting period	$196,000	+25% ($49,000 profit)
End of month	$245,000	

In this case, the net profit/loss for the entire month would be:

$$+ \$10,000 - \$52,000 + \$49,000 = +\$7,000$$

and the time-weighted adjusted BNAV would be

$$\$100,000 + 2/3\,(\$150,000) - 1/3\,(\$12,000) = \$196,000$$

Hence, the time-weighted return would be

$$\$7,000 \div \$196,000 = 3.57\%$$

compared with an unadjusted return of

$$\$7,000 \div \$100,000 = 7\%$$

Thus, in this case, the unadjusted calculation yields a closer estimate of the 15 percent "actual" return—the return that would have been realized by an investment held throughout the month without additions or withdrawals—than does the time-weighted calculation. As this example illustrates, there is no reason to assume that time-weighting will even provide an improvement over an unadjusted return figure, let alone yield a reasonable approximation of actual return.

SUMMARY REMARKS REGARDING ADDITIONS AND WITHDRAWALS

Time-weighting and the OAT method are by far the most widely used of the four alternative ROR calculations permitted by the CFTC,[8] no doubt because these approaches require far less computation than the compounded ROR and ADE methods. Although both the OAT method and time-weighting represent simple computational processes that do not place any undue burden on the CTA, *the OAT method yields ROR figures that precisely reflect actual returns, whereas time-weighting is subject to extreme distortions.* Therefore, I can see no reason—other than statistical ignorance—for the existence of time-weighting as an acceptable method of computation. My recommendation is that the CFTC acknowledge this simple fact and adopt the OAT method as the single uniform approach for calculating ROR data when there are intramonth additions or withdrawals. The compounded ROR, which is generally far more accurate than time-weighting, should be retained as an acceptable alternative calculation method in the event that there are no other similar accounts available to allow the application of the OAT method.

The foregoing proposed change in accepted ROR calculation procedures should be *voluntary* in regards to *past* performance numbers, since revising historical performance figures could entail significant accounting costs. It would be unfair to penalize CTAs who were in compliance with prevailing reporting procedures for an *ex post* change in regulations. In those cases in which the ROR numbers in a performance table are based on two different procedures (e.g., time-weighting for historical figures and the OAT method for new figures), that fact could be cited as an accompanying note to the table.

NOTIONAL FUNDING

The vast majority of CTAs trade position sizes with margin requirements of less than 50 percent of the account size. Therefore, in most cases, it is not necessary for a managed futures account to be fully funded. This is why many investors only partially fund managed futures accounts, utilizing the

---

[8]The CFTC will also consider, and has occasionally accepted, other proposed methods for handling additions and withdrawals in performance reporting.

remaining monies for investments they consider more attractive than the approximate T-bill rates received on excess funds in a futures account. In effect, such partially funded accounts consist of *actual funds* plus *notional funds*, wherein *notional funds* are the amount by which the *nominal account size* exceeds the actual funds deposited. (The *nominal account size*, which is also called the *notional account size*, is the dollar amount a CTA and its customers have agreed in writing will determine the level of trading in an account regardless of the amount of actual funds.)

In the case of partially funded accounts, the question then becomes, should rates of return be based on actual funds alone or on actual funds plus notional funds? There is only one reasonable answer: *Insofar as return levels should reflect only a CTA's performance and not the portion of funds deposited by the investor, return calculations should be based on actual funds plus notional funds.* For example, if a CTA has two $1.0 million accounts, one that is fully funded and the other that is funded with $500,000, and he earns $100,000 in each, the appropriate return level is 10 percent in each case. If returns were based on actual funds only, the return for the second account would be defined as 20 percent, even though it was traded identically to the first account—an absurd proposition.

Arthur Bell, who is regarded by many as the managed futures industry's foremost accounting expert, states that the notional funding issue is basically a matter of "investor performance" versus "CTA performance." Problems arise when the focus is on investor performance, which can vary from investor to investor. He emphasizes that decisions to less than fully fund an account are *always* investor driven. In fact, the use of notional funding will always negatively impact the CTA by reducing interest income, thereby diminishing the CTA's returns.

The CFTC's recognition of the misleading nature of measuring return relative to actual funds alone is expressed by its policy of permitting partially funded accounts to be excluded from performance calculations and instead allowing performance to be based on a *fully funded subset* of accounts. This approach provides an ideal solution *when fully funded accounts exist.* However, with notional funding becoming increasingly prevalent, and CTAs often trading multiple programs, situations in which there are no fully funded accounts in a CTA program are becoming more common. In such circumstances, calculating returns based on actual funds would be very misleading. On the other hand, in the absence of any fully funded accounts, and hence the linkage between such accounts and notional accounts, there may be no evidence of the validity of nominal account sizes. Investors therefore need to take great care in determining the assumptions used in calculating returns for CTA programs without any fully funded accounts.

There is an obvious solution to the ambiguity problem that is currently inherent in trading programs that have no fully funded accounts. The CFTC already requires documentation of a notionally funded account in its advisory letter dated February 8, 1993. The advisory specifies relevant details about the notionally funded account to be explicitly stated such as name of the CTA program, nominal account size, how profits/losses and additions/withdrawals are treated, and the amount of actual funds in the account. In addition to providing verification, this advisory could obviate the need for a fully funded subset to calculate representative performance results. The CFTC is currently moving in that direction on a case-by-case basis, which seems to be a commonsense solution to the problem.

HYPOTHETICAL AND SIMULATED RESULTS

Hypothetical (or simulated) results show how a system or method that was never actually traded would have performed in the past. If rigorous restrictions against the use of hindsight are applied (e.g., developing systems on one set of data and testing them on another), hypothetical results can be useful to the system developer. However, hypothetical results are all but useless, and potentially misleading, to the investor, because it is impossible for the investor to tell how much hindsight was used in generating the hypothetical results. Hindsight can be used in selecting the system, defining the parameters used in the system, deciding which markets are traded, and specifying the leverage used. With this much potential use of hindsight, it is a simple matter to construct hypothetical results showing triple-digit returns and little risk (for the past, that is).

The CFTC recognizing that "hypothetical results are based on hindsight and can be readily manipulated"[9] requires that such results be accompanied by the following prominently displayed, explicit disclaimer:

> Hypothetical performance results have many inherent limitations, some of which are described below. No representation is being made that any account will or is likely to achieve profits or losses similar to those shown. In fact, there are frequently sharp differences between hypothetical performance results and the actual results subsequently achieved by any particular program.
>
> One of the limitations of hypothetical performance results is that they are generally prepared with the benefit of hindsight. In addition, hypothetical trading does not involve financial risk, and no hypothetical trading record can completely account for the impact of financial risk in actual trading. For example, the ability to withstand losses or to adhere to a particular trading program in spite of trading losses are material points which can also

---

[9]*Federal Register,* Vol. 60, No. 142, pg. 38168, July 25, 1995.

adversely affect actual trading results. There are numerous other factors related to the markets in general or to the implementation of any specific trading program which cannot be fully accounted for in the preparation of hypothetical performance results and all of which can adversely affect actual trading results.

The following paragraph must also be included if the CTA has "less than one year experience in directing customer accounts or trading proprietary accounts":

[The member] has had little or no experience in trading actual accounts for itself or for customers. Because there are no actual trading results to compare to the hypothetical performance results, customers should be particularly wary of placing undue reliance on these hypothetical trading results.

The CTFC also requires that this disclaimer and actual results (if any exist) must be displayed at least as prominently as hypothetical performance results. In addition, hypothetical performance results are prohibited for any program that has three months of actual performance.

The term "simulated results" is often used synonymously with "hypothetical results." Unfortunately, the term "simulated results" is also used in an entirely different context. In this alternative usage, simluated results refer to results based on trades generated in real time, but not placed as actual trades. A prime example would be results based on trades placed with a simulated brokerage firm (or trade verification service), such as AUDI-TRACK, which takes real time orders from clients (but does not actually place the orders), estimates a fill price based on prevailing market prices, and issues daily and monthly confirmation statements. (Somewhat less rigorous examples of real-time simulated trades would include time-verifiable tape-recorded trade recommendation services and newsletter trade recommendation programs.)

Real-time simulated trade results still differ from actual trade results in two significant respects:

1. Although fill prices can be estimated, with the exception of limit orders, there is no way of knowing what the exact fill price would have been. In actual trading, the execution price on an order can frequently differ from the fill price that might have been assumed based on the prevailing price quote on a screen, particularly in the case of large orders or stop orders. (This difference is commonly referred to as "slippage.")

2. Although a service such as AUDITRACK seeks to reproduce the actual trading experience, the "trader" is not trading real money. Such "paper trading" cannot duplicate the psychological stress of trading real money. Even in the case of a fully computerized trading approach, there is no way of knowing whether the trader would have

overridden the system during a losing period if the losses had involved real money.

These two limitations notwithstanding, there is no question that there is an enormous difference between such real-time simulated trading and hypothetical results. Real-time simulated trades at least offer some approximation of actual trades, whereas hypothetical results are virtually meaningless to all but the system developer using appropriately rigid testing assumptions. Therefore, it certainly would not be fair to lump real-time simulated results together with hypothetical results. Unfortunately, the treatment of real-time simulated results is a gray area that is not explicitly addressed in government regulations.

The crux of the problem is that both hypothetical and real-time simulated trades are referred to as "simulated trades." This state of affairs creates unnecessary confusion. My suggestion is that the industry should adopt the term "real-time simulated trades" or another suitable term to differentiate such trades from hypothetical trades. Such a labeling distinction appears to be the logical first step. The CFTC then needs to consider the appropriate treatment of real-time simulated trades, or whatever they end up being called, as separate from the rules regulating hypothetical results.

EXTRACTED RESULTS

Extracted results refer to trading results based on actual trades but limited to only a subset of markets in an existing trading program. A track record based on actual currency trades *drawn from a diversified trading program* is an example of extracted results, in contrast to the track record of actual currency trades *in a currency trading program*. Although extracted results are based on actual trades, it is easy for such track records to be greatly distorted because hindsight can be used in two important ways:

1. *Market Selection.* Given any portfolio of markets, simply by chance there will always be market sectors and individual markets that perform significantly better. Therefore, a CTA can always extract a subset from a diversified portfolio that will show far superior *past* returns. Of course, these markets will not necessarily perform better in the future. Although no CTA would be naive enough to form an extracted portfolio of unrelated markets simply because they performed best in the past (say, for example, a British pound, heating oil, and soybean portfolio), there is still a wide choice of reasonable sector portfolios that could be formed. Here is a partial list: currencies, interest rates, precious metals, currencies plus interest rates, currencies plus interest rates plus precious metals, energy, agricultural markets.

Hindsight could be used to select the sector portfolio with the best performance and then create a new trading program based on this portfolio, generating a stellar track record in the process.

2. Leverage Specification. Percent returns depend not only on dollar profit/loss, but also on the amount of funds traded. It is impossible to determine the amount of funds that would have been allocated in the past to trade any given subset in a broader portfolio. By reducing the assumed amount of funds that would have been used to trade the extracted markets, a CTA could proportionately increase the return of the resulting portfolio.

Hypothetical results and extracted results differ only in a matter of degree. Hypothetical results allow the CTA to use hindsight in selecting the following four items: (1) systems traded; (2) parameter sets used in those systems; (3) markets traded; and (4) leverage used in each market. Extracted results allow hindsight to be used in the last two items: market selection and leverage definition. This opens the door to a tremendous potential impact from the use of hindsight. An unscrupulous (or naive) CTA could easily double or triple past performance using hindsight to construct an extracted performance table!

At one time, the rules governing the reporting of extracted trade results were unclear, and extracted performance tables were sometimes presented in a manner that an investor could mistake for actual results. The CFTC, however, correctly recognizing the potential for abuse in this area, now requires that extracted results be accompanied by the same strong disclaimer mandated for hypothetical results. Investors should be cautioned not to dismiss the disclaimer in the case of extracted results because "they are based on actual trades." A sensible guideline is that investors should assume that the performance of an extracted portfolio is no better than the performance of the portfolio from which it was extracted.

COMPOSITE ACCOUNT DISTORTIONS

Performance tables in disclosure documents are usually based on a composite of accounts. When these accounts are traded similarly (for example, roughly similar commissions, fees, and market portfolios), this factor does not present a problem. However, if the composite combines disparate accounts (for example, accounts that differ significantly in markets traded or leverage used), it may be very difficult for an individual investor to draw meaningful comparisons. Therefore, it is important for the investor to ascertain that composite tables in a disclosure document were based on homogeneous rather than heterogeneous accounts.

3   Measuring Trading Performance[1]

THE NEED TO NORMALIZE GAIN[2]

Too many investors make the mistake of focusing solely on return when they evaluate money managers.[3] It is critical to also incorporate some measure of risk as part of the evaluation process.

Consider the equity streams of the accounts of Manager A and Manager B in Figure 3.1. Although Manager A produces the larger return for the period as a whole, he can hardly be considered the superior performer—note the many sharp retracements in equity.

This is not a negative feature merely because investors with Manager A will have to ride out many distressing periods. Even more critical is the consideration that investors who start with Manager A at the wrong time—and that is not hard to do—may actually experience significant losses. In fact, assuming that accounts will be closed once 25–50 percent of the initial equity is lost, there is a significant chance investors with Manager A will be knocked out of the game before the next rebound in performance.

It seems reasonable to assume that most investors would prefer Manager B to Manager A because the modestly lower return of Manager B is more

---

[1]Insofar as performance measurement is essential to both the topics of trading systems and managed trading, there is significant overlap between this chapter and the similarly titled chapter in *Technical Analysis* (the second volume of this series). There are, however, two differences between the two chapters:

1. The chapter in *Technical Analysis* covered performance measurement as it applied to both trading systems and money managers, whereas this chapter focuses only on the latter.
2. This chapter covers a wider range of performance measurements.

[2]The sections "The Need to Normalize Gain" and "Negative Sharpe Ratios" (pages 32–33) are adapted from J. Schwager, "Alternative to Sharpe Ratio Better Measure of Performance," *Futures,* pp. 56–57, March 1985.

[3]In the futures industry, most money managers (i.e., those registered with the Commodity Futures Trading Commission) are called "commodity trading advisors" (CTAs), an unfortunately inappropriate choice of names. In this book we use both the terms *CTAs* and *money managers*. These terms are equivalent and can be read interchangeably.

Figure 3.1
THE NEED TO NORMALIZE GAIN

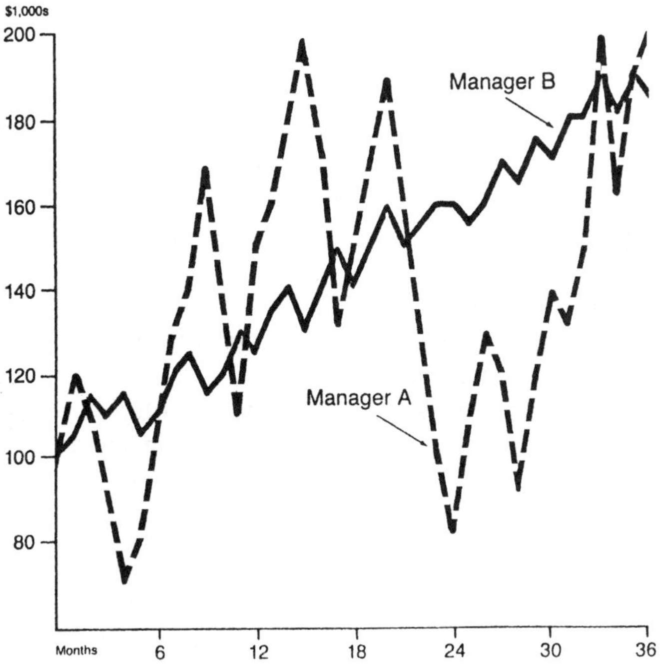

(*Source:* J. Schwager, "Alternative to Sharpe Ratio Better Measure of Performance," *Futures,* p. 56, March 1985. Reproduced by permission.)

than compensated by the apparent much lower risk. Moreover, if Manager B had used a modestly higher margin–equity ratio, she could have exceeded Manager A's return while still having much smaller retracements. (For money management reasons, all managers will limit the number of positions so that total margin requirements are well below total available equity; typically, the margin–equity ratio will be approximately 0.15–0.40.)

Clearly, Manager B has the better performance record. As illustrated by this example, any performance evaluation method must incorporate a risk measure to be meaningful.

THE SHARPE RATIO

The need to incorporate risk in evaluating performance has long been recognized. The classic return/risk measure is the Sharpe Ratio, which can be expressed as follows:

$$SR = \frac{E - I}{\text{sd}}$$

where E = the expected return
     I = risk-free interest rate
   sd = standard deviation of returns

    E is typically stated in terms of percent return. Normally, the expected return is assumed to equal the average past return. In view of this fact, although E always refers to the expected return (i.e., applies to a future period), we will use it synonymously with the average past return.

    The incorporation of I in the Sharpe Ratio recognizes that an investor could always earn a certain return *risk free*—for example, by investing in T bills. Thus, the return in excess of this risk-free return is more meaningful than the absolute level of the return.

    The standard deviation is a statistic that is intended to measure the degree of dispersion in the data. The formula for the standard deviation is

$$\text{sd} = \sqrt{\frac{\sum\limits_{i=1}^{N}(X_i - \overline{X})^2}{N - 1}}$$

where $\overline{X}$ = mean
    X_i = individual data values
    N = the number of data values

In the Sharpe Ratio application, N is equal to the number of time intervals. For example, if monthly time intervals are used for a three-year survey period, $N = 36$.

    In calculating the standard deviation, it is always necessary to choose a time interval for segmenting the total period equity data (e.g., weekly, monthly). If, for example, the percent return data for a given year were broken down into weekly figures, the standard deviation would be very high if the return of many of the individual weeks deviated sharply from the average for the period. Conversely, the standard deviation would be low if the individual weeks tended to cluster around the average. Figure 3.2 illustrates two sets of data with the same average weekly return but substantially different standard deviations.

    The basic premise of the Sharpe Ratio is that the standard deviation is a measure of risk. That is, the more widespread the individual returns from the average return, the riskier the investment. In essence, the standard deviation measures the ambiguity of the return. It should be intuitively clear that if the standard deviation is low, it is reasonable to assume that the actual return will be close to the expected return (assuming, of course, that the expected return is a good indicator of actual return). On the other hand, if the standard

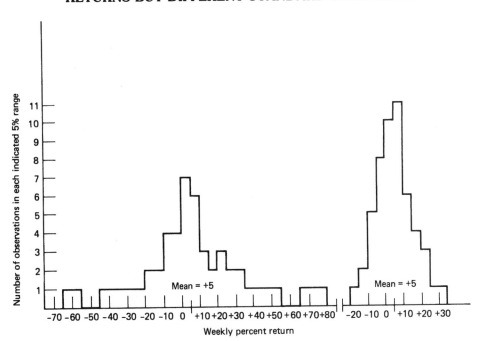

Figure 3.2
COMPARISON OF TWO MANAGERS WITH EQUAL AVERAGE
RETURNS BUT DIFFERENT STANDARD DEVIATIONS

deviation is high, it suggests that there is a good chance that the actual return may vary substantially from the expected return.

THE MODIFIED SHARPE RATIO

One alternative form of the Sharpe Ratio drops the risk-free return from the calculation. This "modified" form of the Sharpe Ratio can be expressed as

$$SR = \frac{E}{sd}$$

Besides the benefit of simplification (by avoiding the need for incorporating a risk-free return series in the calculations), the modified Sharpe Ratio actually has an important theoretical justification: For comparisons of commodity trading advisors (CTAs) with each other, as well as with a CTA index, the modified Sharpe Ratio is actually more meaningful because the performance ranking will be independent of the choice of leverage. In other words, the conventional Sharpe Ratio will increase as a CTA increases leverage, whereas the modified Sharpe Ratio will be unaffected.

For example, assume the annualized average return equals 12 percent, the annualized standard deviation equals 16 percent, and the risk-free return equals 4 percent. In this case, the Sharpe Ratio equals 0.50, whereas the modified Sharpe Ratio equals 0.75.

$$\text{Sharpe Ratio} = (12 - 4)/16 = 0.50$$
$$\text{Modified Sharpe Ratio} = 12/16 = 0.75$$

Now assume the CTA doubles the leverage. In this case, both the return and the standard deviation double. Although the modified Sharpe Ratio would be unaffected by such a change, the Sharpe Ratio would increase to 0.625:

$$\text{Sharpe Ratio} = (24 - 4)/32 = 0.625$$
$$\text{Modified Sharpe Ratio} = 24/32 = 0.75 \text{ (see ftn. 4)}$$

The modified Sharpe Ratio thus eliminates the Sharpe Ratio's inherent bias toward reflecting improved performance on increased leverage.

Because of this theoretical advantage of the modified Sharpe Ratio, as well as to help clarify the exposition, the examples in the remainder of this chapter assume the modified form of the Sharpe Ratio. This simplifying assumption does not meaningfully alter any of the theoretical or practical points discussed.

NEGATIVE SHARPE RATIOS

It should be stressed that negative Sharpe Ratio values are completely ambiguous and should be ignored. Given only the Sharpe Ratio values of two managers with negative Sharpe Ratios, it is impossible to say which manager has the inferior performance record. This is because the more negative Sharpe Ratio could be due to either a more negative return—an undesirable attribute—or to lower volatility—a desirable attribute.

An example should help clarify this point. Consider the three managers in Table 3.1. Both Manager B and Manager C have more negative Sharpe

---

[4]To be precise, doubling the leverage would only exactly double the return and standard deviation (and, hence, leave the modified Sharpe Ratio unchanged) if the return data did not include interest income and management fees (components of the return calculation that do not change when leverage changes)—an assumption that is rarely applicable. Nevertheless, since interest income and management fees influence return in opposite directions, the impact of leverage on the modified Sharpe Ratio will be small as long as these two items are relatively close in value. For larger differences between interest income and management fees, however, leverage can impact the modified Sharpe Ratio as much as or even more than the Sharpe Ratio, depending on the specific data series.

Table 3.1
MISLEADING NATURE OF NEGATIVE SHARPE RATIOS

Manager	Annualized Return	Annualized Standard Deviation	Modified Sharpe Ratio
A	–5	10	–0.5
B	–10	10	–1.0
C	–5	5	–1.0

Ratios than Manager A. As would be implied by the more negative Sharpe Ratio value, Manager B's performance is indeed worse than Manager A's: an equivalent volatility level (as measured by the standard deviation), but double the average annual loss. In contrast to the implication of the more negative Sharpe Ratio value, however, Manager C's performance is better than Manager A's: an equivalent negative return, but half the volatility (as measured by the standard deviation).

Because both a more negative return and a lower volatility level will result in a more negative Sharpe Ratio, negative Sharpe Ratios are meaningless and should be ignored. The implication is that in the case of managers with negative returns, return and risk *must* be evaluated separately. It should be noted that the ambiguity of negative values is not merely a quirk of the Sharpe Ratio, but would be true of any return/risk measure.

It is fairly common to see Sharpe Ratio-based rankings of CTAs that extend the rankings through negative Sharpe Ratio values. It is important to understand that these rankings are completely misleading for the portion of the list containing CTAs with negative Sharpe Ratios. For reasons detailed in this section, lower ranked CTAs (i.e., CTAs with a more negative Sharpe Ratio) might actually have better performance than higher ranked CTAs (i.e., CTAs with a less negative Sharpe Ratio).

How would one rank a list of managers by Sharpe Ratios if the list included managers with negative ratios? This problem actually arises in the performance ranking tests detailed in Chapter 8. Perhaps the simplest solution—and the one employed in Chapter 8—is to use the Sharpe Ratio to rank all managers with positive Sharpe Ratios, and to rank the remaining managers using a return measure.

THREE PROBLEMS WITH THE SHARPE RATIO

Although the Sharpe Ratio is a useful measurement, it does have a number of potential drawbacks:

1. *The Gain Measure of the Sharpe Ratio.* This measure—the annualized average monthly (or other interval) return is more attuned to assessing the probable performance for the next interval than the performance for an extended period. For example, assume that a fund manager has six months of 40 percent gains and six months of 30 percent losses in a given year. The annualized average monthly return would be 60 percent (12 × 5%). However, if position size is adjusted to existing equity, as is done by most managers, the actual return for the year would be −11 percent. That is because, for each dollar of equity at the start of the period, only $0.8858 would remain at the end of the period—$(1.40)^6 \times (0.70)^6 = 0.8858$.

As this example illustrates, if you are concerned about measuring the potential performance for an extended period rather than just the following month or other interval, then the gain measure used in the Sharpe Ratio can lead to extreme distortions. This problem can be circumvented, however, by using an annualized geometric (as opposed to arithmetic) mean rate of return for the numerator of the Sharpe Ratio, as is frequently done. The annualized geometric return is precisely equivalent to the average annual compounded return, which is discussed in the section on the return retracement ratio later in this chapter.

2. *The Sharpe Ratio Does Not Distinguish between Upside and Downside Fluctuations.* The Sharpe Ratio is a measure of volatility, not risk. The two are not necessarily synonymous.

In terms of the risk calculation employed in the Sharpe Ratio—that is, the standard deviation of return—upside and downside fluctuations are considered equally bad. Thus, the Sharpe Ratio would penalize a manager who had sporadic sharp increases in equity, even if the equity retracements were small.

Figure 3.3 compares the hypothetical equity streams of Manager C, who has intermittent surges in equity and no equity retracements, and Manager D, who experiences several equity retracements. Although both managers realize equal gains for the period as a whole and Manager D goes through several retracements while Manager C doesn't have any, the Sharpe Ratio would rate Manager D higher (see Table 3.2). This outcome is a direct consequence of the fact that the Sharpe Ratio penalizes upside volatility exactly the same as downside volatility.

3. *The Sharpe Ratio Does Not Distinguish between Intermittent Losses and Consecutive Losses.* The risk measure in the Sharpe Ratio (the standard deviation) is independent of the order of various data points.

Figure 3.4 depicts the hypothetical equity streams of $100,000 accounts handled by Manager E and Manager F. Each earns a total of

Figure 3.3
PERFORMANCE COMPARISON: MANAGER WITH
LARGE UPSIDE VOLATILITY AND NO RETRACEMENTS
VERSUS MANAGER WITH RETRACEMENTS

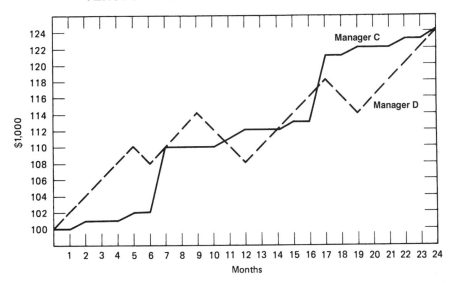

Figure 3.4
COMPARISON OF TWO MANAGERS WITH EQUAL RETURNS
AND STANDARD DEVIATIONS BUT DIFFERENT SEQUENCE
OF MONTHLY GAINS

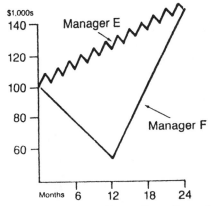

(*Source:* J. Schwager, "Alternative to Sharpe Ratio Better Measure of Performance," *Futures,* p. 56, March 1985.)

Table 3.2
COMPARISON OF MONTHLY RETURNS FOR TWO MANAGERS

	Manager C		Manager D	
Month	Equity Change	Cumulative Equity Change	Equity Change	Cumulative Equity Change
1	0	0	2,000	2,000
2	1,000	1,000	2,000	4,000
3	0	1,000	2,000	6,000
4	0	1,000	2,000	8,000
5	1,000	2,000	2,000	10,000
6	0	2,000	−2,000	8,000
7	8,000	10,000	2,000	10,000
8	0	10,000	2,000	12,000
9	0	10,000	2,000	14,000
10	0	10,000	−2,000	12,000
11	1,000	11,000	−2,000	10,000
12	1,000	12,000	−2,000	8,000
13	0	12,000	2,000	10,000
14	0	12,000	2,000	12,000
15	1,000	13,000	2,000	14,000
16	0	13,000	2,000	16,000
17	8,000	21,000	2,000	18,000
18	0	21,000	−2,000	16,000
19	1,000	22,000	−2,000	14,000
20	0	22,000	2,000	16,000
21	0	22,000	2,000	18,000
22	1,000	23,000	2,000	20,000
23	0	23,000	2,000	22,000
24	1,000	24,000	2,000	24,000

Average monthly return = 1,000   Average monthly return = 1,000

$$SR_C = \frac{E}{sd} = \frac{\dfrac{24{,}000}{2}}{\sqrt{12} \cdot \sqrt{\dfrac{14(1000-0)^2 + 8(1000-1000)^2 + 2(1000-8000)^2}{23}}} = 1.57$$

$$SR_D = \frac{\dfrac{24{,}000}{2}}{\sqrt{12} \cdot \sqrt{\dfrac{18(1000-2000)^2 + 6(1000+2000)^2}{23}}} = 1.96$$

The expected return, E, is equal to total equity gain for the period divided by the number of years, or equivalently, the average monthly return multiplied by 12. The *annualized* standard deviation is equal to the standard deviation of the monthly returns multiplied by $\sqrt{12}$.[a]

[a]To annualize an interval expected (average) return, it is necessary to multiply by the number of intervals in a year (12 for monthly data). To annualize an interval-based standard deviation, it is necessary to multiply by the square root of the number of intervals in a year ($\sqrt{12}$ for monthly data). This standard deviation conversion is a consequence of the fact that if the intervals are independent, the *variance* of return for longer interval data (e.g., year) would be equal to the variance of return for a shorter interval (e.g., month) times the number of shorter intervals in each longer interval (e.g., 12). Thus, the *standard deviation* of return for the longer interval would be equal to the standard deviation of return for the shorter interval times the *square root* of the number of shorter intervals in a longer interval (since the standard deviation is defined as the square root of the variance).

$48,000 or $24,000 per year. However, Manager E alternates $8,000 monthly gains with $4,000 monthly losses, while Manager F first loses $48,000 in the initial 12 months and subsequently gains $96,000 during the remainder of the period.

Both managers would have identical Sharpe Ratios. Despite this fact, few traders would consider the two performance records equivalent in risk. Virtually all traders would agree that Manager F's performance implies a much greater risk level.

SEMIDEVIATION SHARPE RATIO

The problem of the Sharpe Ratio not distinguishing between upside and downside fluctuations can be addressed by using the *semideviation* instead of the standard deviation as the denominator in the Sharpe Ratio. The semideviation is calculated in the same manner as the regular standard deviation, but using only negative data points. The formula for the semideviation is exactly the same as the formula for the standard deviation provided earlier in this chapter. The mean used in the formula is still the mean of *all* the data points, but squared differences from the mean are only summed for the negative terms, and the number of data points (N in the formula) is equal to the number of negative points (not the total number of points). Since positive terms are not used in the calculation, the semideviation will not be affected by large upside excursions in equity. It should be noted, however, that a Sharpe Ratio calculated using the semideviation instead of the standard deviation would still not distinguish between intermittent and consecutive losses.

RETURN RETRACEMENT RATIO

The return retracement ratio (RRR) provides a return/risk measure that avoids the drawbacks of the Sharpe Ratio and also comes closer to defining risk in a manner consistent with the way most traders actually perceive risk. The RRR represents the average annualized compounded return (R) divided by an average maximum retracement (AMR) measure:

$$RRR = \frac{R}{AMR}$$

R is that return that when compounded annually for a period coinciding with a manager's equity stream will yield the same ending equity, given the starting equity. The AMR is equal to the average of the maximum retracement (MR) for each data point (e.g., month), where the MR is equal to the greater of the following two measures:

1. Maximum retracement from a prior equity peak (MRPP); or
2. Maximum retracement to a subsequent low (MRSL).

As the name implies, the MRPP measures the percent decline in equity from the prior high point in equity. In effect, for each data point (e.g., month end) the MRPP reflects the worst retracement that theoretically could have been experienced *by any investor* with an account at that time. The MRPP would be equal to the cumulative loss that would have been realized by an investor starting at the worst possible prior time (i.e., the prior equity peak). Note that if a new equity peak is set in a given month, the MRPP for that point will be equal to 0. One problem with the MRPP is that for early data points the drawdown measure may be understated because there are few prior points. In other words, if more prior data were available, the MRPP for those points would very likely be larger.

As the name implies, the MRSL measures the percent decline in equity to the subsequent lowest equity point. In effect, for each data point (e.g., month end), the MRSL measures the worst retracement that would be experienced *at any time* by investors starting in that month—that is, the cumulative loss that would be realized by such investors at the subsequent low point in equity. Note that if equity never decreases below a level for a given month, the MRSL for that point will be equal to 0. One problem with the MRSL is that for later data points this drawdown measure is likely to be understated. In other words, if more data were available, there is a good chance the MRSL would be greater—that is, the subsequent equity low may not yet have been realized.

The MRPP and MRSL complement each other. Note that each measure is most likely to be understated when the other measure is least likely to be understated. For this reason the MR for each point is defined as the greater of the MRPP and MRSL. In this sense, the MR provides a true worst-case scenario for each point in time (e.g., month end). The AMR simply averages these worst-case values. This approach is far more meaningful than methods that employ only the single worst case—the maximum drawdown.

The mathematical derivation of the RRR is summarized below:

$$RRR = \frac{R}{AMR}$$

where R = average annual compounded return (see below for derivation),

$$AMR = \frac{1}{n} \sum_{i=1}^{n} MR_i$$

where n = number of months in survey period,

$$MR_i = \max(MRPP_i, MRSL_i)$$

where

$$MRPP_i = \frac{PE_i - E_i}{PE_i}$$

$$MRSL_i = \frac{E_i - ME_i}{E_i}$$

where E_i = equity at end of month i
PE_i = peak month-end equity on or prior to month i
ME_i = minimum month-end equity on or subsequent to month i

R, the average annual compounded return, is derived as follows:[5]

$$S(1 + R)^N = E$$

where S = starting equity
E = ending equity
N = number of years
R = annualized compounded return (in decimal terms)

This equation can be reexpressed in terms of the annualized return (R):

$$R = \sqrt[N]{\frac{E}{S}} - 1$$

To facilitate solving this equation for R, it is necessary to reexpress it in terms of logarithms:

$$R = antilog\left[\frac{1}{N}(\log E - \log S)\right] - 1$$

---

[5]The derivation of R through the example where R = 0.30 is from J. Schwager, "Alternative to Sharpe Ratio Better Measure of Performance," *Futures,* p. 58, March 1985.

For example, if a $100,000 account grows to $285,610 in four years, the annualized compounded return would be 0.30 or 30%:

$$R = \text{antilog} \left[\tfrac{1}{4}(\log 285{,}610 - \log 100{,}000) \right] - 1$$
$$R = \text{antilog} \left[\tfrac{1}{4}(5.4557734 - 5) \right] - 1$$
$$R = \text{antilog} \left[0.11394335 \right] - 1 = 0.30$$

A sample EXCEL worksheet for calculating the RRR is provided in Appendix 2 at the end of this book.

ANNUAL GAIN-TO-PAIN RATIO

The annual gain-to-pain ratio (AGPR) represents a simplified type of return/retracement measure. The AGPR is defined as follows:

$$AGPR = AAR \div AAMR$$

where AAR   = arithmetic average of annual returns
      AAMR = average annual maximum retracement, where the maximum retracement for each year is defined as the percent retracement from a prior equity high (even if it occurred in a previous year) to that year's equity low

The RRR is a better return/retracement measure than the AGPR insofar as each data point is incorporated in the risk calculation and the measure does not artificially restrict the data (e.g., calendar year intervals). However, some investors may prefer the AGPR because it requires less computation, and the resulting number has an easy-to-grasp intuitive meaning. For example, an AGPR of 3 would mean that the average annual return is three times as large as the average annual worst retracement (measured from a primary peak).

MAXIMUM LOSS AS A RISK MEASURE

One number of particular interest is the worst-case event—that is, the largest retracement that would have been experienced during the entire survey period if trading was initiated on the worst possible start date. The maximum loss (ML) is merely the largest $MRSL_i$ (or largest $MRPP_i$, the two would be equivalent) and can be expressed as

$$ML = \max(MRSL_i)$$

See the section, "Return Retracement Ratio," for derivation of $MRSL_i$.

The ML is not recommended as a sole risk measure or the risk component in a return/risk ratio because it depends on only a single event and hence may be very unrepresentative of overall performance. Furthermore, because of this characteristic, the value of the ML may be highly contingent on the choice of the survey period. As a related consideration, the use of ML introduces a negative bias for managers with longer track records. However, the ML does provide important information and should be consulted in conjunction with the RRR.

OTHER PERFORMANCE STATISTICS

Some other commonly used statistics include:

1. *Sterling Ratio.* The *Sterling Ratio*, which was developed by Deane Sterling Jones, is defined as the average annual compounded return during the past three years divided by the sum of 10 percent and the average maximum annual drawdown in each of those three years. The Sterling Ratio is somewhat similar to the AGPR. The primary differences are:

- The Sterling Ratio defines the calculation period as three years, whereas the AGPR allows any length time period.
- The AGPR measures annual drawdowns from prior peaks (even if such peaks occurred in a previous year), whereas the Sterling Ratio defines drawdowns within the confines of calendar years.
- The Sterling Ratio uses the average annual compounded return, whereas the AGPR uses the average annual arithmetic return.
- The Sterling Ratio adds 10 percent to the denominator, whereas the AGPR does not contain any corresponding adjustment factor.

Personally, I find the AGPR the preferable of the two measures, because it does not artificially cut off drawdowns by calendar years and because it has the flexibility to be applied to any length period, not just three years. However, the Sterling Ratio is still worth considering because it is widely used.

2. *Correlation Statistics.* Most CTA reporting services indicate the correlation coefficient between each CTA and the CTA index. Correlations range from -1.0 to $+1.0$. The closer the correlation is to $+1.0.$, the more correlated a CTA is to most other CTAs, as measured by a CTA index. Low correlations are desirable because it means the CTA would provide significant diversification when combined in a portfolio with other CTAs. (Negative correlations would be better still, but statistically significant negative correlations between a CTA and a CTA index are virtually unheard of. Therefore, practically speaking, any correlation near 0.0 would be ideal.) Although there are no precise cutoff values, as a general guideline, correlation values above 0.70 could be considered high and those below 0.30 low.

Some services report the r-squared (r^2) value instead of the correlation coefficient. The r^2 is the square of the correlation coefficient. Thus, for example, an r^2 value of 0.7 would be equivalent to a correlation coefficient of 0.49. The r^2 value for a CTA (as measured against a CTA index) has a specific meaning: it is the percentage of the CTA's total variation in month-to-month returns explained by fluctuations in the CTA index.

In addition to indicating correlation coefficients (or r^2 values) for a CTA versus a CTA index, some services also provide correlation statistics between the CTA and stock and bond indexes. These are of far less importance (even for investors looking to incorporate managed futures within a traditional stock/bond portfolio) because most CTAs are fairly uncorrelated with the stock and bond markets.

3. *Return Percentile*. This number is normally shown on an annual basis and represents a CTA's ranking (in terms of return) relative to all CTAs. The lower the number, the better. For example, a percentile rating of 5.0 would indicate that the CTA's return for that year was higher than the returns of 95.0 percent of the CTAs.

4. *Percentage of Winning Months*. This statistic is self-explanatory and is particularly useful as a gauge of a CTA's consistency of performance.

5. *Risk of Ruin*. The risk of ruin is an equation that indicates the probability of reaching a specified percentage loss of capital (e.g., 50 percent). Table 3.3 illustrates the calculation of the risk of ruin for the given sample data. In this example, in which "ruin" is defined as a 50 percent loss, the risk of ruin—that is the probability of losing 50 percent of starting equity by investing with a CTA with the given set of monthly returns—is calculated at 7.45 percent.

6. *Relative Ratings*. Examples of relative ratings are provided by the *Stark Report*, which rates CTAs for four categories: return, risk, risk-adjusted return, and equity under management. A five-star rating scale is used. In each category CTAs who rank in the highest 10 percent of all CTAs surveyed receive five stars; those in the next 22 percent receive four stars; the middle 33 percent receive three stars; the next 22 percent receive two stars; and the lowest 10 percent receive one star. These four rating scores provide a succinct summary of a CTA's relative performance versus the industry.

Table 3.3
RISK OF RUIN EQUATIONS WITH EXAMPLE DATA FOR
EVALUATING THE EQUATIONS

	Data for Example		
Month Number	Percent Return	Month Number	Percent Return
1	27	11	−27
2	−1	12	−5
3	9	13	−23
4	−2	45	6
5	12	15	15
6	13	16	−1
7	−13	17	18
8	42	18	−2
9	−16	19	37
10	35	20	6

	Definitions	
N	Number of time periods per year	12
PW	Probability of a winning period	55
PL	Probability of a losing period	45%
W	Average amount won in a winning period	20%
L	Average amount lost in a losing period	−10%
FC	Fraction of capital loss for ruin	50%
	(The user specifies FC)	
PR	Probability of Ruin	(To be determined below)

Calculations	
$EX = PW * W + PL * L$	= 6.5000
$SQGAM = (PW * W * W + PL * L * L)^{1/2}$	= 16.2788
$P = 0.5 * (1 + EX/SQGAM)$	= 0.6996
$PSI = (1 − P)/P$	= 0.4293
$THETA = FC/SQGAM$	= 3.0715
$PR = (PSI)^{THETA}$	= 0.0745 (7.45%)

Sources: This table was provided by Richard Oberuc, Burlington Hall Asset Management, Inc., Hackensack, N.J. Oberuc cites the following source for the equation: Fred Gehm, *Commodity Market Management*, John Wiley & Sons, 1983. In turn, Gehm in his book cites the following source: Peter Griffin, *Theory of Blackjack*, Gamblers Press, Las Vegas, Nev., 1981.

WHICH PERFORMANCE MEASURE SHOULD BE USED?

By using drawdowns (the worst at each given point in time) to measure risk, the risk component of the RRR (the AMR) comes closer to describing most people's intuitive sense of risk than does the standard deviation in the Sharpe Ratio, which makes no distinction between sudden large gains and sudden sharp losses—two events that are perceived very differently by traders (and investors). The RRR also avoids the Sharpe Ratio's failure to distinguish between intermittent and consecutive losses. (To be precise, however, these two drawbacks will be irrelevant if none of the CTA series being analyzed exhibits any skewness or positive autocorrelation.) For these reasons, the RRR may be a superior return/risk measure to the Sharpe Ratio.

Even so, the RRR is being proposed as an additional rather than replacement return/risk measure to the Sharpe Ratio. Reason: The Sharpe Ratio is a very widely used return/risk measure, whereas, at this writing, the RRR is not used at all. Together the Sharpe Ratio and the RRR provide a very good description of a manager's relative performance.

In addition to these return/risk measures, the maximum loss (ML) figure should be checked to make sure there was no catastrophic losing streak. Also, the AGPR might be calculated as a supplemental measure, which yields a figure that is intuitively meaningful. A thorough performance analysis should also encompass measures of consistency, such as the percentage of winning months and return percentiles.

Finally, if available, relative ratings can be very useful, and correlation statistics would be essential if CTAs are being selected as part of a multi-manager fund or pool.

THE INADEQUACY OF A RETURN/RISK RATIO FOR EVALUATING MONEY MANAGER TRADING PERFORMANCE

Whereas in the case of evaluating trading systems a higher return/risk ratio *always* implies higher percent return,[6] this is not true for the evaluation of money managers. Thus, it is entirely possible for a money manager to have a higher return/risk ratio than another manager, but to also have

---

[6]See Jack D. Schwager, *Schwager on Futures: Technical Analysis,* John Wiley & Sons, New York, 1995, pp. 719–720, for a detailed explanation.

a lower percent return or a higher percent risk. (The reason for this is that in the money manager case, the link between fund requirements and risk is broken—that is, different money managers will differ in the level of risk they will assume for any given level of funds.) Consequently, a return/risk ratio is no longer a sufficient performance measure for choosing between alternative investments. We illustrate this point by using the Sharpe Ratio, but similar conclusions would apply to other return/risk measures. (In the following discussion, we assume that management fees are based entirely on profits and that interest income is not included in money manager return figures, but is received by investors. Consequently, the simplified form of the Sharpe Ratio, which deletes the riskless interest rate, is appropriate.)

Assume we are given the following set of *annualized* statistics for two money managers:

	Manager A	Manager B
Expected gain	$ 10,000	$ 50,000
Standard deviation of gain	$ 20,000	$ 80,000
Initial investment	$100,000	$100,000
Sharpe Ratio	.50	.625

Although Manager B has the higher Sharpe Ratio, not all traders would prefer Manager B, because he also has a higher risk measure (i.e., higher standard deviation). Thus, a risk-averse investor might prefer Manager A, gladly willing to sacrifice the potential for greater gain in order to avoid the substantially greater risk. For example, if annual trading results are normally distributed, for any given year, there would be a 10 percent probability of the return falling more than 1.3 standard deviations below the expected rate. In such an event, an investor would lose $54,000 with Manager B [$50,000 – (1.3 × $80,000)], but only $16,000 with Manager A. For a risk-averse investor, minimizing a loss under negative assumptions may be more important than maximizing gain under favorable conditions.[7]

---

[7]Implicit assumption in this example: The investor can't place a fraction of the stated initial investment with Manager B. In other words, the minimum unit size of investment is $100,000. Otherwise, it would always be possible to devise a strategy in which the investor would be better off with the manager with the higher Sharpe Ratio. For example, placing $25,000 with Manager B would imply the same standard deviation as is the case for a $100,000 investment with Manager A but a higher expected gain ($12,500).

Next, consider the following set of statistics for two other money managers:

	Manager C	Manager D
Expected gain	$ 20,000	$ 5,000
Standard deviation of gain	$ 20,000	$ 4,000
Initial investment	$100,000	$100,000
Sharpe Ratio	1.0	1.25

Although Manager D has a higher Sharpe Ratio, Manager C has a substantially higher percent return. Investors who are not particularly risk-averse might prefer Manager C even though he has a lower Sharpe Ratio. The reason for this is that for the major portion of probable outcomes, an investor would be better off with Manager C. Specifically, in this example, the investor will be better off as long as return does not fall more than .93 standard deviations below the expected rate—a condition that would be met 82 percent of the time (assuming trading results are normally distributed).[8]

Even more striking is the consideration that there are circumstances in which virtually all investors would prefer the money manager with the lower Sharpe Ratio. Consider the following two money managers:[9]

	Manager E	Manager F
Expected gain	$ 10,000	$ 50,000
Standard deviation of gain	$ 2,000	$ 12,500
Initial investment	$100,000	$100,000
Sharpe Ratio	5.0	4.0

[8]Implicit assumption in this example: Borrowing costs for the investor are significantly greater than the interest income return realized by placing funds with a money manager. This assumption prohibits the alternative strategy of borrowing funds and placing a multiple of the initial $100,000 investment with the manager with the higher Sharpe Ratio. If borrowing costs and interest income were equal (an assumption not likely to be valid in the real world), it would always be possible to devise a strategy in which the investor would be better off with the manager with the higher Sharpe Ratio. For example, the strategy of borrowing an additional $400,000 and placing $500,000 with Manager D would imply the same standard deviation as is the case for a $100,000 investment with Manager C, but a higher expected gain ($25,000).

[9]The Sharpe Ratios used in this example are considerably higher than the levels likely to be found in the real world. However, the assumption of such higher Sharpe Ratios elucidates the intended theoretical point.

In this example, virtually all investors (even those who are risk-averse) would prefer Manager F, despite the fact that he has a lower Sharpe Ratio. The reason is that the percent return is so large relative to the ambiguity of that return (standard deviation), that even under extreme adverse circumstances, investors would almost certainly be better off with Manager F. For example, once again assuming that trading results are normally distributed, the probability of a gain more than three standard deviations below the expected gain is only 0.139 percent. Yet even under these extreme circumstances, an investor would still be better off with Manager F: Gain = $12,500/year (12.5 percent) compared with $4,000/year (4 percent) for Manager E. This example illustrates, even more dramatically the fact that, by itself, a return/risk ratio does not provide sufficient information for evaluating a money manager.[10] (This conclusion applies to all return/risk measures, not just the Sharpe Ratio.)

The key point is that in evaluating money managers, it is also important to consider the percent return and risk figures independently rather than merely as a ratio.

TABULAR PERFORMANCE ANALYSIS

Thus far, we have only discussed the interpretation and use of individual performance statistics. For some types of performance data, tabular presentations can be particularly useful. Two excellent examples are provided by *The Barclay Institutional Report:*

1. *Time Window Return Analysis.* As illustrated in Table 3.4, this type of table summarizes the best, worst, and average returns for different length time periods.
2. *Drawdown Analysis.* As illustrated in Table 3.5, this type of table lists drawdowns in descending order of magnitude and indicates their duration, which is broken down into two segments: the number of months to the low point ("length") and the number of months from the low to a new high ("recovery").

These two tables provide a great deal of information about a CTA in very compact form. However, one caveat is that these tables should not be used to compare CTAs with significantly different track-record lengths. Such comparisons will be biased in favor of CTAs with shorter length records, since the longer a CTA trades, the greater the chance that a drawdown of any

---

[10]Comments analogous to footnote 8 also apply here.

Table 3.4
TIME WINDOWS

Length (Months)	Best	Worst	Average
1	108.10%	−21.10%	4.48%
3	189.53%	−24.75%	14.13%
6	287.29%	−24.89%	30.70%
9	561.27%	−26.79%	48.82%
12	507.79%	−26.78%	67.19%
18	503.04%	−23.85%	99.37%
24	1116.63%	−9.85%	145.31%

Source: Reprinted with permission from *The Barclay Institutional Report.* Copyright 1995 by Barclay Trading Group, Ltd.

Table 3.5
DRAWDOWN REPORT

Depth	Length (Months)	Recovery (Months)	Start Date	End Date
28.20	2	3	Feb. 85	Apr. 85
27.75	5	5	May 89	Oct. 89
26.78	9	18	Nov. 90	Aug. 91
26.78	12	2	Apr. 87	Apr. 88
26.60	4	—	May 95	Sep. 95
25.76	11	2	Mar. 86	Feb. 87
15.86	2	1	Dec. 93	Feb. 94

Source: Reprinted with permission from *The Barclay Institutional Report.* Copyright 1995 by Barclay Trading Group, Ltd.

specified amount will be reached, and the lower the worst returns for given intervals will be. (By definition, largest drawdowns and worst interval returns can only increase over time.)

GRAPHIC EVALUATION OF TRADING PERFORMANCE

Graphic depictions can be particularly helpful in comparing the performance of different money managers. Below we consider four types of charts:

1. *Net Asset Value.* The net asset value (NAV) indicates the equity at each point in time (typically, month-end) based on an assumed beginning equity of $1,000. For example, a NAV of 2,000 implies that the original investment was doubled as of the indicated point in time. By definition, the NAV at the start of the survey period is equal to 1,000. Subsequent values would be derived as follows:

End of Month	Monthly Dollar Return Divided by Equity at Start of Month	NAV
1	r_1	$(1,000)(1 + r_1)$
2	r_2	$(1,000)(1 + r_1)(1 + r_2)$
3	r_3	$(1,000)(1 + r_1)(1 + r_2)(1 + r_3)$
.	.	.
.	.	.
.	.	.
n	r_n	$(1,000)(1 + r_1)(1 + r_2)(1 + r_3) \ldots (1 + r_n)$

For example, if a money manager witnesses a +10 percent return in the first month, a −10 percent return in the second month, and a +20 percent return in the third month, the NAV at the end of the third month would be:

$$(1,000)(1 + 0.1)(1 - 0.1)(1 + 0.2) = 1,188$$

Figure 3.5 illustrates the NAV for two money managers during the January 1991–February 1995 period. Figure 3.6 presents the same information using a logarithmic scale for the NAV values. The representation in Figure 3.6 is preferable because it will assure that equal percentage changes in equity will result in equal-magnitude vertical movements. For example, in Figure 3.6, a 10 percent decline in equity when the NAV value equals 2,000 would appear equivalent to a 10 percent decline in equity when the NAV equals 1,000. In Figure 3.5, however, the former decline would appear twice as large. In any case, regardless of the type of scale used to depict NAV curves, it should be stressed that only comparisons based on exactly the same survey period are meaningful.

Although the NAV is primarily a return measure, it also reflects risk. All else being equal, the more volatile a money manager's performance, the lower the NAV. For example, consider the five money managers below who, during a given year, witness the following monthly gains and losses:

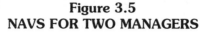

Figure 3.5
NAVS FOR TWO MANAGERS

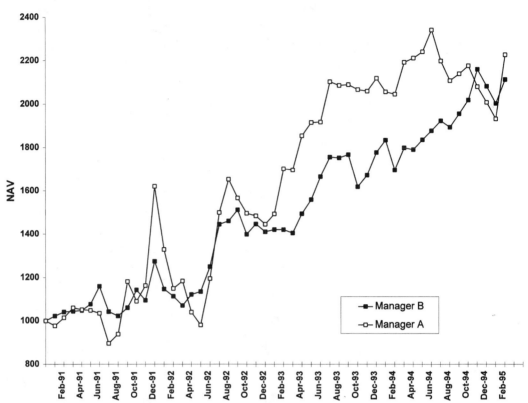

Manager	Six Months of Percentage Gains Equal to:	Six Months of Percentage Losses Equal to:	NAV at End of Year
1	+11%	−1%	$(1,000)(1.11)^6(.99)^6 = 1,760$
2	+21%	−11%	$(1,000)(1.21)^6(.89)^6 = 1,560$
3	+31%	−21%	$(1,000)(1.31)^6(.79)^6 = 1,230$
4	+41%	−31%	$(1,000)(1.41)^6(.69)^6 = 850$
5	+51%	−41%	$(1,000)(1.51)^6(.59)^6 = 500$

Note the dramatic differences between the ending NAV values despite the equal absolute differences between the percentage gains in winning months and percentage declines in losing months.

The degree to which the NAV incorporates risk may not be sufficient for risk-averse investors. For example, although Manager A witnesses a greater ending NAV than Manager B (see Figure 3.6), many investors might still pre-

Figure 3.6
NAVS FOR TWO MANAGERS (LOG SCALE)

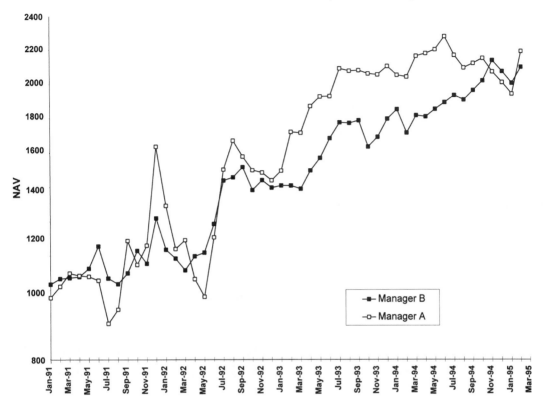

fer Manager B because her performance is less volatile. Clearly a more explicit depiction of risk, such as the "underwater" chart described below, would be helpful as a supplement to the NAV chart.

2. Underwater Curve.[11] The underwater curve depicts the percent drawdown as of the end of each month, measured from the previous equity peak. In other words, assuming beginning-of-month trading start dates, the underwater curve reflects the largest percentage loss as of the end of each month, assuming an account had been initiated at the worst possible prior entry point (i.e., prior equity peak). Insofar as it reflects the maximum possible equity retracement at each point, the underwater curve is conceptually similar to the previously described MRPP in the RRR calculation. Figures 3.7 and 3.8 illustrate the underwater curves for the two money managers depicted in Figures 3.5 and 3.6. (The vertical bars above the zero line indi-

---

[11]The term "underwater curve" was coined by Norman D. Strahm.

Figure 3.7
UNDERWATER CURVE: MANAGER A

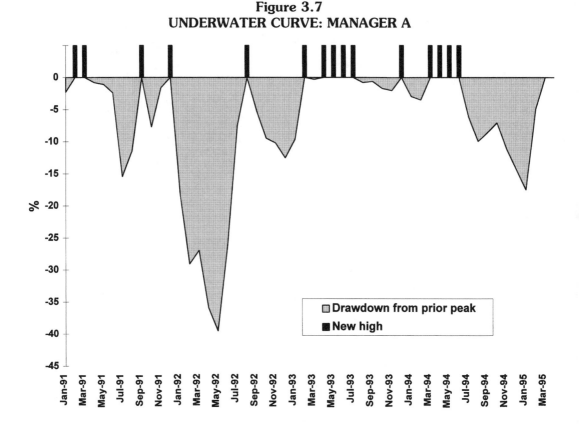

cate that the given month witnessed a new equity high.) These charts clearly demonstrate the greater degree of risk implied by Manager A's performance.

Which manager (A or B) has the better performance? The answer must unavoidably be subjective because Manager A achieves the higher end of period NAV value, but also exhibits more extreme drawdowns.[12] However, the key point is that by using both the NAV and underwater charts, each investor should have sufficient information to choose the money manager he prefers, given his personal return/risk preferences. In fact, given the relative ease with which the NAV and underwater charts can be derived, and the depth of the information they provide, for many investors, the combination of these charts may offer the ideal methodology for money manager performance comparisons.

---

[12]Although this statement is theoretically true, for the example given, it is likely that the vast majority of investors would prefer Manager B because Manager A's marginally higher return hardly seems worth the substantial increase in risk.

Figure 3.8
UNDERWATER CURVE: MANAGER B

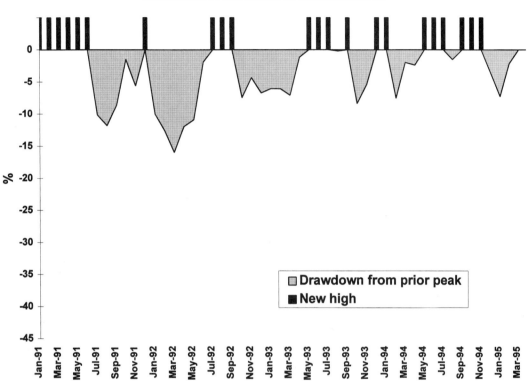

Although this section was described in terms of depicting money manager performance, the same types of charts could be generated for trading systems. The trader would merely have to transform the system's dollar profit/loss figures into percent return figures based on the account size the trader deems necessary to trade the system. The NAV for the system could then be derived by creating a chain multiple of 1,000 and these percent return numbers.

3. *Cumulative Excess Return.* CTA performance is heavily dependent on market conditions. During some periods, market conditions are so favorable for trading that even below-average CTAs may achieve good returns. In contrast, during periods of unfavorable market conditions, a large majority of CTAs may experience negative to mediocre returns. Therefore, a CTA's performance *relative* to an industry standard is far more informative than the CTA's *absolute* performance. For this reason, it is quite useful to superimpose the NAV of a CTA index over the NAV graph for an individual CTA (the chart described in item 1 of this list). Figure 3.9 illustrates such a comparison.

MEASURING TRADING PERFORMANCE

Figure 3.9
NAV: CTA X VERSUS BARCLAY DIVERSIFIED TRADERS INDEX

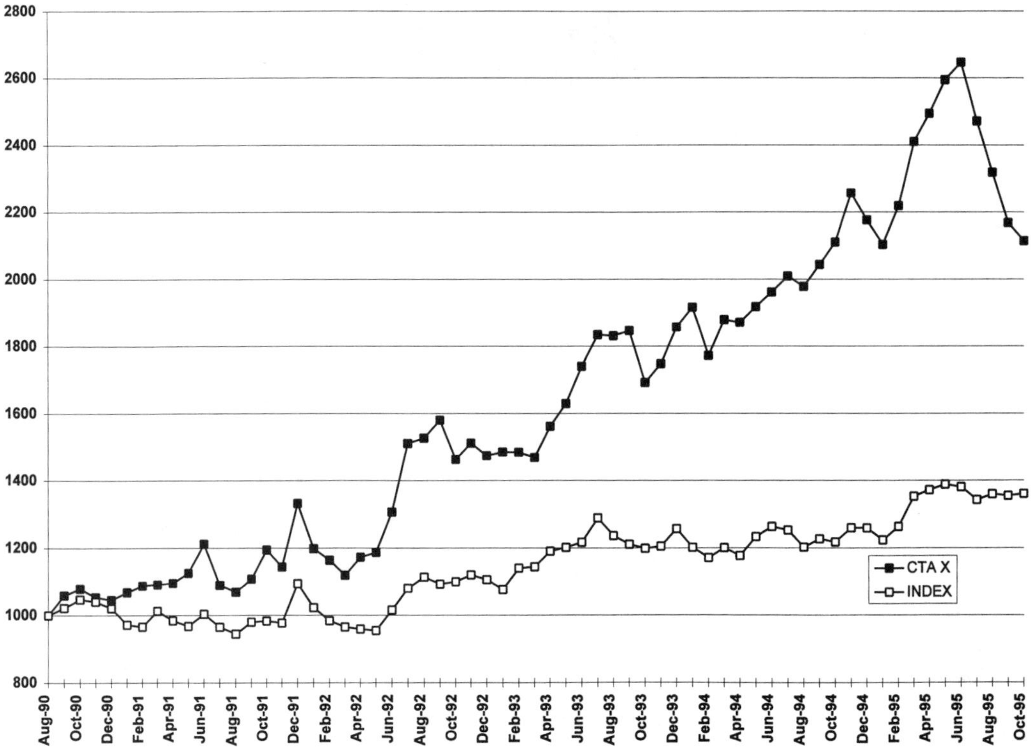

The *cumulative excess return* chart provides another means of depicting a comparison between the CTA and an index. This chart plots the cumulative difference between a CTA's monthly returns and the corresponding index returns. Figure 3.10 illustrates the cumulative excess return of the CTA shown in Figure 3.9. This chart shows that the given CTA generally outperformed the index, but *severely* underperformed the index during the final four months depicted. Of course, for CTAs who underperform the index on balance, the cumulative excess return curve will be negative.

It should be emphasized that NAV comparisons and cumulative excess return curves should employ indexes analogous to the CTA program being analyzed. Thus, for example, if the CTA program being examined traded only currencies, the foregoing charts would use a currency CTA index instead of a diversified CTA index. Figure 3.11 depicts the currency program NAV of the same CTA whose diversified program NAV was shown in Figure 3.9. Note that in this case the comparative index is based on currency traders only. Analogously, the cumulative excess return chart (Figure 3.12) was derived by

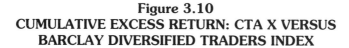

Figure 3.10
CUMULATIVE EXCESS RETURN: CTA X VERSUS
BARCLAY DIVERSIFIED TRADERS INDEX

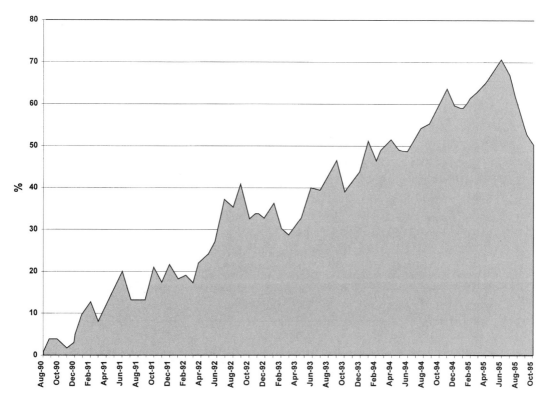

cumulating the differences between the monthly returns of the CTA's currency program and the monthly returns of the currency CTA index.

4. *Rolling 12-Month Return.* This chart shows the returns for the 12-month period ending in each month. (The first available data point in this chart will be for the 12th month of trading.) In effect, this chart depicts annual returns ending in every month, as opposed to the normal artificial constraint of showing annual returns for calendar year intervals only. Figure 3.13 illustrates the rolling 12-month return for the same CTA whose NAV was shown in Figure 3.9. It is interesting to note that despite a number of significant equity drawdowns, all the 12-month-period returns were positive. In addition to the obvious desirability of large positive 12-month returns, relative stability in these returns is a beneficial feature. In other words, if two CTAs had identical average returns, the CTA with more closely clustered 12-month returns would be preferred.

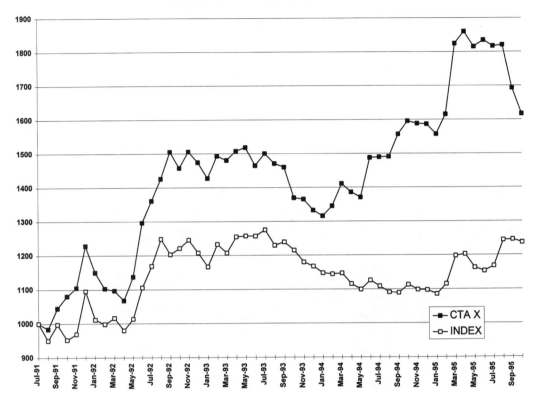

Figure 3.11
**NAV: CTA X CURRENCY PROGRAM VERSUS BARCLAY
CURRENCY TRADERS INDEX**

Of course, rolling return charts could be generated for other time intervals as well. If rolling return charts were plotted for a range of time intervals, the combined graphs would be analogous to the time window return table described earlier, but more informative. (Whereas the table provided information only about the best, worst, and average returns for each time interval, the rolling return charts would depict the returns for every month ending in each time interval.)

SOURCES OF CTA
PERFORMANCE INFORMATION

There are three major sources of *printed* CTA evaluations. Each issues a comprehensive quarterly report that contains a wide range of statistics and charts for all CTAs surveyed. All three publications are excellent, and inter-

Figure 3.12
CUMULATIVE EXCESS RETURN: CTA X VERSUS BARCLAY CURRENCY TRADERS INDEX

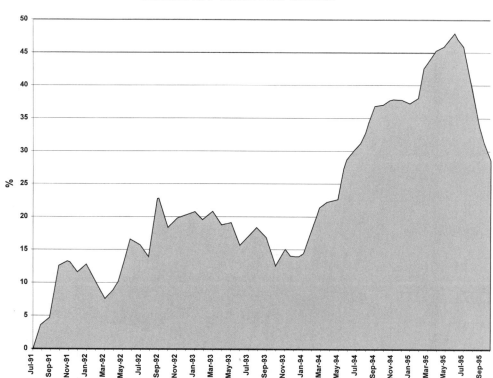

ested readers should sample each in order to determine a personal preference. The three sources are deliberately listed in *alphabetical order* to avoid any implication of ranking:

1. Barclay Trading Group, Fairfield, Iowa (515) 472-3456.
2. Managed Account Reports, New York, New York (212) 213-6202.
3. Stark Research Inc., La Jolla, California (619) 459-0818.

There are four major sources of *electronic* CTA data. All are comprehensive. Again, listed alphabetically, they are:

1. Barclay Trading Group, Fairfield, Iowa, (515) 472-3456.
2. Managed Account Reports, New York, New York, (212) 213-6202.
3. Refco Information Services, New York, New York, (212) 693-7397
4. TASS, London, U.K., (44) (171) 233-9797.

Figure 3.13
CTA X: ROLLING 12-MONTH RETURN (%)

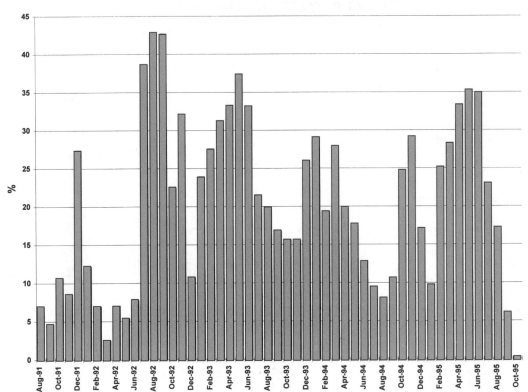

CONCLUSIONS

1. By itself, percent return is an insufficient measure for evaluating the performance of a money manager.
2. The Sharpe Ratio has several potential drawbacks as a trading performance measure:

   a. Failure to distinguish between upside and downside fluctuations;
   b. Failure to distinguish between intermittent and consecutive losses;
   c. Potential distortions in the gain measure in assessing performance for an extended period.

3. The RRR is an alternative performance measure that seems to be preferable to the Sharpe Ratio in that it appears to reflect more closely the behavioral preferences of the investor (that is, investors are generally concerned about *downside* volatility in equity rather

than volatility in equity). However, the Sharpe Ratio should still be considered as a supplemental measure because it is the most widely used return/risk measure, a distinction it enjoys because the measure is derived from Modern Portfolio Theory and plays an important role in that context.

4. The AGPR is a useful supplemental measure insofar as it has a clear intuitive interpretation and requires far less computation than the RRR.

5. Although not suitable as a sole risk measure, the ML provides important additional information.

6. Two measures of performance consistency are the percentage of winning months and return percentiles.

7. Low correlation with a CTA index is an important performance characteristic if CTAs are being selected for inclusion in a multi-manager pool or fund.

8. In the case of money managers, a return/risk ratio is not a fully adequate performance measure. Rather, return and risk should also be evaluated independently. The specific ordering of managers on the basis of these figures will be subjective (i.e., dependent on the individual investor's risk/reward preferences).

9. Two types of tabular data displays that are particularly useful in evaluating performance are time-window return analysis and drawdown analysis.

10. The NAV, underwater curve, cumulative excess return, and rolling 12-month return are four types of charts that are particularly helpful for analyzing money manager performance.

4   The Apples and
        Oranges Pitfall

Compare Figures 4.1 and 4.2, two charts that were extracted from a quarterly compilation of commodity trading advisor (CTA) programs published by a leading performance evaluation service.[1] Which trading program is better? Sounds like a ridiculous question, doesn't it? Trading program A seems to have superlative performance, witnessing steady, huge gains and far outpacing the industry average. Trading program B, however, seems mediocre at best, barely exceeding the lackluster industry average return during the period depicted. If presented with Figures 4.1 and 4.2, probably 100 out of 100 people would readily agree that trading program A is tremendously superior—and they would all be wrong. In fact, Trading programs A and B were both managed by the same CTA, using *identical*, fully computerized trading systems.

Why then the incredible performance difference between the two programs depicted in Figures 4.1 and 4.2? The explanation lies in the fact that the results shown in these two charts differ in two critical respects:

1. **Commissions.** Trading program B was subject to an extremely high $120 round turn commission rate for its first 20 months of trading. Trading program A, on the other hand, was subject to only a $10 round-turn commission rate during much of the same period—a 12-fold difference! The service from which Figures 4.1 and 4.2 were reproduced bases all its performance tables and charts on commissions and fees charged in the past, even if such costs are no longer representative. Thus it is possible for identical trading programs to appear radically different due to differences in their *past* cost structures. In other words, *apparent* performance differences may reflect trading costs rather than performance.

2. **Markets.** Trading program B traded a diversified group of markets, while trading program A traded a financial subset consisting of interest rates, currencies, and precious metals. As it turned out, during the period depicted, these markets were particularly advanta-

---

[1]In order to customize the scale for clarity and ease of comparison, these charts were recreated rather than reproduced from the originals.

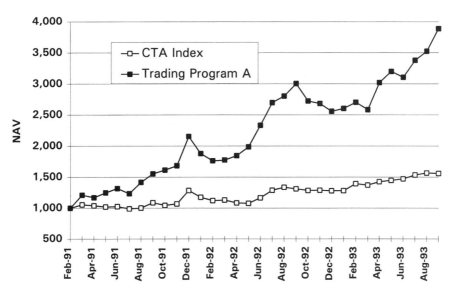

Figure 4.1
TRADING PROGRAM "A" VERSUS CTA INDEX

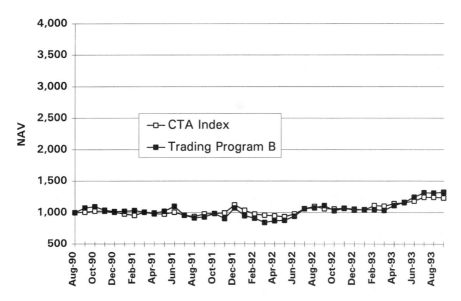

Figure 4.2
TRADING PROGRAM "B" VERSUS CTA INDEX

geous for computerized, trend-oriented approaches. (Sharp-eyed readers may have noticed that the CTA indexes in Figures 4.1 and 4.2 were different. Reason: Each chart depicted an industry subindex to match the particular market portfolio, that is, diversified and financial. Mention of this point was deliberately deferred until after the foregoing discussion regarding the market portfolio differences between the two programs.)

It should be stressed that both of the preceding advantages enjoyed by trading program A over trading program B for the period shown in Figures 4.1 and 4.2 do not imply any edge for trading program A in regards to *future* performance, which after all is the essential issue that concerns a new investor. To explain this contention, we again examine the two factors just discussed:

1. **Commissions.** The radically different cost structures between the two programs was entirely *historical* in nature (due to a high commission account in trading program B that was eventually dropped[2]). At the time the charts shown in Figures 4.1 and 4.2 were published, new investors actually faced identical cost structures in the two trading programs; hence, past cost differences were irrelevant.
2. **Markets.** Although the group of markets in trading program A provided better performance than the group of markets in trading program B in the *past*, there is no reason to assume that this pattern would continue in the *future*.

Therefore, in terms of *expected future* performance, the trading programs represented by Figures 4.1 and 4.2 are equivalent, despite an apparent striking difference between the two charts. The preceding example highlights the importance of the principle of comparing apples and apples. This illustration vividly demonstrates that comparisons of performance results derived using different sets of assumptions could easily lead to wildly inaccurate conclusions.

To draw meaningful performance comparisons, the results for the trading programs being compared should be based on the following identical assumptions:

1. **Commissions.** Performance results should be based on commission rates that are representative of what a current investor might pay. It should be emphasized that the commission rates new investors can expect to pay can differ radically from the historical commission rates charged in a trading program. Historical commission rates could have been much higher (as was the case in the example of trading program B just detailed) or much lower, say, for example, if the track record is based on an account managed by a floor trader and charged only floor commission rates, which are far lower than retail rates. Since the commission charged on a managed account

---

[2]The advisor had agreed to manage the account despite the high commission rate stipulated by the brokerage firm, because it represented the first account in the trading program, and as such was needed by the advisor to establish a track record. However, once other accounts were opened under the same program, this need was eliminated, and the disadvantageous high-commission-rate account was dropped by the advisor .

will usually depend on the broker, not the CTA, it makes sense to adjust for significant differences in historical commission charges when comparing different trading programs.

2. _Management Fees._ For each trading program being compared, the assumed management and profit incentive fees should be representative of the charges a new investor could expect to pay. Historical fees could have been much higher or lower (in some cases even equal to zero) than current fees.

It should be noted that when historical costs (any combination of management fee, incentive fee, and commissions) are widely divergent from the current cost structure (i.e., the costs a new investor could be expected to incur), the CTA will typically display _pro forma_ tables, which are a recalculation of historical results using actual trades and current costs. These tables are provided as a supplement to actual tables, which are based on fees and commissions actually charged in the past, even if substantially different from current levels. In such cases, the investor should almost invariably use the pro forma tables and ignore the so-called "actual" tables, which can be subject to substantial distortions (viewed from the perspective of the new investor). Thus, ironically, pro forma tables are usually far more meaningful than the more solid-sounding "actual" tables. This point was fully detailed in Chapter 1.

3. _Interest Income._ Interest income should either be included or excluded for _all_ programs being compared. The degree to which investors are paid interest typically has nothing to do with the CTA. Yet a CTA who managed pools or funds that paid partial or no interest income could appear inferior to CTAs whose performance results included interest income, even if his or her trading performance was actually significantly superior. New investors, however, would only be interested in performance comparisons based on trading results, _excluding differences in interest income collected by past investors._

4. _Markets._ Trading program comparisons should involve programs trading similar market portfolios. Otherwise, superior performance could easily be due to a more fortuitous basket of markets for the period being compared. In fact, differences in the markets traded could have a much greater impact on performance than differences in the trading systems or methodologies being used. For example, in 1992/1993, foreign interest rate markets witnessed enormous sustained trends. During the same period, domestic agricultural markets were generally subject to choppy price movements. It is hardly surprising that some of the best performance records during this period were registered by trading programs that had a significant involvement in the foreign interest rate sector. The fact that a CTA trading a foreign interest rate portfolio did better than a CTA trading a domestic agricultural program during this period would say very little about which CTA achieved the better performance. To summarize, if the portfolios being traded are significantly different, then there is simply insufficient information to draw any inferences about relative performance. Thus currency programs should be compared with currency programs, energy programs with energy programs, and so on.

5. *Time Period.* Trading programs must also be compared over identical time periods, as there can be tremendous variations between the relative market conditions during different time periods. For example, consider comparing two CTAs at the end of 1994, both trading similar domestic market portfolios. Assume that one CTA began trading at the start of 1990 and the other at the beginning of 1991. The significance of this difference in start dates is that 1990 was a very favorable year for most traders, as many markets witnessed major trends. In contrast, excluding foreign markets, the 1991–1994 period generally experienced significantly choppier trading conditions. Consequently, if the entire available track record were used for each CTA, it would bias the results in favor of the earlier starting CTA. This potential bias is underscored by the industry average performance figures. For example, Barclay Trading Group's broad-based CTA index rose by 21 percent in 1990, but averaged only a paltry 3 percent average annual gain in 1991–1994. Similarly, Managed Account Report's broad-based CTA index was up an impressive 27 percent in 1990, but witnessed a much more moderate average annual return of 11 percent during the 1991–1994 period.[3]

The point is that if an investor wishes to compare two trading programs with different-length track records, the comparison should be restricted to the period in which they both traded. This example is a good illustration of the principle that, in some instances, using less data yields more meaningful results.

Some readers may still find it difficult to believe that Figures 4.1 and 4.2 represent the exact same trading program, and may be wondering how I can be so sure that the CTA in question didn't use some different system variations for trading program A than he did for trading program B. Simple—I was the CTA (Wizard Trading). I can assure you that the two trading programs used all the same systems down to the last parameter set. As explained earlier, the trading programs differed only in respect to historical commission costs and the markets traded.

---

[3]There are a number of differences between the MAR and Barclay CTA indexes. Perhaps the most significant difference is that the MAR index is dollar weighted (i.e., returns for each CTA are weighted by the amount under management), whereas the Barclay index is equally weighted. The MAR index returns will usually be higher insofar as there is some tendency for the CTAs managing more money to also register higher returns. The MAR index is probably more representative of total profits (losses) realized by existing investors, but the Barclay index may be more relevant to new investors, since a number of the CTAs managing large sums—and hence having the greatest impact on the index—are not open to new investment.

5 Why All Conventional CTA Indexes Are Misleading

IN SEARCH OF A BENCHMARK

In the stock market, defining a benchmark is relatively straightforward. Both stock indexes and conventional mutual funds (as opposed to hedge funds) consist only of unleveraged long positions in a portfolio of stocks. Therefore the stock index that most closely conforms to the stock composition of a given portfolio or fund would provide a very appropriate benchmark comparison. For example, the S&P 500 index would provide a fitting benchmark for evaluating the performance of funds investing in diversified portfolios of high capitalization stocks.

For managed futures, however, the choice of an appropriate benchmark is far from obvious. The types of indexes that have been considered as performance benchmarks for managed futures can be classified into four categories:

1. Commodity Indexes. As the name implies, these indexes consist of commodity market prices. Some of the more common commodity indexes include the Commodity Research Bureau Index (CRB), Goldman Sachs Commodity Index (GSCI), and the Dow Jones Futures and Spot Commodity Index. These indexes differ in the mix of commodity markets included and the relative weightings assigned to each market. For example, the CRB uses an equal-weighting scheme, whereas the GSCI weights markets in proportion to the dollar value of their world production.

Commodity indexes are totally inappropriate for making any performance evaluation comparisons for two key reasons. First, by their very construction, commodity indexes assume a long position in each market in the index, whereas managed futures trading involves both long and short positions in approximately equal frequency. Second, commodity indexes do not include any financial markets, whereas financial markets account for over two-thirds of all futures trading.

2. *Generic Trading Index.* The single exponent of this type of approach is the BARRA/MLM index. Although this index avoids the major bias detailed in the next section, its appropriate application is limited. The BARRA/MLM index is discussed in detail in the appendix of this chapter.

3. *Pool/Fund Indexes*. These indexes consist of commodity pool and fund returns, with some indexes using only pool data or fund data alone, and some indexes combining the two.[1] Pool/fund indexes are also available for various classifications. For example, Managed Account Reports (MAR) compiles all of the following pool/fund indexes: dollar-weighted, equal-weighted, public funds, private pools, offshore, guaranteed, multiadvisor, and single-advisor. CTA indexes, which are discussed next, are more appropriate than pool/fund indexes for individual CTA performance comparisons. One suitable use for pool/fund indexes is as proxies for managed futures in a multisector portfolio (e.g., stock/bond/managed futures portfolio). In this application, however, pool/fund indexes would still be subject to the same bias described in the following section for CTA indexes.

4. *CTA Indexes.* There are a number of CTA indexes including those constructed by MAR, Barclay Trading Group, TASS, Refco Information Services, and Stark Research Inc. Some of these services compile sector indexes as well as overall commodity indexes. Some of the ways in which CTA indexes differ from each other include:

- Requirements for a CTA's inclusion in the index
- Types of trading programs included (e.g., all or specific sector)
- The weighting scheme (e.g., equal-weighted or dollar-weighted)

Conceptually, CTA indexes provide the appropriate benchmark for managed futures performance comparisons, particularly if the index is cho-

---

[1]The distinction between pools and funds is summarized by the following excerpt taken from Charles Epstein, *Managed Futures in the Institutional Portfolio*, John Wiley & Sons, New York, 1992:

> "Fund" generally refers to a public offering registered with the Securities and Exchange Commission (SEC) in which the units are publicly offered for a limited period. There is generally no subsequent offering of units once the original period has expired. Funds generally have the smallest minimum investment requirements and as such have been largely used by individual investors. "Pools" generally refer to private limited partnerships that are subject to securities regulations affecting private placements. Pools are developed by a CPO and are offered by private placement to a limited number of nonaccredited investors and to an unlimited number of accredited investors. (An accredited investor is one who meets predefined suitability and income guidelines.)

sen to resemble the portfolio or trading program in the performance evaluation. However, as discussed in the next section, all CTA indexes are subject to a significant bias.

THE BIAS IN CTA INDEXES FROM AN INVESTOR PERSPECTIVE

All conventional CTA indexes are misleading in that they significantly understate risk and, hence, overstate return/risk measures. The crux of the problem is that an investor can't replicate the performance of a CTA index by investing in all the CTAs in the index. The significant minimum investment required, which often equals or exceeds $500,000 per individual CTA, makes it impossible for virtually all investors to diversify among even a significant subset of the CTAs in the index, let alone all the CTAs. (Although smaller investors can achieve some diversification by investing in a multi-manager futures fund, this still leaves open the question of how closely the selected fund comes to matching the diversification of the entire index.) In contrast, in the stock market, investors can indeed replicate the index performance by placing their money in index-based funds, which own appropriately weighted shares of all the stocks in a given index (e.g., S&P 500).

If a CTA index is constructed by calculating the average monthly return of all CTAs in the index (a common methodology[2]), the return will equal the expected return of a randomly selected CTA. Thus, a CTA index will yield an unbiased measure of monthly return, even though the index can't be duplicated in a practical sense. The problem lies on the risk side of the equation. A series created by averaging all CTA returns will *always* have a lower standard deviation than the average standard deviation of all CTAs.[3] In other words, the conventionally calculated CTA index will tend to understate, often by a significant margin, the expected risk level *for an investor placing funds with only a single CTA*. As a result, such an index will also tend to overstate the expected return/risk measure for the *single CTA investor*.[4]

---

[2]Another common approach that weights the CTAs in the average by the amount of funds they have under management will be subject to the same flaw described below.

[3]The standard deviation, which was defined in Chapter 3, is used as a measure of risk. The discussion in this chapter would apply to other risk measures as well.

[4]An implicit assumption made in this chapter is that the method used by the investor for selecting a CTA does not have an edge over a random selection process—an assumption that may be closer to reality than generally realized (see Chapter 8). In turn, such an assumption would imply that the average of all CTA returns (i.e., the index return) would provide a better estimate of expected return than the average return of the CTA actually selected. (Surprisingly, there is strong evidence that this assumption may be entirely valid—see Chapter 6.)

Table 5.1
MONTHLY RETURNS OF THREE CTAs AND
CORRESPONDING INDEX (%)

Month	CTA1	CTA2	CTA3	Index
Jan 90	−14.1	−1.5	−13.6	−9.7
Feb 90	14.7	−4.5	−15.9	−1.9
Mar 90	24.7	−0.8	4.3	9.4
Apr 90	26.0	−2.8	3.5	8.9
May 90	−12.2	3.8	13.1	1.6
June 90	3.6	4.8	2.0	3.5
Jul 90	10.0	−4.0	0.1	2.0
Aug 90	14.2	18.1	4.7	12.3
Sep 90	10.8	−5.2	12.4	6.0
Oct 90	−5.5	7.9	−18.9	−5.5
Nov 90	−1.8	2.8	−1.9	−2.2
Dec 90	−7.9	3.2	12.2	2.5
Jan 91	−13.4	2.4	13.3	0.8
Feb 91	3.6	−2.2	−0.2	0.4
Mar 91	7.1	3.8	−3.2	2.6
Apr 91	−2.6	1.0	1.4	−0.1
May 91	5.5	−5.1	6.5	2.3
Jun 91	6.2	−5.3	4.4	1.8
Jul 91	−19.2	8.3	4.5	−2.1
Aug 91	−12.1	−6.2	4.2	−4.7
Sep 91	−3.2	3.4	−6.9	−2.2
Oct 91	2.1	−3.2	11.1	3.3
Nov 91	−0.9	−1.2	1.5	−0.2
Dec 91	34.0	1.9	9.3	15.1
Jan 92	−14.7	7.6	−2.0	−3.0
Feb 92	−15.3	−3.3	−4.3	−7.6
Mar 92	−11.8	0.4	−11.4	−7.6
Apr 92	7.6	−5.0	0.6	1.1
May 92	1.8	2.8	6.1	3.6
Jun 92	10.0	4.1	2.6	5.6
July 92	15.9	6.7	1.2	7.9
Aug 92	9.5	1.5	−3.7	2.4
Sep 92	−8.6	−0.2	−4.1	−4.3
Oct 92	−4.7	0.5	7.0	0.9
Nov 92	2.3	−1.6	2.2	1.0
Dec 92	1.4	0.1	1.4	1.0
Jan 93	−7.3	−6.1	5.5	−2.6
Feb 93	9.9	2.5	0.7	4.4
Mar 93	7.9	−6.5	1.7	1.0
Apr 93	5.4	5.1	−6.8	1.2
May 93	2.6	−8.5	3.9	−0.7

TABLE 5.1 (continued)

Month	CTA1	CTA2	CTA3	Index
Jun 93	−1.0	12.6	1.3	4.3
Jul 93	18.9	−0.5	1.6	6.7
Aug 93	−15.9	1.5	3.5	−3.6
Sep 93	−8.9	−4.3	5.8	−2.5
Average Return	1.66	0.52	1.34	1.17
Standard Deviation	12.06	5.34	7.12	5.02
Modified Sharpe Ratio	0.48	0.33	0.65	0.81

An illustration will help clarify the bias inherent in a CTA index. Table 5.1 details the returns for three actual CTA trading programs and an index based on these three sets of returns.[5] Note that although the average monthly return of the index is equal to the average of the three CTA average monthly returns, the standard deviation of the index is lower than the lowest standard deviation among the CTAs—far lower in the case of two of the three CTAs.

Figures 5.1–5.3 compare the net asset values (NAVs) of each of the CTAs against the index. The NAV simply shows the equity value per $1,000 initial investment at each point in time, given the corresponding set of monthly returns. In examining these three charts, it is clear that the index, which is supposed to be representative of the CTAs that it comprises, actually exhibits a better performance profile than any of the CTAs. The index has a higher ending NAV than CTA1, with far lower volatility (equivalent to lower risk). The index has a far higher ending NAV than CTA2, with modestly lower volatility. (Although not readily apparent in the chart, the index volatility is lower as measured by the variability in monthly returns.) Finally, although CTA3 has a slightly higher ending NAV than the index, this modest differential is far outweighed by a much higher volatility level. Of course, in broader-based indexes, the index will not have better performance (in terms of risk/return measures) than *all* the elements in the index, as was the case in the foregoing example; however, there will be a built-in bias for the index to outperform a significant majority of the individual CTAs.

---

[5]To clarify the exposition, we are assuming that the universe of CTAs consists of only three CTAs. The general principles demonstrated, however, would apply whether there are three CTAs in the index or 500.

Figure 5.1
NAV: CTA1 VERSUS CONVENTIONAL INDEX

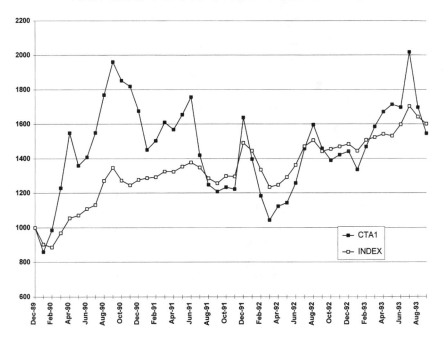

Figure 5.2
NAV: CTA2 VERSUS CONVENTIONAL INDEX

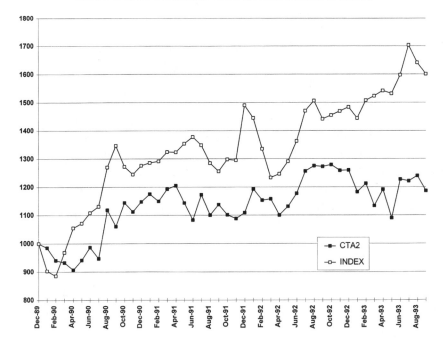

Figure 5.3
NAV: CTA3 VERSUS CONVENTIONAL INDEX

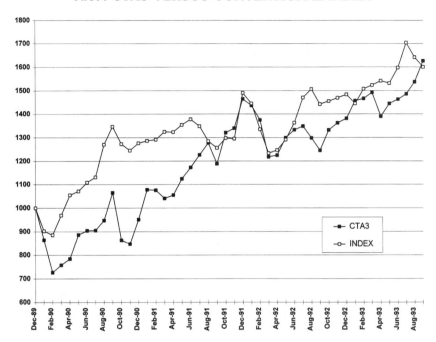

THE IMPACT OF VOLATILITY ON RETURN

It should be emphasized that increased volatility not only increases the risk measure (e.g., standard deviation), but also reduces return. For example, the combination of a 10 percent gain and a 5 percent loss would be a net gain of 4.5 percent ($1.10 \times 0.95 = 1.045$), whereas the combination of a 30 percent gain and a 25 percent loss would a 2.5 percent loss ($1.30 \times 0.75 = 0.975$)—yet both pairs of numbers are equal to an average monthly return of +2.5 percent. As another example of the same point, the net result of a back-to-back 50 percent gain and 50 percent loss (in either order) is not a break-even situation—as many people naively assume—but rather a 25 percent loss ($1.50 \times 0.50 = 0.75$). This effect explains why CTA1, whose performance is quite volatile, actually ends up with a lower NAV than the index, despite an average monthly return that significantly exceeds the industry return (1.66 percent versus 1.17 percent). Thus, the averaging process used in constructing an index will not only tend to understate risk (i.e., the variability of return), but it will also tend to overstate cumulative return as reflected by the ending NAV.

THE BIAS IN CTA INDEXES AS BASELINE COMPARISON MEASURES

The primary purpose of a stock index is to provide a baseline performance comparison for managers who invest in other baskets of stocks. In this application, the tendency of an index to dampen variability, which will reduce risk and increase cumulative return vis-à-vis the individual stocks that make up the index, is not a problem, since the diversification used by most managers will produce similar effects. The situation is completely different in the case of a CTA index. In this instance, due to the volatility reduction that results from the averaging process inherent in its construction, the index provides a very biased baseline comparison against which to measure individual manager performance. The appropriate stock market analogy would be to use a stock index as a performance comparison *if stock managers typically invested in only one stock* (which, of course, is not the case).

As an example of the degree of bias, for the three-year period ending in the third quarter 1995 (the most recent data available), 59 percent of the CTAs in MAR's equal-weighted CTA index had a lower Sharpe Ratio than the index. Moreover, this figure is actually significantly understated because it is only based on CTAs still in the index at the end of the survey period. A substantial number of CTAs terminated their trading activity during the course of the survey period. It is a safe assumption that all of these CTAs underperformed the industry index. If these "nonsurviving" CTAs are included in the count—as they should be—the percentage of CTAs with lower Sharpe Ratios than the index rises to 75 percent (assuming all the nonsurvivors underperformed the index).

DERIVING AN UNBIASED CTA INDEX: METHOD 1

As demonstrated in the preceding section, if a CTA index is intended to be used as a baseline performance measure for evaluating individual CTAs or as a representative measure for investors placing money with single CTAs, conventionally derived indexes will introduce gross distortions. It is intuitively obvious that an index that is supposed to be representative of its individual elements and reflects better performance than a substantial majority of those elements is fundamentally flawed. Clearly, some alternative index derivation methodologies are needed to yield unbiased measures in the previously cited applications.

One possible approach is to construct an index whose standard deviation is equal to the average standard deviation of all the CTAs in the index (in addition to the standard trait of having an average monthly return equal to the average return of all the CTAs in the index). This type of index can be constructed by the following steps:

1. Calculate the returns of a conventional CTA index. (Each month's index return is equal to that month's average return of all CTAs in the index.)
2. Calculate the standard deviation of the returns in a conventional index.
3. Calculate the standard deviation of return for each CTA in the index, and then find the average standard deviation.
4. Divide the average standard deviation by the standard deviation of the conventional index returns.
5. Multiply each monthly return of the conventional index by the ratio obtained in step 4.
6. Calculate the difference between the average monthly return of the series obtained in step 5 and the average monthly return of the conventional index.
7. Subtract this difference from each monthly return in step 5.

The index constructed using these steps will have both an average monthly return and a standard deviation equal to the corresponding averages of all CTAs in the index. Note that step 5 yields a series with a standard deviation equal to the average standard deviation of all the CTAs (since multiplying a series by a constant will multiply the standard deviation by that same constant), but at the same time causes the average monthly return of the index to deviate from the average of all CTAs by the same multiple. Step 7 effectively brings the index average monthly return back into line with the average return of all CTAs, while leaving the standard deviation unaffected (since subtracting or adding a constant to a series does not affect the standard deviation of the series).

Table 5.2 illustrates the preceding methodology for a hypothetical index consisting of the three CTAs in Table 5.1. Of course, an actual CTA index would consist of hundreds of CTAs, but the approach would be exactly the same. By multiplying the conventional index monthly returns by the indicated ratio (8.170/5.018), the next to last column yields a series of monthly returns with a standard deviation equal to the average standard deviation of all CTAs. The last column then subtracts the difference between the average monthly return of this series and the average monthly return of the conventional index (1.908 − 1.172 = 0.736) to obtain the standard-deviation-adjusted index—an index with the same average monthly return as the conventional index and a standard deviation equal to the average of all CTA deviations.

Table 5.2
STANDARD-DEVIATION-ADJUSTED INDEX DERIVATION (%)

Month	CTA1	CTA2	CTA3	Conventional Index (CI)	CI × Ratio	Adjusted Index
Jan 90	−14.1	−1.5	−13.6	−9.7	−15.8	−16.6
Feb 90	14.7	−4.5	−15.9	−1.9	−3.1	−3.8
Mar 90	24.7	−0.8	4.3	9.4	15.3	14.6
Apr 90	26.0	−2.8	3.5	8.9	14.5	13.7
May 90	−12.2	3.8	13.1	1.6	2.5	1.8
June 90	3.6	4.8	2.0	3.5	5.6	4.9
Jul 90	10.0	−4.0	0.1	2.0	3.3	2.6
Aug 90	14.2	18.1	4.7	12.3	20.1	19.3
Sep 90	10.8	−5.2	12.4	6.0	9.8	9.0
Oct 90	−5.5	7.9	−18.9	−5.5	−9.0	−9.7
Nov 90	−1.8	−2.8	−1.9	−2.2	−3.5	−4.3
Dec 90	−7.9	3.2	12.2	2.5	4.1	3.4
Jan 91	−13.4	2.4	13.3	0.8	1.3	0.5
Feb 91	3.6	−2.2	−0.2	0.4	0.7	−0.1
Mar 91	7.1	3.8	−3.2	2.6	4.2	3.4
Apr 91	−2.6	1.0	1.4	−0.1	−0.1	−0.9
May 91	5.5	−5.1	6.5	2.3	3.7	3.0
Jun 91	6.2	−5.3	4.4	1.8	2.9	2.1
Jul 91	−19.2	8.3	4.5	−2.1	−3.5	−4.2
Aug 91	−12.1	−6.2	4.2	−4.7	−7.7	−8.4
Sep 91	−3.2	3.4	−6.9	−2.2	−3.7	−4.4
Oct 91	2.1	−3.2	11.1	3.3	5.4	4.7
Nov 91	−0.9	−1.2	1.5	−0.2	−0.4	−1.1
Dec 91	34.0	1.9	9.3	15.1	24.5	23.8
Jan 92	−14.7	7.6	−2.0	−3.0	−4.9	−5.7
Feb 92	−15.3	−3.3	−4.3	−7.6	−12.4	−13.1
Mar 92	−11.8	0.4	−11.4	−7.6	−12.4	−13.1
Apr 92	7.6	−5.0	0.6	1.1	1.7	1.0
May 92	1.8	2.8	6.1	3.6	5.8	5.1
Jun 92	10.0	4.1	2.6	5.6	9.1	8.3
July 92	15.9	6.7	1.2	7.9	12.9	12.2
Aug 92	9.5	1.5	−3.7	2.4	4.0	3.2
Sep 92	−8.6	−0.2	−4.1	−4.3	−7.0	−7.7
Oct 92	−4.7	0.5	7.0	0.9	1.5	0.8
Nov 92	2.3	−1.6	2.2	1.0	1.6	0.9
Dec 92	1.4	0.1	1.4	1.0	1.6	0.8
Jan 93	−7.3	−6.1	5.5	−2.6	−4.3	−5.0
Feb 93	9.9	2.5	0.7	4.4	7.1	6.4
Mar 93	7.9	−6.5	1.7	1.0	1.7	1.0
Apr 93	5.4	5.1	−6.8	1.2	2.0	1.3

TABLE 5.2 (continued)

Month	CTA1	CTA2	CTA3	Conventional Index (CI)	CI × Ratio	Adjusted Index
May 93	2.6	-8.5	3.9	-0.7	-1.1	-1.8
Jun 93	-1.0	12.6	1.3	4.3	7.0	6.3
Jul 93	18.9	-0.5	1.6	6.7	10.8	10.1
Aug 93	-15.9	1.5	3.5	-3.6	-5.9	-6.7
Sep 93	-8.9	-4.3	5.8	-2.5	-4.0	-4.8
Average Return	1.658	0.516	1.342	1.172	1.908	1.172
Standard Deviation (sd)	12.056	5.339	7.115	5.018	8.170	8.170
Average sd of all CTAs	8.170					
Ratio of average sd to						
Conventional Index sd	1.628					

DERIVING AN UNBIASED CTA INDEX: METHOD 2

Another possible adjustment method would be to derive an index with the same monthly return as the conventional index and a Sharpe Ratio equal to the average Sharpe Ratio of all CTAs. It should be noted that in the following discussion we will be using a modified Sharpe Ratio, which we define as the annualized average return divided by the annualized standard deviation. In other words, the modified Sharpe Ratio does not subtract the risk-free return from the average return:

$$\text{Sharpe Ratio} = \frac{(\text{Annualized return} - \text{Risk-free return})}{\text{standard deviation}}$$

$$\text{Modified Sharpe Ratio} = \frac{\text{Annualized return}}{\text{standard deviation}}$$

Besides the benefit of simplification (by avoiding the need for incorporating a risk-free return series in the calculations), the modified Sharpe Ratio actually has an important theoretical justification: For comparisons of CTAs with each other, as well as with a CTA index, the modified Sharpe Ratio is actually more meaningful because the performance ranking will be independent of the choice of leverage. In other words, the conventional Sharpe Ratio will increase as a CTA increases leverage, whereas the modified Sharpe Ratio will be unaffected. This point was demonstrated in Chapter 3.

Table 5.3
MODIFIED-SHARPE-RATIO-ADJUSTED INDEX DERIVATION (%)

Month	CTA1	CTA2	CTA3	Conventional Index (CI)	CI × Ratio	Adjusted Index
Jan 90	−14.1	−1.5	−13.6	−9.7	−16.1	−16.9
Feb 90	14.7	−4.5	−15.9	−1.9	−3.2	−3.9
Mar 90	24.7	−0.8	4.3	9.4	15.6	14.8
Apr 90	26.0	−2.8	3.5	8.9	14.7	14.0
May 90	−12.2	3.8	13.1	1.6	2.6	1.8
June 90	3.6	4.8	2.0	3.5	5.7	5.0
Jul 90	10.0	−4.0	0.1	2.0	3.4	2.6
Aug 90	14.2	18.1	4.7	12.3	20.4	19.6
Sep 90	10.8	−5.2	12.4	6.0	10.0	9.2
Oct 90	−5.5	7.9	−18.9	−5.5	−9.1	−9.9
Nov 90	−1.8	−2.8	−1.9	−2.2	−3.6	−4.4
Dec 90	−7.9	3.2	12.2	2.5	4.2	3.4
Jan 91	−13.4	2.4	13.3	0.8	1.3	0.5
Feb 91	3.6	−2.2	−0.2	0.4	0.7	−0.1
Mar 91	7.1	3.8	−3.2	2.6	4.2	3.5
Apr 91	−2.6	1.0	1.4	−0.1	−0.1	−0.9
May 91	5.5	−5.1	6.5	2.3	3.8	3.0
Jun 91	6.2	−5.3	4.4	1.8	2.9	2.2
Jul 91	−19.2	8.3	4.5	−2.1	−3.5	−4.3
Aug 91	−12.1	−6.2	4.2	−4.7	−7.8	−8.6
Sep 91	−3.2	3.4	−6.9	−2.2	−3.7	−4.5
Oct 91	2.1	−3.2	11.1	3.3	5.5	4.8
Nov 91	−0.9	−1.2	1.5	−0.2	−0.4	−1.1
Dec 91	34.0	1.9	9.3	15.1	25.0	24.2
Jan 92	−14.7	7.6	−2.0	−3.0	−5.0	−5.8
Feb 92	−15.3	−3.3	−4.3	−7.6	−12.6	−13.4
Mar 92	−11.8	0.4	−11.4	−7.6	−12.6	−13.4
Apr 92	7.6	−5.0	0.6	1.1	1.7	1.0
May 92	1.8	2.8	6.1	3.6	5.9	5.1
Jun 92	10.0	4.1	2.6	5.6	9.2	8.5
July 92	15.9	6.7	1.2	7.9	13.1	12.3
Aug 92	9.5	1.5	−3.7	2.4	4.0	3.3
Sep 92	−8.6	−0.2	−4.1	−4.3	−7.1	−7.9
Oct 92	−4.7	0.5	7.0	0.9	1.5	0.8
Nov 92	2.3	−1.6	2.2	1.0	1.6	0.9
Dec 92	1.4	0.1	1.4	1.0	1.6	0.8
Jan 93	−7.3	−6.1	5.5	−2.6	−4.4	−5.1
Feb 93	9.9	2.5	0.7	4.4	7.2	6.4
Mar 93	7.9	−6.5	1.7	1.0	1.7	1.0
Apr 93	5.4	5.1	−6.8	1.2	2.0	1.3
May 93	2.6	−8.5	3.9	−0.7	−1.1	−1.9

TABLE 5.3 (continued)

Month	CTA1	CTA2	CTA3	Conventional Index (CI)	CI × Ratio	Adjusted Index
Jun 93	−1.0	12.6	1.3	4.3	7.1	6.4
Jul 93	18.9	−0.5	1.6	6.7	11.0	10.3
Aug 93	−15.9	1.5	3.5	−3.6	−6.0	−6.8
Sep 93	−8.9	−4.3	5.8	−2.5	−4.1	−4.9
Average Return	1.658	0.516	1.342	1.172	1.942	1.172
Standard Deviation	12.056	5.339	7.115	5.018	8.316	8.316
Modified Sharpe Ratio (MSR)	0.476	0.335	0.653	0.809	0.809	0.488
Avg. MSR of all CTAs	0.488					
Ratio of Index MSR to Avg. MSR	1.657					

The method for deriving a modified Sharpe-Ratio-adjusted index is analogous to the method used for deriving the standard-deviation-adjusted index:

1. Calculate the returns of a conventional CTA index. (Each month's index return is equal to that month's average return of all CTAs in the index.)
2. Calculate the modified Sharpe Ratio of the returns in a conventional index.
3. Calculate the modified Sharpe Ratio of return for each CTA in the index, and then find the average modified Sharpe Ratio.
4. Divide the modified Sharpe Ratio of the conventional index returns by the average modified Sharpe Ratio. (Note that, in contrast to the preceding standard deviation adjustment procedure, this ratio is calculated by dividing the index measure by the average measure.)
5. Multiply each monthly return of the conventional index by the ratio obtained in step 4.
6. Calculate the difference between the average monthly return of the series obtained in step 5 and the average monthly return of the conventional index.
7. Subtract this difference from each monthly return in step 5.

Table 5.3 illustrates the preceding methodology for a hypothetical index consisting of the three CTAs in Table 5.1. The next to last column is derived by multiplying the conventional index monthly returns by the indicated ratio (0.809/0.488). The last column then subtracts the difference between the average monthly return of this series and the average monthly return of the conventional index $(1.942 - 1.1172 = 0.770)$ to obtain the modified-Sharpe-Ratio-adjusted index—an index with the same average monthly return as the conventional index and a modified Sharpe Ratio equal to the average of all CTA modified Sharpe Ratios.

COMPARING THE INDIVIDUAL CTAs TO AN UNBIASED INDEX

Figures 5.4–5.6 compare the three individual CTAs to a standard-deviation-adjusted index (Method 1). Note that, whereas in Figures 5.1–5.3, the conventional index exhibited better performance than each of the individual CTAs (in return/risk terms), the adjusted index does not reflect such a superiority bias. CTA1 finished with a greater cumulative return than the adjusted index, albeit with significantly higher volatility (see Figure 5.4). CTA2 witnessed a substantially lower cumulative return than the adjusted index but also exhibited lower volatility (see Figure 5.5). CTA3 is clearly superior to the

Figure 5.4
NAV: CTA1 VERSUS STANDARD-DEVIATION-ADJUSTED INDEX

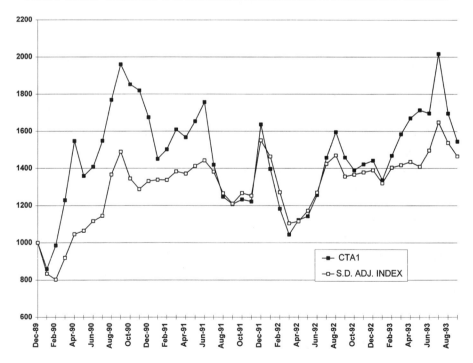

Figure 5.5
NAV: CTA2 VERSUS STANDARD-DEVIATION-ADJUSTED INDEX

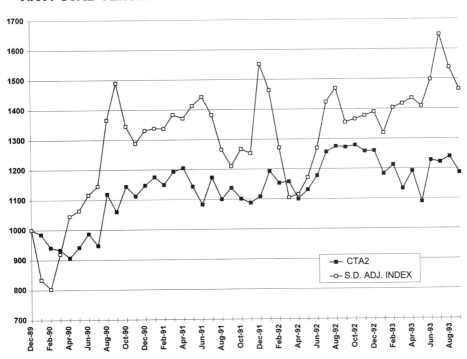

Figure 5.6
NAV: CTA3 VERSUS STANDARD-DEVIATION-ADJUSTED INDEX

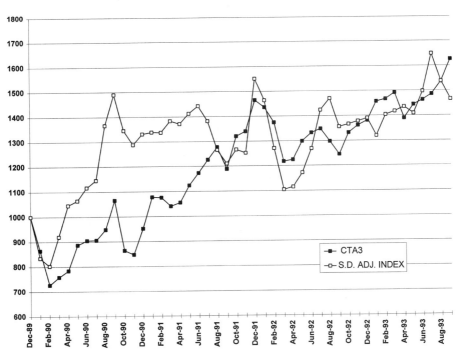

adjusted index, finishing with a greater cumulative return and reflecting somewhat lower volatility (see Figure 5.6). In contrast, CTA3 (by far the best performing of the three CTAs) finished with only a slightly higher cumulative return and a significantly higher volatility than the conventional index (see Figure 5.3).

The fact that an index has return/risk characteristics equivalent to (or better than) the top-performing CTAs used to construct the index—as is the case for the conventional index in our example—demonstrates a critical measurement bias. (Although in an actual CTA index, which includes hundreds of CTAs, the index will not outperform the top CTAs in the index, it will still outperform a significant majority of CTAs.) The average standard-deviation-adjusted index, on the other hand, appears far more representative of the CTAs used to construct the index. A similar conclusion would have been evident if the modified-Sharpe-Ratio-adjusted index (Method 2) had been used as the comparison measure in Figures 5.4–5.6 (instead of the standard-deviation-adjusted index).

ALTERNATIVE INDEX RETURN/RISK MEASURES

Dividing the average annual returns of the adjusted indexes derived in the preceding section by their corresponding standard deviations will yield alternative index-based return/risk measures to the Sharpe Ratios or modified Sharpe Ratios of the conventional (i.e., unadjusted) indexes. These return/risk measures will be analogous to, but lower than, the modified Sharpe Ratios of the conventional indexes: the numerators will be the same in all cases, but the denominators (i.e., standard deviations) of the adjusted-index-based return/risk measures will be higher (because they adjust for the bias of an index standard deviation always being below the average standard deviation of the elements in the index).

OTHER DISTORTIONS IN CONVENTIONAL CTA INDEXES

There are two additional sources of distortions in conventional CTA indexes:

Implicit Rebalancing Assumption.   The use of a monthly average of CTA returns not only assumes an equal investment with each CTA but also implicitly assumes that the investment is rebalanced each month to maintain an equal allocation among CTAs—an assumption not met in the real world.[6] Even the largest and most diversified pool operators only rebalance portfolios intermittently, and then usually not for the purpose of maintaining equal allocations.

The monthly rebalancing assumption can be removed by using an average of NAVs as opposed to an average of percent returns. The index calculation can include periodic rebalancing. For example, if the assumption is that portfolios are rebalanced at the start of each year, the index would be constructed as follows:[7]

1. Set NAV = 1,000 for each CTA at start.
2. Average NAVs for all CTAs in each month.
3. At the end of the year, reset all CTA NAVs to the average NAV for all CTAs.
4. Repeat preceding steps through time.

Closed Investment Bias.   In real life, the most successful CTAs often reach the limit of the funds they are willing to manage due to performance-related equity growth and a high influx of new investment. (The reason for a self-imposed limit is that beyond a given point, which is different for each CTA, the amount of money managed may become unwieldy in terms of order execution, thereby impeding performance.) These CTAs will therefore be closed to new investors. Thus a CTA index that is based on all CTAs, without regard to their availability, may be biased in terms of its implications for new investors. This problem will be exacerbated in the case of equity-weighted indexes, which will give the greatest weight to the very CTAs most likely to be closed to new investors, that is, those with the greatest amount of funds under management.

SUMMARY

The two adjusted indexes described in this chapter and the return/risk measures based on these series are clearly preferable to their conventional index counterparts for the following two applications:

---

[6]An equity-weighted index would embed a similar distortion, except in this case the implicit assumption would be that the index is rebalanced monthly to maintain the assumed weighted allocation—an equally unrepresentative assumption.

[7]Such an index would only be representative for a very broadly diversified portfolio of CTAs that is similarly rebalanced. For the case of a single-CTA investor, or for the purpose of creating a benchmark against which to measure individual CTAs, the adjusted index calculation discussed earlier would be more appropriate.

1. Comparing the performance of an individual CTA to a representative industry return/risk measure (since the conventional index will yield upwardly biased return/risk measures relative to the individual elements in the index);

2. Providing a representative index and return/risk measure for the investor placing funds with only one or two CTAs (for such an investor the Sharpe Ratio of the conventional index will tend to overstate the relative performance of managed futures to other components in the portfolio, such as stocks and bonds).[8]

A distinction, however, must be made for the investor who divides his managed futures investment among a widely diversified group of CTAs (either directly or by means of a multimanager fund or pool). Given a sufficiently large and diversified group of CTAs, the standard deviation (and as a result the Sharpe Ratio) of an index based on the combined investment would more closely approximate the corresponding measure of a conventional index than that of the two adjusted indexes derived in this chapter and based on the implicit assumption of a single CTA investment.

APPENDIX: THE BARRA/MLM INDEX

The BARRA/MLM index is the sole existing example of what can best be described as a "generic trading" index. The premise of the index is that futures markets embed a net positive return to investors as an inducement to accept risk transfer from hedgers and that this return can be captured by simple trend-following methods. The total return of the index consists of two components: (1) interest income (since the overwhelming portion of money in a futures account earns interest), and (2) an unleveraged trading profit based on a very simple trading rule.

The index consists of 25 equal-weighted markets,[9] with the market composition of the index for each year defined at the end of the preceding year and then left unchanged for the duration of the year. The primary consider-

---

[8]An implicit assumption here is that the individual investor does not have an edge in picking a CTA that will have better-than-average performance in the *future*. This assumption is actually quite sound—see Chapter 8.

[9]Since 1993 the index has been defined to contain 25 markets. In prior years the index consisted of varying numbers of markets ranging from 8 in 1961 to 34 in 1992. (As more liquid markets became available during this period, the number of markets in the index was increased.) Beginning with 1993, it was decided to reduce and maintain the index at 25 markets in order to make it easier to implement the index as a component in an overall investment portfolio.

ation in selecting the markets to be included in the index is liquidity, although other factors, such as maintaining a desired mix among different sectors, also play a role. Although there is some arbitrariness in the portfolio selection, the process is conducted in real time.[10]

The index assumes that a long or short position is held in each of the 25 markets, with the determination of whether a market's position is long or short made at the end of the preceding month based on a simple algorithm. Specifically, an index is constructed for each market, with the month-ending market index values reflecting the percentage price changes in the given market. For example, if a market index is 1,000 at the start and the price changes in that market during the next two months are +2 percent and −1 percent, the market index values would be 1,020 and 1,009.8, respectively. This index is calculated each month using the closing price on the next-to-last day of the month.[11] If the current index value is greater than the 12-month moving average, a long position is indicated for the following month; if it is less than the moving average, a short position is indicated. This system is always in the market, with the position being reversed whenever the rule just described indicates a position opposite to the one currently held.

The BARRA/MLM index return is defined to equal the risk-free (T-bill) return plus the average of the 25 market percentage returns, assuming unleveraged positions in each. (The percentage return for a given market will be equal to the absolute percentage price change in that market, with the sign of the return being positive if the indicated position was in the same direction as the price change and negative otherwise.) In effect, the BARRA/MLM index implicitly assumes that available funds are allocated equally to each of the markets in the index. The number of contracts held in each market will be equal to one-twenty-fifth of the equity divided by the value of the contract. For example, given a $10 million account, a market with a contract value of $50,000 would trade 8 contracts ($10,000,000 ÷ 25 ÷ 50,000 = 8).[12]

---

[10]The index composition has been defined in real time since the end of 1990 (for 1991).

[11]In other words, monthly price changes are defined as changes from the close on the *next-to-last day* of one month to the close on the *next-to-last day* of the next month. The reason for using next-to-last days instead of the last days to calculate price changes and market index values is that it allows the position for the following month to be determined as of the close of the current month (instead of the first day of the following month).

[12]Although this approach makes sense for most markets, it will lead to distortions in interest rate markets. For example, assuming equal price levels, the allocation definition will result in the same number of contracts being traded in T-notes as in T-bonds (both of which are included in the index and have $100,000 face values), despite the fact that T-bonds are significantly more volatile.

The BARRA/MLM index corrects the two primary problems inherent in traditional *commodity* indexes:

1. It allows both long and *short* positions, as is representative of the industry.
2. It includes *financial* markets as well as commodity markets.

In addition, the BARRA/MLM index is not subject to the upward bias of return/risk measures as is the case for unadjusted CTA indexes.

It should be noted, however, that for individual CTA relative performance comparisons, the applicability of the BARRA/MLM index would seem limited to CTAs trading a similar mix of markets as the index: a diversified portfolio of *domestic* markets. In most cases, however, a CTA subindex or a market-sector BARRA/MLM subindex will provide a more meaningful benchmark comparison. For example, a currency trading program should ideally be compared with a subindex of currency traders or the BARRA/MLM currency subindex. In regard to this point, it should be emphasized that the market composition of a portfolio has a tremendous influence on performance results—often a much more important impact than the trading methodologies used.

Although the BARRA/MLM index does represent a plausible proposal for an industry benchmark, it does have a serious limitation: For analysis of the effect of including managed futures in conventional stock/bond portfolios, it is only appropriate *if the managed futures portion is actually invested in the BARRA/MLM index*.[13] If the managed futures portion is invested in CTAs instead, as is more likely, the use of CTA indexes would appear more appropriate.

---

[13]A managed investment based on the index is offered by the Mount Lucas Corporation in Princeton, New Jersey.

Part Two

IS PAST PERFORMANCE PREDICTIVE OF FUTURE PERFORMANCE?

6 Are Prospectus Returns Indicative of Future Performance?

The following scenario is typical: An investor receives a prospectus for a commodity futures pool (fund).[1] He checks the performance tables and finds that the same combination of commodity trading advisors (CTAs) selected for the pool, trading in the same percentage allocations and at the same cost structure indicated for the pool (i.e., pro forma performance results), would have realized an average annual return of 45 percent during the past three years.

Thinking that these results look too good to be true, and being sophisticated enough to be aware of the dangers of performance simulations, he checks the footnotes of the performance tables very carefully. To be extra cautious, he even reads the disclosure document! He verifies that the prospectus performance numbers are indeed based on the *actual* trading results of the CTAs. Reasoning that even if the future average annual return only equaled half the prospectus return, it would still represent a very favorable outcome, he decides to invest in the pool.

Two years later, with the pool having eked out a minuscule 2 percent cumulative return, compared with 25 percent for the S&P 500 index during the same interim, the investor decides to bail out.

"Just my luck," he mutters to himself. "What are the odds," he thinks "that managers with an average annual return of 45 percent before I invested with them would see their return plunge to only 1 percent annually?"

Well, the odds are a lot higher than our investor realizes. The truth is that the evidence for the postoffering returns of pools falling drastically below prospectus returns is nothing short of compelling. In this chapter, we will first examine the evidence demonstrating that pool performance routinely deteriorates dramatically below the prospectus levels, which are based on the *actual* past results of the CTAs included in the pool. We will then explain the reasons for this phenomenon.

---

[1]The terms *pool* and *fund* are commonly used interchangeably. In this chapter the former is used to match the terminology of the two studies cited. These studies use the term *pool* to refer to a *public pool*, which is synonymous with the term *fund* (not pool), as defined in footnote 1 in Chapter 5.

THE EDWARDS AND MA STUDY

The Edwards and Ma study[2] examined the relationship between past and future relative performance for 55 public commodity pools. In the first part of their study Edwards and Ma examined whether performance for a pool in the 36 months prior to its going public (that is, performance as represented by the CTAs in that pool) was related to that pool's performance in the following 24 months. Obviously, this comparison involved different definitions of prepublic and postpublic periods for different pools.

Table 6.1, which is reprinted from the Edwards and Ma study, compares the monthly and annual returns of these 55 funds in their respective prepublic and postpublic periods. As this table vividly demonstrates, Edwards and Ma found past performance to be worse than useless in predicting future performance levels. Specifically, the average annualized return of the 55 pools during the 36-month period prior to going public (that is, based on the past performance of the individual CTAs selected for that pool) was a strikingly high 47.99 percent. In stark contrast, the average annualized return of these same pools in the postpublic period was −1.15 percent! Moreover, the correlation between prepublic and postpublic returns was not only negative, but also statistically significant. In other words, higher prepublic returns were actually correlated with lower postpublic returns.

The irrelevance of past performance to future performance was so extreme—in some cases actually implying an inverse relationship—that Edwards and Ma raised the question of whether performance reporting should even be required by the Commodity Futures Trading Commission (CFTC):

> Should the government (in this case the CFTC) require the disclosure of prepublic performance information? Merely by requiring its disclosure the CFTC may indirectly suggest to investors that such information has value. If so, the CFTC may be responsible for encouraging investors to rely on this information, despite the legal disclaimers found in all prospectuses. It is undoubtedly difficult for investors to comprehend that the government might require the disclosure of useless information.

Edwards and Ma, however, stopped short of recommending the prohibition of past-performance reporting—an alternative they found "offensive to fundamental principles of free enterprise."

---

[2]Franklin R. Edwards and Cindy Ma, "Commodity Pool Performance: Is the Information Contained in Pool Prospectuses Useful?" *Journal of Futures Markets* 8(5): 589–616 (1988).

THE IRWIN STUDY

A study by Scott H. Irwin[3] examined the question of whether the CTA returns reported in the prospectuses of multiple-CTA public commodity pools provided useful information regarding potential future performance. Irwin based his study on 36 pools offered during the 1980–1989 period. Irwin compared the prospectus prepublic returns of these pools to their returns in the one-, two-, and three-year periods after going public. He found that prepublic returns drastically overstated postpublic returns: For the one-year holding period, the prepublic average annualized return was a towering 49.6 percent versus only 10.8 percent in the postpublic period. Results for the two-year and three-year holding periods were similar: 49.7 percent versus 9.2 percent, and 47.5 percent versus 10.3 percent, respectively (see the first row of Table 6.2). (The modest differences in the prepublic returns for the different holding period comparisons is a consequence of variations in the number of pools used in the analyses—data availability is smaller for the longer holding periods.) In short, prepublic returns tended to overstate postpublic returns by a factor of approximately 5 to 1 in all three cases!

Irwin also performed the same analysis, segmenting the pool data into two subperiods, as well as three classifications based on the number of CTAs in the pool (two, three, or more than three). Across the three holding periods, these five data segments provided an additional 15 prepublic/postpublic comparisons. The results of these tests are summarized in rows 2–6 of Table 6.2. Once again, in all cases, prepublic returns dwarfed postpublic returns. In these tests, the ratios of prepublic to postpublic returns ranged from a low of 2.5:1 to a high of 9.2:1.

Irwin also examined using the returns of a pool index[4] in the prepublic period (as opposed to a pool's individual performance during that period) as the indicator for a pool's postpublic return. The results of this comparison are shown in Table 6.3. The contrast with Table 6.2 is striking. Note that for all three holding periods, the average prepublic return (based on the pool index) and the average postpublic return are relatively close.[5] The implica-

---

[3]Scott H. Irwin, "Further Evidence of the Usefulness of CTA Performance Information in Public Commodity Pool Prospectuses and a Proposal for Reform." In *Advances in Futures and Options Research,* Don M. Chance and Robert R. Trippi, Eds. JAI Press, Greenwich, Conn., 1994, pp. 251–265.

[4]An equally weighted index based on all public commodity pools trading at the beginning of each year (including those that failed in the given year).

[5]The low t-statistic values shown in the table indicate that the differences between average prepublic pool index returns and average postpublic individual pool returns are not statistically significant in any of the three holding periods.

Table 6.1
COMPARISON OF PREPUBLIC AND POSTPUBLIC RATES OF RETURNS FOR 55 POOLS

Pool	Starting Date	Initial Equity (Million)	Average 36 Prepublic Monthly Return (%)	Average 24 Postpublic Monthly Return (%)	Average 36 Prepublic Annualized Return (%)	Average 24 Postpublic Annualized Return (%)
(1)	7808	10.153	2.31	4.49	27.72	53.88
(2)	7907	12.710	2.63	3.70	31.56	44.4
(3)	8312	7.370	1.02	1.86	12.24	22.32
(4)	8310	21.402	2.19	1.76	26.28	21.12
(5)	8001	16.122	-0.30	1.76	-3.60	21.12
(6)	8010	30.355	2.79	1.54	33.48	18.48
(7)	8312	2.380	1.48	1.39	17.76	16.68
(8)	8401	1.055	4.51	1.22	54.12	14.64
(9)	8002	3.936	2.83	1.18	33.96	14.16
(10)	8011	14.397	3.32	1.12	39.84	13.44
(11)	7903	4.539	6.64	1.09	79.68	13.08
(12)	8210	3.659	7.62	0.90	91.44	10.8
(13)	8308	2.386	3.46	0.89	41.52	10.68
(14)	8303	2.033	0.31	0.89	3.72	10.68
(15)	8211	6.189	1.81	0.59	21.72	7.08
(16)	8201	5.662	8.63	0.43	103.56	5.16
(17)	8002	19.951	3.99	0.40	47.88	4.8
(18)	8309	0.712	2.95	0.39	35.40	4.68
(19)	8301	1.046	8.77	0.32	105.24	3.84
(20)	8210	11.693	3.52	0.31	42.24	3.72
(21)	8011	11.218	4.71	0.31	56.52	3.72
(22)	8307	1.049	1.80	0.26	21.60	3.12
(23)	8106	14.403	5.10	0.24	61.20	2.88
(24)	8112	8.490	7.62	0.17	91.44	2.04
(25)	8001	4.868	2.91	0.15	34.92	1.8
(26)	8105	5.408	5.34	0.12	64.08	1.44

(27)	8308	12.601	3.84	0.08	46.08	0.96
(28)	8109	4.209	1.14	0.02	13.68	0.24
(29)	8111	12.992	1.69	-0.01	20.28	-0.12
(30)	8103	9.648	4.18	-0.11	50.16	-1.32
(31)	8002	3.301	1.46	-0.21	17.52	-2.52
(32)	8102	7.902	1.34	-0.24	16.08	-2.88
(33)	8204	35.406	3.44	-0.25	41.28	-3
(34)	8303	9.831	9.96	-0.31	119.52	-3.72
(35)	8212	48.775	2.98	-0.32	35.76	-3.84
(36)	8103	0.300	3.22	-0.44	38.64	-5.28
(37)	8106	4.214	5.47	-0.63	65.64	-7.56
(38)	8307	25.144	4.39	-0.84	52.68	-10.08
(39)	8108	5.201	1.86	-0.86	22.32	-10.32
(40)	8212	32.865	3.49	-1.11	41.88	-13.32
(41)	8307	1.350	2.88	-1.13	34.56	-13.56
(42)	8103	9.854	14.43	-1.14	173.16	-13.68
(43)	8208	16.639	2.79	-1.29	33.48	-15.48
(44)	8111	12.769	1.14	-1.37	13.68	-16.44
(45)	8208	3.313	5.03	-1.48	60.36	-17.76
(46)	8212	6.551	4.84	-1.56	58.08	-18.72
(47)	8203	3.492	3.44	-1.68	41.28	-20.16
(48)	8110	4.796	0.59	-1.69	7.08	-20.28
(49)	8010	4.427	6.29	-1.75	75.48	-21
(50)	8008	5.414	6.07	-1.75	72.84	-21
(51)	8304	14.670	2.49	-1.87	29.88	-22.44
(52)	8101	9.070	2.78	-2.11	33.36	-25.32
(53)	8104	2.894	6.31	-2.18	75.72	-26.16
(54)	8211	2.791	5.03	-2.44	60.36	-29.28
(55)	8111	1.105	9.42	-4.06	113.04	-48.72
Mean		9.722	4.00	-0.10	47.99	-1.15

Source: Franklin Edwards and Cindy Ma, "Is the Information Contained in Pool Prospectuses Useful?" *The Journal of Futures Markets* 8(5), 596–597 (1988). Copyright © 1988 by John Wiley & Sons, Inc. Reprinted by permission of John Wiley & Sons, Inc.

Table 6.2
BIAS TEST RESULTS BY INITIAL POSTPUBLIC TRADING DATE AND NUMBER OF CTAs EMPLOYED[a]

	One-year Holding Period				Two-year Holding Period				Three-year Holding Period			
	Number of Pools	Average Prepublic Return[a]	Average Postpublic Return	t-Statistic[b]	Number of Pools	Average Prepublic Return	Average Postpublic Return	t-Statistic	Number of Pools	Average Prepublic Return	Average Postpublic Return	t-Statistic
Panel A: Initial Postpublic Trading Date of Pool												
1. Feb. 1980–Apr. 1989	36	49.63	10.83	5.35[c]	35	49.62	9.17	5.57[c]	29	47.64	10.27	4.84[c]
2. Feb. 1980–Dec. 1985	11	59.85	18.08	2.88[c]	11	59.85	9.61	3.24[c]	11	59.85	13.03	2.82[c]
3. Jan. 1986–Apr. 1989	25	45.13	7.64	4.42[c]	24	44.93	8.97	4.53[c]	18	40.17	8.58	4.30[c]
Panel B: Number of CTAs Employed by Pool												
4. Two	10	57.03	12.49	2.71[c]	10	57.03	12.10	2.88[c]	9	56.81	10.29	2.63[c]
5. Three	11	39.55	15.80	1.62	11	39.55	10.95	2.08	9	37.32	13.45	1.51
6. Four or more	15	52.09	6.09	5.46[c]	14	52.24	5.68	4.71[c]	11	48.57	7.64	5.96[c]

Source: Scott H. Irwin, "Further Evidence on the Usefulness of CTA Performance Information in Public Commodity Pool Perspectuses and a Proposal for Reform." In *Advances in Futures and Options Research*, Vol. 7, p. 258, JAI Press, Greenwich, Conn., 1994. Reproduced by permission.

[a]Annualized monthly, %.
[b]The *t*-statistic is calculated to test the null hypothesis of no significant difference between the average prepublic return and the average postpublic return.
[c]Statistical significance at the 5 percent level.

Table 6.3

COMPARISON OF PREPUBLIC POOL INDEX RETURNS AND POSTPUBLIC RETURNS OF MULTIPLE-CTA PUBLIC COMMODITY POOLS

Holding Period	Bias Results[a]				Correlation Regression Results[c]			
	Number of Pools	Average Prepublic Return	Average Postpublic Return	t-Statistic[b]	a	ß	R^2	F
One year	33	13.84	9.74	1.07	12.50[d] (1.99)	−0.20 (−0.52)	0.009	0.27
Two years	32	13.67	8.75	1.64	13.45[d] (3.49)	−0.34 (−1.46)	0.066	2.13
Three years	26	13.45	10.36	0.91	15.26[d] (4.32)	−0.36 (−1.72)	0.110	2.96

Source: Scott H. Irwin, "Further Evidence on the Usefulness of CTA Performance Information in Public Commodity Pool Perspectuses and a Proposal for Reform." In *Advances in Futures and Options Research*, Vol. 7, p. 260, JAI Press, Greenwich, Conn., 1994. Reproduced by permission.

[a]Annualized monthly, %.
[b]The *t*-statistic is calculated to test the null hypothesis of no significant difference between the average prepublic return and the average postpublic return.
[c]The figures in parentheses are t-statistics. F refers to the regression F-statistic.
[d]Statistically significant at the 5 percent level.

tion of this table is that, on average, an investor would be *far* better off using the returns of a pool index in recent years to predict the performance of a *specific* pool than the past returns of that pool itself (that is, the past return of the CTAs included in the pool).

On the basis of these and other tests, Irwin concluded that CTA returns reported in the prospectuses for commodity pools did not provide any useful information in terms of gauging future returns. In fact, prepublic returns were so lacking in any usefulness that Irwin argued that the CFTC should not require disclosure of CTA returns in pool prospectuses: "As Edwards and Ma point out, the disclosure requirement may have the perverse effect of indirectly suggesting that CTA return information is valuable. Why else would a federal government agency require disclosure?" This consideration, as well as the fact that average postpublic returns were far closer to the average prepublic return of a pool index than to the prepublic return based on the CTAs in the given pool, led Irwin to the following policy suggestion:

> In view of this discussion, a modified version of the neutrality policy is suggested. The policy involves a two-part presentation of performance data in prospectuses. In the first and *required* part, the actual returns of a public commodity pool index over the most recent three-year period would be presented. The index would reflect the performance of all public pools and would be free of significant bias. The construction and updating of the index would be the responsibility of the CFTC. In the second and *optional* part, historical CTA performance data would be presented at the discretion of the CPO. It would be clear to investors that data in the first part are required by the CFTC, whereas this is not the case in the second.

WHY PROSPECTUS RETURNS OVERSTATE FUTURE RETURNS

Edwards and Ma's and Irwin's conclusion that a pool's prospectus return is useless as an indicator of the pool's potential future return is certainly a valid assessment. In fact, while neither Edwards and Ma nor Irwin state it in such stark terms, although they certainly imply it, the evidence suggests that prospectus returns are not merely *useless*, but, more accurately, *misleading*. This aspect of prospectus data is no doubt a consequence of the role of *hindsight* in selecting CTAs for pools. Since it is obviously easier to market superior performance than inferior performance, pools will almost invariably select CTAs with well-above-average returns for the recent past. These CTAs, however, are unlikely to maintain their relative rankings. Why?

In any given period, some CTAs will significantly outperform the industry average. Although some of this superior performance might be due to a greater skill level, a very substantial portion can be attributed to market conditions during the given period being particularly favorable for the markets and strategies traded by those CTAs. There is no reason to assume that future market conditions will favor the same markets or strategies. Consequently, it is almost inevitable that the top-performing CTAs of one period will see some deterioration in their relative performance—even if their performance remains above average. Therefore, the understandable bias for picking top-performing CTAs for inclusion in pools will lead to an inevitable bias for pool prospectuses grossly overstating potential future returns.

To avoid misinterpretation, it should be noted that the foregoing discussion is certainly not intended to imply that commodity pool operators (CPOs) would be better off selecting CTAs with average or below-average past returns when constructing pools. Rather, the intended implication is that pools containing top-performing CTAs of the prior period will have the greatest scope for deterioration in future returns, although it is still possible such returns may exceed the corresponding industry average. The question of whether better performing pools (or CTAs) in a common past period are more likely to witness above-average performance in a subsequent period is examined in the next chapter.

CONCLUSION

The following are the essential points of this chapter:

- The empirical evidence that prospectus returns are biased toward substantially overstating potential future performance is overwhelming.
- This phenomenon is an inevitable consequence of the hindsight used in determining the CTA composition of a pool, and therefore is likely to continue to prevail in the future.
- Therefore, generally speaking, investors should not expect prospectus returns to be even remotely approached.
- Past returns of an industry average, such as a pool index, provide a much better predictor of a given pool's potential future return than the past returns of the CTAs in the given pool. Therefore, investors should use such an index as a more reliable gauge of the approximate returns they are likely to realize.
- This chapter demonstrated why actual pool return levels have typically fallen far short of prospectus return levels in the past and why they are likely to continue to do so in the future. The question of whether *relatively* better past returns (during a common comparison period) are at all predictive of *relatively* better future returns (even if such returns are far below past actual levels) has not been considered, but is addressed in the next chapter.

7   Is Past Performance Predictive of Future Performance? A Brief Review of Academic Studies

Most of the studies summarized in this chapter covered multiple issues. It should be noted, however, that this chapter focuses only on the aspects of these studies that deal directly with the question of whether past performance is predictive of future performance.

THE ELTON, GRUBER, AND RENTZLER STUDY

The study, "Professionally Managed, Publicly Traded Commodity Funds," by Edwin J. Elton, Martin J. Gruber, and Joel C. Rentzler (EGR),[1] used public commodity fund[2] data to examine two aspects of the relationship between past and future performance:

1. **Predictability.** Can past performance be used to predict future performance?
2. **Consistency.** Do funds that performed relatively better in one period tend to exhibit superior performance in a subsequent period?

To test predictability, EGR compared using a fund's past period performance as the prediction for the next period versus using a naive forecast. For example, for return, the prediction that the next period's return would

---

[1]*Journal of Business* 60(2), 175–199 (1987).

[2]EGR use the term "public commodity *funds*," whereas other studies use the term "public commodity *pools*." These terms refer to identical investment vehicles and are interchangeable.

equal the prior period's return was compared with the naive forecast that the next period's return would equal zero. A similar test was performed using the Sharpe Ratio and standard deviation, with the naive forecast for the Sharpe Ratio defined as zero and the naive forecast for the standard deviation defined as the average standard deviation of all funds in the prior period.

The comparison between forecasts equal to the past period levels and naive forecasts was conducted for five pairs of adjacent years (July 1979–June 1980 versus July 1980–June 1981 through July 1983–June 1984 versus July 1984–June 1985) for each fund for which data were available in the given pair of years. (The number of funds used ranged from a low of 10 in the first pair of years to 67 in the final pair of years.)

In terms of return and return/risk, EGR found that past values did not provide any improvement over the naive prediction of zero. In fact, in terms of return, the naive forecast provided the better projection in all five years, with the difference statistically significant at the 5 percent level in four out of five years.[3] In the case of the return/risk ratio (i.e., Sharpe Ratio), predictions based on prior period levels were almost as dismal, with the naive forecast of zero providing a better projection than past Sharpe Ratios in four out of five years (one year at a statistically significant level). Only in regards to risk (as measured by the standard deviation) did past levels (for each individual fund) provide a better guideline than the naive forecast (a standard deviation equal to the average standard deviation of *all* funds during the prior period). The prior period standard deviation (for each given fund) provided a better prediction than the naive forecast in three out of five years, although never at a statistically significant level.

Even though EGR's results conclusively demonstrated that past performance could not be used to predict future performance, it was still possible that past relative performance rankings might be useful in projecting future relative rankings. In other words, even though one couldn't gauge the future performance of funds based on their past performance, perhaps it might be still possible to predict which funds were likely to do *relatively* better (gain more or lose less). This question was addressed by EGR's tests of consistency.

EGR first tested whether past fund rankings were correlated to future fund rankings using the same five pairs of years. In terms of return, they found positive correlation between past and future rankings in all five of the paired years, two at statistically significant levels (5 percent). In terms of the Sharpe Ratio, four out of five years showed positive rank correlations, two at statistically sig-

---

[3]Levels of statistical significance are sometimes stated in terms of the probability that the stated result is false (that is, the probability that the result could be due to chance rather than the stated hypothesis) and sometimes in terms of the probability that the stated result is true. Thus, 5 percent and 95 percent refer to equivalent levels of statistical significance. In this chapter, levels of statistical significance are stated in terms of the former convention (e.g., 5 percent).

nificant levels. Although these results seemed to imply that there was some correlation between past return (return/risk) rankings and future return (return/risk) rankings, EGR downplayed this interpretation and focused instead on the fact that the average rank correlation coefficients (for the five periods combined) were relatively low (0.21 for return and 0.18 for the Sharpe Ratio) and not statistically significant in the majority of years.

In terms of risk, as measured by the standard deviation, EGR found strong evidence of correlation between past and future rankings. The rank correlation coefficient was positive in all five test periods, statistically significant in four out of five years, and equal to a relatively high average value of 0.51 for the five periods combined. Therefore they concluded that there was consistency in standard deviation rankings.

In addition to testing ranking correlations across all funds, from period to period, EGR also looked at the consistency of performance among only the best and worst performers. In other words, even though they concluded that there was no consistency in return and return/risk rankings across all funds, they considered the question whether it was possible that there was consistency in the performance of the best and worst funds. To answer this question, they tested rankings based on segmenting the data into thirds as well as based on the top and bottom three performers in each period.

Although funds with returns in the top third during the prior period performed significantly better than funds with returns in the middle or bottom thirds, beating both of these groups four out of five times, they discounted the reliability of this result because of the near identical returns realized on average by both the top three and bottom three performers in each period. In terms of the Sharpe Ratio, they found that, on average, the top third (and top three), as defined by prior period results, outperformed the middle and bottom thirds (and bottom three). Once again, they discounted the significance of these findings, noting that despite the average results, in two out of five years the bottom three performers (in the prior period) realized a higher Sharpe Ratio than the top three in the subsequent period. As in the other tests, the strongest evidence of consistency emerged for risk, as measured by the standard deviation, with the best (i.e., lowest standard deviation) third exhibiting the same placement in all five years.

Finally, EGR tested whether a fund's prior period ranking in terms of risk (standard deviation) was a useful predictor of its future return/risk (Sharpe Ratio), an investigation prompted by the strong evidence of persistence in relative risk levels. They found that a low standard deviation in one year was positively correlated with a higher Sharpe Ratio in the subsequent year in all five periods and statistically significant (at the 5 percent level) in three out of five years. They also found that in four out of five years the best-performing third of funds, in terms of the Sharpe Ratio, was the group with the lowest standard deviation in the prior period. In light of these results, they concluded that while past return/risk (i.e., Sharpe Ratio) rankings were of questionable value in predicting future return or return/risk rankings, past standard deviation did seem to provide useful information regarding future relative return/risk performance.

In summary, EGR concluded that although past performance was useless in predicting future performance, past *relative* performance was helpful in predicting future *relative* performance, at least to some extent. Specifically, they found strong evidence that funds with lower risk (standard deviation) in one period tended to exhibit lower risk levels, and to a more limited extent higher return/risk (Sharpe Ratio) levels, in the next period. Although EGR's tests also revealed net positive correlations between past and future returns and past and future return/risk levels, they viewed these results as statistically insignificant. Ironically, while the results of their study appeared to support the idea that there was some correlation between past and future performance rankings (albeit to a limited extent), EGR chose to stress the negative side in their concluding comments: "When we examined whether we could select a superior commodity fund on the basis of past performance, the answer was probably not."

This conclusion, however, does seem to ignore results in their own study that, while not statistically conclusive, at least lean in the opposite direction. In reading their paper, one almost gets the impression that the quoted conclusion is the one they *preferred* to find, and when the results of their very thorough research didn't quite fit this view precisely, they found reasons for qualifying such contradictory evidence—putting the best spin on the interpretation, so to speak.

Although quite thorough, the EGR study does leave open a number of questions:

1. EGR used one-year intervals for both the past and forecast periods. It seems reasonable to argue that one year may be too short a time period to exhibit meaningful performance patterns. Perhaps if longer survey or longer forecast periods were used, or both, a greater correlation between past and future performance might become evident.
2. The EGR study was based on data only through 1985 (10 years ago as of this writing), and therefore the issue needs to be reexamined in light of more recent data.
3. As explained later in the summary of McCarthy's study, analysis based on fund data (as opposed to individual commodity trading advisor (CTA) data) is seriously biased by double-counting. This point raises the question of whether different results would have been obtained if EGR had based their statistical tests on individual CTA data.

THE EDWARDS AND MA STUDY

In the first part of their study, "Commodity Pool Performance: Is the Information Contained in Pool Prospectuses Useful?" which was detailed in the previous chapter, Franklin R. Edwards and Cindy Ma (EM)[4] showed that prepublic pool returns were highly biased indicators of postpublic performance, with the average annual prepublic return of the 55 pools surveyed being 48.0 percent, compared with an average annual postpublic return of −1.2 percent.

To determine whether past performance might be a more useful indicator of future performance if combined with other explanatory variables, EM tested various regression equations incorporating additional inputs. The additional variables tested in these various equations included management fees, percentage changes in indexes for commodity futures, financial futures and currency futures, trend measures for these same indexes, and interest rates. These variables were combined in three different regression equations. In all three equations, however, the estimated coefficient for the variable representing prepublic returns was statistically insignificant from zero. A similar analysis using Sharpe Ratios instead of returns yielded equivalent results. Specifically, prepublic Sharpe Ratios were uncorrelated with postpublic Sharpe Ratios. Finally, a similar analysis using standard deviations did find statistically significant correlation between prepublic and postpublic levels. In other words, even though a pool's prepublic return and return/risk ratio were uncorrelated with corresponding postpublic levels, prepublic riskiness was related to postpublic riskiness.

The fact that past return (and return/risk) *levels* are uncorrelated with future return (return/risk) levels (where the definition of past and future periods differ for each pool) does not necessarily imply that past *relative* performance is uncorrelated with future relative performance. EM therefore used a subsample of 23 pools to test whether the difference between a pool's prepublic performance and the average public pool performance *during the identical time period* was correlated with the corresponding performance difference in the pool's postpublic period.[5] EM tested analogous regression equations using these *relative* performance variables and arrived at a similar conclusion: "There is no relationship between relative prepublic performance and relative postpublic performance." They also indicated that rank correlation tests further confirmed these findings.

---

[4]*Journal of Futures Markets* 8(5), 589–616 (1988).

[5]The smaller sample (23 versus 55) was dictated by the availability of data for average public pool returns for the 36-month period prior to individual pools going public. Such comparison data were not available for pools that went public during the first 36 months of the data period used in the study.

In summary, EM concluded that not only were past performance *levels* (return and return/risk) useless in predicting future performance levels, but past *relative* performance also offered no guideline for future relative performance. (The only minor exception regarding the usefulness of past performance was that there appeared to be some relationship between a pool's past risk level, as measured by the standard deviation, and its future risk level.) In fact, as was detailed in the previous chapter, the irrelevance of past performance to future performance was so extreme that EM seriously raised the question of whether performance reporting should even be required by the Commodity Futures Trading Commission (CFTC).

It is critical to emphasize that the EM study is only relevant to the specific question of whether *prepublic* pool returns are predictive of *postpublic* returns (nominal or relative) and not the more general question of whether *past* performance is predictive of *future* performance. The reason for this is that using prepublic versus postpublic results represents a very biased selection of survey and test periods. Specifically, since pools are likely to be constructed using CTAs who have had particularly favorable performance in the recent past (since obviously such pools would be far easier to market than pools with CTAs exhibiting subpar performance), the prepublic returns of these pools are likely to be grossly biased to the upside. Therefore, the lack of positive correlation between prepublic and postpublic returns cannot be used to generalize that past performance is unrelated to future performance in a broader sense.

In addition, since the EM study was based on pool as opposed to individual CTA data, it also embeds the double-counting bias detailed in the McCarthy study discussed later in this chapter. Finally, it should be noted that the EM study was based on data through 1987. Therefore, even without the aforementioned biases, it would still be necessary to reexamine the relationship between past and future relative performance using more recent data.

THE IRWIN, KRUKEMEYER, AND ZULAUF STUDY

Only a small section of the study "Are Public Commodity Pools a Good Investment?" by Scott H. Irwin, Terry R. Krukemeyer, and Carl R. Zulauf (IKZ),[6] addressed the question of the predictability of performance. In it, the authors examined the correlation between a pool's return in one year and its return in

---

[6]*Managed Futures: Performance Evaluation and Analysis of Commodity Funds, Pools and Accounts,* Carl C. Peters, Ed., Probus Publishing Company, Chicago, 1992, pp. 403–434.

the subsequent year. A similar correlation analysis was performed using the standard deviation and Sharpe Ratio. The study was based on all available public pool (i.e., fund) data for paired years beginning with 1979/1980 and ending with 1988/1989. In all, there were a total of 596 such paired pool years in the database. In addition to calculating correlation coefficients based on all pools, Irwin, Krukemeyer, and Zulauf (IKZ) also derived correlation coefficients based on data segments stratified by the top third, middle third, and bottom third of pools. (For each paired year, this designation was based on a given pool's ranking in terms of the specified performance measure in the earlier year.)

All the correlation coefficients derived by IKZ for return and the Sharpe Ratio were either negative or far too low to be statistically significant. Only in the case of the standard deviation (using all pools, as opposed to the segmented data) was the correlation coefficient high enough to be meaningful: 0.45.

Similar to every other study cited in this chapter, IKZ concluded that past and future risk levels, as measured by the standard deviation, were correlated. Their conclusion that past and future return and return/risk levels were uncorrelated, while no doubt valid, has limited applicability, because their study focused on *absolute* performance as opposed to *relative* performance. IKZ derived their correlation coefficients based on the data of *all the 2-year periods combined* rather than separate correlation coefficients based on *each individual 2-year period.* Calculated in this manner, the correlation coefficients reflect the degree to which the performance *level* in one year is related to the performance level in the following year, rather than the degree to which the performance *ranking* in one year is related to the ranking in the next year. Given the wide variability of pool returns from year to year, it is hardly surprising that return and return/risk levels in one year were uncorrelated to the corresponding levels in the following period.

In essence, the fact that a pool's return (or return/risk) in one year has no predictive value for that performance measure in the following year can be taken as a given. However, this focus bypasses the essential and unresolved question: Is a pool's *relative* return (or return/risk) in one period correlated with its relative performance in the next period? Or equivalently, is there any tendency for better performing pools in one period to achieve above-average performance in the following period? This critical question was left unaddressed in this study.

THE IRWIN STUDY

A portion of "Further Evidence of the Usefulness of CTA Performance Information in Public Commodity Pool Prospectuses and a Proposal for Reform," by Scott H. Irwin,[7] was detailed in the previous chapter. It will be recalled that Irwin found that prepublic returns overstated postpublic returns by a factor of approximately 5 to 1 in all three holding periods surveyed. Moreover, Irwin showed that, on average, the return of a pool index during the prepublic period actually provided a much closer approximation of the postpublic return of an individual pool than did the past returns of the given pool itself.

Although prepublic returns are highly biased, Irwin next considered whether they could still be useful because of the possibility that prepublic returns might nonetheless be correlated with postpublic returns. In other words, it is possible that, even though prepublic returns severely overstate potential postpublic returns, higher prepublic returns are correlated with higher postpublic returns (measured relative to all pools). To test for such a possible correlation, Irwin derived 18 regression equations (one corresponding to each segmentation of the data detailed in the previous chapter), in which the prepublic returns of CTAs in the pools were used as the explanatory variables for the postpublic returns of the pools. Only 1 out of 18 of these equations yielded a statistically significant result. Ironically, in this sole exception, the correlation between prepublic and postpublic returns was negative—in other words, higher prepublic returns implied lower postpublic returns!

On the basis of these various tests, Irwin concluded that CTA returns reported in the prospectuses for commodity pools did not provide any useful information in terms of gauging future returns. In fact, prepublic returns were so lacking in any usefulness that, as detailed in the previous chapter, Irwin argued that the CFTC should not require disclosure of CTA returns in pool prospectuses.

The foregoing notwithstanding, it should be emphasized that Irwin's study does not prove that past and future *relative* performance are uncorrelated in a more general sense. Reason: Irwin's analysis of the correlation between past and future returns defines these two time periods separately for each pool (based on its prospectus and public offering dates). Given the extremely high dependence of return on the period chosen, the fact that different pools are being compared for different time periods would tend to swamp the effect of any possible tendency for the relative rankings of pools in a *common* time period to be indicative of their relative rankings in a subsequent *common* time period. Therefore, while Irwin's study conclusively demonstrates that there is no correlation between prepublic and postpublic returns, it does not address the question of whether there is any persistence of relative performance rankings across different time periods.

---

[7]*Advances in Futures and Options Research,* Don M. Chance and Robert R. Trippi, Eds., JAI Press Inc., Greenwich, Conn., 1994, pp. 251–265.

Moreover, not only are the time periods different for each pool, but the selection of time periods is a very biased one. As was previously noted, studies in which survey periods are defined on the basis of pool launch dates are particularly biased because such pools are almost invariably constructed with hindsight to include CTAs with particularly high returns in the immediately preceding years—returns that are unlikely to be equaled in a subsequent period. Any meaningful test of the stability of performance must therefore be based on a neutral definition of time periods, that is, common time periods for all pools (or CTAs) in the survey.

THE McCARTHY STUDY

David F. McCarthy's study, "Consistency of Relative Commodity Trading Advisor Performance,"[8] differs from most others reviewed in this chapter in that it uses individual CTA data instead of fund[9] data. This choice is quite deliberate, because as McCarthy points out, the use of fund data introduced a bias by double-counting the results of CTAs included in multiple funds. (The term "double-counting" is used to refer to counting the same data two or more times.) Since a small number of CTAs accounted for a large percentage of the funds analyzed in other studies, this bias is a serious one. The extent of this bias is illustrated by Tables 7.1 and 7.2, which are taken from McCarthy's study. Table 7.1 shows that 80 out of 120 of the funds surveyed were managed by single advisors and that only 31 CTAs accounted for all single advisor funds. Table 7.2 highlights the participation levels of the 10 most prominent CTAs. Note that CTA A alone participated in 21 funds, 6 of them single advisor funds. Also note that these 10 CTAs accounted for more than half (42) of all single-advisor funds, which as a group represented two-thirds of all funds (including multiadvisor funds). As a result of the severe double-counting embedded in fund performance data, McCarthy points out that "any analysis that considers rankings is going to be subject to biases resulting from treating observations as independent."

In his study, McCarthy compared the performance of 52 CTAs in a 36-month period (January 1985–December 1987) with the performance in the subsequent 48-month period (January 1988–December 1991). McCarthy first examined whether performance in the earlier period was a biased predictor of performance in the later period. McCarthy found a significant deterioration of returns from the earlier to later period: 1.91 percent per month in 1985–1987 versus only 0.46 percent in 1988–1991, with a statistical test showing the

---

[8]University College Dublin, Dublin, Ireland, unpublished thesis, 1995.
[9]Referred to as "pool" in some of the studies.

Table 7.1
PARTICIPATION BY INDEPENDENT CTAs IN PUBLIC
COMMODITY FUNDS

	1987
Total number of funds	120
Number of funds managed by single CTA	80
Number of CTAs managing single-advisor funds	31

Source: David McCarthy, unpublished thesis, University College Dublin, Dublin, Ireland, 1995; based on data from Managed Account Reports, "Quarterly Performance Report," IV, 1987.

means for the two periods to be significantly different (at the 5 percent level). Thus, similar to other studies, McCarthy found that past performance was a biased predictor of future performance.

The deterioration in performance levels noted by McCarthy was a consequence of the early period being more favorable to CTA performance than the later one. Conceivably, a future comparison of two periods could show the reverse outcome, that is, higher return levels in the later period. (The lack of correlation between past and future return levels, however, will likely persist.) In contrast, the more extreme deterioration between past and future return levels noted by EGR and Irwin was primarily a consequence of the previously discussed bias in prepublic returns. (For example, in Irwin's study

Table 7.2
EXAMPLE OF 10 INDIVIDUAL CTAs' PARTICIPATION IN
MULTIPLE PUBLIC COMMODITY FUNDS—1991

CTA	Number of Public Commodity Funds for Which CTA Trades (Including Multiadvisor Funds)	Number of Public Commodity Funds: CTA Acts as Sole Advisor
A	15	6
B	9	4
C	9	2
D	8	5
E	7	7
F	7	6
G	6	3
H	5	3
I	3	3
J	3	3

Source: David McCarthy, unpublished thesis, University College Dublin, Dublin, Ireland, 1995; based on data from Managed Account Reports, "Quarterly Performance Report," IV, 1987.

the gap between past and future performance was modest when past performance was defined by a pool index, as opposed to the prepublic returns of individual pools.) The implication is that in the case where past and future periods are defined in terms of prepublic–postpublic periods (which will be different for each pool), as opposed to common periods for all pools, future comparisons would *always* be expected to show sharply lower returns for the later period.

As previously noted, the fact that past performance levels are poor predictors of future performance does not imply a lack of correlation in relative performance. McCarthy, therefore, also examined whether performance rankings in the earlier period were correlated with rankings in the later period. Here he found significant correlation between past and future performance. Although the rank correlation coefficient for return was only borderline significant (i.e., significant at the 10 percent level) and modestly low at 0.24, the Sharpe Ratio rank correlation coefficient of 0.42 was significant at well beyond the 1 percent level. As in all the other studies, past and future standard deviation levels were highly correlated, with a very high rank correlation coefficient of 0.70 (significant at better than the 0.01 percent level).

McCarthy also tested a series of regression equations modeled after those used by Edwards and Ma. In contrast to Edwards and Ma, however, McCarthy found that the variables corresponding to the early-period CTA performance levels (return and return/risk measures, as well as standard deviation) were uniformly significant as explanatory variables for the corresponding CTA performance measure in the later period (for both absolute and relative performance measures).

McCarthy considered why his results differed so starkly from those of Edwards and Ma. He cites two explanations:

1. His study used CTA data instead of fund data.
2. His analysis covered a different time period, with little overlap with the Edwards and Ma study. He acknowledged that if a common time period had been used, the results between the two studies might have been more similar (notwithstanding the first difference cited).

In addition, I would add a third important difference: By using common survey and test periods, as opposed to defining time periods separately for each element, McCarthy avoided the previously cited bias toward overstated early-period (i.e., prepublic) returns that resulted by defining time periods individually for each pool based on the public offering date.

One weakness of the McCarthy study is that it analyzed the correlation between only a single pair of periods. Since performance correlation results can vary substantially between periods, the limited temporal span of the analysis cautions against drawing generalized conclusions based on the results.

THE IRWIN, ZULAUF, AND WARD STUDY

The study by Scott H. Irwin, Carl R. Zulauf, and Barry W. Ward (IZW), "The Predictability of Managed Futures Returns,"[10] avoided many of the deficiencies of other studies. Similar to McCarthy, the IZW study employed individual CTA data, as opposed to pool data, thereby avoiding the double-counting error cited by McCarthy. However, whereas McCarthy analyzed only a single pair of periods, IZW applied their performance correlation tests to four pairs of periods. Moreover, IZW used a significantly larger CTA database: as many as 134 in the latest period comparison, versus only 52 in McCarthy's study. Also, whereas EGR, who also tested multiple period pairs, used one-year units for their time periods—a time definition that arguably appears too short for establishing meaningful performance rankings and judging performance correlations—IZW examined one-, two-, and three-year holding periods. For these reasons, in respect to the question of whether past- and future-period performance rankings are correlated, this study appears to be the most comprehensive and least biased of the various studies cited in this chapter, suggesting its conclusions be given the greatest weight.

IZW calculated rank correlation coefficients between four adjacent two-year holding periods. (Although one- and three-year holding periods were also analyzed, the results were not detailed, because the authors indicated that the results were similar to those of the two-year holding period.) IZW found that the rank correlation coefficient for return was statistically significant (at the 5 percent level) in only one of the four holding periods. Standard deviation rankings, however, were far more stable, with three of the four periods yielding statistically significant rank correlation coefficients for this performance measure.

To examine whether performance might be more predictable for a given segment (e.g., top performers) than for the entire CTA data list, IZW also analyzed the data by decile rankings, comparing the relative rankings of CTAs in each decile in a past period with their average decile ranking in the forward period (see Table 7.3). IZW concluded:

> There is modest evidence of consistency in average return performance for the top decile of CTA programs. CTAs in decile 1 have an average rank of 3.333 in subsequent two-year holding periods. Average annual return for the top decile is higher than the return for all CTAs (19.714% versus 13.128%). In contrast, average annual returns for deciles 2 through 10 appear to be randomly scattered around the average return for all CTAs . . . .
>
> Confirming earlier findings, there is strong evidence of consistency in standard deviation, especially for the first six deciles. CTAs in decile 1 have

---

[10]*Journal of Derivatives*, 20–27, Winter 1994.

Table 7.3

PREDICTABILITY OF THE AVERAGE RETURN AND STANDARD DEVIATION OF CTA PROGRAM RETURNS, BY DECILE, TWO-YEAR HOLDING PERIODS, 1982–1989

Performance Decile Rank in Period t	Average Return		Standard Deviation	
	Average Decile Rank in $t + 1$	Average Return in $t + 1$ (annual %)	Average Decile Rank in $t + 1$	Average Standard Deviation in $t + 1$ (annual %)
1	3.333	19.714	1.667	12.353
2	6.333	14.725	2.333	15.756
3	5.667	16.752	3.333	15.732
4	7.333	8.911	4.000	19.095
5	6.000	13.208	4.333	21.522
6	7.667	7.184	5.333	22.519
7	4.333	12.778	10.000	30.241
8	5.667	12.467	7.667	25.838
9	3.333	16.385	9.000	27.574
10	5.333	9.151	7.000	25.099
All CTAs		13.128		21.573

Source: Scott H. Irwin, Carl R. Zulauf, and Barry W. Ward, "The Predictability of Managed Futures Returns," *Journal of Derivatives*, Winter 1994. This copyrighted material is reprinted with permission from the Journal of Derivatives, a publication of Institutional Investor, Inc., 488 Madison Avenue, New York, NY 10022.

an average rank of 1.667 and an annual standard deviation of 12.353% in subsequent two-year holding periods. In contrast, CTAs in deciles 7 through 10 have an average rank of at least 7.00 and a standard deviation of at least 25.099%.

In summary, similar to all the other studies, IZW found strong evidence of persistence in standard deviation rankings, and as with most other studies, they found no evidence of statistically significant correlation between past and future returns. Unfortunately, IZW did not test for the stability of rankings in return/risk measures, such as the Sharpe Ratio. Although IZW did uncover a tendency for CTAs in the top decile of return in a given period to experience significantly above-average returns in the following period, they placed little confidence in these results because of the lack of superior performance persistence at the individual CTA level, citing that no CTA placed in the top decile in all three periods,[11] and only one CTA placed in the top decile in two of these periods.

---

[11]The earliest of the four period pairs was not used in the decile analysis because of insufficient data.

SUMMARY

There was unanimous agreement among the studies that past performance levels do not provide a reliable indication of future performance levels (and in the case of prepublic returns, are biased as well). However, even accepting this conclusion, it still leaves open the question of whether the *relative rankings* of past performance provide useful information regarding the relative rankings of future performance. In other words, even though a manager's (or pool's) past performance does not provide any guide to future performance, are managers (pools) with relatively better performance in the past more likely to exhibit relatively better performance in the future (even if that performance level is very different from past levels)?

All the studies agreed that in terms of risk (as measured by the standard deviation), there was a substantive correlation between past and future relative rankings—that is, managers (or pools) that are the riskiest (most volatile) in the past tend to remain the riskiest in the future (and those that are the least risky remain least risky). Thus past performance is useful in identifying high- and low-risk managers (pools).

The foregoing two points (regarding the lack of correlation between past and future performance *levels* and the stability in relative risk rankings) were about as far as universal agreement among the researchers went. There were major contradictions in the findings regarding the more important question of whether past *relative* performance provides a guideline to future relative performance in terms of return and return/risk measures—a far more pertinent matter to most investors than the stability of relative risk. All the studies employing pool data failed to find any evidence that past relative returns were indicative of future relative returns (or at least evidence they deemed statistically significant). In other words, these studies implied that you were as likely to select a pool that would generate above-average returns by picking from among the worst or middling past-performing pools as the best. Similarly, these studies found an equal paucity of evidence regarding any relationship between the relative rankings of past and future return/risk levels for pools.

It should be noted, however, that although dismissed by the authors as not being statistically significant, the EGR study did contain some evidence of positive correlation between past and future relative performance rankings. (Examples of such tendencies were cited in the prior discussion of their study.) Also, as pointed out by McCarthy, pool data introduces severe double-counting in the data. This consideration, of course, raises the question of whether past relative rankings of returns or return/risk measures provide a guideline for future relative rankings in the case of individual managers. Only two of the studies cited—Irwin ("The Predictability of Managed Futures Returns") and McCarthy—considered this question, and they reached very different conclusions.

IZW concluded that past relative returns did not provide a useful indicator of future relative returns—the same conclusion found by the studies using pool data. IZW's study, however, still left some open questions. First, they found that managers in the top decile of past performance had a tendency to exhibit above-average returns in the future period, suggesting that past rankings of returns might contain some useful information, even if overall past and future relative rankings were uncorrelated. Second, IZW did not examine whether there was any correlation between past and future relative rankings based on a return/risk measure. It is entirely possible that past and future relative rankings could be correlated in terms of return/risk, even if they are uncorrelated in terms of return.

McCarthy considered both return and return/risk ratios in his study and found statistically significant correlations between past and future relative rankings for each type of measure. Thus McCarthy's findings regarding CTA relative rankings of return contradicted IZW's conclusions, whereas his observations regarding return/risk relative rankings were not addressed by IZW.

The contradictory conclusions reached by IZW and McCarthy could probably be explained by the fact that they used different sets of CTA data and more importantly conducted their empirical tests over different time periods. (McCarthy, in fact, only conducted performance comparisons across a single pair of periods.) As a general rule, empirical studies of performance are highly dependent on the time period chosen.

The bottom line, though, is that even after all these studies, the answer to the critical question of whether an investor is more likely to achieve above-average returns (or above-average return/risk results) by selecting superior *past* performing managers (as opposed to selecting mangers randomly) remains inconclusive.

8 Is Past Performance Predictive of Future Performance? A CTA-Based Analysis

In this chapter we reexamine the question of whether past performance is a useful indicator of future performance. In other words, are the best past performing managers more likely to do better in the future than their poorer performing counterparts?

Why is it necessary to revisit this question in view of the numerous academic studies that have dealt with this topic and whose results were summarized in the previous chapter? There are four key reasons:

1. Most of the previous studies were based on public pool (fund) performance (as opposed to the performance of individual commodity trading advisors (CTAs). As McCarthy pointed out in his study, this approach introduces serious distortion due to the double-counting of results for CTAs who manage assets for numerous pools (or funds).

2. The two studies that did focus on individual CTA performance reached opposite conclusions regarding the correlation between past and future relative performance rankings. Also, only one of these studies looked at return/risk (the most significant measure).

3. This chapter incorporates data several years beyond the end dates of the studies cited in Chapter 7.

4. As implied in Chapter 7, results of tests of performance stability are highly dependent on the survey periods chosen. This chapter examines a much greater number of period combinations than the studies cited in Chapter 7, enhancing the validity of the conclusions found.

PERFORMANCE MEASURES

The study detailed in this chapter looks at the correlation between past and future relative rankings based on five separate performance measures of CTAs.

Average Monthly Returns

Many investors focus primarily on average monthly returns. However, by itself, this statistic is a flawed measure. For one thing, the degree of volatility in monthly returns can significantly affect the return actually realized by an investor. For example, Table 8.1 compares the hypothetical monthly returns and net asset values (NAVs) of two managers with identical average monthly returns during the period shown, but significantly different variability of return. As can be seen, the final return realized by manager B (the lower-volatility manager), as represented by the ending NAV value, is far higher, even though that manager witnessed the same average monthly return. In addition, the average monthly return also shares the drawbacks detailed for the average geometric return (average annual compounded return), which is detailed next.

Table 8.1
THE IMPACT OF VOLATILITY ON RETURN

Month	Manager A Return	Manager B Return		Manager A NAV	Manager B NAV
Dec				1000.0	1000.0
Jan	15.0	6.0		1150.0	1060.0
Feb	28.0	2.0		1472.0	1081.2
Mar	−7.0	−3.0		1369.0	1048.8
Apr	12.0	8.0		1533.2	1132.7
May	−26.0	−3.0		1134.6	1098.7
Jun	−17.0	2.0		941.7	1120.7
Jul	14.0	8.0		1073.6	1210.3
Aug	22.0	9.0		1309.7	1319.2
Sep	−18.0	−4.0		1074.0	1266.5
Oct	10.0	−1.0		1181.4	1253.8
Nov	19.0	5.0		1405.8	1316.5
Dec	−21.0	2.0		1110.6	1342.8
Average Monthly Return	2.58	2.58	Cumulative Return	11.06	34.28

Average Monthly Geometric Return
(Average Annual Compounded Return)

The average monthly geometric return is that return that when compounded monthly will yield the ending NAV given the starting NAV. The geometric return is calculated by taking the *n*th root of the product of the monthly returns expressed as factors of 1. This concept will be a lot clearer if we use an example. Table 8.2 illustrates how to calculate a geometric mean return for a hypothetical series of 12 monthly returns. The procedure can be broken down into the following steps:

1. Express monthly returns as factors of 1 (e.g., 2% = 1.02).
2. Calculate the chain multiple of these returns (1.02 × 0.96 × 1.06 × . . . × 0.94).
3. Find the geometric mean: Take the *n*th root of the chain multiple (12th root in this example).
4. To express the geometric mean in terms of a monthly percent return, subtract 1.0 and multiply by 100.

Table 8.2
CALCULATING THE MONTHLY GEOMETRIC MEAN RETURN

Month	Percent Return	Return as Factor of 1	NAV
			1,000
1	2	1.02	1,020
2	−4	0.96	979
3	6	1.06	1,038
4	−3	0.97	1,007
5	−2	0.98	987
6	8	1.08	1,066
7	7	1.07	1,140
8	−5	0.95	1,083
9	−1	0.99	1,072
10	10	1.10	1,180
11	4	1.04	1,227
12	−6	0.94	1,153

Chain multiple = (1.02) (0.96) ⋯ (0.94) = 1.153175
Geometric mean = 12th root of chain multiple =1.011947 (1.1947% expressed in terms of monthly return)
Note that starting NAV (1,000) multiplied by $(1.011947)^{12}$ = ending NAV (1,153)

As can be seen in Table 8.2, compounding the starting NAV monthly by the geometric mean return yields the ending NAV. An average compounded return (geometric mean return) is the relevant calculation if the CTA adjusts trading leverage for the account size each month, as is typically the case. (The arithmetic mean return would only be the appropriate measure if the CTA kept leverage constant at the starting NAV level, which would be highly atypical.) It should be noted that the monthly geometric mean return and the average annual compounded return are exactly equivalent. (Annualizing the average monthly geometric return will yield the average annual compounded return.)

Although the average geometric return avoids the aforementioned distortion in the average monthly return—that is, in contrast to the average monthly return, a higher average geometric return will always imply a higher cumulative return for the investment period—it doesn't fully incorporate the risk impact of greater volatility. In other words, two managers could have the same average geometric return, and hence identical cumulative returns over the holding period, but differ in terms of risk considerations. For example, Figure 8.1 compares two managers with equal geometric returns as evidenced by the identical starting and ending NAV values, but significantly different volatility levels. Obviously, manager B would be preferred by any investor because he realizes the same cumulative return, but does so with much smaller equity drawdowns.

Although some investors may think, "All I care about is which manager will give me the greatest cumulative return. I am willing to accept the interim risk," this type of thinking is flawed for two reasons. First, there is a significantly greater chance that investors will abandon a manager with high volatility during one of his drawdown periods, and hence never realize the potentially higher cumulative return. In this sense, the lower the volatility, the greater the chance that the implied return will actually be realized, instead of a much lower return or even loss due to premature liquidation of the account.

Second, by using notional funding[1], an investor can always increase the leverage of a manager who has both lower return and risk (but a higher return/risk ratio) to yield a higher cumulative return at an equivalent (or lower) risk level (relative to a manager with higher return but lower

---

[1]Notional funding refers to the funding of an account at less than the nominal account size. For example, an investor might provide a CTA with $500,000 and the instruction that it be traded as a nominal $1,000,000 account (in effect doubling the leverage on the money actually provided). Since CTAs typically only use a fraction of funds for margin requirements (fully allocating the money would result in excessive leverage), they will usually accept notional funding.

Figure 8.1
TWO MANAGERS WITH IDENTICAL GEOMETRIC RETURNS
BUT DIFFERENT VOLATILITY

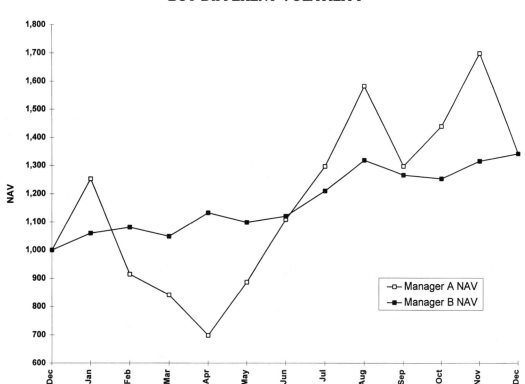

return/risk). In this sense, return/risk is always a more meaningful measure than return alone.

Standard Deviation

By itself, standard deviation, which is a proxy for risk, is an inadequate measure. There are, however, two reasons for considering standard deviation independently. First, as was detailed in Chapter 3, viewing return and risk measures independently provides more information than a return/risk ratio. As was shown in an example in that chapter, it is theoretically possible for a manager to have a lower Sharpe Ratio than another manager and yet be preferred by virtually all investors. Second, as was detailed in the previous chapter, prior studies have shown that risk measures, such as the standard deviation, tend to be far more stable from period to period than return measures.

Modified Sharpe Ratio

For reasons detailed in Chapter 3, we use the modified Sharpe Ratio—that is, the Sharpe Ratio calculated without an adjustment for a risk-free return—in this chapter as well. Generally speaking, given the drawbacks for return measures, which were previously discussed in this section, a return/risk measure is a far more meaningful gauge for investors than return alone. Again, even if an investor places a greater importance on return than return/risk, he can use notional funding to realize a higher return at an equivalent risk level with a manager who exhibits a higher return/risk ratio (and presumably a lower return) than with a manager reflecting the opposite characteristics.

Modified Sharpe Ratio Using Geometric Return

Typically, the numerator of the Sharpe Ratio is calculated using the average arithmetic return. However, the geometric mean return is more meaningful because it corresponds to the cumulative return that will actually be realized by an investor, whereas the average arithmetic return does not. (As an example, in Table 8.1, a geometric mean return would precisely reflect the performance difference between the two managers, whereas the arithmetic mean return is the same for both.) Consequently, this form of the Sharpe Ratio is preferred.

Use of Performance Measures in Testing

This chapter will examine the degree of correlation between each of these five performance measures in a prior period and the values witnessed in the forward period. In addition, the correlation between past standard deviations and future Sharpe Ratios (geometric return based) is also examined following the implications of the Elton, Gruber, and Rentzler (EGR) study. (It will be recalled that EGR found past standard deviation to be a better predictor of future return/risk than past return/risk itself.) In other words, we will seek to answer the question: Do managers that exhibit relatively better past performance (as reflected by these measures) continue to achieve relatively better future performance?

TEST PERIODS

As was illustrated in the previous chapter, the results of tests of performance stability are highly dependent on the particular periods chosen. Given this variability, it is desirable to examine as many diverse survey periods as possible. Specifically, we will examine the issue of performance stability using prior three-year periods as indicators for the subsequent two- and three-year periods, prior four-year periods as indicators for the subsequent two-, three-, and four-year periods, and prior five-year periods as indicators for the subsequent two- and three-year periods. Prior survey periods are defined beginning with mid-1987, the approximate start date of data availability from the source used, and ending in mid-1995 (the latest available data at this writing).

DATA

The analysis in this chapter employed the Refco CTA Database.[2] For each combination of periods, performance rankings were calculated for all CTAs in this database that were managing at least $1 million as of the first month of the earlier period. Generally speaking, in cases in which the database contained several programs for a single CTA, only a single program was used (typically the one with the greatest equity), because these programs were usually highly correlated. An exception was made for two CTAs, each of whom had two programs that were relatively uncorrelated. (One of these CTAs had many programs, but only one that was significantly uncorrelated with the main program.)

It should be emphasized that while the database contained data for a large number of CTA programs, it was by no means all-inclusive, especially for the earlier years in our analysis. The following are the number of CTA programs in the database exceeding the specified $1 million threshold as of midyear in each of the following initial-period start years: 1987—25; 1988—34; 1989—41; and 1990—86. (The CTA lists for each of these periods are contained in Appendix 3 at the end of the book.) While not all-inclusive, it is assumed that this database was probably sufficiently comprehensive for the conclusions reached to be representative of the industry as a whole. In other words, if the same analysis were conducted over a hypothetically complete CTA database, the precise results would, of course, differ, but it is assumed that the same general patterns and conclusions would emerge.

---

[2]Refco Information Services, Inc., One World Financial Center, 200 Liberty Street, New York.

One potential source of distortion in the database used, as well as virtually all available CTA databases, is that it did not include defunct CTAs. In this respect, the database is not representative of the CTAs existent during the time periods being analyzed. Errors related to this data gap are termed *survivorship bias*. For some types of analysis, survivorship bias can significantly distort results. For example, a CTA index in which past data did not include CTAs that subsequently went defunct would invariably tend to overstate CTA performance (since such an index would systematically exclude a class of poorly performing CTAs—those who did badly enough to go out of business). For the application employed in this chapter—comparisons of relative performance rankings in different periods—survivorship bias is probably not a problem, as demonstrated by the following explanation.

The question of survivorship bias was examined in a study by Thomas Schneeweis and Richard Spurgin.[3] They found that the primary difference between nonsurvivor returns and the average return of survivors during corresponding periods was concentrated in the final year, and especially the final few months, of trading by nonsurvivors (a period during which, not surprisingly, nonsurvivors drastically underperformed survivors). Excluding their final 12 months of trading, however, the difference between the two groups was far smaller. For the purposes of this discussion, however, Schneeweis and Spurgin's key finding was that the nonsurvivors underperformed in each of the three survey periods examined. Thus, the implication is that, if anything, our analysis, which does not include nonsurvivors, would tend to understate correlations between past and future period performance rankings. Therefore, any evidence of correlations between past and future performance can safely be assumed to still be valid if nonsurvivor data had been included in the analysis.

METHODOLOGY

Rank Correlation Analysis

For each performance measure, managers are ranked for a defined past period. For example, if there are 50 managers, the manager with the best performance measure would be assigned a rank of 1, the manager with the second best performance measure a rank of 2, and so on, with the manager with

---

[3]Thomas Schneeweis and Richard Spurgin, "Survivor Bias in Commodity Trading Advisor Performance," University of Massachusetts, Amherst, 1995.

the worst performance measure receiving a rank of 50.[4] Next, the managers would be ranked for the same performance measure in a subsequent period. A rank correlation coefficient would then be derived for these two sets of numbers.[5] If there were perfect correlation between past and future relative rankings, the rank correlation coefficient would equal 1.0 (the best performing manager in the past period would also be the best in the future period, the second best in the past would also be the second best in the future, and so on). If there were no relation between past and future rankings (that is, a manager with a high past ranking would be about as likely to have a high future ranking as a low one), the rank correlation coefficient would be near zero.

The rank correlation coefficient is used instead of the raw correlation coefficient because it eliminates the distortional impact of outliers. A perfect illustration of this point was provided in the Irwin, Zulauf, and Ward (IZW) study.[6] In one instance, they found a statistically significant *negative* correlation between the CTA returns in a two-year period and returns in the next two-year period, a result that seemed to imply that CTAs with poor returns in the past were more likely to witness superior returns in the future. IZW demonstrated that this odd result was entirely a consequence of one extreme outlier.[7] (See Figure 8.2, which is reproduced from IZW's original article.) When IZW transformed the raw data into rankings, the correlation coefficient between the two periods was transformed from

---

[4]Two points need to be clarified:
1. For the standard deviation, the lowest value would be assigned a rank of 1, since the lower the volatility, the better.
2. While the rankings for average monthly return, average monthly geometric return, and standard deviation would be assigned in the straightforward fashion described, rankings for the Sharpe Ratio measures are complicated by the fact that negative Sharpe Ratio values are completely ambiguous and should be ignored. As was explained in Chapter 3, a more negative Sharpe Ratio could be due to a more negative return or to lower volatility, with the implications of each being 180 degrees apart. Consequently, in our analysis, negative Sharpe Ratios are ignored for the purpose of assigning rank values. Specifically, rank values for positive Sharpe Ratios are assigned in normal fashion, but the ranking order of the negative Sharpe Ratio values are determined by geometric return values. For example, if there are 50 managers and 8 have negative Sharpe Ratios, the assignment of the rank values 43–50 would be determined on the basis of geometric return—the manager with the least negative geometric return would receive a rank of 43, and so on.

[5]A rank correlation coefficient is simply a correlation coefficient calculated on rankings instead of the raw data.

[6]Scott H. Irwin, Carl R. Zulauf, and Barry W. Ward, "The Predictability of Managed Futures Returns," *Journal of Derivatives,* 20–27, Winter 1994.

[7]Although in IZW's study, the cited instance of a statistically significant inverse relationship between past and future performance was due to a statistical quirk, as will be seen later in this chapter, such a seeming odd result is a genuine phenomenon for some survey periods (even if rank correlations are used instead of raw correlations).

Figure 8.2
CTA RETURNS IN 1980/1981 AND 1982/1983

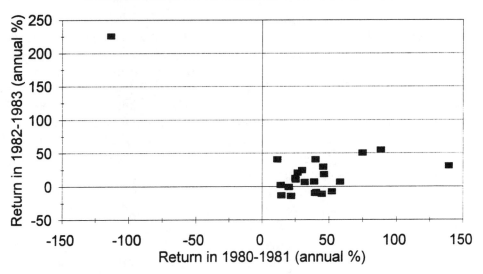

Source: Scott H. Irwin, Carl R. Zulauf, and Barry W. Ward, "The Predictability of Managed Futures Returns," *Journal of Derivatives,* Winter 1994. This copyrighted material is reprinted with permission from the Journal of Derivatives, a publication of Institutional Investor, Inc., 488 Madison Avenue, New York, NY 10022.

Figure 8.3
CTA RANKINGS IN 1980/1981 AND 1982/1983

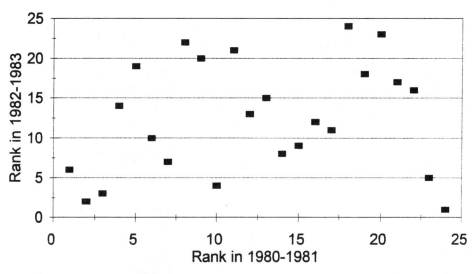

Source: Scott H. Irwin, Carl R. Zulauf, and Barry W. Ward, "The Predictability of Managed Futures Returns," *Journal of Derivatives,* Winter 1994. This copyrighted material is reprinted with permission from the Journal of Derivatives, a publication of Institutional Investor, Inc., 488 Madison Avenue, New York, NY 10022.

–0.55 to +0.19, eliminating the anomalous result. Figure 8.3, which is also taken from IZW's study, shows how a scatter diagram based on ranks (instead of raw data) dramatically reduces the influence of the outlier observation in Figure 8.2.

Another advantage of using rank correlations instead of raw correlations is that tests of statistical significance based on the rank correlation coefficient do not require the restrictive assumption that the data are normally distributed, as is the case for the raw correlation coefficient.[8] Therefore, if some of the distributions of CTA performance being analyzed deviate from a normal curve distribution, statistical tests of significance based on the rank correlation coefficient would be theoretically more sound.[9]

Quintile Analysis

Even if rank correlations are not stable across all CTAs, it is possible that there may be stability among the top performing CTAs. In other words, the top quintile performers in a past period may have a tendency to witness above-median results in the subsequent period, even if the rank correlation between past and future performance based on *all* CTAs is not statistically significant. In fact, IZW's study (which segmented data into deciles as opposed to quintiles) strongly hinted at this possibility. Even though all the rank correlation coefficients (of CTA rankings in two periods) derived by IZW were statistically insignificant, they found that the top decile performers did evidence enough persistence to show above-median results in the following period. If such a pattern of persistence can be demonstrated, it would indicate that past performance provides useful information for selecting future managers, even if the rank correlation coefficients based on all CTAs (in the database being used) was consistently near zero.

For each combination of periods we therefore calculate the average future period ranking of CTAs in each quintile, as defined by performance in the prior period.[10] If the top quintile performers of a past period tend to wit-

---

[8]To be precise, this advantage is related to the aforementioned advantage of diminishing the impact of outliers, since the existence of outliers is evidence of a nonnormal distribution.

[9]The rank correlation method, however, will not correct for heteroskedasticity, which is a potential source of distortion when dealing with CTA data, because CTA performance distributions will have different variances.

[10]When the number of CTAs is not a multiple of 5, the following approach is used: The total number of CTAs is divided by 5 and rounded down to the nearest integer. This is the minimum number of CTAs in each quintile, with an extra CTA in the number of top quintiles equal to the remainder. For example, if the total number of CTAs is 34, the first four quintiles would have 7 CTAs apiece, while the lowest quintile would have 6 CTAs (34 ÷ 5 = 6 with a remainder of 4).

ness above-average future quintile rankings, it would suggest the possibility that selecting managers from the top quintile may be a viable strategy for beating the industry average performance in a future period.

SOURCES OF BIAS
AND DISTORTION AVOIDED
BY DESCRIBED METHODOLOGY

Before turning to a discussion of the results of our study, it is worth highlighting the aspects of our analysis that are aimed at avoiding the sources of bias, distortion, and incompleteness of data that were present in some of the past studies detailed in the previous chapter. These key methodological features include:

1. **CTA Data.** Using CTA data instead of pool data avoids the severe double-counting error cited by McCarthy.
2. **Common Comparison Periods.** As was explained in Chapter 7, comparing all elements (CTA trading programs in this instance) over the same past and forward periods avoids the strong upward bias in past performance that results from defining past periods individually based on pool offering dates.
3. **Broad Range of Comparison Periods.** Our analysis uses 16 combinations of past and future survey periods, substantially more than the studies summarized in the previous chapter. Since tests of performance stability are highly dependent on the periods chosen—just how much so will become strikingly evident later in this chapter—the use of a significantly larger number of comparison periods enhances the likelihood that the results obtained will be representative rather than due to a quirk.
4. **Past Performance Periods Are at Least Three Years Long.** Some of the studies cited in Chapter 7 used periods as short as one year to define past relative performance. It can be reasonably argued that one year is far too short a time frame to establish relative performance comparisons. Moreover, since most investors are likely to view past performance over longer periods in the process of selecting a CTA or pool, one-year comparisons are of questionable relevance to real-world decision making.
5. **Return/Risk Measures Are Used to Evaluate the Stability of Relative Performance.** As was explained earlier in this chap-

ter, return/risk measures, as opposed to return measures, are the critical performance gauge. Therefore, our analysis examines return/risk measures directly as opposed to only considering return and risk independently, as was done in some of the cited studies.

6. ***Quintile Rankings Examined as a Supplement to Total Data Rankings.*** Demonstrating that past and future performance rankings are not statistically significant does not necessarily prove that past performance can't be used to pick above-average future performers. Reason: It can be argued that top performers exhibit some performance stability from period to period, even if the total group of CTAs does not. A quintile analysis addresses this possibility.

7. ***Adjustment for Negative Sharpe Ratios.*** As was explained in Chapter 3, negative Sharpe Ratios are completely ambiguous and should be ignored. Our analysis corrects for this statistical distortion (see footnote 4 in this chapter).

THE RANK CORRELATION COEFFICIENT TEST RESULTS

Table 8.3 summarizes all the rank correlation coefficients for five different performance measures and one combination of measures across 16 period comparisons. In effect, this single table distills the results of 96 correlation tests! Each indicated value represents the rank correlation coefficient between the two indicated periods for the specific performance measure.

As can be seen, there was striking consistency between past and future standard deviation rankings. All 16 rank correlation coefficients for this measure were statistically significant at better than the 0.1 percent level! This result confirms the similar findings of all the other studies.

The situation, however, was quite different for the return and return/risk measures. Based on the averages for all the indicated periods, the rank correlation coefficients for return (both arithmetic and geometric) and return/risk (two types of Sharpe Ratios, one of which is compared against both its own past value and the past standard deviation level) were remarkably close to zero. In the case of the return measures, not a single period showed a result significant at even the 5 percent level. In the case of the return/risk measures, however, the near-zero average rank correlation coefficients were a consequence of statistically significant *negative* correla-

Table 8.3
RANK CORRELATION SUMMARY TABLE

Past Period	Forward Period	Number of Years Past Period	Number of Years Forward Period	Arithmetic Return	Geometric Return	Standard Deviation	Modified Sharpe Ratio	Geometric Return Modified Sharpe Ratio	SD versus Modified Sharpe Ratio
7/87–6/90	7/90–6/92	3	2	0.11	−0.07	0.78[c]	−0.15	−0.12	0.05
7/87–6/90	7/90–6/93	3	3	0.09	−0.08	0.79[c]	−0.25	−0.23	−0.01
7/87–6/91	7/91–6/93	4	2	−0.05	−0.21	0.81[c]	−0.42[a]	−0.42[a]	−0.15
7/87–6/91	7/91–6/94	4	3	−0.14	−0.37	0.81[c]	−0.53[b]	−0.49[a]	−0.02
7/87–6/91	7/91–6/95	4	4	−0.14	−0.29	0.82[c]	−0.37	−0.33	0.08
7/87–6/92	7/92–6/94	5	2	−0.14	−0.26	0.71[c]	−0.43	−0.45	−0.17
7/87–6/92	7/92–6/95	5	3	−0.02	−0.12	0.72[c]	−0.22	−0.16	0.03
7/88–6/91	7/91–6/93	3	2	0.07	−0.06	0.82[c]	−0.04	−0.02	0.00
7/88–6/91	7/91–6/94	3	3	0.02	−0.08	0.81[c]	−0.01	0.00	0.04
7/88–6/92	7/92–6/94	4	2	0.09	0.08	0.66[c]	0.15	0.18	−0.02
7/88–6/92	7/92–6/95	4	3	0.11	0.12	0.67[c]	0.23	0.35[a]	0.17
7/88–6/93	7/92–6/95	5	2	0.08	0.14	0.70[c]	0.25	0.34[a]	0.31
7/89–6/92	7/92–6/94	3	2	0.27	0.23	0.70[c]	0.28	0.24	−0.05
7/89–6/92	7/92–6/95	3	3	0.26	0.25	0.72[c]	0.32[a]	0.32[a]	0.06
7/89–6/93	7/93–6/95	4	2	0.21	0.20	0.76[c]	0.32[a]	0.33[a]	0.22
7/90–6/93	7/93–6/95	3	2	0.22	−0.02	0.76[c]	0.12	0.12	0.29[a]
Average for All Periods:				0.07	−0.03	0.75	−0.10	−0.14	0.04

[a]Significant at between the 1% and 5% level.
[b]Significant at better than the 1% level.
[c]Significant at better than the 0.1% level.

tions between past and future rankings in the earlier periods counterbalancing statistically significant positive correlations in the later periods. Six of the return/risk rank correlation coefficients for periods including a past period beginning in 1987 were statistically significant at better than the 5 percent level. All six of these coefficients were negative, implying an *inverse* relationship between past and future performance. Seven of the rank correlation coefficients for periods including a past period beginning in 1988 or later were statistically significant at better than the 5 percent level. These correlations all had the more intuitively plausible positive sign, implying that superior past performance, in terms of return/risk, was indicative of above-average future performance.

Figures 8.4–8.15 provide graphic depictions of the relationship between past and future performance. Each chart compares the correlation between past and future rankings of the indicated performance measure for a specific period. Rather than generate a chart for each period, which would have resulted in 96 charts (6 performance measure comparisons for 16 pairs of time periods), we reproduce only the periods that exhibited the highest and lowest rank correlation coefficients for each performance measure (12 in all).

The points depicted in Figures 8.4–8.15 represent different CTAs, with a point's placement along the horizontal axis corresponding to the given CTA's ranking (in terms of the indicated performance measure) for an earlier period, and the point's vertical placement corresponding to the same CTA's performance ranking in the subsequent period. Thus, for example, in Figure 8.4, point A indicates that the top ranking (1) CTA in the earlier period was also the top-ranking CTA in the later period, while point B indicates that the lowest-ranking (41) CTA in the earlier period was also near the bottom of the list (39) in the later period. Although the placement of these two points corresponds perfectly with the commonly held notion that past superior performing CTAs are likely to exhibit superior future performance, the placement of other points are highly counterintuitive. For example, point C indicates that the third-worst (39) CTA in the first period was the second-best (2) in the subsequent period, while point D indicates that the eighth-best (8) CTA in the earlier period was the second-worst (40) in the later period.

On balance, Figure 8.4 shows a modest positive correlation between past and future rankings as measured by the average monthly return. The correlation is so modest that it is difficult to see. (The reader can better visualize the correlation by covering up some of the extreme outlier points, such as C, D, E.) It should be emphasized that Figure 8.4 represents the *best* correlation between past and future arithmetic returns among all 16 pairs of periods tested! In other words, all other tested periods showed even lower correlations (or negative correlations). Figure 8.5 illustrates the correlation between past and future rankings of arithmetic returns for the period combination exhibiting the most negative correlation (a not meaningfully different from zero r value of $-.14$).

Figures 8.6 and 8.7 are the counterpart charts to Figures 8.4 and 8.5, using geometric rather than arithmetic returns. Here, too, Figure 8.6, which represents the best-case example, shows only a modest correlation between past and future relative rankings. Moreover, the absolute value of the rank correlation coefficient in Figure 8.7 ($-.37$) is greater than the corresponding value in Figure 8.6 (.25). In other words, the period pair with the strongest correlation for geometric returns is the one that implies that past and future returns are *inversely* related. Clearly, Figures 8.4–8.7 indicate that there is little correlation between past relative returns and future relative returns.

Figures 8.8 and 8.9 illustrate the correlation between past and future relative standard deviation rankings. Note that for standard deviation, high rankings (low ranking numbers) correspond to *low* standard deviation values, since low standard deviations are desirable. In these charts, the correlation between past and future relative rankings is clearly evident, even in the lowest correlation case (Figure 8.9). In fact, the lowest correlation for standard deviation ($r = .66$) was higher than the highest correlation for any other measure in any other period.

Figures 8.10–8.13 provide the corresponding charts for the Sharpe Ratio (both arithmetic-return- and geometric-return-based). Here the best-case examples (Figures 8.10 and 8.12) show borderline statistically significant positive correlation. However, at the other extreme, Figures 8.11 and 8.13 show even stronger *negative* correlation. In other words, even though some periods provide evidence of positive correlation between past and future Sharpe Ratio relative rankings, other periods show even stronger evidence of negative correlation. Therefore, on balance, there is no meaningful pattern between past and future relative Sharpe Ratios.

Finally, Figures 8.14 and 8.15 illustrate the correlation between past relative standard deviations and future relative Sharpe Ratios. Since CTAs with the best (lowest) standard deviations of the past tended to exhibit the best standard deviations in the future, it raised the question whether such CTAs would also be more likely to achieve above-average return/risk levels in the future. Here, too, the correlations ranged between modestly positive to modestly negative. Only one of the 16 period combinations showed a statistically significant positive correlation between past relative standard deviations and future relative Sharpe Ratios. And, even in this instance, the correlation was relatively low ($r = .29$), with statistical significance only achieved because of the greater number of observations (Figure 8.14).

Figure 8.4
ARITHMETIC RETURN: MOST POSITIVE CORRELATION
BETWEEN PAST AND FORWARD PERIODS

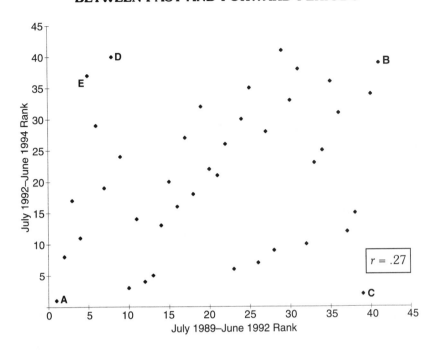

Figure 8.5
ARITHMETIC RETURN: MOST NEGATIVE CORRELATION
BETWEEN PAST AND FORWARD PERIODS

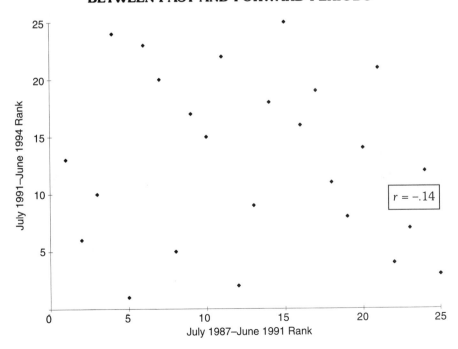

Figure 8.6
**GEOMETRIC RETURN: MOST POSITIVE CORRELATION
BETWEEN PAST AND FORWARD PERIODS**

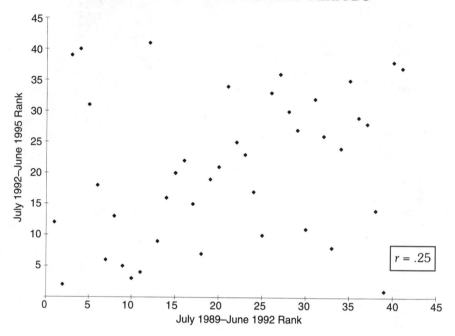

Figure 8.7
**GEOMETRIC RETURN: MOST NEGATIVE CORRELATION
BETWEEN PAST AND FORWARD PERIODS**

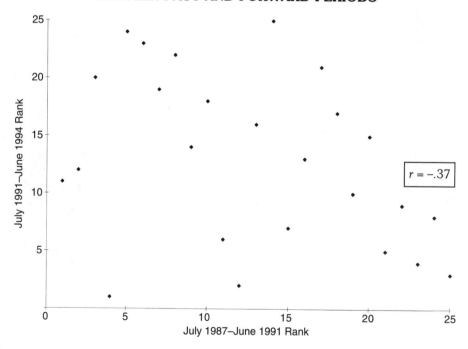

Figure 8.8
STANDARD DEVIATION: HIGHEST CORRELATION BETWEEN
PAST AND FORWARD PERIODS

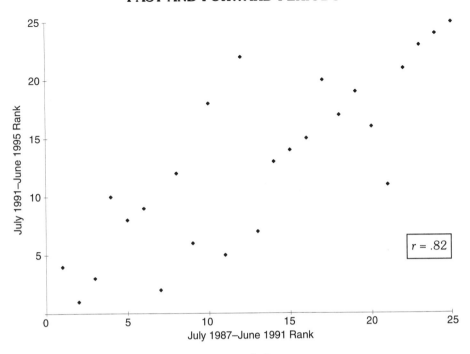

Figure 8.9
STANDARD DEVIATION: LOWEST CORRELATION BETWEEN
PAST AND FORWARD PERIODS

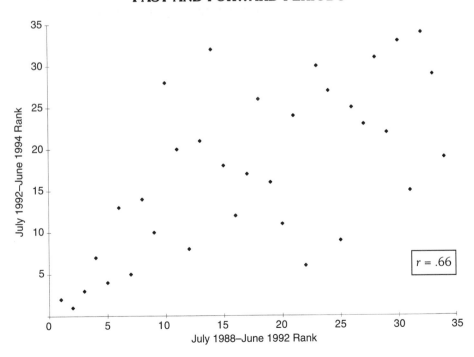

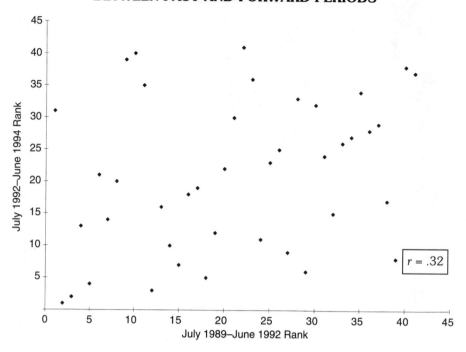

Figure 8.10
MODIFIED SHARPE RATIO: MOST POSITIVE CORRELATION BETWEEN PAST AND FORWARD PERIODS

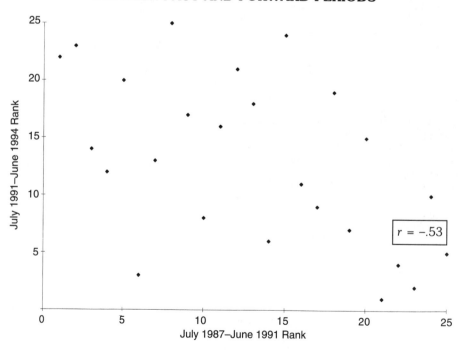

Figure 8.11
MODIFIED SHARPE RATIO: MOST NEGATIVE CORRELATION BETWEEN PAST AND FORWARD PERIODS

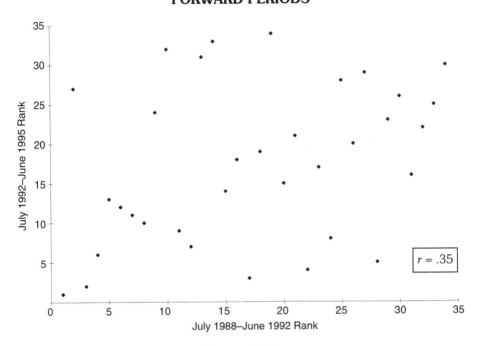

Figure 8.12
MODIFIED SHARPE RATIO (GEOMETRIC-RETURN-BASED):
MOST POSITIVE CORRELATION BETWEEN PAST AND
FORWARD PERIODS

$r = .35$

July 1988–June 1992 Rank

July 1992–June 1995 Rank

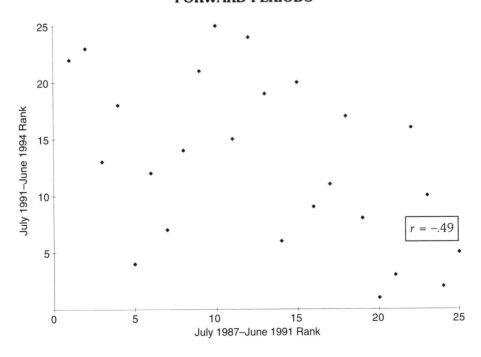

Figure 8.13
MODIFIED SHARPE RATIO (GEOMETRIC-RETURN-BASED):
MOST NEGATIVE CORRELATION BETWEEN PAST AND
FORWARD PERIODS

$r = -.49$

July 1987–June 1991 Rank

July 1991–June 1994 Rank

131

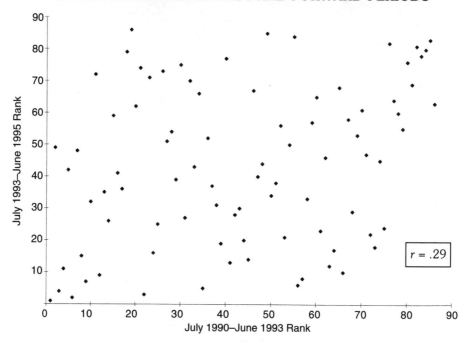

Figure 8.14
STANDARD DEVIATION VERSUS MODIFIED SHARPE RATIO
(GEOMETRIC-RETURN-BASED): MOST POSITIVE
CORRELATION BETWEEN PAST AND FORWARD PERIODS

$r = .29$

July 1993–June 1995 Rank

July 1990–June 1993 Rank

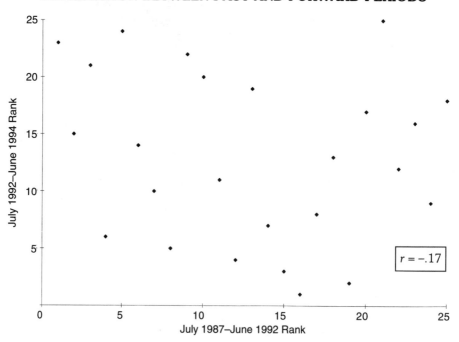

Figure 8.15
STANDARD DEVIATION VERSUS MODIFIED SHARPE RATIO
(GEOMETRIC-RETURN-BASED): MOST NEGATIVE
CORRELATION BETWEEN PAST AND FORWARD PERIODS

$r = -.17$

July 1992–June 1994 Rank

July 1987–June 1992 Rank

THE QUINTILE TEST RESULTS

Thus far, our analysis has shown that in terms of return/risk (as well as return), superior past relative performance does not provide any reliable indication of future relative performance. However, even though there is no significant correlation in the data viewed as a whole, one reasonable question is whether perhaps the *top* past performers continue to exhibit above-average future performance. To answer this question, we examined the average rankings of quintiles defined by past-performance rankings. Thus, for example, if the performance of top-ranking CTAs tends to be more stable than the performance of CTAs overall, we would expect the top quintile in each comparison period (a designation based on past performance) to exhibit better-than-average rankings (i.e., relatively low-ranking numbers).

In the top half of Table 8.4, the data in each row is segmented by the rankings of CTAs in the past period. Thus, for example, looking at the first row, the CTAs who had an arithmetic average monthly return among the top 20 percent of all CTAs during July 1987–June 1990 (i.e., quintile 1) had an average rank (based on this same performance measure) of 5.8 during the subsequent July 1990–June 1992 period. Since average rankings will be affected by the number of CTAs, which differ from period to period, it is necessary to reexpress the quintile average ranking figures as percentages of the average ranking for that period. Thus, since the average ranking value for the pair of periods in the first row was 13.0, the 5.8 average ranking for quintile 1 was equal to 44.6 percent of the average ranking. This figure implies that the CTAs in quintile 1 (i.e., the CTAs in the top one-fifth of past performers), on average, had much better rankings (lower ranking numbers) in the subsequent period.

Although the single result in the example just cited conformed to the notion that the best (worst) past performers will tend to achieve above-average (below-average) performance in the future, note the anomalous result for quintile 5, which also had a much better than average ranking. In effect, the results for the first period combination (top row of lower half of Table 8.4) imply that in order to pick CTAs who are likely to experience the highest future returns, one should select from among the best and *worst* past performers— an obviously nonsensical conclusion. This example provides a good illustration of the extreme dependence of past/future performance correlation tests on the periods chosen and highlights the critical importance of basing conclusions on as large a number of period comparisons as possible.

To get more meaningful figures, the quintile average rankings for individual periods are averaged. Specifically, for each quintile, the average rank-

Table 8.4
QUINTILE AVERAGE RANKINGS: ARITHMETIC RETURN

Past Period	Forward Period	Number of Years Past Period	Number of Years Forward Period	Quintile 1	Quintile 2	Quintile 3	Quintile 4	Quintile 5	Average
7/87–6/90	7/90–6/92	3	2	5.8	17.2	15.2	18.2	8.6	13.0
7/87–6/90	7/90–6/93	3	2	7.4	16.0	15.8	15.2	10.6	13.0
7/87–6/91	7/91–6/93	4	2	10.0	15.0	16.2	12.2	11.6	13.0
7/87–6/91	7/91–6/94	4	3	10.8	16.0	15.2	13.6	9.4	13.0
7/87–6/91	7/91–6/95	4	4	11.8	14.4	16.2	11.8	10.8	13.0
7/87–6/92	7/92–6/94	5	2	12.4	17.0	10.2	16.0	9.4	13.0
7/87–6/92	7/92–6/95	5	3	13.0	13.8	11.6	15.6	11.0	13.0
7/88–6/91	7/91–6/93	3	2	15.4	19.0	17.0	18.9	17.2	17.5
7/88–6/91	7/91–6/94	3	3	15.7	18.9	16.6	21.7	14.2	17.5
7/88–6/92	7/92–6/94	4	2	20.4	12.7	15.3	21.1	18.0	17.5
7/88–6/92	7/92–6/95	4	3	21.6	13.3	13.7	17.4	22.2	17.5
7/88–6/93	7/93–6/95	5	2	18.6	14.4	14.3	20.4	20.2	17.5
7/89–6/92	7/92–6/94	3	2	20.7	12.8	23.8	23.6	24.3	21.0
7/89–6/92	7/92–6/95	3	3	23.2	10.3	22.0	24.0	24.9	21.0
7/89–6/93	7/93–6/95	4	2	19.3	21.8	15.8	24.3	24.1	21.0
7/90–6/93	7/93–6/95	3	2	49.9	34.9	40.9	45.6	45.8	43.5

QUINTILE AVERAGE RANKINGS AS PERCENTAGE OF PERIOD
AVERAGE RANKINGS: ARITHMETIC RETURN

Period	Period							
7/87–6/90	7/90–6/92	3	2	44.6	132.3	116.9	140.0	66.2
7/87–6/90	7/90–6/93	3	2	56.9	123.1	121.5	116.9	81.5
7/87–6/91	7/91–6/93	4	2	76.9	115.4	124.6	93.8	89.2
7/87–6/91	7/91–6/94	4	3	83.1	123.1	116.9	104.6	72.3
7/87–6/91	7/91–6/95	4	4	90.8	110.8	124.6	90.8	83.1
7/87–6/92	7/92–6/94	5	2	95.4	130.8	78.5	123.1	72.3
7/87–6/92	7/92–6/95	5	3	100.0	106.2	89.2	120.0	84.6
7/88–6/91	7/91–6/93	3	2	88.0	108.6	97.1	108.0	98.3
7/88–6/91	7/91–6/94	3	3	89.7	108.0	94.9	124.0	81.1
7/88–6/92	7/92–6/94	4	2	116.6	72.6	87.4	120.6	102.9
7/88–6/92	7/92–6/95	4	3	123.4	76.0	78.3	99.4	126.9
7/88–6/93	7/93–6/95	5	2	106.3	82.3	81.7	116.6	115.4
7/89–6/92	7/92–6/94	3	2	98.6	61.0	113.3	112.4	115.7
7/89–6/92	7/92–6/95	3	3	110.5	49.0	104.8	114.3	118.6
7/89–6/93	7/93–6/95	4	2	91.9	103.8	75.2	115.7	114.8
7/90–6/93	7/93–6/95	3	2	114.7	80.2	94.0	104.8	105.3
Average for All Periods:				93.0	98.9	99.9	112.8	95.5

ings for the 16 periods shown are averaged to yield a single average ranking, expressed as a percent of the period average ranking (bottom row in Table 8.4). These 16-period average rankings are illustrated in Figure 8.16. The virtually flat distribution of these rankings shows that there is no consistent pattern for CTAs with returns in the higher quintiles of one period to achieve better returns in the next period.

Table 8.5 and Figure 8.17 show the results of similar calculations using geometric returns rather than arithmetic returns. Once again, there is no discernible pattern among the quintile rankings. As can be seen in Figure 8.17, the differences among all five quintiles are relatively small and, in fact, the quintile with the best ranking (lowest ranking number) is quintile 5—the CTAs with the worst past performance.

The average quintile rankings for the standard deviation are derived in Table 8.6 and depicted in Figure 8.18. Here the pattern in quintile rankings is not merely obvious, but striking. The quintile with the lowest past standard deviation (quintile 1) has the lowest (best) ranking, quintile 2 has the second lowest, and so on in virtually perfect stair-step fashion. Clearly, CTAs with low past standard deviations tend to continue to display below-average standard deviations, while those with high past standard deviations continue to exhibit above-average standard deviations. In colloquial terms, low-risk managers remain low risk and high-risk managers remain high risk.

Tables 8.7 and 8.8 derive the average quintile rankings for the two versions of the Sharpe Ratio. The results are illustrated in Figures 8.19 and 8.20. Once again, the rankings across all five quintiles are relatively flat. Finally, Table 8.9 and Figure 8.21 show the average Sharpe Ratio rankings for a quintile breakdown based on past standard deviation rankings. Although in this case the quintile of worst past performers (CTAs with the highest past standard deviations) also exhibits the worst ranking (highest ranking number) in the subsequent period, the significance of this observation is questionable since the next-to-worst quintile had the best ranking.

Since our rank correlation coefficient tests showed significantly different results between earlier and later periods, we also break down our quintile results by two segments: past periods starting in 1987 and past periods starting in 1988–1990. Table 8.10 shows the quintile average rankings for each of the performance measures for these two time classifications. These results are depicted graphically in Figures 8.22–8.27.

The quintile patterns exhibited by the two Sharpe Ratios (Figures 8.25 and 8.26) are particularly noteworthy. In each case, for past periods beginning in 1988–1990, quintile 1 had the best ranking (lowest ranking number) and quintile 5 the worst. These results seem to confirm the common assumption that the best past performers will tend to remain among the best

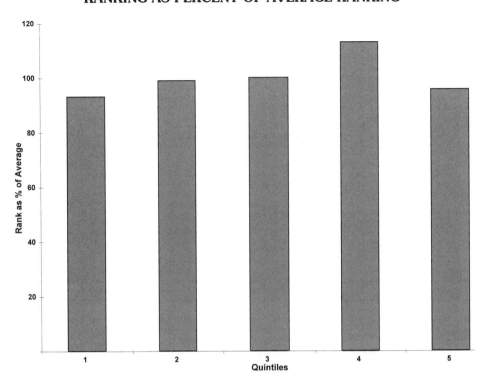

Figure 8.16
ARITHMETIC RETURN: ALL PERIOD AVERAGE QUINTILE
RANKING AS PERCENT OF AVERAGE RANKING

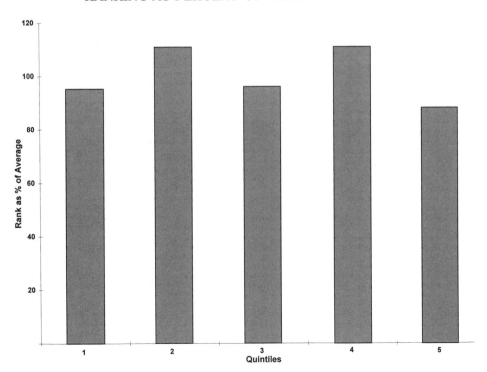

Figure 8.17
GEOMETRIC RETURN: ALL PERIOD AVERAGE QUINTILE
RANKING AS PERCENT OF AVERAGE RANKING

Table 8.5
QUINTILE AVERAGE RANKINGS: GEOMETRIC RETURN

Past Period	Forward Period	Number of Years Past Period	Number of Years Forward Period	Quintile 1	Quintile 2	Quintile 3	Quintile 4	Quintile 5	Average
7/87–6/90	7/90–6/92	3	2	11.0	13.8	17.0	15.4	7.8	13.0
7/87–6/90	7/90–6/93	3	2	12.4	14.2	15.2	12.8	10.4	13.0
7/87–6/91	7/91–6/93	4	2	11.8	19.4	11.6	15.0	7.2	13.0
7/87–6/91	7/91–6/94	4	3	13.6	19.2	11.2	15.2	5.8	13.0
7/87–6/91	7/91–6/95	4	4	13.6	18.4	11.8	13.0	8.2	13.0
7/87–6/92	7/92–6/94	5	2	12.8	17.0	10.6	18.8	5.8	13.0
7/87–6/92	7/92–6/95	5	3	13.6	13.0	11.8	17.8	8.8	13.0
7/88–6/91	7/91–6/93	3	2	18.4	17.3	19.1	16.1	16.3	17.5
7/88–6/91	7/91–6/94	3	3	18.0	19.3	17.3	18.4	14.0	17.5
7/88–6/92	7/92–6/94	4	2	16.3	18.1	14.3	20.9	18.0	17.5
7/88–6/92	7/92–6/95	4	3	17.0	18.0	13.0	17.7	22.5	17.5
7/88–6/93	7/93–6/95	5	2	13.7	20.3	14.1	17.6	22.5	17.5
7/89–6/92	7/92–6/94	3	2	15.6	20.0	22.1	23.8	24.3	21.0
7/89–6/92	7/92–6/95	3	3	18.4	16.3	19.5	25.4	25.8	21.0
7/89–6/93	7/93–6/95	4	2	20.0	18.1	21.6	21.5	23.9	21.0
7/90–6/93	7/93–6/95	3	2	46.2	42.2	44.8	38.4	45.6	43.5

QUINTILE AVERAGE RANKINGS AS PERCENTAGE OF PERIOD AVERAGE RANKINGS: GEOMETRIC RETURN

Period								
7/87–6/90	7/90–6/92	3	2	84.6	106.2	130.8	118.5	60.0
7/87–6/90	7/90–6/93	3	2	95.4	109.2	116.9	98.5	80.0
7/87–6/91	7/91–6/93	4	2	90.8	149.2	89.2	115.4	55.4
7/87–6/91	7/91–6/94	4	3	104.6	147.7	86.2	116.9	44.6
7/87–6/91	7/91–6/95	4	4	104.6	141.5	90.8	100.0	63.1
7/87–6/92	7/92–6/94	5	2	98.5	130.8	81.5	144.6	44.6
7/87–6/92	7/92–6/95	5	3	104.6	100.0	90.8	136.9	67.7
7/88–6/91	7/91–6/93	3	2	105.1	98.9	109.1	92.0	93.1
7/88–6/91	7/91–6/94	3	3	102.9	110.3	98.9	105.1	80.0
7/88–6/92	7/92–6/94	4	2	93.1	103.4	81.7	119.4	102.9
7/88–6/92	7/92–6/95	4	3	97.1	102.9	74.3	101.1	128.6
7/89–6/92	7/93–6/95	5	2	78.3	116.0	80.6	100.6	128.6
7/89–6/92	7/92–6/94	3	2	74.3	95.2	105.2	113.3	115.7
7/89–6/93	7/92–6/95	3	3	87.6	77.6	92.9	121.0	122.9
7/89–6/93	7/93–6/95	4	2	95.2	86.2	102.9	102.4	113.8
7/90–6/93	7/93–6/95	3	2	106.2	97.0	103.0	88.3	104.8
Average for All Periods:				95.2	110.8	95.9	110.9	87.9

Table 8.6
QUINTILE AVERAGE RANKINGS: STANDARD DEVIATION

Past Period	Forward Period	Number of Years Past Period	Number of Years Forward Period	Quintile 1	Quintile 2	Quintile 3	Quintile 4	Quintile 5	Average
7/87–6/90	7/90–6/92	3	2	5.6	9.4	10.4	17.2	22.4	13.0
7/87–6/90	7/90–6/93	3	2	5.6	9.2	10.4	17.6	22.2	13.0
7/87–6/91	7/91–6/93	4	2	5.0	9.2	11.4	18.2	21.2	13.0
7/87–6/91	7/91–6/94	4	3	4.6	10.6	11.4	17.4	21.0	13.0
7/87–6/91	7/91–6/95	4	4	5.2	9.4	12.2	17.4	20.8	13.0
7/87–6/92	7/92–6/94	5	2	4.2	10.4	14.6	17.2	18.6	13.0
7/87–6/92	7/92–6/95	5	3	4.6	9.0	16.0	16.4	19.0	13.0
7/88–6/91	7/91–6/93	3	2	4.1	13.6	20.3	22.9	28.2	17.5
7/88–6/91	7/91–6/94	3	3	4.3	15.3	18.4	23.0	28.0	17.5
7/88–6/92	7/92–6/94	4	2	5.0	19.0	17.7	21.6	25.3	17.5
7/88–6/92	7/92–6/95	4	3	4.3	18.9	18.6	22.0	24.8	17.5
7/88–6/93	7/93–6/95	5	2	4.9	17.4	17.0	24.7	24.5	17.5
7/89–6/92	7/92–6/94	3	2	7.3	19.1	23.6	23.3	33.4	21.0
7/89–6/92	7/92–6/95	3	3	6.8	19.3	22.8	24.1	33.9	21.0
7/89–6/93	7/93–6/95	4	2	7.6	17.4	22.1	24.9	34.8	21.0
7/90–6/93	7/93–6/95	3	2	15.6	35.0	42.6	59.5	66.5	43.5

QUINTILE AVERAGE RANKINGS AS PERCENTAGE OF PERIOD
AVERAGE RANKINGS: STANDARD DEVIATION

7/87–6/90	7/90–6/92	3	2	43.1	72.3	80.0	132.3	172.3
7/87–6/90	7/90–6/93	3	2	43.1	70.8	80.0	135.4	170.8
7/87–6/91	7/91–6/93	4	2	38.5	70.8	87.7	140.0	163.1
7/87–6/91	7/91–6/94	4	3	35.4	81.5	87.7	133.8	161.5
7/87–6/91	7/91–6/95	4	4	40.0	72.3	93.8	133.8	160.0
7/87–6/92	7/92–6/94	5	2	32.3	80.0	112.3	132.3	143.1
7/87–6/92	7/92–6/95	5	3	35.4	69.2	123.1	126.4	146.2
7/88–6/91	7/91–6/93	3	2	23.4	77.7	116.0	130.9	161.1
7/88–6/91	7/91–6/94	3	3	24.6	87.4	105.1	131.4	160.0
7/88–6/92	7/92–6/94	4	2	28.6	108.6	101.1	123.4	144.6
7/88–6/92	7/92–6/95	4	3	24.6	108.0	106.3	125.7	141.7
7/89–6/93	7/93–6/95	5	2	28.0	99.4	97.1	141.1	140.0
7/89–6/92	7/92–6/94	3	2	34.8	91.0	112.4	111.0	159.0
7/89–6/92	7/92–6/95	3	3	32.4	91.9	108.6	114.8	161.4
7/89–6/93	7/93–6/95	4	2	36.2	82.9	105.2	118.6	165.7
7/90–6/93	7/93–6/95	3	2	35.9	80.5	97.9	136.8	152.9
Average for All Periods:				33.5	84.0	100.9	129.2	156.5

Table 8.7
QUINTILE AVERAGE RANKINGS: MODIFIED SHARPE RATIO

Past Period	Forward Period	Number of Years Past Period	Number of Years Forward Period	Quintile 1	Quintile 2	Quintile 3	Quintile 4	Quintile 5	Average
7/87–6/90	7/90–6/92	3	2	13.2	11.6	18.2	12.4	9.6	13.0
7/87–6/90	7/90–6/93	3	2	16.2	10.6	17.6	8.6	12.0	13.0
7/87–6/91	7/91–6/93	4	2	17.2	12.6	16.4	12.4	6.4	13.0
7/87–6/91	7/91–6/94	4	3	18.2	13.2	17.0	12.2	4.4	13.0
7/87–6/91	7/91–6/95	4	4	18.4	11.2	15.4	12.6	7.4	13.0
7/87–6/92	7/92–6/94	5	2	18.8	12.4	15.2	10.6	8.0	13.0
7/87–6/92	7/92–6/95	5	3	17.6	11.0	11.6	14.8	10.0	13.0
7/88–6/91	7/91–6/93	3	2	17.9	17.9	20.7	13.6	17.5	17.5
7/88–6/91	7/91–6/94	3	3	15.3	19.3	21.9	16.0	14.7	17.5
7/88–6/92	7/92–6/94	4	2	13.0	21.9	15.9	17.4	19.7	17.5
7/88–6/92	7/92–6/95	4	3	13.4	20.4	15.6	15.6	23.2	17.5
7/88–6/93	7/93–6/95	5	2	15.1	16.6	15.9	17.9	22.8	17.5
7/89–6/92	7/92–6/94	3	2	15.1	20.8	24.4	19.3	26.3	21.0
7/89–6/92	7/92–6/95	3	3	16.1	18.5	22.5	21.3	27.3	21.0
7/89–6/93	7/93–6/95	4	2	16.4	20.0	19.8	22.0	27.4	21.0
7/90–6/93	7/93–6/95	3	2	35.3	45.4	49.0	42.3	45.2	43.5

QUINTILE AVERAGE RANKINGS AS PERCENTAGE OF PERIOD AVERAGE RANKINGS: MODIFIED SHARPE RATIO

Period	Period							
7/87–6/90	7/90–6/92	3	2	101.5	89.2	140.0	95.4	73.8
7/87–6/90	7/90–6/93	3	2	124.6	81.5	135.4	66.2	92.3
7/87–6/91	7/91–6/93	4	2	132.3	96.9	126.2	95.4	49.2
7/87–6/91	7/91–6/94	4	3	140.0	101.5	130.8	93.8	33.8
7/87–6/91	7/91–6/95	4	4	141.5	86.2	118.5	96.9	56.9
7/87–6/92	7/92–6/94	5	2	144.6	95.4	116.9	81.5	61.5
7/87–6/92	7/92–6/95	5	3	135.4	84.6	89.2	113.8	76.9
7/88–6/91	7/91–6/93	3	2	102.2	102.2	118.2	77.6	99.9
7/88–6/91	7/91–6/94	3	3	87.3	110.2	125.0	91.3	83.9
7/88–6/92	7/92–6/94	4	2	74.2	125.0	90.8	99.3	112.4
7/88–6/92	7/92–6/95	4	3	76.5	116.4	89.0	89.0	132.4
7/88–6/93	7/93–6/95	5	2	86.2	94.7	90.8	102.2	130.1
7/89–6/92	7/92–6/94	3	2	71.9	99.0	116.2	91.9	125.2
7/89–6/92	7/92–6/95	3	3	76.7	88.1	107.1	101.4	130.0
7/89–6/93	7/93–6/95	4	2	78.1	95.2	94.3	104.8	130.5
7/90–6/93	7/93–6/95	3	2	81.1	104.4	112.6	97.2	103.9
Average for All Periods:				103.4	98.2	112.6	93.6	93.3

Table 8.8
QUINTILE AVERAGE RANKINGS: MODIFIED SHARPE RATIO
(GEOMETRIC-RETURN-BASED)

Past Period	Forward Period	Number of Years Past Period	Number of Years Forward Period	Quintile 1	Quintile 2	Quintile 3	Quintile 4	Quintile 5	Average
7/87–6/90	7/90–6/92	3	2	12.8	10.4	20.0	12.0	9.8	13.0
7/87–6/90	7/90–6/93	3	2	17.2	9.2	18.2	8.8	11.6	13.0
7/87–6/91	7/91–6/93	4	2	18.0	13.4	14.8	9.2	9.6	13.0
7/87–6/91	7/91–6/94	4	3	16.0	15.8	16.8	9.2	7.2	13.0
7/87–6/91	7/91–6/95	4	4	14.8	13.6	16.8	10.8	9.0	13.0
7/87–6/92	7/92–6/94	5	2	18.8	13.8	12.6	11.8	8.0	13.0
7/87–6/92	7/92–6/95	5	3	16.8	9.4	15.2	13.2	10.4	13.0
7/88–6/91	7/91–6/93	3	2	18.0	14.4	23.7	14.1	17.2	17.5
7/88–6/91	7/91–6/94	3	3	14.7	16.7	24.3	16.7	14.7	17.5
7/88–6/92	7/92–6/94	4	2	12.1	20.9	18.0	17.3	19.5	17.5
7/88–6/92	7/92–6/95	4	3	10.3	20.9	17.7	15.9	23.7	17.5
7/88–6/93	7/93–6/95	5	2	12.1	17.3	17.9	17.9	23.2	17.5
7/89–6/92	7/92–6/94	3	2	15.6	23.0	21.6	19.3	26.3	21.0
7/89–6/92	7/92–6/95	3	3	15.2	19.9	21.0	21.6	28.0	21.0
7/89–6/93	7/93–6/95	4	2	17.0	20.0	21.0	20.0	27.5	21.0
7/90–6/93	7/93–6/95	3	2	31.5	53.4	43.1	45.3	44.9	43.5

QUINTILE AVERAGE RANKINGS AS PERCENTAGE OF PERIOD AVERAGE RANKINGS: MODIFIED SHARPE RATIO
(GEOMETRIC-RETURN-BASED)

7/87–6/90	7/90–6/92	3	2	98.5	80.0	153.8	92.3	75.4
7/87–6/90	7/90–6/93	3	2	132.3	70.8	140.0	67.7	89.2
7/87–6/91	7/91–6/93	4	2	138.5	103.1	113.8	70.8	73.8
7/87–6/91	7/91–6/94	4	3	123.1	121.5	129.2	70.8	55.4
7/87–6/91	7/91–6/95	4	4	113.8	104.6	129.2	83.1	69.2
7/87–6/92	7/92–6/94	5	2	144.6	106.2	96.9	90.8	61.5
7/87–6/92	7/92–6/95	5	3	129.2	72.3	116.9	101.5	80.0
7/88–6/91	7/91–6/93	3	2	103.0	82.4	135.6	80.7	98.4
7/88–6/91	7/91–6/94	3	3	84.1	95.5	139.0	95.5	84.1
7/88–6/92	7/92–6/94	4	2	69.2	119.6	103.0	99.0	111.6
7/88–6/92	7/92–6/95	4	3	58.9	119.6	101.3	91.0	135.6
7/88–6/93	7/93–6/95	5	2	69.2	99.0	102.4	102.4	132.7
7/89–6/92	7/92–6/94	3	2	74.3	109.5	102.9	91.9	125.2
7/89–6/92	7/92–6/95	3	3	72.4	94.8	100.0	102.9	133.3
7/89–6/93	7/93–6/95	4	2	81.0	95.2	100.0	95.2	131.0
7/90–6/93	7/93–6/95	3	2	72.4	122.8	99.1	104.1	103.2
Average for All Periods:				97.8	99.8	116.4	90.0	97.5

Table 8.9
QUINTILE AVERAGE RANKINGS: STANDARD DEVIATION
VERSUS MODIFIED SHARPE RATIO
(GEOMETRIC-RETURN-BASED)

Past Period	Forward Period	Number of Years Past Period	Number of Years Forward Period	Quintile 1	Quintile 2	Quintile 3	Quintile 4	Quintile 5	Average
7/87–6/90	7/90–6/92	3	2	11.2	15.6	11.4	15.4	11.4	13.0
7/87–6/90	7/90–6/93	3	2	12.2	14.0	13.0	13.8	12.0	13.0
7/87–6/91	7/91–6/93	4	2	13.2	18.2	8.8	12.0	12.8	13.0
7/87–6/91	7/91–6/94	4	3	13.6	15.8	8.8	10.4	16.4	13.0
7/87–6/91	7/91–6/95	4	4	11.8	16.4	10.4	10.4	16.0	13.0
7/87–6/92	7/92–6/94	5	2	17.8	14.2	8.8	8.2	16.0	13.0
7/87–6/92	7/92–6/95	5	3	14.4	10.6	14.4	10.8	14.8	13.0
7/88–6/91	7/91–6/93	3	2	17.9	20.1	18.0	10.1	22.0	17.5
7/88–6/91	7/91–6/94	3	3	19.1	16.0	20.1	8.4	24.8	17.5
7/88–6/92	7/92–6/94	4	2	21.3	15.3	18.0	8.1	26.0	17.5
7/88–6/92	7/92–6/95	4	3	15.7	17.3	18.1	11.0	26.7	17.5
7/88–6/93	7/93–6/95	5	2	12.7	18.4	19.0	11.3	27.3	17.5
7/89–6/92	7/92–6/94	3	2	24.2	19.9	21.9	14.4	24.3	21.0
7/89–6/92	7/92–6/95	3	3	20.6	20.1	23.8	16.5	24.1	21.0
7/89–6/93	7/93–6/95	4	2	16.4	22.6	21.4	20.6	24.5	21.0
7/90–6/93	7/93–6/95	3	2	32.7	43.3	36.2	58.0	47.9	43.5

QUINTILE AVERAGE RANKINGS AS PERCENTAGE OF PERIOD
AVERAGE RANKINGS: STANDARD DEVIATION VERSUS
MODIFIED SHARPE RATIO (GEOMETRIC-RETURN-BASED)

Period							
7/87–6/90	3	2	86.2	120.0	87.7	118.5	87.7
7/87–6/90	3	2	93.8	107.7	100.0	106.2	92.3
7/87–6/91	4	2	101.5	140.0	67.7	92.3	98.5
7/87–6/91	4	3	104.6	121.5	67.7	80.0	126.2
7/87–6/91	4	4	90.8	126.2	80.0	80.0	123.1
7/87–6/92	5	2	136.9	109.2	67.7	63.1	123.1
7/87–6/92	5	3	110.8	81.5	110.8	83.1	113.8
7/88–6/91	3	2	102.3	114.9	102.9	57.7	125.7
7/88–6/91	3	3	109.1	91.4	114.9	48.0	141.7
7/88–6/92	4	2	121.7	87.4	102.9	46.3	148.6
7/88–6/92	4	3	89.7	98.9	103.5	62.9	152.6
7/88–6/93	5	2	72.6	105.1	108.6	64.6	156.0
7/89–6/92	3	2	115.2	94.8	104.3	68.6	115.7
7/89–6/92	3	3	98.1	95.7	113.3	78.6	114.8
7/89–6/93	4	2	78.1	107.6	101.9	98.1	116.7
7/90–6/93	3	2	75.2	99.5	83.2	133.3	110.1
Average for All Periods:			99.2	106.3	94.8	80.1	121.7

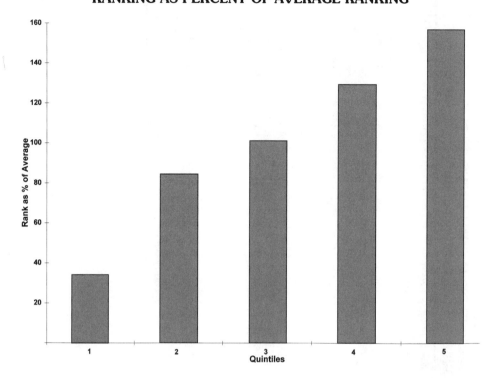

Figure 8.18
STANDARD DEVIATION: ALL PERIOD AVERAGE QUINTILE
RANKING AS PERCENT OF AVERAGE RANKING

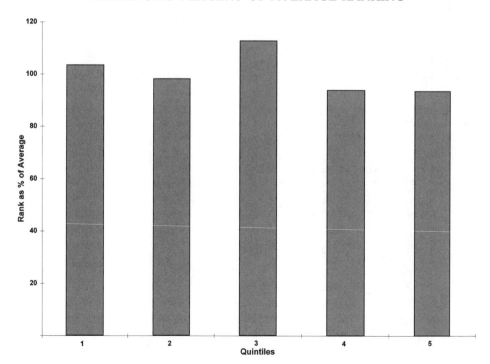

Figure 8.19
MODIFIED SHARPE RATIO: ALL PERIOD AVERAGE QUINTILE
RANKING AS PERCENT OF AVERAGE RANKING

Figure 8.20
MODIFIED SHARPE RATIO (GEOMETRIC-RETURN-BASED): ALL PERIOD AVERAGE QUINTILE RANKING AS PERCENT OF AVERAGE RANKING

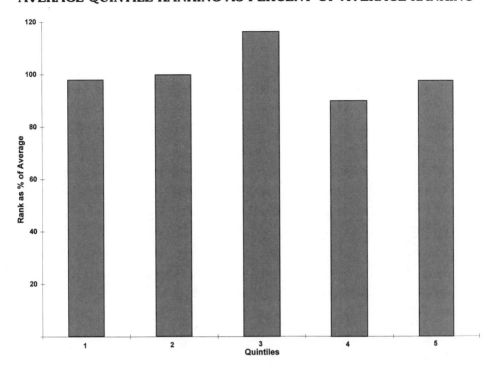

Figure 8.21
STANDARD DEVIATION VERSUS MODIFIED SHARPE RATIO (GEOMETRIC-RETURN-BASED): ALL PERIOD AVERAGE QUINTILE RANKING AS PERCENT OF AVERAGE RANKING

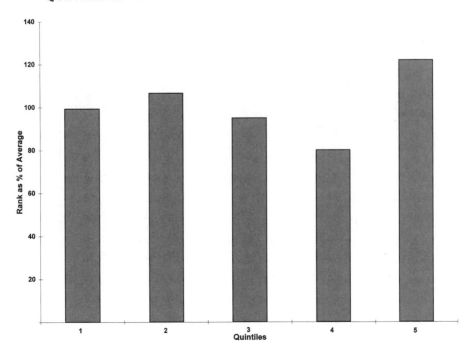

Table 8.10
QUINTILE AVERAGE RANKINGS AS PERCENTAGE OF PERIOD AVERAGE RANKINGS

	Quintile 1	Quintile 2	Quintile 3	Quintile 4	Quintile 5
Arithmetic return					
Average for past periods starting 1987	78.2	120.2	110.3	112.7	78.5
Average for past periods starting 1988–1990	104.4	82.4	91.9	112.9	108.8
Geometric return					
Average for past periods starting 1987	97.6	126.4	98.0	118.7	59.3
Average for past periods starting 1988–1990	93.3	98.6	94.3	104.8	110.0
Standard deviation					
Average for past periods starting 1987	38.2	73.8	94.9	133.4	159.6
Average for past periods starting 1988–1990	29.8	91.9	105.5	126.0	154.1
Modified Sharpe Ratio					
Average for past periods starting 1987	131.4	90.8	122.4	91.9	63.5
Average for past periods starting 1988–1990	81.6	103.9	104.9	95.0	116.5
Modified Sharpe Ratio (Geometric-Return-Based)					
Average for past periods starting 1987	125.7	94.1	125.7	82.4	72.1
Average for past periods starting 1988–1990	76.1	104.3	109.2	95.9	117.2
Standard deviation versus Sharp Ratio					
Average for past periods starting 1987	103.5	115.2	83.1	89.0	109.2
Average for past periods starting 1988–1990	95.8	99.5	103.9	73.1	131.3

Figure 8.22
ARITHMETIC RETURN: SEGMENTED PERIOD AVERAGE
QUINTILE RANKING AS PERCENT OF AVERAGE RANKING

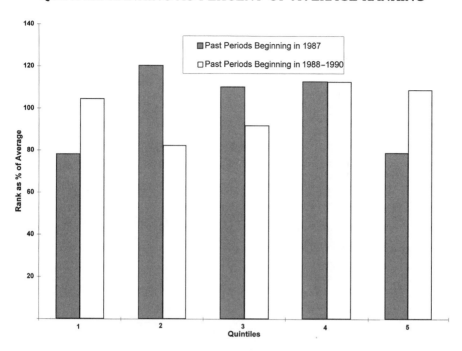

Figure 8.23
GEOMETRIC RETURN: SEGMENTED PERIOD AVERAGE
QUINTILE RANKING AS PERCENT OF AVERAGE RANKING

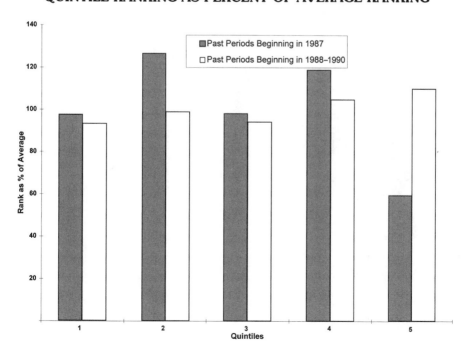

151

Figure 8.24
STANDARD DEVIATION: SEGMENTED PERIOD AVERAGE
QUINTILE RANKING AS PERCENT OF AVERAGE RANKING

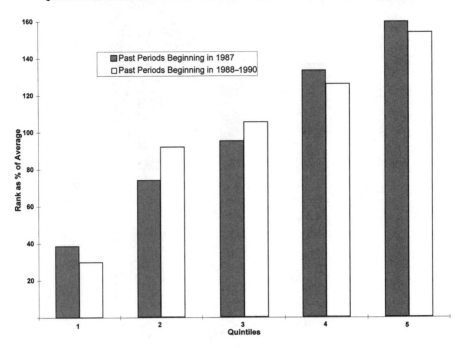

Figure 8.25
MODIFIED SHARPE RATIO: SEGMENTED PERIOD AVERAGE
QUINTILE RANKING AS PERCENT OF AVERAGE RANKING

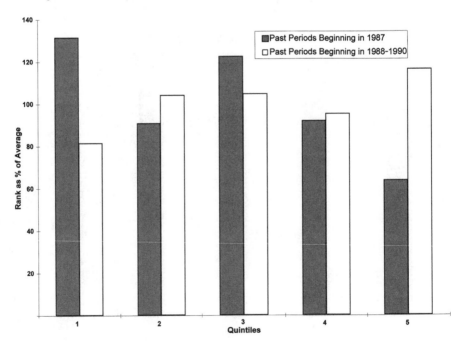

Figure 8.26
MODIFIED SHARPE RATIO (GEOMETRIC-RETURN-BASED): SEGMENTED PERIOD AVERAGE QUINTILE RANKING AS PERCENT OF AVERAGE RANKING

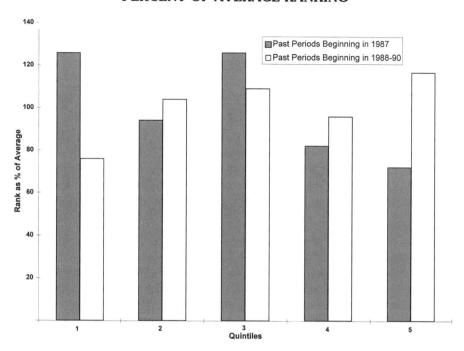

Figure 8.27
STANDARD DEVIATION VERSUS MODIFIED SHARPE RATIO (GEOMETRIC-RETURN-BASED): SEGMENTED PERIOD AVERAGE QUINTILE RANKING AS PERCENT OF AVERAGE RANKING

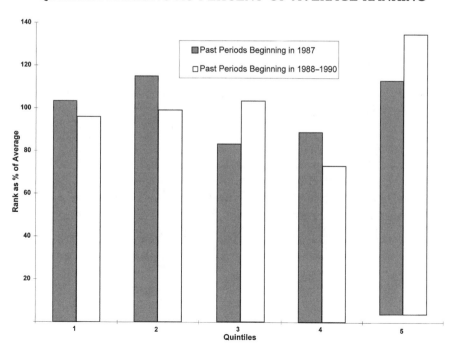

153

in the future, while the worst past performers will tend to remain among the worst in the future. However, note that the quintile patterns for periods beginning in 1987 imply the exact opposite conclusion. Here the best rankings are obtained by the lowest quintiles and the worst rankings by the highest quintiles. In other words, a researcher examining only the earlier period combinations would have concluded that the best way to achieve superior future performance is to pick from among the CTAs with the *worst* past performance! The fact that the quintile patterns for the two time segments are completely contradictory means that neither can be deemed reliable. Perhaps the most important point indicated by this time-segmented quintile analysis is that performance correlation results are critically dependent on the survey periods selected.

Viewed as a whole, the implication of the foregoing quintile analysis is that there is no more predictability between past and future performance among the top (or bottom) past performers than for the group of all CTAs. With the exception of the standard deviation, which also demonstrated an extremely strong correlation between past and future levels in our rank correlation coefficient tests, none of the performance measures showed any meaningful quintile patterns.

IMPLICATIONS OF RANKING CORRELATION AND QUINTILE TESTS

Relative risk is highly predictable as evidenced by both the consistently high rank correlation coefficients for standard deviation and the stair-step pattern of standard deviation quintile rankings. The fact that past riskiness, as measured by the standard deviation, is such a reliable indicator of future riskiness is not really surprising. After all, risk levels are directly correlated with the amount of leverage used—a factor that is totally controllable by the CTA. Insofar as CTAs who use low leverage are unlikely to abruptly switch to high leverage, and vice versa, there is a strong likelihood that past and future risk levels will be significantly correlated.

The fact that relative risk is predictable is of limited use. Although, intuitively it might appear that CTAs with past low standard deviation levels would be more likely to have higher future Sharpe Ratio levels, since standard deviation is the denominator in the Sharpe Ratio, the evidence does not bear this out. Overall, the correlations between past standard deviations and future Sharpe Ratios were not significantly different from zero, and quintiles based on past standard deviations showed no tendency for higher quintiles registering higher future Sharpe Ratios.

Why doesn't picking low standard deviation CTAs result in above-average future return/risk levels? There are two reasons: First, low standard deviation CTAs are no more likely to have positive returns than high standard deviation CTAs. Second, while low standard deviation CTAs with negative returns (for the future period) will lose less than their high standard deviation counterparts, low standard deviation CTAs with positive returns will also make less than high standard deviation managers. Therefore, on balance, past low standard deviation levels are not correlated with better Sharpe Ratios.

Return (both arithmetic and geometric) did not even show a hint of any relationship between past and future levels. All 32 return rank correlation coefficients were statistically indistinguishable from zero and none of the past return-based quintile segmentations of the data showed any pattern of higher quintiles tending to have better (lower number) rankings.

The test results using return/risk measures were a bit odd. On average, similar to return, the return/risk correlations were remarkably close to zero. However, a breakdown of the results by periods showed some periods with statistically significant positive correlations (as is commonly assumed) and some periods with statistically significant *negative* correlations (a highly counterintuitive result). These contrasting results were mirrored by the time-segmented quintiles, which showed the highest quintiles doing worst for past periods beginning in 1987 and best for past periods beginning in 1988–1990. Why?

A plausible explanation is that two factors affect the correlation between past and future return/risk levels: (1) skill level, and (2) time period. All else being equal, the skill effect (that is, the idea that some managers are more skillful than others, just as some tennis players are more skillful than others) would always result in some tendency for the best past performers to also be among the best future performers (positive correlation). However, the evidence suggests that the skill effect may be dominated by the time-period effect: the fact that any approach and any market portfolio will perform better in some market conditions than others. Therefore, when the time-period effect works in the opposite direction, it can swamp the skill effect, leading to the seemingly paradoxical result of negative correlation between past and future performance, even assuming that the skill-level effect is quite real.

Moreover, although the time-period effect can work in either direction, it seems plausible to assume that it will have a tendency toward negative correlations between the past and future. Why? Because market conditions go through transformations, wherein the most profitable markets and strategies of one period may become particularly unfavorable in the next—perhaps as a consequence of too many market participants having gravitated to these markets and methods. Similarly, markets and strategies that have been highly unprofitable, and thus fall out of favor, may have the best chance for superior future performance. The existence of such a tendency could explain why the average correlation between past and future return/risk rankings across all period comparisons is close to zero, even though the skill-level effect is always positive.

Finally, it should be noted that this chapter has only shown the difficulty of predicting performance based on past return and risk data. However, the question of whether it is possible to utilize other types of information to predict returns remains open. Such alternative measures might be quantitative (e.g., years of trading experience, amount of money managed) or qualitative (e.g., trading method).

CONCLUSION

To be honest, when I began the research for this chapter, I assumed that if I corrected for the biases contained in previous studies, conducted correlation tests for a large number of period combinations, and used return/risk performance measures to determine rankings, I would be able to demonstrate that past and future relative performance are correlated. I was surprised to find that, viewed across all periods, correlations between past and future relative performance were remarkably close to zero for all the return and return/risk measures considered. It is ironic that a number of past studies that found some evidence of net positive correlation between past and future relative performance dismissed the results as statistically insignificant, whereas I set out to prove such a correlation and found a more complete absence of correlation between past and future performance than any of the studies considered. I can only imagine how emphatically EGR or IZW might have denounced the relevance of past performance to future performance if they had found the results detailed in this chapter.

The bottom line is that even if past and future relative performance are related—and certainly the analysis of this chapter failed to provide any evidence that they are (except for standard deviation)—the degree of correlation is far smaller than generally assumed. However, there are three reasons why I would stop short of concluding that past and future relative performance are completely uncorrelated:

1. As was demonstrated by a number of examples in this chapter, correlation test results are highly dependent on the period combination used. In fact, the rank correlation coefficients for return/risk ranged from statistically significant positive levels for some period combinations to statistically significant negative levels for others. Given the extreme impact of the periods chosen on test results, even the 16 period combinations examined in this chapter seem insufficient to draw broad generalizations.

2. The database used in our analysis did not include nonsurvivors. Since the study by Schneeweis and Spurgin mentioned earlier found nonsurvivors to be consistent underperformers across periods, it is possible that their inclusion might have resulted in higher correlations between past and future performance.

3. The database we used was far from a complete representation of all CTAs existent at the specified time periods (beyond the already mentioned exclusion of nonsurvivors). Although it was assumed that our database was sufficiently large to be representative of all CTAs managing more than $1 million at the specified times, it is possible that a more complete database might have yielded meaningfully different results.

Of these three factors, I would consider the first by far the most important and the only definite significant influence. The other two items are only factors that *might* have affected the results.

DIRECTIONS FOR FUTURE RESEARCH

In our tests, instances of statistically significant negative correlations between past and future relative return/risk levels were about equally prevalent with statistically significant positive correlations. Is one of these outcomes an aberration? Unfortunately, there are insufficient data to answer this question. Although there is always a temptation for a researcher to provide definitive conclusions, one of the greatest errors a researcher can make is to reach conclusions when there are simply insufficient data to do so.

The answer to whether past relative return/risk levels are more likely to be positively correlated, negatively correlated, or uncorrelated must await more years of data accumulation. As more years of data collect, tests similar to those described in this chapter can be applied to an ever-increasing list of period comparisons, eventually revealing whether there are any consistent tendencies in the relationship between past and future return and return/risk levels.[10] For now, however, it does seem safe to assume that if any positive correlation does exist, it is far smaller than generally believed.

---

[10]Additional tests can also be conducted for periods prior to the beginning of the earliest time period surveyed in this chapter (mid-1987). However, insofar as the studies summarized in the previous chapter used such earlier data and as a group failed to find any consistent patterns between past and future performance, it is questionable whether such earlier-year data extensions of our study would provide worthwhile additional information, even if such an analysis corrected for the biases noted earlier in this chapter.

On balance, however, these past studies showed a definite tendency toward positive correlations between past and future performance, albeit such findings were frequently dismissed by their authors as not being statistically significant. This consideration would suggest that the periods of statistically significant *negative* correlations that emerged in our study may have been aberrations. Such an assumption, however, still does not imply that past and future performance are positively correlated as opposed to uncorrelated. The bottom line is that earlier data are still likely to leave the essential question regarding the relationship between past and future performance unanswered.

Part Three

INVESTMENT AND PORTFOLIO ISSUES

9 We Have Met the Enemy

"We has met the enemy, and it is us." This famous quote from Walt Kelly's cartoon strip, *Pogo*, would serve as a fitting universal motto for investors. In my experience, investors are truly their own worst enemy. The natural instincts of most investors lead them to do exactly the wrong thing with uncanny persistence.

In a nutshell, the heart of the investor blunder is the tendency to commit to an investment right after it has done very well and to liquidate an investment right after it has done very poorly. Although these types of investment decisions may sound perfectly natural, even instinctive, they are also generally wrong. This chapter contains several empirical studies that demonstrate the folly of following hot streaks and dumping investments right after they have plummeted. However, first I would like to relate two personal experiences that made me appreciate this general principle in very real terms.

The first occurred about a decade ago, when I worked for a firm where part of my job responsibilities included evaluating commodity trading advisors (CTAs). I made the striking discovery that the majority of closed accounts showed a net loss for virtually all the CTAs I reviewed—*even those who had no losing years!* The obvious implication was that investors were so bad in timing their investment entry and exit that most of them lost money even when they chose a consistently winning CTA.

During the past five years, as an active CTA, I have been able to experience this phenomenon firsthand. Although I could relate many relevant episodes, one in particular stands out. At my CTA firm, we trade three different programs. These programs employ an identical computerized methodology and differ only in the markets traded. The vast majority of the equity under management is contained in the most diversified program; however, the narrower portfolio programs are maintained to fulfill a specialized niche of investor demand.

Several years ago, we had a private investor open an account in one of these smaller portfolios: the currency program. He opened the account when the program was near an all-time high. In the ensuing period, all the currency markets went through extended phases of choppy, directionless trading—conditions generally adverse to trading profitability, particular for computerized approaches. During this time many currency trading programs witnessed enormous losses, with drawdowns of 30 percent, 40 percent, 50 percent and even more quite common. Our own program also lost money, but in a more moderate fashion, gradually drifting down 12 percent from its peak over the course of 14 months.

At this point, it became clear that the investor was getting very anxious about the account. Since at the time this was the only account trading the currency program, I became very concerned that our track record for the program would be disrupted if the account were closed. I discussed the situation with my partner, Louis Lukac, and we decided to open a standby account in our own name that could be activated instantaneously if our one existing client currency account were closed.

Sure enough, about a week or two later, the currency program had a particularly adverse day. At the time, the program was long in the European currencies and the Japanese yen, and those currencies broke sharply, finishing the day near recent lows. On that same afternoon, after the market closed, the investor called instructing us to close the account immediately. We wired funds to activate our own currency account, and on the next morning's opening we simultaneously implemented the positions for our account and liquidated the same positions in the investor's account. That day's opening proved to be almost the exact low of the currencies. Our own account never witnessed so much as a $1 decline relative to the account initiation level. In other words, after staying with the account for 14 months, the investor managed to close the account on the exact low day! Within 8 months of the day the investor closed the account, the currency program had rebounded to a new all-time high, and in the 14 months following that date it gained nearly 50 percent.

Of course, not every investor's timing will be this bad, but the foregoing example is not all that unrepresentative. It is remarkable how many investors open accounts when a CTA is near a peak and close accounts when a CTA is near a bottom. The problem is that many investors first wait for the CTA they select to prove himself or herself with a winning streak before they open an account. They then compound the error by abandoning ship during the first rough period, even if the account has not reached the originally intended bailout point.

COMPARING NAVs AND ASSETS UNDER MANAGEMENT

One way of seeing the relationship between investment flows and CTA performance is to compare a manager's net asset value (NAV)[1] with assets under management. However, one cannot use nominal assets under management for this comparison, because changes in the NAV will also cause the assets under management to change. For example, if the NAV doubled, the assets under management would also double (assuming no additions or withdrawals). What we are interested in, however, are changes in assets under management due to additions or withdrawals, as opposed to changes in the NAV. We can remove the influence of the NAV on assets under management by dividing the assets under management by a NAV-based index. This index value would simply equal the current NAV value divided by the starting NAV. Thus, for example, if the NAV had doubled, the NAV index would equal 2.0.

We define assets under management divided by the NAV index as the "adjusted assets under management." The adjusted assets under management will be unaffected by changes in the NAV. Thus, for example, if the NAV doubled and there were no additions or withdrawals, the adjusted assets under management would be unchanged (since both nominal assets under management and the NAV index would have doubled). Therefore, the adjusted assets under management will reflect only asset changes due to additions or withdrawals. If both the NAV and the adjusted assets under management are rising, it means that assets under management are rising faster than the NAV, implying net additions in equity. Similarly, if both the NAV and the adjusted assets under management are falling, it means that assets under management are declining faster than the NAV, implying net withdrawals in equity.

Figures 9.1–9.7 compare the NAVs and adjusted assets for seven CTAs. These charts vividly illustrate just how bad investors can be in timing both the entry and exit of their investments. The CTA in Figure 9.1 saw assets under management explode from nominal levels and then collapse back to nominal levels only about two years later. Note that assets did not begin to build until *after* the strong performance in 1990. Assets were not far from their all-

---

[1]The NAV at the end of any given month is equal to the starting NAV value (usually assumed to be 1,000, but sometimes set at 1.0 or 100) multiplied by the product of all returns expressed as factors of 1.0. For example, if the starting NAV value is 1,000 and the first three monthly returns are +4 percent, −2 percent, and +3 percent, the NAV at the end of the third month would equal 1,049.776 ($1,000 \times 1.04 \times 0.98 \times 1.03 = 1049.776$). In effect, the NAV shows the value of each \$1,000 invested at the start date as of the end of each subsequent month.

Figure 9.1
CTA 1: NAV VERSUS ADJUSTED ASSETS ($MIL./NAV INDEX)

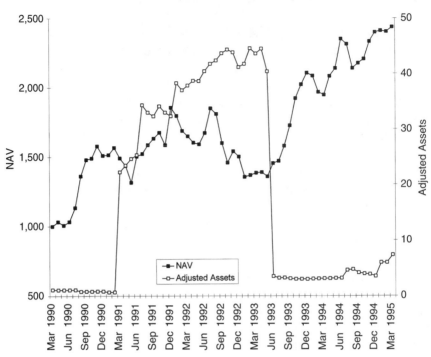

time high when the mid-1992 to early 1993 drawdown began. Assets then plunged, returning almost all the way back to the 1990 levels, just in the nick of time to miss the entire steep advance in the NAV during mid-1993 through early 1995. Thus, although the CTA experienced a cumulative return in excess of 140 percent for the five-year period shown, it is clear from the chart that the bulk of invested funds suffered a net loss!

In Figure 9.2, adjusted assets climbed steadily along with NAV during mid-1991 to early 1992, peaking three months after the high point in the NAV. Assets then just as steadily followed the NAV downward, reaching a low point just one month before the NAV low. Once again, investors were most heavily invested near the performance peak and all but completely absent at the NAV low points.

In Figure 9.3, the CTA experienced a dramatic growth in assets under management during a period of essentially sideways performance. Assets then steadily eroded as sideways performance continued. By the time the CTA witnessed a period of sustained performance gains, with the NAV more than doubling in about one and a half years, the majority of the prior net additions to assets had been withdrawn. Assets did not begin to rebuild until the NAV was already within a few months of its ultimate peak.

Figure 9.2
CTA 2: NAV VERSUS ADJUSTED ASSETS ($MIL./NAV INDEX)

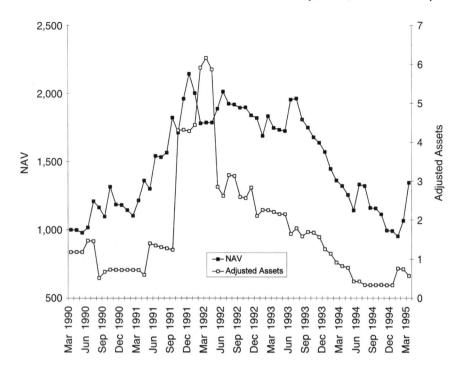

Figure 9.3
CTA 3: NAV VERSUS ADJUSTED ASSETS ($MIL./NAV INDEX)

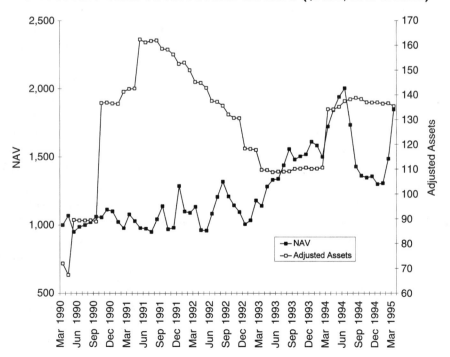

In Figure 9.4 adjusted assets remained near nominal levels throughout the entire late 1991 to mid-1992 steep advance in NAV. Assets then grew dramatically during late 1992 through 1993, a period during which the NAV witnessed little net change. The peak in adjusted assets occurred when the NAV was relatively close to its high. As the NAV slid sharply lower in 1994, adjusted assets dropped even more precipitously. By the time the NAV exploded to the upside in early 1995, nearly recovering to its prior high in the short span of two months, adjusted assets had fallen to less than 25 percent of their level only one year earlier. Again we see the same pattern of low assets under management during periods of strong performance and large assets at the performance peak.

In Figure 9.5, adjusted assets increased fivefold during the period the NAV steadily rose. The NAV peak occurred with assets very close to their eventual high. As the NAV then slid steadily, falling all the way back to its early 1992 level, so did adjusted assets. Thus, by the time the NAV surged again in early 1995, adjusted assets were near their low for the period depicted.

In Figure 9.6, we see the familiar pattern of adjusted assets building steadily as the NAV rises, reaching a high nearly coincident with the NAV peak, and then contracting sharply as NAV falls. Note that although the early 1995 surge carried the NAV back most of the way to its prior high, this steep two-month advance occurred with adjusted assets equal to less than half their level at the 1993 peak.

In Figure 9.7 the first three-quarters of the mid-1992 to mid-1994 slide in the NAV transpired at a time when adjusted assets were in the upper third of their range for the period shown. The incredible performance surge during late 1994 to early 1995, in which the NAV more than tripled in only six months, occurred with adjusted assets near the low end of their range. Incidentally, this final six-month period also provides a perfect example for illustrating the difference between adjusted assets and nominal assets. The flat line formed by adjusted assets during this six-month period indicates that there were no net additions or withdrawals during this time. If nominal assets had been used, the asset curve would have exactly paralleled the advance in the NAV, duplicating the performance information and telling us nothing about investment flows.

A careful examination of Figures 9.1–9.7 should make it easy to understand how it is possible for the majority of investors to lose money with a profitable CTA, even one who is wildly profitable. It must be acknowledged, however, that Figures 9.1–9.7 hardly represent a scientific sample. I deliberately selected these charts because they clearly illustrated the tendency for investors to jump on board *after* profitable performance surges and to abandon their investments *after* large losses had already been realized—often just *before* an ensuing sharp recovery. Of course, not all CTAs will experience investment flows as ill-timed as those illustrated in this section. Nevertheless, the selected examples do reflect investor patterns that are quite common,

Figure 9.4
CTA 4: NAV VERSUS ADJUSTED ASSETS ($MIL./NAV INDEX)

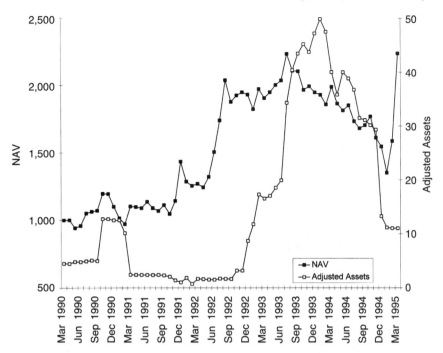

Figure 9.5
CTA 5: NAV VERSUS ADJUSTED ASSETS ($MIL./NAV INDEX)

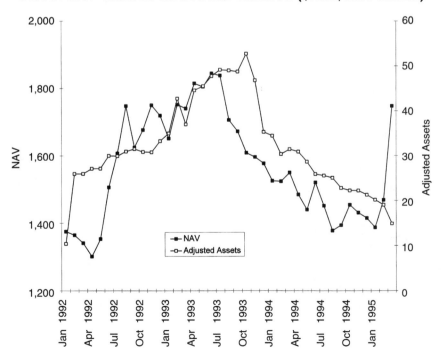

Figure 9.6
CTA 6: NAV VERSUS ADJUSTED ASSETS ($MIL./NAV INDEX)

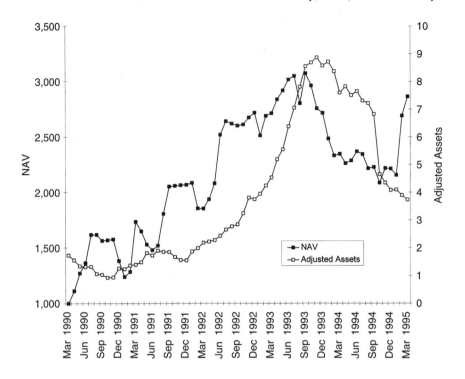

Figure 9.7
CTA 7: NAV VERSUS ADJUSTED ASSETS ($MIL./NAV INDEX)

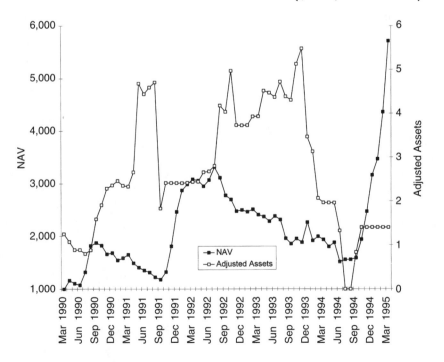

168

even if not always as egregious. Also, while I believe it would be easy to find many other examples of adjusted assets building sharply near performance peaks and reaching relative lows near NAV bottoms, I believe it would be very difficult, if not impossible, to find examples of the opposite pattern combination: assets expanding dramatically before steep NAV advances and contracting substantially before NAV slides.

Insofar as Figures 9.1–9.7 were hand-picked, these charts don't *prove* anything. However, they were not intended as proof; they were only intended as illustrations. For proof, we turn to the two empirical studies that follow.

EMPIRICAL STUDY 1

All my experiences support the assumption that most investors open their accounts after a manager has done particularly well and tend to take a wait-and-see attitude if his or her recent performance has been subpar. I believe a comprehensive study of CTA additions/withdrawals data would support this view. The interesting question is what would happen if investors instead opened their accounts when CTAs were in the midst of significant draw-downs. To answer this question, we compare the results of using the following two investment initiation strategies:

Entry Strategy 1:   Initiate an account after the selected CTA experiences a hot streak, which we define as a 12-month return greater than 50 percent.

Entry Strategy 2:   Initiate an account after the selected CTA experiences a significant drawdown, which we define as a decline of 25 percent or more from a prior month-end peak.

It is safe to assume that Entry Strategy 1 would far more closely resemble the decision process of most investors.

To conduct this study, we employ the same list of 41 CTAs that were used in Chapter 8 for the analysis of periods beginning in 1989 (see third table in Appendix 3 at the end of the book). For each CTA we assume the perspective of an investor beginning in July 1989. If the 12-month return as of the end of June 1989 was greater than 50 percent, it is assumed that an investor following Strategy 1 would open the account immediately.[2] If the condition was not met, it is assumed that the investor would place the investment funds in T bills, checking the 12-month return in each ensuing month.

---

[2]Note that the calculation of a 12-month return requires data back to at least July 1988. For those CTAs that began trading after this date, the 12-month return condition will not be determinable until some point after the assumed July 1989 start point (1 to 12 months later, depending on the start date).

On the first month in which the 12-month return exceeded 50 percent, it is assumed that the account would be activated as of the start of the following month. Thus, the monthly returns realized by an investor employing Strategy 1 would equal T-bill returns until the CTA experienced a 12-month return greater than 50 percent and that CTA's monthly returns thereafter.

Analogously, an investor following Strategy 2 would check the CTA's equity as of the end of June 1989. If the equity was down at least 25 percent from a prior month-end peak, it is assumed that the investor would open the account immediately (July 1989). If the condition was not met, it is assumed that the funds would be kept in T-bills until the first month in which the ending equity was down at least 25 percent from a prior month-end peak, with the account being activated as of the start of the following month. Thus, the monthly returns realized by an investor employing Strategy 2 would equal T-bill returns until the CTA experienced a drawdown greater than 25 percent and that CTA's monthly returns thereafter.

Of course, in some instances one or both strategy conditions will not be met at any time, in which case an investor following that strategy would merely earn a T-bill return for the entire period.

Table 9.1 illustrates the foregoing approach for a sample CTA. In this example, the first month in which the 12-month return exceeds 50 percent is September 1990. It is therefore assumed that an investor using Strategy 1 would open the account in October 1990. Thus, as can be seen, the monthly returns for Strategy 1 are equal to T-bill returns through September 1990 and the CTA's returns thereafter.

The first month to experience a cumulative drawdown greater than 25 percent is October 1989 (the month-end equity on October 1989 was 25.2 percent lower than the prior peak equity set in May 1989). Therefore, an investor following Strategy 2 would initiate an account in November 1989. Thus, as can be seen, the monthly returns for Strategy 2 are equal to T-bill returns through October 1989 and the CTA's returns thereafter.

The bottom of Table 9.1 shows two key statistics for each strategy:

1. **Annualized Geometric Return.** The annualized geometric return is the average annual compounded return, that is, that percent return that if compounded annually would yield the ending equity given the starting equity. (The last two columns in Table 9.1—the decimal return counterparts to the two preceding columns—are needed to calculate the annual geometric return.)

2. **Maximum Drawdown from Entry.** As the name implies, this statistic indicates the worst percentage loss that would have been realized relative to the account starting level as of the end of any subsequent month. If the month-end equity in every month following the account initiation is greater than the month-end equity in the month preceding the account start, then this value would equal 0. In other

words, a 0 value doesn't imply there are no drawdowns, but rather that the investor doesn't experience a month-end equity lower than the starting point.

In this particular example, the annualized geometric return for Strategy 1 is equal to 10.72 percent, compared with 19.66 percent for Strategy 2. The maximum drawdown from entry for Strategy 1 is 10.72 percent (coincidentally, the same magnitude as the annualized geometric return), while the figure for Strategy 2 is equal to 0. Obviously, in this particular example, Strategy 2 fares far better, realizing nearly double the return and no drawdown from entry versus a near 11 percent drawdown for Strategy 1.

This same procedure is used for each of the 41 CTAs, in effect producing a counterpart to Table 9.1 for each CTA. The resulting annualized geometric return and maximum drawdown from entry figures for each CTA (one set of figures for each strategy) are then compiled in a summary table (see Table 9.2). The careful reader will note that there are fewer than 41 CTAs listed. The reason for this is that in the case of some CTAs, neither strategy triggered an entry. In other words, both strategies would have resulted in T-bill returns for the entire period. Such information is hardly useful and when averaged would tend to bias the overall results. Consequently, these CTAs (10 out of 41) are deleted from the list.

As can be seen, Strategy 2 (investing on drawdowns) far outperforms Strategy 1. The average return for Strategy 2 is 14 percent higher—13.24 percent versus 11.59 percent—if data for all CTAs in the table are used, and 46 percent higher—16.77 percent versus 11.48 percent—if comparisons are restricted to only CTAs in which both strategies resulted in an entry. The contrast is far starker on the risk side. Here it only makes sense to compare CTAs with entries for both strategies, because no-entry situations will automatically result in zero maximum drawdown from entry figures, since T-bill returns are never negative. The maximum drawdown from entry was nearly three times as large for Strategy 1 as for Strategy 2: 17.55 percent versus 6.40 percent.

The last four columns of Table 9.2 indicate which of the two strategies was best for each CTA. Strategy 2 outperformed Strategy 1 the vast majority of the time. Including all CTAs in the table, Strategy 2 had the higher return 23 out of 31 times. Excluding those CTAs in which one of the strategies failed to yield an entry, the results were even more lopsided, with Strategy 2 coming out on top 20 out of 23 times![3] On the risk side, the results were equally dramatic, with Strategy 2 also having the lower maximum drawdown from entry 20 out 23 times!

---

[3]The absence of nonsurvivors in our database, however, could have introduced a bias in the analysis. The magnitude of this bias is impossible to gauge, but a mitigating factor is that the effect is not unidirectional—that is, for some nonsurvivors, entering on an upside excursion would still yield a worse outcome than entering on a drawdown.

Table 9.1
SAMPLE ILLUSTRATION FOR CALCULATING ANNUAL RETURN
AND MAXIMUM DRAWDOWN FROM ENTRY
(FOR ENTRY STRATEGIES 12-MONTH ROLLING RETURN > 50% AND DRAWDOWN > 25%)

	Month-end Equity	Monthly Return	Peak Equity	Drawdown from Most Recent Peak	12-Month Rolling Return	Entry Strategy 1: 12-Month R.R. > 50%	Entry Strategy 2: Drawdown > 25%	Decimal Return 12-Month R.R. > 50%	Decimal Return Drawdown > 25%
	1,000.0		1,000.0						
Jul 88	987.0	-1.30	1,000.0	-1.30		0.56	0.56	1.0056	1.0056
Aug 88	1,020.6	3.40	1,020.6	0.00		0.59	0.59	1.0059	1.0059
Sep 88	1,045.1	2.40	1,045.1	0.00		0.60	0.60	1.0060	1.0060
Oct 88	1,044.0	-0.10	1,045.1	-0.10		0.61	0.61	1.0061	1.0061
Nov 88	1,109.8	6.30	1,109.8	0.00		0.64	0.64	1.0064	1.0064
Dec 88	1,158.6	4.40	1,158.6	0.00		0.67	0.67	1.0067	1.0067
Jan 89	1,100.7	-5.00	1,158.6	-5.00		0.69	0.69	1.0069	1.0069
Feb 89	1,106.2	0.50	1,158.6	-4.53		0.71	0.71	1.0071	1.0071
Mar 89	1,160.4	4.90	1,160.4	0.00		0.74	0.74	1.0074	1.0074
Apr 89	1,100.0	-5.20	1,160.4	-5.20		0.73	0.73	1.0073	1.0073
May 89	1,239.8	12.70	1,239.8	0.00		0.70	0.70	1.0070	1.0070
Jun 89	1,191.4	-3.90	1,239.8	-3.90	19.14	0.69	0.69	1.0069	1.0069
Jul 89	1,192.6	0.10	1,239.8	-3.80	20.83	0.66	0.66	1.0066	1.0066
Aug 89	1,065.0	-10.70	1,239.8	-14.10	4.35	0.66	0.66	1.0066	1.0066
Sep 89	1,038.4	-2.50	1,239.8	-16.24	-0.64	0.64	0.64	1.0064	1.0064
Oct 89	927.3	-10.70	1,239.8	-25.21	-11.18	0.64	0.64	1.0064	1.0064
Nov 89	959.7	3.50	1,239.8	-22.59	-13.52	0.64	3.50	1.0064	1.0350
Dec 89	1,093.1	13.90	1,239.8	-11.83	-5.65	0.64	13.90	1.0064	1.1390
Jan 90	1,083.3	-0.90	1,239.8	-12.62	-1.58	0.64	-0.90	1.0064	0.9910

Feb 90	1,140.7	5.30	1,239.8	-7.99	3.12	0.65	5.30	1.0065	1.0530
Mar 90	1,208.0	5.90	1,239.8	-2.56	4.10	0.66	5.90	1.0066	1.0590
Apr 90	1,321.5	9.40	1,321.5	0.00	20.13	0.65	9.40	1.0065	1.0940
May 90	1,206.6	-8.70	1,321.5	-8.70	-2.68	0.65	-8.70	1.0065	0.9130
Jun 90	1,258.4	4.30	1,321.5	-4.77	5.63	0.65	4.30	1.0065	1.0430
Jul 90	1,357.9	7.90	1,357.9	0.00	13.86	0.64	7.90	1.0064	1.0790
Aug 90	1,562.9	15.10	1,562.9	0.00	46.75	0.62	15.10	1.0062	1.1510
Sep 90	1,584.8	1.40	1,584.8	0.00	52.62	0.62	1.40	1.0062	1.0140
Oct 90	1,633.9	3.10	1,633.9	0.00	76.21	3.10	3.10	1.0310	1.0310
Nov 90	1,655.1	1.30	1,655.1	0.00	72.46	1.30	1.30	1.0130	1.0130
Dec 90	1,643.6	-0.70	1,655.1	-0.70	50.36	-0.70	-0.70	0.9930	0.9930
Jan 91	1,554.8	-5.40	1,655.1	-6.06	43.53	-5.40	-5.40	0.9460	0.9460
Feb 91	1,522.2	-2.10	1,655.1	-8.03	33.44	-2.10	-2.10	0.9790	0.9790
Mar 91	1,628.7	7.00	1,655.1	-1.60	34.83	7.00	7.00	1.0700	1.0700
Apr 91	1,526.1	-6.30	1,655.1	-7.80	15.48	-6.30	-6.30	0.9370	0.9370
May 91	1,507.8	-1.20	1,655.1	-8.90	24.97	-1.20	-1.20	0.9880	0.9880
Jun 91	1,559.1	3.40	1,655.1	-5.81	23.89	3.40	3.40	1.0340	1.0340
Jul 91	1,468.6	-5.80	1,655.1	-11.27	8.16	-5.80	-5.80	0.9420	0.9420
Aug 91	1,437.8	-2.10	1,655.1	-13.13	-8.01	-2.10	-2.10	0.9790	0.9790
Sep 91	1,522.6	5.90	1,655.1	-8.01	-3.92	5.90	5.90	1.0590	1.0590
Oct 91	1,516.5	-0.40	1,655.1	-8.38	-7.18	-0.40	-0.40	0.9960	0.9960
Nov 91	1,522.6	0.40	1,655.1	-8.01	-8.01	0.40	0.40	1.0040	1.0040
Dec 91	1,798.2	18.10	1,798.2	0.00	9.41	18.10	18.10	1.1810	1.1810
Jan 92	1,654.3	-8.00	1,798.2	-8.00	6.40	-8.00	-8.00	0.9200	0.9200
Feb 92	1,574.9	-4.80	1,798.2	-12.42	3.47	-4.80	-4.80	0.9520	0.9520
Mar 92	1,508.8	-4.20	1,798.2	-16.09	-7.36	-4.20	-4.20	0.9580	0.9580
Apr 92	1,440.9	-4.50	1,798.2	-19.87	-5.58	-4.50	-4.50	0.9550	0.9550
May 92	1,414.9	-1.80	1,798.2	-21.31	-6.16	-1.80	-1.80	0.9820	0.9820
Jun 92	1,477.2	4.40	1,798.2	-17.85	-5.25	4.40	4.40	1.0440	1.0440

TABLE 9.1 (continued)

	Month-end Equity	Monthly Return	Peak Equity	Drawdown from Most Recent Peak	12-Month Rolling Return	Entry Strategy 1: 12-Month R.R. > 50%	Entry Strategy 2: Drawdown > 25%	Decimal Return 12-Month R.R. > 50%	Decimal Return Drawdown > 25%
Jul 92	1,570.3	6.30	1,798.2	-12.67	6.92	6.30	6.30	1.0630	1.0630
Aug 92	1,689.6	7.60	1,798.2	-6.04	17.51	7.60	7.60	1.0760	1.0760
Sep 92	1,556.1	-7.90	1,798.2	-13.46	2.20	-7.90	-7.90	0.9210	0.9210
Oct 92	1,526.6	-1.90	1,798.2	-15.11	0.66	-1.90	-1.90	0.9810	0.9810
Nov 92	1,547.9	1.40	1,798.2	-13.92	1.66	1.40	1.40	1.0140	1.0140
Dec 92	1,472.1	-4.90	1,798.2	-18.13	-18.13	-4.90	-4.90	0.9510	0.9510
Jan 93	1,458.8	-0.90	1,798.2	-18.87	-11.82	-0.90	-0.90	0.9910	0.9910
Feb 93	1,577.0	8.10	1,798.2	-12.30	0.13	8.10	8.10	1.0810	1.0810
Mar 93	1,580.2	0.20	1,798.2	-12.12	4.73	0.20	0.20	1.0020	1.0020
Apr 93	1,651.3	4.50	1,798.2	-8.17	14.60	4.50	4.50	1.0450	1.0450
May 93	1,723.9	4.40	1,798.2	-4.13	21.84	4.40	4.40	1.0440	1.0440
Jun 93	1,605.0	-6.90	1,798.2	-10.75	8.65	-6.90	-6.90	0.9310	0.9310
Jul 93	1,768.7	10.20	1,798.2	-1.64	12.64	10.20	10.20	1.1020	1.1020
Aug 93	1,731.5	-2.10	1,798.2	-3.71	2.48	-2.10	-2.10	0.9790	0.9790
Sep 93	1,660.5	-4.10	1,798.2	-7.65	6.71	-4.10	-4.10	0.9590	0.9590
Oct 93	1,627.3	-2.00	1,798.2	-9.50	6.60	-2.00	-2.00	0.9800	0.9800
Nov 93	1,671.3	2.70	1,798.2	-7.06	7.97	2.70	2.70	1.0270	1.0270
Dec 93	1,815.0	8.60	1,815.0	0.00	23.29	8.60	8.60	1.0860	1.0860

						Strategy 1: 12 mo. > 50%	Strategy 2: M.D. > 25%		
Jan 94	1,744.2	-3.90	1,815.0	-3.90	19.56	-3.90	0.9610	0.9610
Feb 94	1,665.7	-4.50	1,815.0	-8.22	5.63	-4.50	0.9550	0.9550
Mar 94	1,867.3	12.10	1,867.3	0.00	18.17	12.10	1.1210	1.1210
Apr 94	1,871.0	0.20	1,871.0	0.00	13.31	0.20	1.0020	1.0020
May 94	2,063.7	10.30	2,063.7	0.00	19.71	10.30	1.1030	1.1030
Jun 94	2,294.9	11.20	2,294.9	0.00	42.98	11.20	1.1120	1.1120
Jul 94	2,164.0	-5.70	2,294.9	-5.70	22.35	-5.70	0.9430	0.9430
Aug 94	2,021.2	-6.60	2,294.9	-11.92	16.73	-6.60	0.9340	0.9340
Sep 94	2,047.5	1.30	2,294.9	-10.78	23.30	1.30	1.0130	1.0130
Oct 94	1,951.3	-4.70	2,294.9	-14.97	19.91	-4.70	0.9530	0.9530
Nov 94	2,117.1	8.50	2,294.9	-7.74	26.68	8.50	1.0850	1.0850
Dec 94	2,148.9	1.50	2,294.9	-6.36	18.40	1.50	1.0150	1.0150
Jan 95	1,985.6	-7.60	2,294.9	-13.48	13.84	-7.60	0.9240	0.9240
Feb 95	2,096.8	5.60	2,294.9	-8.63	25.88	5.60	1.0560	1.0560
Mar 95	2,329.5	11.10	2,329.5	0.00	24.75	11.10	1.1110	1.1110
Apr 95	2,453.0	5.30	2,453.0	0.00	31.10	5.30	1.0530	1.0530
May 95	2,607.5	6.30	2,607.5	0.00	26.35	6.30	1.0630	1.0630
Jun 95	2,651.8	1.70	2,651.8	0.00	15.56	1.70	1.0170	1.0170
Annualized geometric return						10.72	19.66	
Maximum drawdown from entry						-10.72	0.00	

Table 9.2
ENTRY STRATEGY COMPARISON: 12-MONTH ROLLING RETURN > 50% VERSUS DRAWDOWN > 25%
(EXCLUDES CTAs WITH NO ENTRY FOR BOTH STRATEGIES)

CTA	Annual Geometric Return (%)		Maximum Drawdown after Entry		Best Return = 1		Smallest Drawdown = 1	
	Entry Strategy 1: 12-Month Rolling Return >50%	Entry Strategy 2: Drawdown >25%	Entry Strategy 1: 12-Month Rolling Return >50%	Entry Strategy 2: Drawdown >25%	Entry Strategy 1: 12-Month Rolling Return >50%	Entry Strategy 2: Drawdown >25%	Entry Strategy 1: 12-Month Rolling Return >50%	Entry Strategy 2: Drawdown >25%
Beacon	5.18 (N.E.)	6.71	No Entry	-6.60	0	1	No Entry	N.A.
Campbell	8.99	8.96	-12.09	0.00	1	0	0	1
Cristo	4.47	7.94	0.00	-2.55	0	1	1	0
Dunn	10.64	17.17	-13.78	0.00	0	1	0	1
EMC	24.78	31.21	-39.14	-19.30	0	1	0	1
Fairfield	-1.14	5.60	-32.52	-5.76	0	1	0	1
ICSC	0.67	5.81	-12.05	-11.67	0	1	0	1
JPD	10.72	19.66	-10.72	0.00	0	1	0	1
Knilo	5.18 (N.E.)	11.15	No Entry	-3.59	0	1	No Entry	N.A.
Little Brook	16.74	18.07	-26.23	-22.80	0	1	0	1
Millburn	7.43	15.24	-9.19	0.00	0	1	0	1
Miss	0.80	2.17	-22.94	-22.53	0	1	0	1
Rabar	30.38	37.63	-25.83	0.00	0	1	0	1

Sunrise	4.70	14.31	-18.10	0.00	0	1	0	1
Tactical	13.60	28.71	-34.34	0.00	0	1	0	1
Visioneering	7.90	17.02	-37.62	-1.13	0	1	0	1
Waldner	11.23	6.83	-9.40	0.00	1	0	N.A.	No Entry
Chesapeake	23.84	5.18 (N.E.)	-20.58	0.00	1	0	N.A.	No Entry
Crow	14.27	5.18 (N.E.)	-9.31	No Entry	1	0	No Entry	N.A.
Dallas	5.18 (N.E.)	-8.30	No Entry	-44.38	0	1	0	1
Gaicorp	-0.40	5.99	-30.25	0.00	0	1	1	0
Hawksbill	34.40	48.08	0.00	-20.62	0	1	0	1
Hyman Beck	12.94	22.82	-2.68	0.00	0	1	0	1
Northfield	10.33	14.02	-11.22	0.00	1	0	1	0
Pragma	10.71	2.26	0.00	-15.51	0	1	0	1
Saxon	15.54	22.40	-34.78	-16.54	1	0	N.A.	No Entry
SJO	31.15	5.18 (N.E.)	-6.45	No Entry	0	1	No Entry	N.A.
Trendlogic	5.18 (N.E.)	5.87	No Entry	-11.64	0	1	0	1
Trendstat	3.92	6.13	-7.94	-3.10	1	0	No Entry	N.A.
Willowbridge(R)	5.18 (N.E.)	-6.17	No Entry	-55.19	0	1	0	1
Willowbridge(V)	24.72	27.63	-12.85	-5.68	1	0	0	1
Average (All CTAs)	11.59	13.24	N.A.	N.A.	Total — 8	Total — 23	N.A.	N.A.
Average (Excluding CTAs with a N.E.)	11.48	16.77	-17.55	-6.40	3	20	3	20

N.E. = No Entry.
N.A. = Not Applicable.

What if less extreme returns and drawdowns were used? We repeated the same analysis using a 30 percent 12-month return (as opposed to 50 percent) and a 15 percent drawdown (as opposed to 25 percent) as the triggers for initiating accounts. Table 9.3 illustrates this approach using the same CTA as the one employed in Table 9.1. In this case, the 12-month return condition is reached one month earlier than in the prior example. (The 30 percent or greater 12-month return condition is met as of the end of August 1990, and the account is activated in September 1990.) The less restrictive 15 percent drawdown condition is also fulfilled one month earlier than the prior 25 percent threshold. Using these less restrictive conditions, the summary statistics at the bottom of the table show that Strategy 2 still provided a considerably higher return, but in this instance Strategy 1 had the lower maximum drawdown from entry.

Table 9.4 is the counterpart summary table to Table 9.2 for the less restrictive (30 percent 12-month return and 15 percent drawdown) entry conditions. Strategy 2 still comes out better than Strategy 1 in all the comparison categories, but the degree of improvement is more muted.

The general implication is that opening accounts after a CTA has experienced a drawdown will tend to provide higher returns at lower risk levels than initiating accounts after a CTA has witnessed an upside excursion in equity. The performance difference also seems to be greater for more extreme entry conditions (i.e., higher returns versus greater drawdowns). Of course, there is a limit to how extreme the entry conditions can be, since if the threshold levels are set too wide, entry conditions will often fail to be met.

EMPIRICAL STUDY 2

The previous study demonstrated that *for any given CTA*, an investor would generally be better off initiating an account after a drawdown as opposed to after a period of strong gains. One obvious question is whether *for any given start date*, an investor would generally be better off selecting a CTA with a large drawdown as opposed to a CTA with a large recent gain. To test this question, for each month beginning in July 1989, we compared the results achieved by selecting the CTA with the largest return in the prior 12-month period versus the CTA with the largest drawdown from a prior equity peak. The last start month used was June 1992, in order to allow at least three years of subsequent data to compare performance.

A separate table (similar to Tables 9.1 and 9.3) needs to be constructed for each of the two strategies, *for each start date*. The annualized geometric return and maximum drawdown from entry figures derived in each of these tables is then combined in a summary table (Table 9.5). The results suggest that an investor would generally be better off selecting the CTA with the largest prevailing drawdown than the CTA with the largest 12-month return. The average return of the maximum drawdown CTAs was moderately higher than the average return of the maximum 12-month return CTAs—21.58 percent versus 18.42 percent—while the maximum drawdown from entry was much lower at 9.93 percent versus 18.49 percent. The ratio of the average annualized geometric return to the average maximum drawdown from entry was more than twice as high for the maximum drawdown CTAs: 2.17 versus 1.00. The drawdown strategy was also the better approach 21 out of 36 times in terms of return and 21 out of 33 times in terms of the maximum drawdown from entry.[4]

If the same analysis were extended to end in June 1993, instead of June 1992, leaving only two years for the performance comparison of the last data point, selecting the maximum drawdown CTA (as opposed to the maximum 12-month return CTA) still proved to the better strategy, but by a lesser margin. In this case, the ratio of the average annualized geometric return to the average maximum drawdown from entry was less than 50 percent higher for the maximum drawdown CTAs: 1.84 versus 1.25. In this instance, the advantage of selecting the maximum drawdown CTA is offset by the fact that one of the CTAs witnessed a huge drawdown and never recovered. This CTA was picked in every month of the extended year and underperformed the best 12-month return CTA in every case.

Although this study seems to imply that investors would usually be better off selecting the CTA with the largest prevailing drawdown than the CTA with the largest 12-month return, one danger in the foregoing approach is that the CTA with the worst drawdown may never recover (as was the case in the example just cited). However, the intended implication is not that one should necessarily select the CTA with the *worst* drawdown, albeit such an assumption provided an easy means of testing the general concept, but rather that a strategy of selecting from among CTAs with large prevailing drawdowns is likely to be a better strategy than choosing from among CTAs with high recent returns. Moreover, if it is feasible to invest with several CTAs, the potential impact of selecting a CTA who does not recover would be significantly mitigated.

The foregoing study is also not intended to imply that the worst past performer will do better than the best past performer, since we are not evaluating broad past records, but only recent performance. The study, however, does appear to imply that an investor would generally be better off investing with a CTA who is in a slump than one who is in a hot streak.

---

[4]There are fewer total observations for the drawdown comparisons because the two approaches were tied for three start dates.

The actual advantage in selecting the maximum drawdown CTA is smaller than the various foregoing statistics imply because the database used for analysis did not include nonsurvivors. Although it is impossible to gauge the impact of this nonsurvivor bias in the data, the performance gap between the two entry strategies was so wide that it is assumed that the drawdown entry strategy would still have maintained some edge even if nonsurvivor data had been included.

Table 9.3
SAMPLE ILLUSTRATION FOR CALCULATING ANNUAL RETURN AND MAXIMUM DRAWDOWN FROM ENTRY
(FOR ENTRY STRATEGIES 12-MONTH ROLLING RETURN > 30% AND DRAWDOWN > 15%)

	Month-end Equity	Monthly Return	Peak Equity	Drawdown from Most Recent Peak	12-Month Rolling Return	Entry Strategy 1: 12-Month Rolling Return > 30%	Entry Strategy 2: Drawdown > 15%	Decimal Return 12-Month Rolling Return > 30%	Decimal Return Drawdown > 15%
	1,000.0		1,000.0						
Jul 88	987.0	-1.30	1,000.0	-1.30		0.56	0.56	1.0056	1.0056
Aug 88	1,020.6	3.40	1,020.6	0.00		0.59	0.59	1.0059	1.0059
Sep 88	1,045.1	2.40	1,045.1	0.00		0.60	0.60	1.0060	1.0060
Oct 88	1,044.0	-0.10	1,045.1	-0.10		0.61	0.61	1.0061	1.0061
Nov 88	1,109.8	6.30	1,109.8	0.00		0.64	0.64	1.0064	1.0064
Dec 88	1,158.6	4.40	1,158.6	0.00		0.67	0.67	1.0067	1.0067
Jan 89	1,100.7	-5.00	1,158.6	-5.00		0.69	0.69	1.0069	1.0069
Feb 89	1,106.2	0.50	1,158.6	-4.53		0.71	0.71	1.0071	1.0071
Mar 89	1,160.4	4.90	1,160.4	0.00		0.74	0.74	1.0074	1.0074
Apr 89	1,100.0	-5.20	1,160.4	-5.20		0.73	0.73	1.0073	1.0073
May 89	1,239.8	12.70	1,239.8	0.00		0.70	0.70	1.0070	1.0070
Jun 89	1,191.4	-3.90	1,239.8	-3.90	19.14	0.69	0.69	1.0069	1.0069
Jul 89	1,192.6	0.10	1,239.8	-3.80	20.83	0.66	0.66	1.0066	1.0066
Aug 89	1,065.0	-10.70	1,239.8	-14.10	4.35	0.66	0.66	1.0066	1.0066
Sep 89	1,038.4	-2.50	1,239.8	-16.24	-0.64	0.64	0.64	1.0064	1.0064
Oct 89	927.3	-10.70	1,239.8	-25.21	-11.18	0.64	-10.70	1.0064	0.8930
Nov 89	959.7	3.50	1,239.8	-22.59	-13.52	0.64	3.50	1.0064	1.0350
Dec 89	1,093.1	13.90	1,239.8	-11.83	-5.65	0.64	13.90	1.0064	1.1390

Jan 90	1,083.3	-0.90	1,239.8	-12.62	-1.58	0.64	-0.90	1.0064	0.9910
Feb 90	1,140.7	5.30	1,239.8	-7.99	3.12	0.65	5.30	1.0065	1.0530
Mar 90	1,208.0	5.90	1,239.8	-2.56	4.10	0.66	5.90	1.0066	1.0590
Apr 90	1,321.5	9.40	1,321.5	0.00	20.13	0.65	9.40	1.0065	1.0940
May 90	1,206.6	-8.70	1,321.5	-8.70	-2.68	0.65	-8.70	1.0065	0.9130
Jun 90	1,258.4	4.30	1,321.5	-4.77	5.63	0.65	4.30	1.0065	1.0430
Jul 90	1,357.9	7.90	1,357.9	0.00	13.86	0.64	7.90	1.0064	1.0790
Aug 90	1,562.9	15.10	1,562.9	0.00	46.75	0.62	15.10	1.0062	1.1510
Sep 90	1,584.8	1.40	1,584.8	0.00	52.62	1.40	1.40	1.0140	1.0140
Oct 90	1,633.9	3.10	1,633.9	0.00	76.21	3.10	3.10	1.0310	1.0310
Nov 90	1,655.1	1.30	1,655.1	0.00	72.46	1.30	1.30	1.0130	1.0130
Dec 90	1,643.6	-0.70	1,655.1	-0.70	50.36	-0.70	-0.70	0.9930	0.9930
Jan 91	1,554.8	-5.40	1,655.1	-6.06	43.53	-5.40	-5.40	0.9460	0.9460
Feb 91	1,522.2	-2.10	1,655.1	-8.03	33.44	-2.10	-2.10	0.9790	0.9790
Mar 91	1,628.7	7.00	1,655.1	-1.60	34.83	7.00	7.00	1.0700	1.0700
Apr 91	1,526.1	-6.30	1,655.1	-7.80	15.48	-6.30	-6.30	0.9370	0.9370
May 91	1,507.8	-1.20	1,655.1	-8.90	24.97	-1.20	-1.20	0.9880	0.9880
Jun 91	1,559.1	3.40	1,655.1	-5.81	23.89	3.40	3.40	1.0340	1.0340
Jul 91	1,468.6	-5.80	1,655.1	-11.27	8.16	-5.80	-5.80	0.9420	0.9420
Aug 91	1,437.8	-2.10	1,655.1	-13.13	-8.01	-2.10	-2.10	0.9790	0.9790
Sep 91	1,522.6	5.90	1,655.1	-3.92	-3.92	5.90	5.90	1.0590	1.0590
Oct 91	1,516.5	-0.40	1,655.1	-8.38	-7.18	-0.40	-0.40	0.9960	0.9960
Nov 91	1,522.6	0.40	1,655.1	-8.01	-8.01	0.40	0.40	1.0040	1.0040
Dec 91	1,798.2	18.10	1,798.2	0.00	9.41	18.10	18.10	1.1810	1.1810
Jan 92	1,654.3	-8.00	1,798.2	-8.00	6.40	-8.00	-8.00	0.9200	0.9200
Feb 92	1,574.9	-4.80	1,798.2	-12.42	3.47	-4.80	-4.80	0.9520	0.9520
Mar 92	1,508.8	-4.20	1,798.2	-16.09	-7.36	-4.20	-4.20	0.9580	0.9580
Apr 92	1,440.9	-4.50	1,798.2	-19.87	-5.58	-4.50	-4.50	0.9550	0.9550
May 92	1,414.9	-1.80	1,798.2	-21.31	-6.16	-1.80	-1.80	0.9820	0.9820

TABLE 9.3 (continued)

	Month-end Equity	Monthly Return	Peak Equity	Drawdown from Most Recent Peak	12-Month Rolling Return	Entry Strategy 1: 12-Month Rolling Return > 30%	Entry Strategy 2: Drawdown > 15%	Decimal Return 12-Month Rolling Return > 30%	Decimal Return Drawdown > 15%
Jun 92	1,477.2	4.40	1,798.2	-17.85	-5.25	4.40	4.40	1.0440	1.0440
Jul 92	1,570.3	6.30	1,798.2	-12.67	6.92	6.30	6.30	1.0630	1.0630
Aug 92	1,689.6	7.60	1,798.2	-6.04	17.51	7.60	7.60	1.0760	1.0760
Sep 92	1,556.1	-7.90	1,798.2	-13.46	2.20	-7.90	-7.90	0.9210	0.9210
Oct 92	1,526.6	-1.90	1,798.2	-15.11	0.66	-1.90	-1.90	0.9810	0.9810
Nov 92	1,547.9	1.40	1,798.2	-13.92	1.66	1.40	1.40	1.0140	1.0140
Dec 92	1,472.1	-4.90	1,798.2	-18.13	-18.13	-4.90	-4.90	0.9510	0.9510
Jan 93	1,458.8	-0.90	1,798.2	-18.87	-11.82	-0.90	-0.90	0.9910	0.9910
Feb 93	1,577.0	8.10	1,798.2	-12.30	0.13	8.10	8.10	1.0810	1.0810
Mar 93	1,580.2	0.20	1,798.2	-12.12	4.73	0.20	0.20	1.0020	1.0020
Apr 93	1,651.3	4.50	1,798.2	-8.17	14.60	4.50	4.50	1.0450	1.0450
May 93	1,723.9	4.40	1,798.2	-4.13	21.84	4.40	4.40	1.0440	1.0440
Jun 93	1,605.0	-6.90	1,798.2	-10.75	8.65	-6.90	-6.90	0.9310	0.9310
Jul 93	1,768.7	10.20	1,798.2	-1.64	12.64	10.20	10.20	1.1020	1.1020
Aug 93	1,731.5	-2.10	1,798.2	-3.71	2.48	-2.10	-2.10	0.9790	0.9790
Sep 93	1,660.5	-4.10	1,798.2	-7.65	6.71	-4.10	-4.10	0.9590	0.9590
Oct 93	1,627.3	-2.00	1,798.2	-9.50	6.60	-2.00	-2.00	0.9800	0.9800
Nov 93	1,671.3	2.70	1,798.2	-7.06	7.97	2.70	2.70	1.0270	1.0270
Dec 93	1,815.0	8.60	1,815.0	0.00	23.29	8.60	8.60	1.0860	1.0860

Month								
Jan 94	1,744.2	-3.90	1,815.0	-3.90	19.56	-3.90	0.9610	0.9610
Feb 94	1,665.7	-4.50	1,815.0	-8.22	5.63	-4.50	0.9550	0.9550
Mar 94	1,867.3	12.10	1,867.3	0.00	18.17	12.10	1.1210	1.1210
Apr 94	1,871.0	0.20	1,871.0	0.00	13.31	0.20	1.0020	1.0020
May 94	2,063.7	10.30	2,063.7	0.00	19.71	10.30	1.1030	1.1030
Jun 94	2,294.9	11.20	2,294.9	0.00	42.98	11.20	1.1120	1.1120
Jul 94	2,164.0	-5.70	2,294.9	-5.70	22.35	-5.70	0.9430	0.9430
Aug 94	2,021.2	-6.60	2,294.9	-11.92	16.73	-6.60	0.9340	0.9340
Sep 94	2,047.5	1.30	2,294.9	-10.78	23.30	1.30	1.0130	1.0130
Oct 94	1,951.3	-4.70	2,294.9	-14.97	19.91	-4.70	0.9530	0.9530
Nov 94	2,117.1	8.50	2,294.9	-7.74	26.68	8.50	1.0850	1.0850
Dec 94	2,148.9	1.50	2,294.9	-6.36	18.40	1.50	1.0150	1.0150
Jan 95	1,985.6	-7.60	2,294.9	-13.48	13.84	-7.60	0.9240	0.9240
Feb 95	2,096.8	5.60	2,294.9	-8.63	25.88	5.60	1.0560	1.0560
Mar 95	2,329.5	11.10	2,329.5	0.00	24.75	11.10	1.1110	1.1110
Apr 95	2,453.0	5.30	2,453.0	0.00	31.10	5.30	1.0530	1.0530
May 95	2,607.5	6.30	2,607.5	0.00	26.35	6.30	1.0630	1.0630
Jun 95	2,651.8	1.70	2,651.8	0.00	15.56	1.70	1.0170	1.0170

	Strategy 1: 12 mo. >30%	Strategy 2: M.D.> 15%
Annualized geometric return	10.86	17.30
Maximum drawdown from entry	-9.47	-10.70

Table 9.4
ENTRY STRATEGY COMPARISON: 12-MONTH ROLLING
RETURN > 30% VERSUS DRAWDOWN > 15%
(EXCLUDES CTAs WITH NO ENTRY FOR BOTH STRATEGIES)

CTA	Annual Geometric Return (%)		Maximum Drawdown after Entry		Best Return = 1		Smallest Drawdown = 1	
	Entry Strategy 1: 12-Month Rolling Return >30%	Entry Strategy 2: Drawdown >15%	Entry Strategy 1: 12-Month Rolling Return >30%	Entry Strategy 2: Drawdown >15%	Entry Strategy 1: 12-Month Rolling Return >30%	Entry Strategy 2: Drawdown >15%	Entry Strategy 1: 12-Month Rolling Return >30%	Entry Strategy 2: Drawdown >15%
AZF	3.56	6.08	-0.14	-1.71	0	1	1	0
Beacon	3.69	3.10	-22.82	-23.06	1	0	1	0
Campbell	11.56	10.75	0.00	0.00	1	0	N.A.	N.A.
Com. Cap.	5.18 (N.E.)	5.54	No Entry	-5.29	0	1	No Entry	N.A.
Cristo	4.47	5.68	0.00	-13.72	0	1	1	0
Dunn	11.17	17.17	-10.21	0.00	0	1	0	1
EMC	24.78	29.33	-39.14	-25.51	0	1	0	1
Fairfield	0.96	2.94	-23.14	-12.64	0	1	0	1
Fundam.	6.28	10.46	-9.82	0.00	0	1	0	1
ICSC	0.69	2.73	-11.38	-25.52	0	1	1	0
JPD	10.86	17.30	-9.47	-10.70	0	1	1	0
Knilo	5.63	6.65	-3.07	-20.85	0	1	1	0
LaSalle	5.18 (N.E.)	7.77	No Entry	0.00	0	1	No Entry	N.A.
Little Br.	16.74	18.07	-26.23	-22.80	0	1	0	1
Millburn	8.96	12.63	0.00	-11.73	0	1	1	0
Miss	3.96	-0.20	-24.89	-30.98	1	0	1	0

CTA								
Rabar	30.38	34.58	−25.83	−11.47	0	1	0	1
RXR	9.30	11.79	−10.94	0.00	0	1	0	1
Sunrise	9.04	10.94	0.00	−15.38	0	1	1	0
Tactical	16.69	21.84	−22.38	−27.10	0	1	1	0
Visioneering	7.90	11.39	−37.62	−25.95	1	1	0	1
Waldner	11.67	9.06	−6.59	0.00	0	1	0	1
Chesap	26.00	29.10	−11.33	0.00	1	0	0	1
Crow	15.33	5.18 (N.E.)	−3.48	No Entry	1		N.A.	No Entry
DF	11.04	5.52	0.00	0.00	1	0	N.A.	N.A.
Dallas	5.18 (N.E.)	−9.85	No Entry	−48.83	1	0	No Entry	N.A.
Gaicorp	−1.00	5.99	−32.29	0.00	0	1	0	1
Hawksbill	34.40	48.08	0.00	−20.62	0	1	1	0
Hyman Beck	16.08	20.92	−13.24	−8.36	0	1	0	1
Northfield	11.77	20.60	−3.46	−4.20	0	1	1	0
Pragma	10.71	2.37	0.00	−5.47	1	0	1	0
Saxon	17.82	18.90	−22.82	−27.71	0	1	1	0
SJO	31.15	12.43	−6.45	0.00	1	0	0	1
Strategic	5.18 (N.E.)	4.88	No Entry	−6.35	1	0	No Entry	N.A.
Trendlogic	−2.07	2.96	−43.59	−24.78	0	1	0	1
Trendstat	3.92	5.32	−7.94	−2.16	0	1	0	1
Willowbridge(R)	−9.99	−6.22	−62.24	−50.43	0	1	0	1
Willowbridge(V)	27.48	28.80	−13.39	−6.03	0	1	0	1
Average (All CTAs)	11.50	12.04	N.A.	N.A.	Total 10	Total 28	N.A.	N.A.
Average (Excl. CTAs with a N.E.)	11.38	13.24	−15.16	−13.00	Total 7	Total 26	14	17

N.E. = No Entry.
N.A. = Not Applicable.

Table 9.5

CTA SELECTION STRATEGY COMPARISON: CTA WITH MAXIMUM 12-MONTH ROLLING RETURN VERSUS CTA WITH MAXIMUM DRAWDOWN AT DIFFERENT START DATES

Start date	Annual Geometric Return (%)		Maximum Drawdown after Entry		Best Return = 1		Smallest Drawdown = 1	
	Selection Strategy 1: Maximum 12-Month Rolling Return	Selection Strategy 2: Maximum Drawdown	Selection Strategy 1: Maximum 12-Month Rolling Return	Selection Strategy 2: Maximum Drawdown	Selection Strategy 1: Maximum 12-Month Rolling Return	Selection Strategy 2: Maximum Drawdown	Selection Strategy 1: Maximum 12-Month Rolling Return	Selection Strategy 2: Maximum Drawdown
Jul 89	7.90	10.46	-37.62	0.00	0	1	0	1
Aug 89	24.08	3.03	-42.20	-23.06	1	0	0	1
Sep 89	7.02	49.41	-41.28	-20.62	0	1	0	1
Oct 89	11.54	22.68	-25.95	-6.48	0	1	0	1
Nov 89	13.64	24.51	-0.60	0.00	0	1	0	1
Dec 89	13.16	7.65	-3.96	0.00	1	0	0	1
Jan 90	13.64	8.33	-2.70	0.00	1	0	0	1
Feb 90	37.53	7.23	0.00	-0.32	1	0	1	0
Mar 90	33.66	6.52	0.00	-4.32	1	0	1	0
Apr 90	31.23	7.37	0.00	-0.81	1	0	1	0
May 90	25.18	6.74	-13.26	-4.35	1	0	0	1
Jun 90	28.31	7.79	-3.51	0.00	1	0	0	1
Jul 90	26.04	7.83	-13.54	0.00	1	0	0	1

Aug 90	19.10	5.04	-35.81	-9.95	1	0	0	1
Sep 90	14.66	2.92	-47.34	-18.68	1	0	0	1
Oct 90	7.42	2.42	-61.82	-20.71	1	0	0	1
Nov 90	7.84	12.08	-61.35	-3.59	0	1	0	1
Dec 90	9.33	-9.62	-59.10	-39.24	1	0	0	1
Jan 91	11.15	6.24	-56.26	-7.07	1	0	0	1
Feb 91	21.68	25.08	-6.11	-26.98	0	1	1	0
Mar 91	16.34	27.77	-18.69	-21.40	0	1	1	0
Apr 91	-3.35	24.62	-54.52	-30.75	0	1	0	1
May 91	-0.61	29.39	-24.70	-20.49	0	1	0	1
Jun 91	23.18	33.18	-3.17	-12.43	0	1	1	0
Jul 91	24.28	30.12	-1.40	-22.09	0	1	1	0
Aug 91	25.31	36.07	0.00	-9.20	0	1	1	0
Sep 91	25.50	40.47	0.00	0.00	0	1	N.A.	N.A.
Oct 91	22.94	38.09	0.00	-5.90	0	1	1	0
Nov 91	21.08	41.43	0.00	0.00	0	1	N.A.	N.A.
Dec 91	21.45	42.42	0.00	0.00	0	1	N.A.	N.A.
Jan 92	18.31	-4.10	-5.63	-16.55	1	0	1	0
Feb 92	32.79	37.35	-15.90	-16.57	0	1	1	0
Mar 92	36.41	44.65	-10.18	-3.44	0	1	0	1
Apr 92	18.88	43.14	-4.75	-9.50	0	1	1	0
May 92	20.11	47.75	-3.00	-2.90	0	1	0	1
Jun 92	-3.67	50.75	-11.34	0.00	0	1	0	1
Average	18.42	21.58	-18.49	-9.93	15	21	12	21
G.R./M.D. Ratio	1.00	2.17						

N.A. = Not Applicable (the drawdown is the same for both straegies, namely 0).

IMPLICATIONS REGARDING PERFORMANCE EVALUATION

The studies in this chapter should make it clear that performance measures that are affected by the timing of investor entry and liquidation can be extraordinarily misleading in respect to their implications regarding CTA performance. Two such measures are worth noting:

    1. *Percentage of Accounts Closed at a Profit.* As was shown in numerous examples, the predilection of investors to initiate accounts in the general vicinity of NAV relative highs and to liquidate accounts in the general vicinity of NAV relative lows can easily result in a majority of accounts being closed at a net loss, even if the CTA is highly profitable. In short, the percentage of accounts closed at a profit is a statistic that is a lot more informative about the relative skill level (or lack thereof) of investors than the skill level of CTAs. Ironically, in the recently adopted capsule reporting format, which was generally a sensible improvement over the previous format, the Commodity Futures Trading Commission (CFTC) required the inclusion of this statistic. Although there may have been many performance statistics that deserved consideration for inclusion in the capsule format, the percentage of accounts closed at a profit was not one of them. At best, this statistic is useless; at worst, it is highly misleading. In my opinion, the CFTC erred in requiring its inclusion. Hopefully, the CFTC will reverse this decision in the future.

    2. *Cumulative Dollar Profit/Loss Curves.* This type of curve would simply show the cumulative net profits or losses realized by a CTA. There is a perfectly valid rationale for considering the total dollar profits/losses earned by a CTA: Some CTAs may do well with small amounts of money, but do far more poorly when they are managing large amounts of money. Reasons for this phenomenon might include a trading strategy that can't accommodate large size (e.g., trading in thin markets, the use of stops, which may be vulnerable to greater slippage on large orders), or a psychological block in managing large sums. Conceivably, such CTAs could lose money on balance, even if they have favorable NAV curves. The contention is that using a cumulative dollar profit/loss measure would flag such CTAs. The only problem with this argument is that the timing of investor additions and withdrawals will usually have a much greater impact on cumulative dollar profits/losses than will the influence of asset size on a CTA's performance. The CTAs in Figures 9.1–9.7 probably would not have very attractive cumulative dollar profit/loss curves. However, this fact says more about their investors than it does about their performance. In short, the potential for a cumulative dollar profit/loss curve to be heavily influenced by investor timing makes it a measure prone to extreme distortion, and therefore one that should generally not be used. (One exception would be track record segments in which additions and withdrawals are relatively minor.)

CONCLUSION

The empirical studies described in this chapter strongly imply that one would be better off investing with CTAs after they have experienced a drawdown as opposed to after they have witnessed a winning streak.[5] In fact, the common dual tendency of many people to initiate an account after a manager has already had a large winning streak and to liquidate an account in the midst of a drawdown probably represents the single worst investor blunder.

To be fair, it must be acknowledged that the studies in this chapter do not conclusively prove that investing on drawdowns is significantly superior to investing after upswings in equity. We only examined data for 41 CTAs for two different sets of entry strategies. It is conceivable that employing data for other CTAs and different numerical values for the threshold entry levels would yield different results. Nevertheless, the performance differentials were so pronounced and consistent for the data studied that barring future evidence to the contrary, it seems safe to assume that initiating CTA investments on drawdowns is far preferable to launching accounts right after highly profitable performance periods.

It goes against human nature to invest in what has been going down instead in what has been going up. However, this counterintuitive approach appears to be the definitively superior strategy. The message of this chapter should not be confused with implying that one should invest with losing CTAs as opposed to winning CTAs. Rather the intended message is that one should first select a CTA (by whatever method) and then invest with that CTA after a losing period as opposed to after a winning period.

If readers of this book absorb only one fact it should be this: *Separate the processes of selecting and timing investments, and once having selected the investment, wait for it to do poorly, not well, before actually initiating the investment.*

---

[5]Although the statement implies that past and future performance are inversely related, it should be stressed that the analysis of this chapter focuses on relatively short time periods (12-month upside excursions, and drawdowns typically of even shorter durations). In contrast, the previous chapter focuses on comparisons between multiyear periods. Therefore, the conclusion of this chapter could still hold even if the performance levels in past and future multiyear periods were positively correlated.

10 Robin Hood Investing: Taking from the Winners and Giving to the Losers

A TRUE STORY

About eight years ago, I worked for a brokerage firm where in addition to being the research director I was also the department "expert" on the quantitative evaluation of commodity trading advisors (CTAs). This job responsibility got me thinking about better methods for constructing multimanager funds. At one point, it became apparent to me that if all the managers had equivalent *expected future* performance, the return/risk would be increased if the total equity were redistributed monthly. (A monthly redistribution implies that equity is redistributed among all the managers at the start of each month so that each manager has an equal equity share.)

The assumption that all managers would have equivalent future performance did not mean that such an outcome was expected literally, but rather that one could not predict anything about the relative ranking order of the *future* performance of the selected managers. (Of course, the *past* ranking order of selected managers was known, but with all managers typically being selected from the top quintile or decile, there was no statistical justification for assuming past performance could be a guide to *future* performance rankings within the selected group. Hence, the assumption that all selected managers were expected to have equivalent performance was quite reasonable. In fact, based on the empirical study described in Chapter 8, this assumption could very well be considered valid even if managers were selected far more broadly.)

The following analogy occurred to me: The assumption of equivalent performance could be thought of as monthly performance results being represented on a series of cards—each card representing one month—with each manager's set of results a different shuffle of the same cards. Since all managers are assumed to have the same set of monthly results (i.e., same set of cards in a different order), and since reduced variability implies increased return[1] and by definition reduced risk, it seemed that the return/risk based on the average of cards in each month—the mathematical equivalent of monthly redistribution—would have to be equal to or higher than the return/risk of any individual set of cards (i.e., the performance of each manager). In other words, if one had no a priori reason to believe that any manager in a selected group would perform better in the *future* than the other managers, a monthly redistribution of equity would yield a higher return/risk.

As a very simple example to provide a feel for the preceding conclusion, assume a two-manager fund with a two-month performance period, in which Manager A makes 10 percent in the first month and loses 5 percent in the second, while Manager B witnesses the reverse order of monthly results. The respective net asset values (NAVs) would then be:

Manager A NAV $= 1,000 \times 1.10 \times 0.95 = 1,045$
Manager B NAV $= 1,000 \times 0.95 \times 1.10 = 1,045$
Monthly Redistribution Fund $= 1,000 \times 1.025 \times 1.025 = 1,050.6$
No Redistribution Fund $= 1,045$

Note in this simple example that the monthly redistribution fund realizes a higher return than the fund that does not redistribute assets.

To check whether the idea of monthly redistribution held up in the real world, I conducted the following empirical experiment. I selected about 30 groups of 6 managers from the available database. For each group, I calculated the NAV over a three-year period for the following two situations:

1. An equal distribution of equity with no further reallocations
2. A monthly redistribution scheme, augmented by a 1.25 leverage factor (since the monthly redistribution scheme reduced risk, part of the benefit was put back on the return side by using increased leverage)

I found that the leveraged/redistribution fund almost invariably outperformed the standard no-reallocation fund. However, even more striking was the observation that the return of the leveraged/redistribution fund was usually about in line with the best or second best manager in the group, while the maximum drawdown and standard deviation (measures of risk) were about in line with the lowest or second lowest figures among the group of managers. In other words, by employing a monthly redistribution scheme, it was possible to approximate the return of the best return managers in the group and the risk of the best (lowest) risk managers in the group. In effect, it was a

---

[1]See, for example, the section "Graphic Evaluation of Trading Performance" in Chapter 3, as well as Table 8.1 and the associated text.

means of optimizing the *future* performance—achieving return/risk characteristics in line with those managers in a selected group that performed best in the *future*.

I was very excited about my discovery. I next tried to convince management at my company of the logic and attractiveness of a multimanager fund that would be structured around the concepts of monthly redistribution and leverage. A number of meetings ensued, but I felt my idea was going nowhere. Then I struck upon the idea of applying my redistribution/leverage scheme to a hypothetical fund consisting of all the firm's single-manager funds, most of which had disappointing track records, and therefore, not surprisingly, were regarded with less than enthusiasm by management. As it turned out, the theoretical multimanager fund I constructed using my scheme had a performance profile that was only slightly inferior to the best manager in the group and far superior to the four other managers. Since the best manager could only have been selected with hindsight, the potential advantage of my approach seemed both obvious and striking.

"This should clinch it," I thought. I made some pretty color charts illustrating these performance comparisons and set up another meeting with the division manager whose approval was vital. After I completed my 15-minute presentation, I leaned back, waiting for the division head to extol the wisdom of my proposal.

Instead he exclaimed, "You mean you want to take from the winners and give it to the losers!" in a tone as if I had just proposed the virtues of matricide.

"No," I replied, "you're missing the point. The assumption is that we believe all the managers in the fund are winners—that's presumably why we picked them in the first place. What we are doing is taking from winners during their winning periods and giving it to other winners during their losing periods." But, all the logic in the world could not prevail. The division head simply could not get beyond the "shocking" nature of my proposal. My idea never went anywhere.

In retrospect, in considering this episode, I realize that it represents yet another facet of William Eckhardt's general contention that the natural human tendency to do what feels comfortable will lead people to do what is wrong in the market.[2] For example, holding on to a losing trade, hoping that it will recover, is more comfortable than getting out of the position and locking in the loss, but it is also usually the wrong thing to do. Similarly, shifting assets in a multimanager fund to those CTAs who are in the midst of an upside excursion is far more comfortable than shifting assets to those CTAs who are experiencing drawdowns, yet I would argue that it is empirically demonstrable that the latter is actually a far superior strategy.

---

[2]Jack Schwager, *New Market Wizards,* HarperCollins, 1992.

I deliberately never published any articles on this concept because I didn't want to give away any trade secrets. Even though the idea of monthly rebalancing of CTAs in a fund had probably been considered by others, I was not aware of any funds or pools employing this strategy. The last thing I wanted to do was write a convincing article persuading others to employ a monthly rebalancing/leverage scheme in a fund or a pool before I had the opportunity to help create such a fund myself.

Two events changed my mind: First I became a CTA, and hence I did not anticipate being in a future position that required CTA selection or participation in the design of futures funds and pools. Second Tom Basso (in conjunction with Bruce Haun) published a brief article in an industry monthly summarizing the results of an exhaustive empirical test of the effect of monthly redistribution. This study, which confirmed the results of my far more cursory analysis eight years earlier, is detailed in the next section.

THE BASSO STUDY[3]

The Test

Tom Basso compared the results of two identical groups of multimanager combinations, each consisting of 79,079 three-manager portfolios. For each group, it was assumed that in every portfolio, each manager received one-third of the assets at the start of trading (January 1983). The two groups differed only in respect as to how assets in the portfolio were divided following the initial allocation. The two methods of asset allocation were:

1. **Static Allocation.** In this approach, following the initial division of assets at the start of trading, *no further allocation adjustments are made.* Over time, each manager's capital would increase or decrease in conjunction with his or her respective profits or losses, with the end result being that better-performing managers would end up controlling a larger percentage of total assets.
2. **Rebalanced (Dynamic) Allocation.** In this approach, assets are rebalanced monthly so that at the start of each month, each manager has one-third of the existing assets. In practice, monthly rebalancing is

---

[3]The material in the remainder of this chapter is based on a study done by Tom Basso, President, Trendstat Capital Management, and on an article describing the study written by Bruce Haun: "Rebalancing Portfolios Lowers Volatility and Stabilizes Return," *Managed Accounts Reports,* June 1994.

a "Robin Hood" approach because it implies that at the end of each month, money is taken from the manager(s) who performed best during the month (that is, won the most or lost the least) and given to the manager(s) who performed worst during the month.

The static allocation represents the status quo, that is, virtually all multimanager funds employ some variation of the static approach. It should be noted, however, that in the initial allocation of funds in the static approach, assets need not necessarily be equally divided among the managers, as was the case in Basso's study; in many multimanager funds, some managers are given a larger percentage of the assets than other managers. Also, it is fairly common for multimanager funds to sporadically adjust the allocation among the existing managers, or replace some of these managers with new managers. Although such changes may appear to be a form of rebalancing, they differ from the rebalanced (dynamic) approach in two critical ways: First, the changes in allocation occur sporadically as opposed to a constant monthly schedule. Second, and most importantly, asset changes almost invariably involve shifting money from poorer-performing managers to better-performing managers, or replacing existing managers with new managers with better performance—*the exact opposite tack of monthly rebalancing, which shifts assets from better-performing managers to poorer-performing managers.*

Data Used

Performance statistics were collected on 720 managers, as reported in *Managed Account Reports*, for January 1983 to December 1993. Of these managers, 79 (10.97 percent) had been in business since the start of 1983. A computer program was written to define and test all combinations of three-manager portfolios that could be formed from these 79 managers—79,079 in all.[4]

As a special note: Of the 79 managers active since January 1983, data became unavailable for 5 of these managers before the end of the survey period (presumably because they had gone out of business). In portfolios that contained one or more of these managers, it was assumed that all assets were allocated to the remaining managers following the point of data unavailability.

---

[4]According to basic probability theory:

$$_{79}C_3 = 79! \div (76!3!) = 79 \times 78 \times 77 \div 6 = 79,079$$

Return and Risk Measures Used

The following performance statistics were calculated for each of the 79,079 portfolios:

> **Annual Compounded Return.**   The annual return that when compounded would yield the same ending equity realized by the manager for the eleven-year survey period.
>
> **Maximum Drawdown.**   The largest month-end to month-end percentage decline in equity during the entire period.
>
> **Return/Maximum Drawdown Ratio.**   The annual compounded return divided by the maximum drawdown.

Results

The key statistical comparisons between rebalanced and static allocation portfolios are summarized in Table 10.1. The average annualized return for all rebalanced portfolios was actually slightly lower than the average for the static allocation portfolios: 12.62 percent versus 13.27 percent (a 5 percent reduction in the average percent return due to rebalancing). This decline in return, however, was more than offset by a larger decline in the maximum drawdown: 28.29 percent versus 34.26 percent (a 17 percent reduction in the average maximum drawdown due to rebalancing). The average return/maximum drawdown ratio for all rebalanced portfolios was 0.53 versus a 0.46 average for the static allocation portfolios. In other words, on average, the rebalanced portfolios achieved a 15 percent higher return/maximum drawdown ratio than the static allocation portfolios. Seventy-two percent of all the portfolio combinations witnessed a higher return/risk ratio with rebalancing. Therefore, in Basso's comprehensive survey, nearly three-quarters of the time the fund operator could have realized a more favorable outcome using rebalancing.

It should be stressed that in performance comparisons, a return/risk ratio, rather than return, is the key measure. The reason for this is that return can always be increased by using greater leverage.[5] Therefore, given

---

[5]Leverage can be increased by the use of notional funding, that is, by instructing the managers that the funds provided represent only a partial allocation of the intended account size (the remainder of the funding being "notional"). For example, to increase the leverage by 20 percent in a fund in which each manager is allocated $1 million, each manager would be instructed (in writing) to trade the account as a $1.2 million account (the $200,000 difference being considered notional funds). Since all CTAs use only a fraction of funds to meet margin requirements (as trading at full margin commitment would imply excessive risk), moderate increases in leverage are always feasible.

Table 10.1
A COMPARISON OF REBALANCED VERSUS
STATIC PORTFOLIOS

Statistic	Static Portfolios			Rebalanced Portfolios		
	Best	Worst	Average	Best	Worst	Average
Annual						
Return (%)	42.75	−13.54	13.27	57.90	−9.81	12.62
Maximum						
Drawdown (%)	2.13	91.29	34.26	1.86	75.98	28.29
Return/Maximum						
Drawdown Ratio	2.50	N.A.	0.46	3.33	N.A.	0.53
Percent of portfolios rebalanced higher return than static						50.94
Percent of portfolios rebalanced lower drawdown than static						76.93
Percent of portfolios rebalanced higher return/drawdown than static						72.01

N.A. = Not Applicable.

two portfolios, one with a higher return/risk ratio and the other with a higher return, the portfolio with the higher return/risk ratio could be leveraged to yield an equivalent return and still have a lower risk, or a higher return at the same risk level. For example, if the rebalanced portfolios in the study were leveraged by a factor of 1.0515, the average annualized return for this group would be identical to the average 13.26 percent return for the static allocation group, while the average maximum drawdown level would be significantly lower at 29.74 percent versus 34.26 percent. Or, if the rebalanced portfolios in the study were leveraged by a factor of 1.211, the average annualized return for this group would be 15.28 percent, well above the 13.26 percent for the static allocation group, while the average maximum drawdown levels would be equivalent at 34.26 percent. The specific choice of leverage—the balance between return and risk—would be dependent on the individual investor (or fund operator in the case of a fund).

Why Basso's Results Are Probably Understated

Although the results of Basso's test unequivocally demonstrate that rebalancing is likely to improve the performance of multimanager portfolios, the implied degree of improvement was probably significantly understated for two key reasons:

1. Basso tested all possible combinations of three-manager portfolios. Many of these combinations included managers whose results were highly correlated. In such circumstances, the benefits of rebalancing would be muted (because for managers with high correlations, the percentage of total portfolio assets controlled will not deviate widely, even if there is no rebalancing). In reality, any fund operator who knows what he or she is doing will make an effort to select managers that are not highly correlated in order to enhance diversification, which reduces risk. In fact, selecting highly correlated managers to trade a fund defeats the whole purpose of a multimanager fund. Therefore, for the types of portfolios that are likely to be selected in the real world, the benefits of rebalancing would almost certainly be greater.

I have no doubt that if Basso had restricted portfolio combinations to managers whose correlations were below a specific threshold level, the degree of performance improvement in the rebalanced group of portfolios would have been even more stark. (Basso and Haun make a virtually identical conjecture in their article: "Our sense is that when multimanager funds are strategically constructed to integrate different and diverse trading methodologies, rebalancing will provide even better results than those found in this study.") In fact, in my previously described empirical test of about 30 six-manager portfolios, which were deliberately constructed to avoid including highly correlated managers in the same portfolio, the improvement provided by rebalancing was far more dramatic. (In statistical terms, however, Basso's results are far more significant because his test included all possible combinations instead of a small, nonrandom sample.)

2. Basso's study contains a statistical bias that results in an understatement of the average rebalanced portfolio return/risk level and an overstatement of the average static portfolio return/risk level. Specifically, Basso's study did not make an adjustment for negative return/risk ratios. As was explained in Chapter 3 for the case of the Sharpe Ratio, negative return/risk ratios can be highly misleading and should not be used. The crux of the problem is that in the case of negative returns, *better* risk levels (e.g., *lower* drawdowns) will have the ironic effect of *reducing* the return/risk ratio (because the lower denominator will make the ratio more negative).

Since rebalancing lowers the drawdown in the vast majority of cases (nearly 77 percent of all portfolios tested), rebalancing will reduce the return/risk ratio for the majority of portfolios with negative return levels.[6] It should be stressed that this reduction in return/risk ratio values is totally arti-

---

[6]Although a breakdown of the results for unprofitable portfolios only was unavailable, with the percentage of lower drawdowns being equal to nearly 77 percent for all portfolios, it is a fairly safe assumption that rebalancing reduced the drawdown for at least a majority of the cases in which the net portfolio returns were negative.

ficial (it occurs even though performance is actually being improved through lower drawdowns) and entirely a consequence of the inappropriate inclusion of negative return/risk levels in the analysis. Due to this statistical quirk, including negative return/risk values in calculating average return/risk levels will bias the average downward in the case of rebalanced portfolios and upward in the case of static portfolios.

The preceding considerations imply that if calculation distortions due to negative return/risk levels are averted and portfolios are constructed to avoid combining highly correlated managers—as is likely to be the case in any sensibly designed portfolio—the performance enhancement provided by rebalancing is likely to be even greater than implied by the results of Basso's test.

WHY REBALANCING WORKS

If the managers in a portfolio had identical performance (defined as identical monthly returns in different orders), it would be a mathematical certainty that rebalancing would improve performance. This point was demonstrated in nonrigorous fashion at the start of this chapter using the card shuffling analogy. Therefore, if there is no strong reason to expect one or more of the selected managers in a portfolio to outperform the other managers in the *future*, rebalancing would provide a mathematical edge.

At different times, market conditions will be favorable for different strategies. A strategy that works particularly well during one period may perform very poorly in another period. For example, if markets are generally experiencing choppy trading-range conditions, countertrend strategies are likely to do very well, while trend-following approaches get whipsawed. If market conditions then change so that there are many prevalent trends, trend-following methods will be very profitable, while countertrend traders suffer losses. Rebalancing keeps the asset allocation among the different market strategies (represented by different managers) equal. Without rebalancing, assets would be most heavily concentrated in the strategies that worked best in the past. If market conditions then changed, the largest asset allocations would be in those strategies that are most vulnerable. In effect, rebalancing helps mitigate the negative impact of the inevitable shifts in market conditions.

Another way of understanding why rebalancing works is that it effectively forces profit taking when a manager witnesses an upside excursion and increases investment when a manager experiences a drawdown. Therefore, when a manager witnesses the inevitable retracement following an especially profitable run, the investment with that manager will be smaller than it would have been without rebalancing. Conversely, when a manager experiences a rebound after a drawdown, the investment with that manager will be greater than it would have been without rebalancing.

CONCLUSION

Theoretical arguments and empirical evidence strongly suggest that monthly rebalancing of equity provides a means of significantly enhancing the expected return/risk of multimanager portfolios. This does not mean that the use of rebalancing would improve the performance (that is, increase the return/risk) of *every* multimanager fund; it does, however, mean that rebalancing would improve the performance of a substantial majority of such funds. In other words, for any given fund, the odds strongly favor that the use of rebalancing would enhance performance. As an analogy, not using rebalancing is like turning down a bet on the toss of a fair coin, where the payoff is $3 for a correct call at a cost of $1 for a wrong call.

Given the apparent strong advantage of rebalancing, why is this method virtually, if not completely, unused? The answer to this question is simple: human nature. The idea of shifting assets from traders who have just performed best in a given portfolio to those who have performed worst goes against natural human instincts. Following these instincts, however, will usually lead to incorrect market decisions. One of the requirements for success in the markets is the ability to make decisions based on evidence, not based on what feels comfortable.

11 Is Diversification Beneficial?

THE DIVERSIFICATION DEBATE

The question of whether diversification is beneficial is a common point of debate among the designers and marketers of funds.[1] Proponents of diversification argue that by using two or more managers, as opposed to a single manager, it is possible to achieve the same return at a lower risk level, or, equivalently, a higher return at the same risk level. Opponents of diversification contend that diversification reduces the chances of stellar performance. In fact, they argue that if diversification is taken to its extreme—that is, diversifying among all commodity trading advisors (CTAs)—the results would replicate the performance of an index consisting of those CTAs, in effect eliminating even the possibility of above-average performance.

Which viewpoint is correct? To put it bluntly, the diversification debate is about as meaningful a controversy as the dispute whether the earth is round or flat: There may be two sides to the argument, but they are hardly of equal merit.

As was explained in the previous chapter, if two managers have exactly equivalent performance (the same set of monthly returns in a different sequence), it is a mathematical certainty that a combined investment in both managers would exhibit a superior return/risk relative to the individual managers. Therefore, the implicit assumption in any single manager fund is that the selected manager has a significant probability of outperforming (in terms of *future* performance) any other manager that could have been selected. Chapter 8 demonstrated that it is highly questionable whether it is even possible to identify a group of managers that are likely to exhibit above-average *future* performance. Single-manager funds not only make this assumption, but make the further assumption that it is possible to identify the *single manager within this group* that is likely to have the *best future* performance. This is obviously a preposterous assumption. Even if such a reliably superior manager existed, it

---

[1]The discussion in this chapter is generally phrased in terms of funds but applies equally to pools (see footnote 1 in Chapter 5 for the distinction between the two).

would be safe to assume that she would be so flooded with funds from eager investors that she would quickly be closed to new investment.

Opponents of diversification might counter with the previously cited argument that diversification carried to the extreme would simply result in index-type returns.[2] So what? First, lesser diversified groupings could well outperform such a hypothetical, fully diversified fund. Second, as was explained in Chapter 5, in terms of return/risk, which is the only type of measure that is relevant, a CTA index will by definition outperform a substantial majority of individual CTAs. Thus, there is nothing wrong with index returns, especially if one assumes that notional funding can be used to increase leverage. Finally, even if one assumed that past performance was a good predictor of future performance—a highly tenuous assumption (as was demonstrated in Part 2)—it would still almost always be possible to use leverage to construct a multimanager fund that would achieve a higher return than any single manager (at an equivalent risk level).

In short, with the possible exception of a manager who has developed several highly diversified trading programs, I can't conceive of any reason why it would ever make theoretical sense to use a single-manager fund instead of a multimanager fund. The following section provides an empirical study that compares the performance of single managers with multimanager portfolios. Of course, in view of the foregoing discussion, the outcome of this study—the conclusion that multimanager portfolios are superior to single-manager investments in terms of return/risk—will hardly come as a surprise. However, the primary importance of this study to the reader is that it illustrates the decisiveness of the edge provided by diversification.

SINGLE-MANAGER VERSUS MULTIMANAGER PORTFOLIOS: AN EMPIRICAL STUDY

In Chapter 8 we saw that in some period combinations, selecting the better-performing managers in the prior period tended to yield above-average performance in the subsequent period, whereas in others, ironically, selecting the poorer-performing managers proved to be the superior approach. In this chapter we evaluate the outcomes that would result from a strategy of selecting multimanager portfolios instead of individual managers, where portfolios are defined by quintiles based on past performance rankings.

---

[2]Recall from Chapter 5 that index returns implicitly assume monthly rebalancing among the CTAs in the index.

The multimanager portfolio monthly returns are defined as equalling the average of the monthly returns of the managers in the portfolio. It should be noted that this definition implicitly assumes monthly rebalancing. While monthly rebalancing is rarely if ever used, the previous chapter made clear that it should be. Since the ultimate goal of our study is to determine guidelines for optimal investing, we base our analysis on multimanager portfolios that employ rebalancing as opposed to static multimanager portfolios.

To encompass widely varying conditions, we choose two period combinations from Chapter 8: July 1987–June 1991/July 1991–June 1995 and July 1989–June 1992/July 1992–June 1995. The first pair of periods exhibited negative correlation between past and future performance ($r = -.33$), while the second pair of periods witnessed equivalent positive correlation ($r = +.32$).[3]

We use the geometric-return-based modified Sharpe Ratio to define quintile rankings in the past period, as well as to evaluate forward period performance. (The definition of this measure, as well as its desirability vis-à-vis other performance measures, was fully detailed in Chapter 8.) Table 11.1 lists 25 CTAs in order of their July 1987–June 1991 performance, as measured by the geometric-return-based modified Sharpe Ratio, and their corresponding rankings in the subsequent July 1991–June 1995 period.[4] Note that since the July 1991–June 1995 rankings incorporate five multimanager portfolios (not shown in this table), along with the 25 individual CTAs, the rankings range between 1 and 30. The table also indicates the average ranking for each quintile.

Table 11.2 lists the CTAs in Table 11.1 and the five multimanager portfolios, as defined by the quintiles in Table 11.1, in descending order of their July 1991–June 1995 performance. The multimanager portfolios are designated as MM#, where the number corresponds to the quintile ranking in the prior period. The extremely high ranking of MM5 (the multimanager portfolio corresponding to the lowest-ranked quintile in the prior period) comes as no particular surprise, since the period was selected to be representative of negative correlation between past and future performance. However, what is noteworthy in this table is the tendency for the multimanager portfolios to cluster in the upper portion of the rankings.

---

[3]The indicated correlation values are the rank correlation coefficients derived using the geometric-return-based modified Sharpe Ratio to rank CTAs.

[4]This CTA list corresponds to the CTA list used in Chapter 8 for the analysis of periods beginning in 1987 (see first table in Appendix 3 at the end of the book).

Table 11.1
CTAs RANKED BY JULY 87–JUNE 91 GEOMETRIC-RETURN-MODIFIED SHARPE RATIOS AND CORRESPONDING JULY 91–JUNE 95 RANKINGS

July 87– June 91 Rank	Advisor Name	July 91– June 95 Rank[a]
1	Cristo Commodities Inc.	29
2	AZF Commodity Management	28
3	Campbell & Company	17
4	Fundamental Futures, Inc.	16
5	Rabar Market Research Inc.	3
	Quintile 1 Average Rank	**18.6**
6	Waldner Financial Corporation	26
7	LaSalle Portfolio Management, Inc.	6
8	EMC Capital Management, Inc.	14
9	Prospective Commodities Inc.	11
10	Anglo Dutch Investments Limited	30
	Quintile 2 Average Rank	**17.4**
11	Millburn Ridgefield Corporation	18
12	Commodity Capital, Inc.	27
13	Sunrise Capital Partners, LLC (Sunrise)	23
14	Dunn Capital Management, Inc.	15
15	Visioneering R & D Co.	24
	Quintile 3 Average Rank	**21.4**
16	JPD Enterprises, Inc.	10
17	Tactical Investment Management Corp.	8
18	ICSC, Inc.	25
19	Mississippi River Investments, Inc.	21
20	RXR Inc.	9
	Quintile 4 Average Rank	**14.6**
21	Knilo International Trading Limited	12
22	Beacon Management Corporation	20
23	Fairfield Financial Group, Inc.	22
24	MC Futures Inc.	4
25	Little Brook Corporation of New Jersey	1
	Quintile 5 Average Rank	**11.8**

[a] Note 1991–1995 rankings incorporate portfolios (not shown). Hence, ranking placements range up to 30.

Table 11.2
RANKINGS OF CTAs AND MULTIMANAGER PORTFOLIOS BASED ON JULY 91–JUNE 95 GEOMETRIC-RETURN-MODIFIED SHARPE RATIOS

Rank Based on July 91–June 95 Geometric Return Sharpe Ratio[a]	Advisor Name	Annualized Geometric Return Sharpe Ratio July 91–June 95
1	Little Brook Corporation of New Jersey	0.924
2	MM5	0.919
3	Rabar Market Research Inc.	0.918
4	MC Futures Inc.	0.791
5	MM1	0.791
6	LaSalle Portfolio Management, Inc.	0.784
7	MM4	0.711
8	Tactical Investment Management Corp.	0.693
9	RXR Inc.	0.631
10	JPD Enterprises, Inc.	0.608
11	Prospective Commodities Inc.	0.605
12	Knilo International Trading Limited	0.587
13	MM2	0.518
14	EMC Capital Management, Inc.	0.469
15	Dunn Capital Management, Inc.	0.456
16	Fundamental Futures, Inc.	0.413
17	Campbell & Company	0.360
18	Millburn Ridgefield Corporation	0.354
19	MM3	0.351
20	Beacon Management Corporation	0.281
21	Mississippi River Investments, Inc.	0.194
22	Fairfield Financial Group, Inc.	0.122
23	Sunrise Capital Partners, LLC (Sunrise)	0.090
24	Visioneering R & D Co.	0.089
25	ICSC, Inc.	0.015
26	Waldner Financial Corporation	0.009
27	Commodity Capital, Inc.	−0.045
28	AZF Commodity Management	−0.052
29	Cristo Commodities Inc.	−0.093
30	Anglo Dutch Investments Limited	−0.130

[a]For negative geometric Sharpe Ratios, rank based on geometric return (which is not shown).
MM1— Multimanager portfolio consisting of CTAs in quintile 1 for June 87–June 91 (as defined in Table 11.1).
MM2—Multimanager portfolio consisting of CTAs in quintile 2 for June 87–June 91 (as defined in Table 11.1).
MM3—Multimanager portfolio consisting of CTAs in quintile 3 for June 87–June 91 (as defined in Table 11.1).
MM4—Multimanager portfolio consisting of CTAs in quintile 4 for June 87–June 91 (as defined in Table 11.1).
MM5—Multimanager portfolio consisting of CTAs in quintile 5 for June 87–June 91 (as defined in Table 11.1).

Table 11.3 demonstrates just how decisively the multimanager portfolios tended to outperform the individual CTAs. Note the following highlights:

- All five of the multimanager portfolios ranked higher than the average rank of the CTAs that they contained, with the average ranking improvement exceeding seven placements (out of a total ranking range of only 30).
- Four out of the five multimanager portfolios exhibited above-median performance.
- Three out of the five multimanager portfolios outperformed 84 percent or more of the individual CTAs.
- All five of the multimanager portfolios outperformed *at least* three out of the five (60 percent) CTAs that they contained.
- Two out of the five multimanager portfolios outperformed *all* of the CTAs in the portfolio.
- On average, the multimanager portfolios outperformed 75 percent of all individual CTAs.
- On average, the multimanager portfolios outperformed 80 percent of all the CTAs in their respective groupings.

The same type of analysis is repeated for July 1989–June 1992/July 1992–June 1995—a period combination exhibiting positive correlation between past and future performance. Table 11.4 lists 41 CTAs in order of their July 1989–June 1992 performance, as measured by the geometric-return-based modified Sharpe Ratio, and their corresponding rankings in the subse-

Table 11.3
MULTIMANAGER PORTFOLIO RANKINGS VERSUS INDIVIDUAL CTA RANKINGS (JULY 91–JUNE 95)[a]

Portfolio	Rank	Average Rank of CTA in Portfolio	Percent of All CTAs Exceeded by Portfolio	Percent of CTAs in Portfolio Exceeded by Portfolio
MM5	2	11.8	96.0	80.0
MM1	5	18.6	88.0	100.0
MM4	7	14.6	84.0	100.0
MM2	13	17.4	64.0	60.0
MM3	19	21.4	44.0	60.0
Median[b]	15.5			
Average:			75.2	80.0

[a]Rankings based on geometric-return-modified Sharpe Ratio.
[b]Median of 25 individual CTAs and 5 portfolios.

Table 11.4
CTAs RANKED BY JULY 89–JUNE 92 GEOMETRIC-RETURN-MODIFIED SHARPE RATIOS AND CORRESPONDING JULY 92–JUNE 95 RANKINGS

July 89–June 92 Rank	Advisor Name	July 92–June 95 Rank[a]
1	D.F. Advisors, Inc.	33
2	Gandon Fund Management Ltd.	1
3	Gateway Investment Advisers Inc.	2
4	SJO, Inc.	19
5	Fundamental Futures, Inc.	26
6	Crow Trading, Inc.	5
7	Northfield Trading L.P.	18
8	Hyman Beck & Company, Inc.	25
9	Cristo Commodities Inc.	39
	Quintile 1 Average Rank	**18.7**
10	PRAGMA, Inc.	45
11	Waldner Financial Corporation	44
12	Chesapeake Capital Corporation	4
13	Campbell & Company	20
14	LaSalle Portfolio Management, Inc.	21
15	Prospective Commodities Inc.	22
16	Rabar Market Research Inc.	8
17	Millburn Ridgefield Corporation	27

Quintile 2 Average Rank		**23.9**
18	AZF Commodity Management	35
19	Willowbridge Associates Inc.	6
20	Commodity Capital, Inc.	41
21	Hawksbill Capital Management	13
22	EMC Capital Management, Inc.	16
23	RXR Inc.	28
24	Gaiacorp Ireland Limited	46
25	Tactical Investment Management Corp.	14
Quintile 3 Average Rank		**24.9**
26	JPD Enterprises, Inc.	12
27	Trendstat Capital Management, Inc.	37
28	Sunrise Capital Partners, LLC (Sunrise)	29
29	Fairfield Financial Group, Inc.	38
30	Dunn Capital Management, Inc.	23
31	Visioneering R & D Co.	31
32	Strategic Investments	30
33	Little Brook Corporation of New Jersey	7
Quintile 4 Average Rank		**25.9**
34	Beacon Management Corporation	32
35	Trendlogic Associates, Inc.	34
36	ICSC, Inc.	40
37	Mississippi River Investments, Inc.	36
38	Knilo International Trading Limited	24
39	Saxon Investment Corporation	9
40	Willowbridge Associates Inc.	43
41	Dallas Commodity Co., Inc.	42
Quintile 5 Average Rank		**32.5**

[a] Note 1992–1995 rankings incorporate portfolios (not shown). Hence, ranking placements range up to 46.

quent July 1992–June 1995 period.[5] Note that since the July 1992–June 1995 rankings incorporate five multimanager portfolios (not shown in this table), along with the 41 individual CTAs, the rankings range between 1 and 46. The table also indicates the average ranking for each quintile.

Table 11.5 lists the CTAs in Table 11.4 and the five multimanager portfolios, as defined by the quintiles in Table 11.4, in descending order of their July 1992–June 1995 performance. In this instance, it is MM1 (the multimanager portfolio corresponding to the highest-ranked quintile in the prior period) that scores particularly high. Analogously, this result comes as no particular surprise, since the period was selected to be representative of positive correlation between past and future performance. Once again, however, the key pattern that should be noted in this table is the pronounced tendency for the multimanager portfolios to cluster in the upper portion of the rankings.

Table 11.6 demonstrates just how decisively the multimanager portfolios tended to outperform the individual CTAs. If anything, the superiority of the multimanager portfolios over the individual CTAs is perhaps even more striking than it was in Table 11.3. In particular, note the following highlights:

- All five of the multimanager portfolios ranked higher than the average rank of the CTAs that they contained, with the *minimum* ranking improvement exceeding 10 placements (out of a total ranking range of only 46).
- All five of the multimanager portfolios outperformed a *minimum* of 68 percent of the individual CTAs.
- Three out of the five multimanager portfolios outperformed 80 percent or more of the individual CTAs.
- All five of the multimanager portfolios outperformed *at least* 75 percent of the CTAs that they contained.
- On average, the multimanager portfolios outperformed nearly 80 percent of all individual CTAs.
- On average, the multimanager portfolios outperformed over 80 percent of all the CTAs in their respective groupings.

Tables 11.3 and 11.6 demonstrate that multimanager portfolios (with monthly rebalancing) have a huge edge over single-manager portfolios. In both instances, on average, the multimanager portfolios beat a minimum of 75 percent of all the individual CTAs and 80 percent of the CTAs in their respective groupings.

---

[5]This CTA list corresponds to the CTA list used in Chapter 8 for the analysis of periods beginning in 1989 (see third table in Appendix 3 at the end of the book).

Table 11.5
RANKINGS OF CTAs AND MULTIMANAGER PORTFOLIOS
BASED ON JULY 92–JUNE 95 GEOMETRIC-RETURN-
MODIFIED SHARPE RATIO

Rank Based on July 92–July 95 Geometric Sharpe Ratio[a]	Advisor Name	Annualized Geometric Return Sharpe Ratio July 92–June 95
1	Gandon Fund Management Ltd.	1.990
2	Gateway Investment Advisers Inc.	1.894
3	MM1	1.827
4	Chesapeake Capital Corporation	1.633
5	Crow Trading, Inc.	1.582
6	Willowbridge Associates Inc.	1.377
7	Little Brook Corporation of New Jersey	1.335
8	Rabar Market Research Inc.	1.258
9	Saxon Investment Corporation	1.061
10	MM3	0.975
11	MM2	0.933
12	JPD Enterprises, Inc.	0.929
13	Hawksbill Capital Management	0.798
14	Tactical Investment Management Corp.	0.786
15	MM4	0.776
16	EMC Capital Management, Inc.	0.749
17	MM5	0.726
18	Northfield Trading L.P.	0.643
19	SJO, Inc.	0.611
20	Campbell & Company	0.606
21	LaSalle Portfolio Management, Inc.	0.602
22	Prospective Commodities Inc.	0.600
23	Dunn Capital Management, Inc.	0.578
24	Knilo International Trading Limited	0.575
25	Hyman Beck & Company, Inc.	0.522
26	Fundamental Futures, Inc.	0.516
27	Millburn Ridgefield Corporation	0.485
28	RXR Inc.	0.466
29	Sunrise Capital Partners, LLC (Sunrise)	0.365
30	Strategic Investments	0.314
31	Visioneering R & D Co.	0.288
32	Beacon Management Corporation	0.262
33	D.F. Advisors, Inc.	0.156
34	Trendlogic Associates, Inc.	0.148
35	AZF Commodity Management	0.142
36	Mississippi River Investments, Inc.	0.102
37	Trendstat Capital Management, Inc.	0.038
38	Fairfield Financial Group, Inc.	0.036

TABLE 11.5 (continued)

Rank Based on July 92–July 95 Geometric Sharpe Ratio[a]	Advisor Name	Annualized Geometric Return Sharpe Ratio July 92–June 95
39	Cristo Commodities Inc.	−0.048
40	ICSC, Inc.	−0.040
41	Commodity Capital, Inc.	−0.099
42	Dallas Commodity Co., Inc.	−0.668
43	Willowbridge Associates Inc.	−0.130
44	Waldner Financial Corporation	−0.189
45	PRAGMA, Inc.	−0.382
46	Gaiacorp Ireland Limited	−0.361

[a]For negative geometric Sharpe Ratios, rank based on geometric return (which is not shown).
MM1— Multimanager portfolio consisting of CTAs in quintile 1 for June 89–June 92 (as defined in Table 11.4).
MM2— Multimanager portfolio consisting of CTAs in quintile 2 for June 89–June 92 (as defined in Table 11.4).
MM3—Multimanager portfolio consisting of CTAs in quintile 3 for June 89–June 92 (as defined in Table 11.4).
MM4—Multimanager portfolio consisting of CTAs in quintile 4 for June 89–June 92 (as defined in Table 11.4).
MM5—Multimanager portfolio consisting of CTAs in quintile 5 for June 89–June 92 (as defined in Table 11.4).

Table 11.6
MULTIMANAGER PORTFOLIO RANKINGS VERSUS INDIVIDUAL CTA RANKINGS (JULY 92–JUNE 95)[a]

Portfolio	Rank	Average Rank of CTAs in Portfolio	Percent of All CTAs Exceeded by Portfolio	Percent of CTAs in Portfolio Exceeded by Portfolio
MM1	3	18.7	95.1	77.8
MM3	10	23.9	80.5	75.0
MM2	11	24.9	80.5	87.5
MM4	15	25.9	73.2	75.0
MM5	17	32.5	68.3	87.5
Median[b]	23.5			
Average:			79.5	80.6

[a]Rankings based on geometric-return-modified Sharpe Ratio.
[b]Median of 41 individual CTAs and 5 portfolios.

Table 11.7 combines the two different period multimanager portfolio rankings (as well as the average rankings of the CTAs they contain) by quintile. In this table, raw rankings are converted into ranking percentiles[6] to allow combining figures for the two periods. (The raw ranking figures cannot be combined, because the total number of elements differ for the two periods: 30 versus 46.) Note that the dramatic superiority of multimanager portfolios holds true whether one selects portfolio groupings of the best-performing managers in the past (MM1 corresponding to quintile 1), worst performing managers in the past (MM5), or anything in between (MM2, MM3, or MM4). For the two periods combined, the minimum percentile ranking improvement for any multimanager combination (versus the corresponding CTA average percentile) is a very substantive 19 percent, with the average improvement exceeding 27 percent.[7]

It should be emphasized that although the superior performance of multimanager portfolios was demonstrated in terms of return/risk, the same conclusion is implied in terms of return alone. Reason: If the return/risk of a portfolio exceeds the return/risk of a CTA (but the return is lower), it implies that if the portfolio is leveraged (through notional funding) so that its risk is equal to the risk of the CTA, the portfolio return would exceed the CTA return (assuming, of course, that the return is positive).

The portfolios in our analysis were constructed without regard to the correlations between the managers in each portfolio. If portfolios were formed with attention to combining managers with low correlations, diversification would be enhanced, reducing risk, and presumably increasing return/risk even further. Although this is a plausible assumption, it is only relevant if CTA correlations are stable, that is, if CTAs with low correlations in one period also tend to exhibit low correlations in the subsequent period. In the next section, we examine whether this premise is empirically justified.

---

[6]The ranking percentile indicates the percentage of elements with ranking numbers equal to or lower than the given ranking. For example, in the 1991–1995 period, which has a total of 30 elements (25 CTAs and 5 multimanager portfolios), a raw rank of 5 would convert to a percentile of 16.67 because 16.67 percent (5 ÷ 30) have equal or lower rank numbers. The lower the percentile, the higher the ranking.

[7]The keen-eyed reader may wonder why the average CTA ranking in each period (the average of the average CTA rank in each portfolio) approximates 55 percent instead of equaling 50 percent. There are two reasons: (1) multimanager portfolios are included in the rankings, and since they tend to outperform most CTAs, the average CTA rank will be worse (higher) than 50 percent; (2) defining percentiles as the percentage of elements with *equal* or lower ranking numbers biases the average ranking slightly upward (by 1.7 percent in the case of 30 elements and by 1.2 percent in the case of 46 elements). This bias approaches 0, as the number of elements increases. (Defining percentiles as the percentage of elements with "lower" instead of "equal or lower" ranking numbers would result in an equivalent bias in the opposite direction.)

Table 11.7
PERCENTILE RANKINGS FOR COMBINED PERIODS:
MULTIMANAGER PORTFOLIOS VERSUS INDIVIDUAL CTAs[a]

Portfolio	Rank as Percentile	Average Rank of CTAs in Portfolio as Percentile	Average Percentile Ranking of CTAs Minus Portfolio Percentile Ranking
		July 1991–June 1995	
MM1	16.67	62.00	45.33
MM2	43.33	58.00	14.67
MM3	63.33	71.33	8.00
MM4	23.33	48.67	25.33
MM5	6.67	39.33	32.67
Average	30.67	55.87	25.20
		July 1992–June 1995	
MM1	6.52	40.65	34.13
MM2	23.91	54.13	30.22
MM3	21.74	51.96	30.22
MM4	32.61	56.30	23.70
MM5	36.96	70.65	33.70
Average	24.35	54.74	30.39
		Average of Two Periods Combined	
MM1	11.59	51.33	39.73
MM2	33.62	56.07	22.44
MM3	42.54	61.64	19.11
MM4	27.97	52.49	24.51
MM5	21.81	54.99	33.18
Average	27.51	55.30	27.80

[a]Rankings based on geometric Sharpe Ratio.

ARE CTA CORRELATIONS STABLE?

For consistency, we use the same two CTA lists and two time period combinations employed in the analysis of the previous section to evaluate the stability of CTA correlations. We begin by ranking all CTA pair correlations for the July 1987–June 1991 period in descending order and listing the corresponding correlation rankings for the subsequent July 1991–June 1995. Since there are 25 CTAs, there are a total of 300 pair correlations.[8] Rather

---

[8]$_{25}C_2 = 25! \div 23!2! = 25 \times 24 \div 2 = 300$.

than show the entire list, Tables 11.8 and 11.9 depict the top 50 and bottom 50 pairs (in terms of the earlier period correlation rankings). As can readily be seen, the 50 highest correlation pairs in the first period exhibit significantly higher correlations (lower rank numbers) in the subsequent period than do the 50 lowest correlation pairs. As implied by these tables, the rank correlation coefficient strongly confirms the correlation between CTA correlations in the two periods: a value of 0.51, which is statistically significant at better than the 0.1 percent level.

The same test is repeated for the list of 41 CTAs, comparing CTA pair correlations in the July 1989–June 1992 and July 1992–June 1995 periods. Since there are 41 CTAs, there are a total of 820 pair correlations.[9] Once again, rather than show the entire list, Tables 11.10 and 11.11 depict the top 50 and bottom 50 pairs (in terms of the earlier period correlation rankings). In this case, the pattern is even more pronounced, with the 50 highest correlation pairs in the first period exhibiting far higher correlations (lower rank numbers) in the subsequent period than do the 50 lowest correlation pairs. The rank correlation coefficient of 0.67 is off the charts in terms of statistical significance.

The foregoing illustrations indicate that there is significant stability in CTA pair correlations. The implication is that past CTA correlations can provide a useful guideline in selecting CTAs that are likely to have low correlations in the future.

Since any portfolio with more than two managers involves multiple CTA pair correlations (for example, a nine-manager portfolio will contain 36 pair correlations), how can we compare different portfolios in regards to their degree of correlation? Perhaps the simplest method is to calculate the average for all the pair correlations in a portfolio. Assuming the CTAs are equally weighted, this simple approach will provide a good approximation of relative diversification. Table 11.12, which depicts a correlation matrix for a nine-manager portfolio, illustrates this method. Generally speaking, portfolios with lower average pair correlations can be considered more diversified than portfolios with higher average pair correlations. The portfolio used for the example in Table 11.12 has an extremely low average pair correlation of 0.07, and hence is very well diversified.

To examine the relationship between the average pair correlation and portfolio performance, Table 11.13 lists the five portfolios shown in Table 11.3 (the July 1991–June 1995 period) in ascending order of their correlations. Two additional columns of information are provided: (1) the corresponding pair correlations for the prior period, and (2) the improvement in rank placement of the portfolios versus the average rank of the CTAs they

---

[9] $_{41}C_2 = 41! \div 39!2! = 41 \times 40 \div 2 = 820.$

Table 11.8
CTA PAIR CORRELATIONS (TOP 50): RANKING COMPARISON
(7/87–6/91 VERSUS 7/91–6/95)

Rank of Pair Correlation 7/87–6/91	CTA 1	CTA 2	Pair Correlation 7/87–6/91	Pair Correlation 7/91–6/95	Rank of Pair Correlation 7/91–6/95
1	Rabar	Tactical	0.887	0.705	27
2	EMC	Rabar	0.878	0.797	7
3	Beacon	ICSC	0.851	0.628	49
4	EMC	Tactical	0.833	0.750	13
5	Beacon	Tactical	0.828	0.593	60
6	ICSC	Little Brook	0.826	0.638	43
7	JPD	Rabar	0.825	0.937	1
8	Campbell	Tactical	0.821	0.684	35
9	Beacon	Campbell	0.816	0.660	39
10	Campbell	Rabar	0.815	0.791	8
11	AZF	Beacon	0.793	0.487	83
12	Little Brook	Sunrise	0.789	0.735	17
13	Millburn	Sunrise	0.785	0.815	5
14	Beacon	Little Brook	0.783	0.706	26
15	Little Brook	Millburn	0.779	0.783	9
16	EMC	JPD	0.776	0.832	3
17	Campbell	RXR	0.774	0.682	36
18	ICSC	Millburn	0.772	0.618	53
19	Campbell	EMC	0.768	0.576	66
20	Campbell	JPD	0.767	0.735	16
21	ICSC	Sunrise	0.767	0.622	52
22	Millburn	Tactical	0.762	0.601	58

214

23	ICSC	Tactical	0.761	0.473	87
24	AZF	Tactical	0.758	0.346	106
25	Sunrise	Tactical	0.758	0.704	29
26	Campbell	Little Brook	0.751	0.667	38
27	JPD	Tactical	0.744	0.704	28
28	Beacon	Sunrise	0.741	0.723	21
29	Beacon	Millburn	0.740	0.585	62
30	EMC	ICSC	0.725	0.366	102
31	Little Brook	Tactical	0.724	0.571	68
32	Beacon	Rabar	0.723	0.692	31
33	Campbell	ICSC	0.718	0.517	79
34	AZF	Campbell	0.711	0.195	144
35	Campbell	Sunrise	0.707	0.853	2
36	Campbell	Millburn	0.698	0.692	32
37	RXR	Tactical	0.692	0.606	56
38	ICSC	Rabar	0.692	0.461	90
39	Beacon	EMC	0.687	0.605	57
40	Millburn	RXR	0.686	0.641	41
41	AZF	ICSC	0.680	0.357	104
42	EMC	Millburn	0.662	0.592	61
43	ICSC	RXR	0.661	0.482	84
44	JPD	MC	0.658	0.718	23
45	Millburn	Rabar	0.657	0.737	15
46	Beacon	RXR	0.655	0.554	72
47	AZF	Rabar	0.654	0.182	148
48	EMC	RXR	0.648	0.718	22
49	AZF	Millburn	0.646	0.124	162
50	Beacon	Fundamental	0.645	-0.011	222

Table 11.9

CTA PAIR CORRELATIONS (BOTTOM 50): RANKING COMPARISON (7/87–6/91 VERSUS 7/91–6/95)

Rank of Pair Correlation 7/87–6/91	CTA 1	CTA 2	Pair Correlation 7/87–6/91	Pair Correlation 7/91–6/95	Rank of Pair Correlation 7/91–6/95
251	Cristo	LaSalle	-0.027	0.040	195
252	Anglo Dutch	Dunn	-0.029	0.116	168
253	Fundamental	Waldner	-0.033	-0.219	294
254	Anglo Dutch	LaSalle	-0.034	0.307	112
255	Cristo	Mississippi River	-0.034	-0.112	262
256	LaSalle	Prospective	-0.048	-0.019	227
257	LaSalle	RXR	-0.050	0.518	78
258	Dunn	Fundamental	-0.051	-0.149	276
259	Fundamental	MC	-0.051	-0.078	251
260	Anglo Dutch	Rabar	-0.052	0.286	116
261	MC	Mississippi River	-0.057	0.124	163
262	JPD	Prospective	-0.062	-0.017	224
263	Cristo	Visioneering	-0.062	0.010	207
264	Cristo	Fairfield	-0.074	0.014	204
265	Dunn	Fairfield	-0.077	0.099	174
266	Anglo Dutch	ICSC	-0.079	0.046	194
267	Anglo Dutch	Sunrise	-0.085	0.254	123
268	Anglo Dutch	EMC	-0.092	0.350	105
269	Anglo Dutch	JPD	-0.094	0.187	146
270	MC	Prospective	-0.103	-0.084	256
271	Anglo Dutch	RXR	-0.111	0.237	130
272	Anglo Dutch	Visioneering	-0.113	0.337	108
273	Anglo Dutch	Beacon	-0.115	0.185	147

274	Commodity Cap.	LaSalle	-0.123	0.092	180
275	Anglo Dutch	Prospective	-0.127	0.182	150
276	Anglo Dutch	Waldner	-0.130	0.129	160
277	LaSalle	Sunrise	-0.130	0.330	109
278	LaSalle	Mississippi River	-0.141	-0.295	297
279	LaSalle	Little Brook	-0.141	0.218	138
280	Cristo	Fundamental	-0.142	-0.398	300
281	Anglo Dutch	Little Brook	-0.143	0.245	126
282	Anglo Dutch	Mississippi River	-0.146	-0.031	231
283	LaSalle	Millburn	-0.152	0.219	137
284	Anglo Dutch	AZF	-0.162	-0.063	243
285	EMC	LaSalle	-0.166	0.473	88
286	Anglo Dutch	Commodity Cap.	-0.166	-0.192	287
287	JPD	LaSalle	-0.168	0.223	134
288	ICSC	LaSalle	-0.176	0.125	161
289	Dunn	Prospective	-0.177	-0.081	255
290	LaSalle	MC	-0.192	0.092	179
291	Fairfield	Visioneering	-0.205	-0.006	216
292	Anglo Dutch	Tactical	-0.208	0.159	155
293	Anglo Dutch	Millburn	-0.224	0.213	140
294	AZF	LaSalle	-0.227	-0.053	240
295	Anglo Dutch	Fundamental	-0.233	-0.207	291
296	Beacon	LaSalle	-0.234	0.231	131
297	Fundamental	LaSalle	-0.237	-0.235	295
298	LaSalle	Tactical	-0.251	0.412	98
299	Campbell	LaSalle	-0.289	0.358	103
300	LaSalle	Rabar	-0.343	0.238	129

Rank Correlation Coefficient:[a]   0.506

[a]Based on all 300 pairs, not just the 100 pairs shown in this table.

Table 11.10
CTA PAIR CORRELATIONS (TOP 50): RANKING COMPARISON
(7/89–6/92 VERSUS 7/92–6/95)

Rank of Pair Correlation 7/89–6/92	CTA 1	CTA 2	Pair Correlation 7/89–6/92	Pair Correlation 7/92–6/95	Rank of Pair Correlation 7/92–6/95
1	JPD	Rabar	0.937	0.934	1
2	EMC	Rabar	0.882	0.754	10
3	JPD	Hyman Beck	0.880	0.726	14
4	EMC	JPD	0.871	0.765	8
5	Rabar	Hawksbill	0.855	0.661	32
6	Campbell	JPD	0.855	0.644	41
7	Rabar	Hyman Beck	0.844	0.702	20
8	JPD	Hawksbill	0.843	0.597	60
9	Campbell	Sunrise	0.839	0.808	3
10	Campbell	Hyman Beck	0.832	0.685	23
11	Rabar	Tactical	0.829	0.674	25
12	Sunrise	Hawksbill	0.820	0.544	88
13	JPD	Sunrise	0.816	0.716	15
14	Sunrise	Tactical	0.813	0.585	67
15	JPD	Chesapeake	0.809	0.664	30
16	Sunrise	Hyman Beck	0.809	0.778	7
17	Tactical	Hawksbill	0.806	0.479	136
18	Beacon	ICSC, Inc.	0.800	0.583	70
19	JPD	Tactical	0.800	0.669	26
20	JPD	Millburn	0.798	0.633	47
21	ICSC, Inc.	Little Brook	0.793	0.640	44
22	Millburn	Rabar	0.792	0.684	24

23	Millburn	Tactical	0.790	0.474	140
24	JPD	Willowbridge (Vulcan)	0.790	0.643	42
25	Beacon	Campbell	0.788	0.542	90
26	Tactical	Hyman Beck	0.787	0.624	54
27	Trendstat	Willowbridge (Vulcan)	0.783	0.466	146
28	Little Brook	Sunrise	0.782	0.578	72
29	Campbell	Willowbridge (Vulcan)	0.780	0.607	58
30	EMC	Hawksbill	0.779	0.512	114
31	Tactical	Willowbridge (Vulcan)	0.776	0.584	69
32	RXR Inc.	Willowbridge (Vulcan)	0.776	0.653	37
33	Campbell	Rabar	0.775	0.746	11
34	Little Brook	Hyman Beck	0.774	0.611	57
35	Rabar	Sunrise	0.771	0.787	6
36	Beacon	EMC	0.770	0.427	172
37	JPD	Gaiacorp	0.770	0.331	243
38	EMC	ICSC, Inc.	0.769	0.194	377
39	Beacon	Hyman Beck	0.768	0.788	5
40	Beacon	JPD	0.764	0.643	43
41	Chesapeake	Gaiacorp	0.761	0.428	170
42	Millburn	Hawksbill	0.760	0.432	165
43	Beacon	Little Brook	0.756	0.658	35
44	Sunrise	Trendstat	0.755	0.478	137
45	Beacon	Rabar	0.753	0.626	52
46	EMC	Chesapeake	0.753	0.666	28
47	Campbell	Little Brook	0.751	0.467	144
48	Hawksbill	Willowbridge (Vulcan)	0.751	0.366	220
49	EMC	Hyman Beck	0.746	0.549	85
50	Campbell	EMC	0.745	0.366	218

Table 11.11
CTA PAIR CORRELATIONS (BOTTOM 50): RANKING
COMPARISON (7/89–6/92 VERSUS 7/92–6/95)

Rank of Pair Correlation 7/89–6/92	CTA 1	CTA 2	Pair Correlation 7/89–6/92	Pair Correlation 7/92–6/95	Rank of Pair Correlation 7/92–6/95
771	Fairfield	Willowbridge (Rex)	-0.188	0.252	325
772	EMC	D.F.	-0.188	0.027	564
773	Sunrise	D.F.	-0.189	-0.132	741
774	Dunn	Fairfield	-0.190	0.193	380
775	D.F.	Saxon	-0.196	-0.213	782
776	ICSC, Inc.	Prospective Comm.	-0.196	0.061	522
777	Mississippi River Inv.	Sunrise	-0.196	0.255	321
778	Campbell	D.F.	-0.198	-0.122	735
779	Beacon	Prospective Comm.	-0.202	-0.001	596
780	Commodity Cap.	Fairfield	-0.204	-0.013	613
781	Dunn	Prospective Comm.	-0.209	0.005	586
782	Gandon	PRAGMA	-0.210	-0.133	743
783	Knilo	Gateway	-0.212	-0.241	792
784	Fundamental Futures	Willowbridge (Vulcan)	-0.215	0.006	585
785	Fundamental Futures	Northfield	-0.218	-0.122	734
786	Gateway	Hyman Beck	-0.222	-0.104	714
787	Fundamental Futures	Strategic	-0.226	0.319	255
788	Commodity Cap.	PRAGMA	-0.226	-0.343	811
789	Little Brook	D.F.	-0.228	-0.065	673
790	Mississippi River Inv.	Chesapeake	-0.234	0.247	327
791	Fundamental Futures	LaSalle	-0.239	-0.052	658
792	JPD	D.F.	-0.240	-0.061	669
793	Knilo	Strategic	-0.243	0.033	553

794	LaSalle	D.F.	-0.246	0.021	572
795	Gateway	PRAGMA	-0.248	0.217	350
796	Mississippi River Inv.	Visioneering	-0.250	0.086	491
797	D.F.	Hyman Beck	-0.253	-0.165	759
798	AZF	LaSalle	-0.264	-0.101	709
799	Milburn	D.F.	-0.265	-0.133	742
800	Fairfield	PRAGMA	-0.266	-0.178	769
801	Mississippi River Inv.	Saxon	-0.268	0.238	330
802	Fundamental Futures	Trendstat	-0.269	-0.186	774
803	Fairfield	Crow	-0.274	-0.079	687
804	D.F.	Dallas	-0.279	-0.057	666
805	Prospective Comm.	PRAGMA	-0.281	0.100	471
806	D.F.	Hawksbill	-0.289	-0.076	685
807	Milburn	Prospective Comm.	-0.294	0.124	445
808	Dallas	SJO, Inc.	-0.300	0.142	427
809	Mississippi River Inv.	Gaiacorp	-0.301	-0.039	644
810	Fundamental Futures	Waldner	-0.314	-0.167	761
811	Gateway	Willowbridge (Rex)	-0.325	-0.103	713
812	Cristo	LaSalle	-0.341	0.056	527
813	Mississippi River Inv.	Strategic	-0.346	0.254	323
814	Prospective Comm.	Trendlogic	-0.359	0.273	300
815	Chesapeake	D.F.	-0.368	-0.089	697
816	Fundamental Futures	PRAGMA	-0.375	0.287	280
817	Milburn	Mississippi River Inv.	-0.383	0.324	251
818	Mississippi River Inv.	Willowbridge (Rex)	-0.449	0.207	364
819	Cristo	Gateway	-0.472	-0.064	671
820	Fairfield	D.F.	-0.516	0.148	415

Rank Correlation Coefficient:[a]   0.667

[a]Based on all 820 pairs, not just the 100 pairs shown in this table.

Table 11.12
SAMPLE CORRELATION MATRIX (MM1: JUNE 89–JULY 92)

	D.F.	Gandon	Gateway	SJO	Fundamental	Crow	Northfield	Hyman Beck
D.F.								
Gandon	0.01							
Gateway	–0.10	0.43						
SJO	0.07	–0.05	0.18					
Fundamental	0.07	0.09	–0.02	0.02				
Crow	0.34	0.17	0.00	0.05	0.01			
Northfield	0.01	0.06	–0.10	0.27	–0.22	0.06		
Hyman Beck	–0.25	0.08	–0.22	0.22	–0.08	0.09	0.70	
Cristo	0.11	–0.12	–0.47	0.15	–0.16	0.08	0.32	0.45
Average:	0.069							

contain. Similarly, Table 11.14 lists the five portfolios shown in Table 11.6 (the July 1992–June 1995 period) in ascending order of their pair correlations, along with the same additional information.

Note the following observations in examining Tables 11.13 and 11.14:

1. Portfolios with low average correlations generally tended to have low correlations in the prior period, while those with high correlations tended to have high correlations in the prior period. For example, in Table 11.14 the correlation ranking order is almost identical for the two periods. The only major anomaly is portfolio MM1 in Table 11.13, which had the lowest average correlation in the July 1991–June 1995 period, but was only the third lowest (the median) in the prior period.

2. The lowest correlation portfolio did extremely well in both periods, achieving the best rank for a portfolio in July 1992–June 1995 (3), and the second best portfolio rank in July 1991–June 1995 (5).

3. The highest correlation portfolio was the lowest ranking portfolio in July 1991–June 1995 (19), and the second lowest ranking portfolio in July 1992–June 1995 (15).

4. Perhaps the most pronounced pattern was the strong inverse relationship between the average correlation level and the improvement of the portfolio's ranking placement relative to the average rank of its constituent CTAs. As can be seen in both Table 11.13 and 11.14, the lower the average pair correlation of the portfolio, the greater the improvement of the portfolio's ranking relative to the ranking of the CTAs in the portfolio. In fact, with the exception of

Table 11.13
**MULTIMANAGER PORTFOLIO RANKINGS LISTED IN
ASCENDING ORDER OF AVERAGE PAIR CORRELATIONS
(JULY 1991–JUNE 1995)**

Portfolio	Average Pair Correlation July 91–June 95	Average Pair Correlation July 87–June 91	Rank	Average Rank of CTA in Portfolio	Percent of All CTAs Exceeded by Portfolio	Percent of CTAs in Portfolio Exceeded by Portfolio	Improvement in Rank Placement of Portfolio Versus Average of CTAs in Portfolio
MM1	0.11	0.36	5	18.6	88.0	100.0	13.6
MM2	0.20	0.05	13	17.4	64.0	60.0	4.5
MM5	0.25	0.29	2	11.8	96.0	80.0	9.8
MM4	0.37	0.57	7	14.6	84.0	100.0	7.6
MM3	0.40	0.37	19	21.4	44.0	60.0	2.4

Table 11.14
**MULTIMANAGER PORTFOLIO RANKINGS LISTED IN
ASCENDING ORDER OF AVERAGE PAIR CORRELATIONS
(JULY 1992–JUNE 1995)**

Portfolio	Average Pair Correlation July 92–June 95	Average Pair Correlation July 89–June 92	Rank	Average Rank of CTA in Portfolio	Percent of All CTAs Exceeded by Portfolio	Percent of CTAs in Portfolio Exceeded by Portfolio	Improvement in Rank Placement of Portfolio Versus Average of CTAs in Portfolio
MM1	0.02	0.07	3	18.7	95.1	77.8	15.7
MM5	0.15	0.22	17	32.5	68.3	87.5	15.5
MM2	0.24	0.28	11	24.9	80.5	87.5	13.9
MM3	0.26	0.50	10	23.9	80.5	75.0	11.6
MM4	0.39	0.47	15	25.9	73.2	75.0	10.9

portfolio MM2 in Table 11.13, the final columns are in perfect descending order.

HOW MUCH DIVERSIFICATION IS ENOUGH?

How many managers must a portfolio typically contain until the benefit of including additional managers provides only a marginal further reduction in risk? Although some studies have suggested the number is as high as 40 or more,[10] practically speaking, the vast portion of the diversification benefit can be achieved with 10 or fewer CTAs.

Table 11.15 illustrates the relationship between risk and the number of CTAs in a portfolio. Although these statistics are based on CTA data for a single year (1989), it is reasonable to assume that the general risk-reduction pattern illustrated is probably representative of any period. In this example, a portfolio consisting of all 218 CTAs reduces risk by 52.9 percent relative to the average single manager portfolio. Note that adding just one CTA (that is, a 2-CTA portfolio) reduces risk by 21.8 percent, which is equal to 41.3 percent of the total possible risk reduction. A 5-CTA portfolio reduces risk by 38.6 percent, which is equal to 72.9 percent of the total possible risk reduction, while a 10-CTA portfolio reduces risk by 45.3 percent, which is equal to 85.6 percent of the total possible risk reduction. In other words, adding the remaining 208 CTAs to a 10-CTA portfolio would reduce risk by only about one-sixth as much as did adding the first nine CTAs! Obviously, the diversification benefit provided by adding CTAs to a portfolio drops quite rapidly as CTAs are added.

Another study of the relationship between risk and the number of CTAs in a portfolio appeared in the fourth quarter, 1993 issue of the *Barclay Managed Futures Report*. Figure 11.1, which is reproduced from the *Barclay* study, plots the standard deviation of a randomly selected portfolio versus the number of CTAs in the portfolio. As can be seen, the standard deviation drops precipitously as the first few CTAs are added, with the curve becoming nearly flat by the point the portfolio reaches eight CTAs.

It should also be noted that Table 11.15 and Figure 11.1 actually understate the degree of diversification achievable with a small number of CTAs because they assume random selection. If the CTAs in a portfolio are deliberately selected so that they are diversified—as they should be—equivalent risk reduction can be achieved with a smaller number of CTAs. In fact, a

---

[10]See, for example, the article by Randall Billingsley and Don Chase in *Managed Account Reports*, July 1994.

Table 11.15
RISK VERSUS NUMBER OF CTAs IN PORTFOLIO

Number of CTAs	Average Portfolio Standard Deviation	Market Standard Deviation	Percent Risk Reduction Versus Average Single CTA Portfolio	Percentages of Total Risk Reduction Achieved
1	30.325	14.281		
2	23.702	14.281	21.8	41.3
3	21.036	14.281	30.6	57.9
4	19.567	14.281	35.5	67.1
5	18.630	14.281	38.6	72.9
6	17.978	14.281	40.7	77.0
7	17.498	14.281	42.3	79.9
8	17.129	14.281	43.5	82.2
9	16.836	14.281	44.5	84.1
10	16.599	14.281	45.3	85.6
11	16.401	14.281	45.9	86.8
12	16.235	14.281	46.5	87.8
13	16.093	14.281	46.9	88.7
14	15.971	14.281	47.3	89.5
15	15.864	14.281	47.7	90.1
16	15.769	14.281	48.0	90.7
17	15.686	14.281	48.3	91.2
18	15.611	14.281	48.5	91.7
19	15.544	14.281	48.7	92.1
20	15.483	14.281	48.9	92.5
21	15.428	14.281	49.1	92.9
22	15.377	14.281	49.3	93.2
23	15.331	14.281	49.4	93.5
24	15.289	14.281	49.6	93.7
25	15.250	14.281	49.7	94.0
50	14.774	14.281	51.3	96.9
100	14.529	14.281	52.1	98.5
218	14.281	14.281	52.9	100.0

Source: Based on an unpublished study by Scott Irwin, Ohio State University. Results based on annual standard deviations of 218 CTAs in 1989.

portfolio of 5–10 well-diversified CTAs could well imply a lower risk level than a portfolio consisting of all CTAs. Why? Because a portfolio consisting of all CTAs might contain a large proportion of highly correlated CTAs (for example, trend-followers) and, hence, might well be less diversified than a portfolio with a small number of CTAs that were selected on the basis of

Figure 11.1
EFFECTS OF RANDOM DIVERSIFICATION: PORTFOLIO RISK VERSUS SIZE OF PORTFOLIO

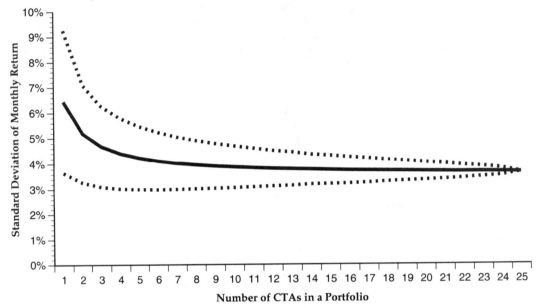

Note: Past results are not necessarily indicative of future results.
Source: Reprinted with permission from "A Random Walk Down LaSalle Street," *Barclay Managed Futures Report* 4(4), 9 (1993). Copyright 1993 by Barclay Trading Group, Ltd.

having low or negative correlations with each other. Keep in mind that the previous section demonstrated that CTAs who are relatively uncorrelated in the past are likely to continue to exhibit low correlation in the future.

In summary, one of the basic criteria in constructing a portfolio is to select CTAs who are relatively uncorrelated with each other. Assuming this is done, full diversification benefits should be achievable with as few as 4 to 7 CTAs.

CALCULATING PROFIT INCENTIVE FEES IN MULTIADVISOR FUNDS

One potential complication in multimanager funds is the payment of profit incentive fees. If the fund pays each CTA a profit incentive fee based on his or her own performance, investors will sometimes pay fees on profits they have not earned (e.g., when one or more CTAs make new highs, while other CTAs lose money in the same quarter). On the other hand, under the same circumstances, if the fund pays profit incentive fees only on the net performance of the fund, some CTAs will experience a deferral in payment (and possibly even loss) on some or all of their profit incentive fees. Although there is no perfect solution, an approach that would be fully equitable to investors, while mitigating the negative impact on CTAs, would meet the following criteria:

1. Investors are charged only on *net* profits earned by the fund.
2. Profit incentive fees charged against the fund are distributed among the CTAs in proportion to their *cumulative* relative performance.

Appendix 4 at the end of this book describes a profit incentive fee distribution methodology that fulfills these conditions for a 2-CTA fund. This appendix also contains a sample EXCEL worksheet and details the EXCEL formulas used. The calculations become significantly more complex when there are three or more CTAs. Appendix 5 at the end of the book contains an EXCEL worksheet example, as well as detailed formulas, for the 3-CTA case.

CONCLUSION

The empirical study presented in this chapter demonstrated that a multimanager combination (employing monthly rebalancing) will invariably tend to outperform a substantial majority of the individual managers within the group. Assuming that it is not possible to select a single manager that has a significant probability of outperforming *all* other managers in the *future*—a highly realistic assumption—there would always exist a multimanager combination with a higher expected return/risk than any single manager. *Therefore, if the stand-alone performance of a fund is the primary criterion, the fund developer would almost always be better served by a multimanager (as opposed to single-manager) structure.*

It should be stressed that the common argument cited to justify using a single-manager approach—that it increases the chances of achieving a well-above-average return (if one is willing to accept the higher risk)—is entirely fallacious. Why? Because by using leverage (through notional funding), it is always possible to add one or more managers to the original manager selected and achieve the *same expected return at a lower risk level.*

In short, the theoretical and empirical evidence supporting the benefits of diversification is overwhelming. Given the obvious advantages of diversification, it is interesting to consider the relative prevalence of single-manager versus multimanager funds. As of late 1995, 57 percent of all funds and pools monitored by *Managed Account Reports* were single manager. Thus, on the premise that action speaks louder than words, apparently *a significant majority of the industry does not believe that diversification is worthwhile!* (The choice of a single-manager structure over a multimanager approach implies the belief either that the disadvantages of diversification outweigh the advantages or, at the very least, that the net benefits of diversification are not sufficient to justify the added costs and work entailed in a multimanager product.) *Therefore, incredibly, the majority of the industry is employing a clearly inferior strategy: single-manager funds.*[11]

To state it bluntly, a single-manager fund often represents an ignorant approach. By definition, a single-manager fund either accepts unnecessary additional risk to achieve a given return or forgoes the potential of a higher return at the same risk level. Therefore, *if a fund developer is primarily guided by the principle of creating a quality stand-alone managed futures product for the investor*, there is rarely a reason to consider a single-manager strategy.[12] One important qualification is that a single-manager fund could be a theoretically justified investment if it is combined with other single-manager funds as part of a broader portfolio (hence the "stand-alone" specification in the previous sentence).

Any fund developer considering a single-manager approach would be guaranteed to construct an investment product with a higher *expected* return/risk by using the following step-by-step approach:

1. Identify other managers of approximately equivalent merit. (It would be absurd to claim that there weren't any.)
2. Calculate the pair correlations for these managers, and select two or more low-correlated managers.
3. Use leverage (through notional funding) if there is a desire to increase return in exchange for a commensurate increase in risk.
4. Rebalance the equity monthly. (Although monthly rebalancing flies in the face of convention, as was detailed in the preceding chapter, there is compelling evidence that this strategy significantly improves performance.)

Will this approach always outperform the single-manager alternative? Of course not, anymore than the house will always win against *every* player at the roulette wheel. However, it is a statistical certainty that the recommended multimanager method will prove to be the better choice a substantial majority

---

[11]To be precise, it is possible that a single-manager fund could include a manager who employs several highly diversified trading programs and in this sense is somewhat similar to a multimanger fund. Such exceptions, however, are probably sufficiently small as to not alter the general conclusion.

[12]Of course, there could be other motivations (that is, reasons unrelated to performance) for choosing the single-manager route. For example, a single-manager structure might be preferred by the fund developer because it is less costly to produce, requires less work, and possibly is easier to market. However, none of these reasons are relevant to the investor.

of the time (just as it is a statistical certainty that the casino will win against most roulette players). In other words, using diversification improves the odds of obtaining a more favorable return/risk outcome. Fund developers who select a single manager as opposed to a multimanager approach are deliberately selecting a strategy with lower odds. The blackjack player who draws on 18 might pull a 3, but he shouldn't confuse luck with wisdom.

12 Should Managed Futures Be Included in Investment Portfolios?

*With respect to managed futures as a portfolio asset, an invest-
ment in an equal-weighted market portfolio of either CTAs or
pools significantly enhances the performance of conventional
stock/bond portfolios.*

Edwards and Park

*The return on commodity funds was considerably lower than on
Treasury bills. This evidence would not support the addition of
commodity funds to a portfolio of bonds and stocks.*

Elton, Gruber, and Rentzler

How can two groups of researchers reach such polar conclusions? As we
will see in the course of this chapter, the apparent paradox implied by
these contradictory statements can be satisfactorily resolved, and the
weight of statistical evidence leads to a completely unambiguous answer as
to whether managed futures should be included in traditional stock/bond
portfolios.

PERFORMANCE COMPARISON
OF INDIVIDUAL SECTORS

To begin, Table 12.1 compares the return, risk (as represented by the standard deviation), and return/risk ratio of the S&P 500, long-term government
bonds, Managed Account Reports (MAR) equal-weighted commodity trading
advisor (CTA) index, and MAR equal-weighted fund/pool index for the past
15-, 10-, and 5-year periods. As can be seen, for the entire 15-year period
(1981–1995), the CTA index exhibits the highest average annual com-

Table 12.1
PERFORMANCE COMPARISONS: SP500, T-BONDS,
CTA INDEX, AND FUND/POOL INDEX

	S&P 500 Total Return	Long-Term Bond Total Return	MAR CTA Index[a]	MAR Fund/Pool Index[b]
1981–1995				
Average annual compounded return	14.75	13.51	18.02	9.47
Annualized standard deviation[c]	14.61	11.44	20.34	18.04
Modified Sharpe Ratio[d]	1.01	1.18	0.89	0.52
1986–1995				
Average annual compounded return	14.76	11.88	14.65	8.42
Annualized standard deviation[c]	15.00	9.77	16.63	15.34
Modified Sharpe Ratio[d]	0.98	1.22	0.88	0.55
1991–1995				
Average annual compounded return	16.41	13.02	6.40	2.71
Annualized standard deviation[c]	10.10	7.92	10.09	10.19
Modified Sharpe Ratio[d]	1.63	1.64	0.63	0.27
Rank				
Rank 1981–1995	2	1	3	4
Rank 1986–1995	2	1	3	4
Rank 1991–1995	2	1	3	4

[a]Managed Accounts Reports equal-weighted CTA index.
[b]Managed Accounts Reports equal-weighted fund/pool index.
[c]Monthly standard deviation multiplied by square root of 12.
[d]Average annual compounded return divided by annualized standard deviation.

pounded return. However, note that its volatility (i.e., standard deviation) is also the highest. In terms of the return/risk (i.e., modified Sharpe Ratio), which is the only relevant criterion, both the S&P 500 and T-bonds surpassed the CTA index. The commodity fund/pool index was by far the worst performer, achieving only about half the return of the CTA index, with only a moderately lower standard deviation.

The performance gap between the stock/bond investments and managed futures was even wider in the 10- and 5-year periods, particularly the latter. Interestingly, in terms of the return/risk ratio, the ranking order of the four sectors was identical in each of the three periods: (1) T-bonds; (2) S&P 500; (3) CTA index; (4) fund/pool index. The superior performance of T-bonds was due to the sector's low volatility relative to the other sectors.

The fact that managed futures consistently underperformed the S&P 500 and T-bonds only indicates relative inferiority as a single-asset investment; no implications can be drawn from these individual asset comparisons regarding the relative merit of managed futures as an *addition* to a stock/bond portfolio. The question of whether managed futures are a beneficial addition to conventional portfolios is the core subject of this chapter and is considered later.

Figure 12.1
NAV: CTA INDEX VERSUS S&P 500 AND T-BONDS

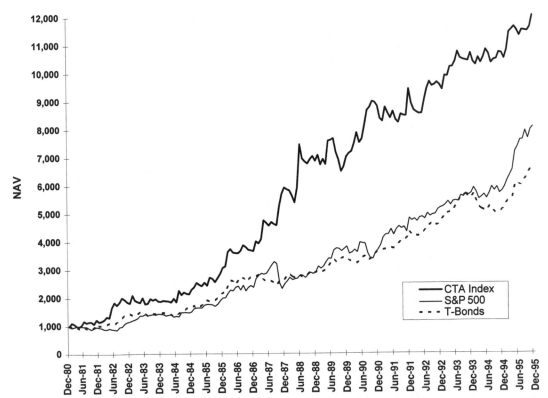

Data sources: S&P and T-bond series: Refco Information Services Inc., One World Financial Center, 200 Liberty Street, New York, NY 10281. CTA index: Managed Account Reports, 220 Fifth Avenue, New York, NY 10001.

Definitions: S&P 500 = S&P 500 total return; T-Bonds = long-term government-bond total return; CTA Index = MAR equal-weighted CTA index.

Figure 12.1 compares the net asset value (NAV) of the MAR CTA index with the NAVs of the S&P 500 total return and the long-term government-bond total return. That Figure 12.1 seems to imply that the CTA index out-performed the S&P 500 and T-bonds is misleading because the CTA index was much more volatile. To visually compare the NAVs of different invest-ments in a meaningful way, it is necessary to adjust the series so that the risk levels are equal. Such a methodology is introduced later in this chapter. Fig-ure 12.2 compares the NAV of the MAR fund/pool index with the NAVs of the S&P 500 total return and the long-term government-bond total return. The fund/pool index not only exhibited significantly greater volatility than the S&P 500 or T-bonds, but it also realized substantially smaller returns, as implied by its much lower NAV.

Figure 12.2
NAV: FUND/POOL INDEX VERSUS S&P 500 AND T-BONDS

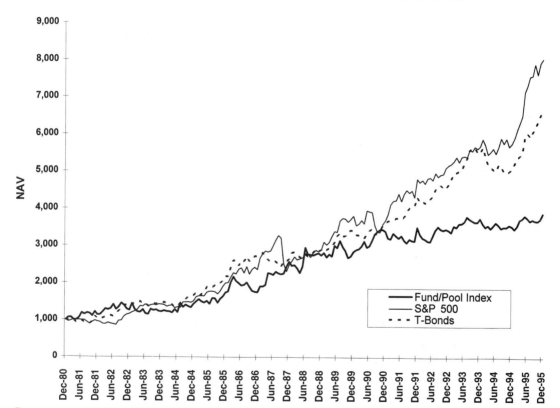

Data sources: S&P and T-bond series: Refco Information Services Inc., One World Financial Center, 200 Liberty Street, New York, NY 10281. Fund/pool index: Managed Account Reports, 220 Fifth Avenue, New York, NY 10001.

Definitions: S&P 500 = S&P 500 total return; T-Bonds = long-term government-bond total return; fund/pool index = MAR equal-weighted fund/pool index.

WHY DOES THE FUND/POOL INDEX UNDERPERFORM THE CTA INDEX?

One striking feature evident in both Table 12.1 and Figures 12.1 and 12.2 is the tremendously poorer performance of the fund/pool index vis-à-vis the CTA index. Why the wide chasm between these two measures, given the fact that public commodity funds and private commodity pools allocate their assets to CTAs? There is no mystery. The primary explanation is that funds and pools (particularly the former) have a significantly higher average cost structure than direct investments with CTAs, which are often held by institutional investors who typically are charged lower fees and substantially lower commissions. In their journal article, "Investment Performance of Public Commodity Pools: 1979–1990," Irwin, Krukemyer, and Zulauf[1] address the issue of the adverse impact of high costs on public commodity pools (i.e., commodity funds):

> Performance problems of public commodity pools frequently have been attributed to high operating costs . . . . Estimates of the total operating costs of public commodity pools range from 17% to 19% of annual equity . . . .
>
> Costs for institutional commodity pools are 10% to 12% of annual equity, approximately seven percentage points less than costs for public commodity pools. The biggest reduction is in commissions . . . .
>
> The cost of investing in public commodity pools is often mentioned as a reason for their unattractive performance. When costs are reduced to the level which large institutional pension funds have been able to obtain, average returns to the market portfolio of pools exceed stock and bond portfolio break-even levels in all cases . . . Therefore, reducing cost to investors has the potential to make a portfolio of public commodity pools a desirable addition to stock and bond portfolios.

This study helps explain the wide gap between the CTA index and fund/pool index returns. The implication is that the subpar performance of the fund/pool index, as summarized in Table 12.1 and illustrated in Figure 12.2, may have more to do with the high cost structure embedded in these results rather than inferior investment performance. Therefore, for investors paying lower fees and commissions, the CTA index results are more relevant than those of the fund/pool index.

Several other factors may also contribute to the significantly lower returns exhibited by the fund/pool index vis-à-vis the CTA index. To begin, as implied by the moderately lower standard deviation of the fund/pool index, on average, funds and pools probably use less leverage than individual CTAs. This factor, however, would not reduce the return/risk ratio, since the lower leverage would reduce risk and return commensurably.

---

[1]Scott H. Irwin, Terry R. Krukemyer, and Carl R. Zulauf, "Investment Performance of Public Commodity Pools: 1979–1990," *The Journal of Futures Markets* 13(7):403–434 (1993).

In addition, it is possible that the CTA selection process used by funds and pools as a group, as well as the timing of their launch dates, may contribute to below-average performance. Some possible examples include:

- The tendency of funds and pools to choose CTAs who are on hot streaks may increase the chances of picking CTAs who experience large retracements in the periods after they have been selected. The research in Chapter 9 supports such a hypothesis.
- The proclivity of funds and pools to select well-established CTAs who already have large assets under management may push the average order size of those CTAs to levels that result in increased slippage, causing them to experience poorer performance than they would have realized with a smaller asset base.
- For marketing reasons, funds and pools are probably most likely to be launched after periods of particularly favorable industry performance and least likely to be started after periods of poor performance. Given the oscillatory nature of managed futures returns, any such timing bias could easily result in below-average performance.

It should be stressed that, in contrast to the cost difference factor, this list of explanations is speculative. Existing data are insufficient to determine whether the performance inferiority of funds and pools vis-à-vis individual CTAs is almost entirely due to cost differences, or whether the CTA selection process used by funds and pools or the timing of their launch dates are also contributing factors. In either event, cost differences are certainly the dominant reason among these possible explanations for the wide performance gap.

Finally, two additional factors that could cause a net upward bias in a CTA index vis-à-vis a pool/fund index are (1) the types of distortions possible in individual CTA returns (as detailed in various sections of Part One); and (2) the possibility that the final month or two of results for some CTAs who do poorly enough to go out of business may be unobtainable and hence may fail to be included in a CTA index. (However, the more serious type of "survivorship bias"—the failure to incorporate data for defunct CTAs—is not a factor.) These two influences are impossible to quantify, but they are probably less significant than the cost–difference effect.

THE CHOICE OF A PERFORMANCE COMPARISON MEASURE

As was fully explained in Chapter 3, return *alone* is an incomplete measure. It is *always* necessary to measure performance by means of both return and risk, either considered independently or as a ratio. It should be stressed that the common perception among some risk-tolerant investors that a higher return investment with a lower return/risk ratio might be preferable to an investment with the reverse characteristics is entirely fallacious. Why? Because by using leverage, the investment with the higher return/risk ratio, but lower return, could always be made to yield a higher return at the same risk level, or equivalently, the same return at a lower risk level. (As will be explained later in this chapter, stock and bond investments can be leveraged through the use of futures, while managed futures can be leveraged through notional funding, as we discussed in Chapter 2.)

In this chapter we use the modified Sharpe Ratio (return divided by standard deviation) as the comparative performance measure. The modified Sharpe Ratio differs from the conventional Sharpe Ratio in that it does not subtract the risk-free return from the investment return in the numerator of the ratio.

The modified Sharpe Ratio is used instead of the Sharpe Ratio because it provides a better *relative* gauge in comparing different portfolios *with each other*. For example, assume Portfolio A has an average annual return of 10 percent and an annualized standard deviation of 10 percent; Portfolio B has an average annual return of 9 percent and the same standard deviation; and the risk-free return is 8 percent. The conventional Sharpe Ratio value of Portfolio A would be double that of Portfolio B [(10 − 8) ÷ 10 = 0.2 versus (9 − 8) ÷ 10 = 0.1], even though its performance is only slightly better. In contrast, the modified Sharpe Ratio would provide a much more representative *relative* performance gauge, showing Portfolio A to be only modestly better than Portfolio B, as is indeed the case (10 ÷ 10 = 1.0 versus 9 ÷ 10 = 0.9).

As a related point, which was illustrated in Chapter 3, the conventional Sharpe Ratio can be significantly affected by changes in leverage, whereas the modified Sharpe Ratio is completely unaffected by leverage. It is obviously undesirable to use a performance measure that can yield different relative performance rankings just because leverage is changed (assuming everything else remains the same).

It should also be noted that the numerator of the modified Sharpe Ratio uses an annualized geometric return (equivalent to the average annual compounded return), as opposed to an annualized arithmetic return. As was discussed in Chapter 8 and illustrated in Table 8.1, an arithmetic return can be misleading. Whereas a geometric return will always show a higher value for the investment with a higher cumulative return, this is not necessarily the case for an arithmetic return. The annualized geometric return is precisely equivalent to the average annual compounded return, that is, the annual return that when compounded yields the ending equity given the starting equity.

STOCK/BOND PORTFOLIOS VIS-À-VIS SINGLE-SECTOR INVESTMENTS

Before examining the effect of adding managed futures to stock/bond portfolios, it is useful to first examine the effect of diversifying between both of these sectors as opposed to investing in only one. Table 12.2 compares 100 percent stock and 100 percent bond investments with various mixed allocations. The results are depicted by year for start dates ranging from 1981 to 1991 (all ending in 1995, the latest available year at this writing). The results are also shown for all possible 10-year periods during 1981–1995. There is

Table 12.2
MODIFIED SHARPE RATIO: STOCK/BOND PORTFOLIOS,
NO REBALANCING[a]

	Portfolio Relative Weights (%)										
S&P 500	100	90	80	70	60	50	40	30	20	10	0
T-bonds	0	10	20	30	40	50	60	70	80	90	100

Start Year	Modified Sharpe Ratio: Periods Ending 12/31/1995										
1981	1.010	1.068	1.128	1.186	1.238	1.280	1.305	**1.309**	1.288	1.244	1.181
1982	1.111	1.173	1.240	1.309	1.378	1.441	1.490	**1.516**	1.509	1.466	1.389
1983	1.109	1.153	1.200	1.251	1.302	1.350	1.387	**1.404**	1.388	1.331	1.231
1984	1.048	1.111	1.178	1.249	1.320	1.385	1.438	**1.467**	1.463	1.422	1.346
1985	1.100	1.154	1.212	1.274	1.338	1.399	1.450	**1.479**	1.476	1.430	1.342
1986	0.985	1.033	1.085	1.143	1.203	1.262	1.312	**1.344**	1.344	1.301	1.216
1987	0.975	1.018	1.068	1.124	1.187	1.254	1.319	1.370	**1.384**	1.339	1.228
1988	1.332	1.380	1.430	1.480	1.528	1.570	1.601	**1.613**	1.600	1.557	1.484
1989	1.288	1.347	1.408	1.472	1.535	1.593	1.640	1.667	**1.667**	1.635	1.571
1990	1.089	1.149	1.212	1.276	1.339	1.396	1.444	1.478	**1.493**	1.487	1.458
1991	1.631	1.693	1.755	1.812	1.861	1.893	**1.903**	1.884	1.832	1.750	1.644

Start Year	Modified Sharpe Ratio: 10-Year Periods Beginning in Given Start Year										
1981	0.846	0.903	0.961	1.019	1.072	1.117	1.147	**1.158**	1.148	1.117	1.068
1982	1.059	1.121	1.189	1.262	1.335	1.406	1.466	1.504	**1.510**	1.476	1.403
1983	1.028	1.069	1.114	1.163	1.214	1.263	1.305	**1.329**	1.322	1.272	1.178
1984	0.960	1.027	1.101	1.181	1.264	1.345	1.417	1.468	**1.485**	1.462	1.399
1985	0.938	0.984	1.033	1.087	1.142	1.196	1.242	1.271	**1.272**	1.236	1.162
1986	0.985	1.033	1.085	1.143	1.203	1.262	1.312	**1.344**	1.344	1.301	1.216

[a]Modified Sharpe Ratio defined as average annual compound return divided by annualized standard deviation. S&P 500 total return used to represent stock return; long-term government-bond total return used to represent T-bond return.

a strong tendency for the 30 percent stock/70 percent bond allocation to be the optimal portfolio in each period. This was true in 9 out of the 16 periods shown. (Note that the 10-year period beginning in 1986 appears in both sections of the table. Therefore, there are a total of 16—not 17—different periods examined.) In six of the remaining seven periods, the 20 percent stock/80 percent bond allocation was the best portfolio.

Note the following two key observations:

1. *All* the stock/bond portfolios have higher modified Sharpe Ratios than the corresponding 100 percent stock and 100 percent bond portfolios in *every* period examined! This is but one more example of the power of diversification. Just as diversifying among multiple CTAs was shown in Chapter 11 to provide a substantive advantage over single-manager investments, diversifying in different sectors provides a consistent advantage over single-sector investments. Recall that a higher return/risk ratio guarantees that a higher return can be achieved at an equivalent risk level by using leverage.
2. The best portfolios weight bonds much more heavily than stocks, even though stocks have a higher return (see Table 12.1). The heavier allocation to bonds can be explained by the fact that bonds are less volatile than stocks (by a greater degree than the return advantage of stocks).

Table 12.3 is the counterpart of Table 12.2 under the assumption that assets are rebalanced monthly to restore the original sector allocations. For example, assume a $1 million portfolio using a 30 percent S&P 500/70 percent T-bond portfolio, which realizes a first month return of +10 percent in the S&P 500 and –5 percent in T-bonds. With no rebalancing, the second month assets would be $330,000 for the S&P 500 and $665,000 for T-bonds. With rebalancing the asset allocation split would be $298,500 for the S&P 500 and $696,000 for T-bonds. In other words, the original 30 percent/70 percent split would be maintained by reallocating assets at the end of each month. In the case of rebalanced portfolios as well, a 30 percent S&P 500/70 percent T-bond split is the optimal allocation in most periods. In this instance, however, the exception periods are approximately evenly divided between the 40 percent S&P 500/60 percent T-bond and the 20 percent S&P 500/80 percent T-bond allocations, as opposed to being concentrated in the latter.

Table 12.4 expresses the modified Sharpe Ratios of the rebalanced portfolios as percentages of their static portfolio counterparts. Percentages greater than 100 imply that rebalancing results in a superior return/risk ratio. Note that only 4 out of the 154 portfolio/period combinations[2] (highlighted

---

[2]Recall that the 1986–1995 period appears in both sections of the table, but is counted only once.

Table 12.3
MODIFIED SHARPE RATIO: STOCK/BOND PORTFOLIOS WITH MONTHLY REBALANCING*[a]*

	Portfolio Relative Weights (%)									
S&P 500	100	90	80	70	60	50	40	30	20	10	0
T-bonds	0	10	20	30	40	50	60	70	80	90	100

Start Year	Modified Sharpe Ratio: Periods Ending 12/31/1995										
1981	1.010	1.079	1.149	1.215	1.272	1.315	**1.338**	1.334	1.305	1.251	1.181
1982	1.111	1.189	1.269	1.350	1.426	1.489	1.532	**1.545**	1.524	1.470	1.389
1983	1.109	1.178	1.247	1.315	1.376	1.422	**1.445**	1.438	1.397	1.325	1.231
1984	1.048	1.126	1.207	1.289	1.368	1.435	1.482	**1.499**	1.481	1.428	1.346
1985	1.100	1.174	1.252	1.330	1.403	1.464	1.505	**1.516**	1.492	1.431	1.342
1986	0.985	1.052	1.124	1.197	1.267	1.327	1.369	**1.383**	1.361	1.303	1.216
1987	0.975	1.043	1.116	1.193	1.270	1.342	1.397	**1.422**	1.402	1.335	1.228
1988	1.332	1.393	1.453	1.510	1.562	1.602	1.626	**1.628**	1.605	1.556	1.484
1989	1.288	1.356	1.427	1.497	1.563	1.621	1.663	1.683	**1.675**	1.637	1.571
1990	1.089	1.153	1.218	1.285	1.349	1.408	1.456	1.489	**1.502**	1.492	1.458
1991	1.631	1.703	1.772	1.834	1.883	1.913	**1.916**	1.890	1.833	1.749	1.644

Start Year	Modified Sharpe Ratio: 10-Year Periods Beginning in Given Start Year										
1981	0.846	0.915	0.984	1.050	1.110	1.157	1.185	**1.190**	1.170	1.128	1.068
1982	1.059	1.138	1.222	1.308	1.391	1.464	1.519	**1.544**	1.533	1.484	1.403
1983	1.028	1.095	1.163	1.231	1.294	1.345	**1.375**	1.374	1.340	1.271	1.178
1984	0.960	1.043	1.132	1.225	1.318	1.403	1.471	1.509	**1.510**	1.471	1.399
1985	0.938	1.003	1.070	1.139	1.204	1.259	1.298	**1.310**	1.291	1.240	1.162
1986	0.985	1.052	1.124	1.197	1.267	1.327	1.369	**1.383**	1.361	1.303	1.216

*[a]*Modified Sharpe Ratio defined as average annual compound return divided by annualized standard deviation. S&P 500 total return used to represent stock return; long-term government-bond total return used to represent T-bond return.

by shading) did better without rebalancing. Once again, rebalancing is shown to be an investment strategy that appears to provide a consistent edge. (It will be recalled that the empirical study cited in Chapter 10 demonstrated that monthly rebalancing of assets among the CTAs in a multimanager pool or fund tended to improve performance in a decisive majority of cases.)

Figure 12.3 compares the NAV of the optimal stock/bond portfolio— 30 percent S&P 500/70 percent T-bond (with rebalancing)[3]—with the

---

[3]Although the 40 percent S&P 500/60 percent T-bond portfolio actually has a slightly higher modified Sharpe Ratio for the maximum length 15-year period, the 30 percent S&P 500/70 percent T-bond portfolio is superior in a large majority of the periods surveyed.

Table 12.4
MODIFIED SHARPE RATIOS: STOCK/BOND REBALANCED
PORTFOLIOS AS % OF CORRESPONDING STATIC PORTFOLIO[a]

S&P 500	90	80	70	60	50	40	30	20	10
T-bonds	10	20	30	40	50	60	70	80	90
Start Year				Portfolios Ending 12/31/95					
1981	101.0	101.8	102.4	102.7	102.8	102.5	102.0	101.3	100.6
1982	101.3	102.4	103.1	103.5	103.4	102.8	102.0	101.0	100.3
1983	102.1	103.9	105.2	105.7	105.3	104.1	102.4	100.6	**99.6**
1984	101.3	102.5	103.2	103.6	103.6	103.1	102.2	101.2	100.4
1985	101.8	103.3	104.4	104.9	104.7	103.8	102.5	101.1	100.1
1986	101.9	103.5	104.7	105.3	105.2	104.3	102.9	101.3	100.1
1987	102.4	104.5	106.1	107.0	107.0	105.9	103.8	101.3	**99.7**
1988	100.9	101.6	102.0	102.2	102.0	101.6	101.0	100.4	100.0
1989	100.7	101.3	101.7	101.8	101.7	101.4	101.0	100.5	100.1
1990	100.3	100.5	100.7	100.8	100.8	100.8	100.7	100.6	100.3
1991	100.6	101.0	101.2	101.2	101.0	100.7	100.3	100.0	**99.9**
Start Year				10-Year Portfolios Beginning in Given Year					
1981	101.3	102.4	103.1	103.6	103.6	103.4	102.7	101.9	100.9
1982	101.5	102.7	103.7	104.2	104.2	103.6	102.7	101.5	100.5
1983	102.4	104.4	105.9	106.6	106.5	105.3	103.4	101.3	**99.9**
1984	101.6	102.9	103.8	104.3	104.3	103.8	102.8	101.7	100.6
1985	102.0	103.6	104.8	105.4	105.3	104.5	103.1	101.5	100.3
1986	101.9	103.5	104.7	105.3	105.2	104.3	102.9	101.3	100.1

[a]Rebalanced portfolios adjusted monthly to maintain indicated relative percentages. Static portfolios start at indicated relative percentages and are not subsequently adjusted.

NAV of a 100 percent S&P 500 investment. In similar fashion, Figure 12.4 compares the NAV of this same stock/bond portfolio with the NAV of a 100 percent T-bond investment. At surface glance, these charts seem to imply that the optimal stock/bond portfolio provides little improvement over the 100 percent stock and 100 percent T-bond investments. In fact, the 100 percent S&P 500 portfolio actually has a higher NAV. Although these charts seem to contradict the superiority of stock/bond portfolios to single-sector investments implied by Table 12.3, there is no inconsistency. The problem is that in both Figures 12.3 and 12.4, the depicted series differ in terms of risk, making visual comparisons of NAVs difficult, if not misleading. This problem can be eliminated by equalizing the risk levels of the series depicted.

Figure 12.3
NAV COMPARISON: BEST STOCK/BOND PORTFOLIO (WITH REBALANCING) VERSUS 100 PERCENT STOCK PORTFOLIO

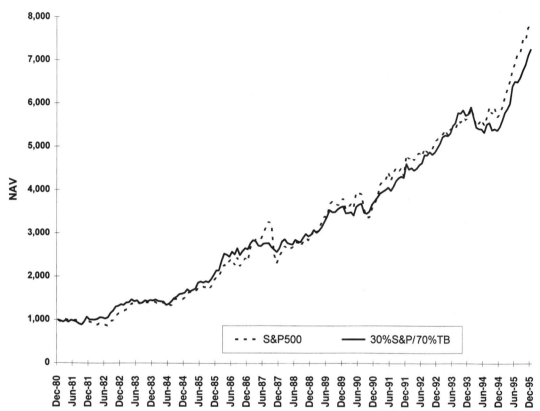

Data sources: S&P and T-bond series: Refco Information Services Inc., One World Financial Center, 200 Liberty Street, New York, NY 10281.

Definitions: S&P 500 = S&P 500 total return; T-Bonds = long-term government-bond total return.

USING LEVERAGE TO EQUALIZE RISK LEVELS

The stock/bond portfolios have lower risk levels (as represented by the standard deviations) than the 100 percent stock or 100 percent bond portfolios. To equalize the risk level of a stock/bond portfolio with the risk level of a single-sector investment, we increase its leverage by the ratio of the standard deviations. For example, for the 1981–1995 period, the standard deviation of a 100 percent S&P 500 portfolio was 4.216, while the standard deviation of the 30 percent S&P 500/70 percent T-bond portfolio was 3.056.

Figure 12.4
NAV COMPARISON: BEST STOCK/BOND PORTFOLIO (WITH REBALANCING) VERSUS 100 PERCENT BOND PORTFOLIO

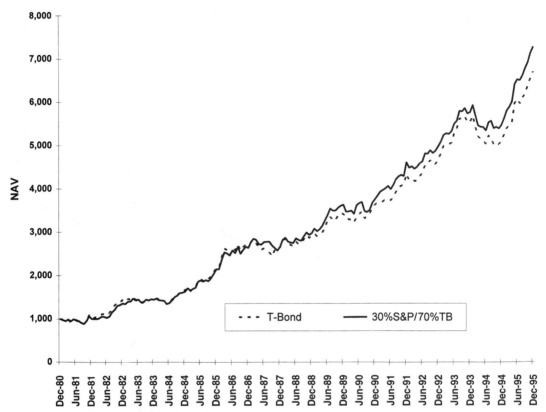

Data sources: S&P and T-bond series: Refco Information Services Inc., One World Financial Center, 200 Liberty Street, New York, NY 10281.

Definitions: S&P = S&P 500 total return; T-Bond and TB = long-term government-bond total return.

The ratio of these standard deviations is equal to 1.38. Therefore by increasing the leverage of the 30 percent S&P 500/70 percent T-bond portfolio by a factor of 1.38, we would have an investment with the same standard deviation (i.e., risk level) as the 100 percent stock investment. The NAV of this leveraged stock/bond portfolio could then be directly compared with the NAV of a 100 percent stock portfolio.

The leverage of a stock/bond portfolio can be easily increased through the use of futures. Before using futures to increase leverage, however, it is first necessary to ascertain that futures provide a close approximation of actual stock and bond positions. The total return of a futures position is approximately equal to the profit/loss due to price changes plus T-bill interest income. The reason for adding T-bill interest income is that a futures position requires only a small percentage of the investment value as margin, and even most of the margin earns interest. Therefore, it is a reasonable assumption that virtually the entire face value of a futures investment will be available to earn interest income. If futures are a good proxy for a stock or bond investment, the total return of the futures position (i.e., profit/loss of the S&P 500 or T-bond futures position plus interest income) should approximately equal the total return of the actual instrument (stocks or bonds).

Figure 12.5 compares the NAVs based on the actual market and futures market total returns for the S&P 500. As can be seen, the two series are closely correlated. The difference between the two series is magnified by the compounding effect and is smaller than it appears. Specifically, the difference between the compounded returns of the two NAV series is only equal to 0.6 percent per annum. Figure 12.6 compares the NAVs based on the actual market and futures market total returns for long-term T-bonds. As can

Figure 12.5
S&P 500 TOTAL RETURN NAV: ACTUAL MARKET VERSUS FUTURES

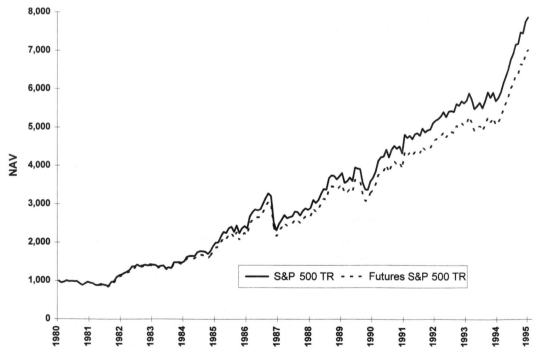

Data sources: S&P and T-bond series: Refco Information Services Inc., One World Financial Center, 200 Liberty Street, New York, NY 10281.

Definitions: S&P 500 TR = S&P 500 total return.

Figure 12.6
**LONG-TERM T-BOND TOTAL RETURN NAV: ACTUAL MARKET
VERSUS FUTURES**

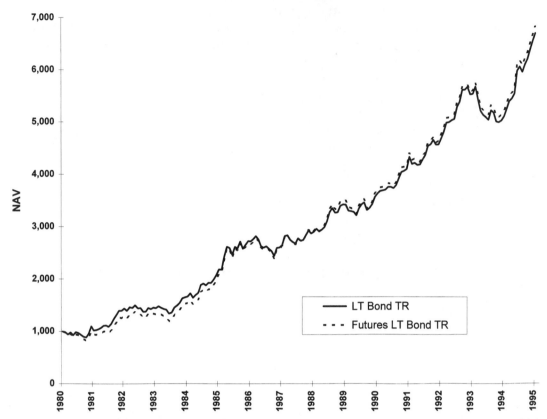

Data sources: S&P and T-bond series: Refco Information Services Inc., One World Financial Center, 200 Liberty Street, New York, NY 10281.

Definitions: LT Bond TR = long-term government-bond total return.

be seen, these two series are very closely correlated. In fact, the difference between the compounded returns of the two NAV series is equal to a minuscule 0.2 percent per annum. Thus, it appears that futures positions provide excellent proxies for actual investments in the S&P 500 and long-term government T-bonds.

In order to leverage a stock or bond position, it is assumed that the increase in leverage beyond a 100 percent investment is achieved by implementing a long futures position equal to the dollar equivalent of the incremental investment. For example, assume an investor with a $1.2 million account wishes to hold an S&P 500 position leveraged by a factor of 1.5:1 (that is, the equivalent of a $1.8 million stock position). The investor can achieve this position by being fully invested in an S&P 500 basket of stocks (or more conveniently, an S&P 500 index-based mutual fund) and buying an S&P 500 futures position equivalent to a face value of $600,000 (e.g., two contracts if the S&P 500 is at 600).[4]

The total income of this leveraged investment will equal the total return of the S&P 500 plus the profit/loss on the futures position. Note that in this type of application, T-bill income is not added to the futures position return. Why? Because all the funds are being used in the actual market investment. Therefore, there are no available funds to earn interest. If, however, the entire position were placed in futures (as opposed to placing the face-value amount in the actual market and just the excess leverage portion in futures), T-bill interest would be added for that segment of the futures position equal to the face value of the investment (the first $1.2 million in the foregoing example).

We are now ready to compare a leveraged stock/bond portfolio with 100 percent stock and 100 percent T-bond investments. As was mentioned earlier in this section, for the entire 15-year period (1981–1995), the standard deviation of a 100 percent S&P 500 portfolio was 4.216, while the standard deviation of the 30 percent S&P 500/70 percent T-bond portfolio was 3.056. To equalize the risk levels of these two investments, we increase the leverage of the stock/bond portfolio by the ratio of these standard deviations (1.38). The monthly percent returns of this leveraged position (assuming rebalancing) will equal 30 percent of the total return of the S&P 500 plus 70 percent of the total return of the long-term T-bond index plus 11.4 percent of the profit/loss of a long S&P 500 futures position ($0.30 \times 0.38 = 0.114$ or 11.4%) plus 26.6 percent of the profit/loss of a long T-bond futures position ($0.70 \times 0.38 = 0.266$ or 26.6%).[5]

Figure 12.7 compares the NAV of this leveraged stock/bond investment with the NAV of a 100 percent stock position. As can be seen, once leverage is applied to eliminate the risk difference between the two investments,[6] the stock/bond portfolio is clearly superior to the pure stock portfolio by a

---

[4]To avoid unnecessarily complicating the exposition, we ignore the margin funds needed for the futures position. This is a justifiable simplification because only a small portion of the face value of the futures position is needed as margin and most of the margin funds earn interest income.

[5]The S&P 500 total return, long-term T-bond index total return, profit/loss in long S&P 500 futures position, and profit/loss in long T-bond position are all expressed as monthly percent returns.

[6]Although it may appear that the leveraged stock/bond portfolio in Figure 12.7 is more volatile than the 100 percent stock position, this is entirely a consequence of the fact that equal percentage equity swings will appear larger in the stock/bond NAV because of its greater value. If the chart had been plotted on a log scale—a graphic representation in which equal *percentage* (as opposed to *nominal*) swings appear to be of equal magnitude—the two NAV curves would have appeared to be equivalent in terms of volatility.

Figure 12.7
NAV COMPARISON: LEVERAGED BEST STOCK/BOND PORTFOLIO (WITH REBALANCING) VERSUS 100 PERCENT STOCK PORTFOLIO

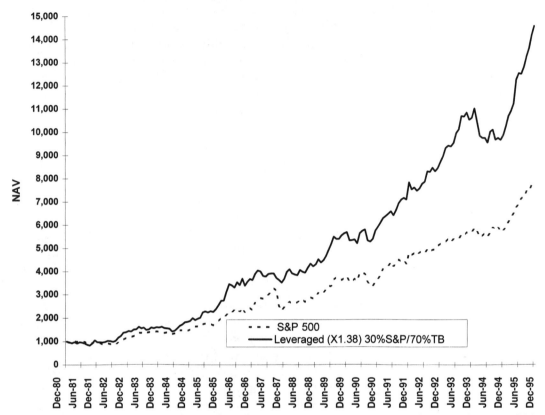

Data sources: S&P and T-bond series: Refco Information Services Inc., One World Financial Center, 200 Liberty Street, New York, NY 10281.

Definitions: S&P 500 = S&P 500 total return; TB = long-term government-bond total return.

Notes: Stock/bond portfolio leveraged by factor (1.38) to equalize standard deviation with 100 percent S&P 500 portfolio.

wide margin—a fact that was hidden in the comparison using an unleveraged stock/bond portfolio (Figure 12.3).

Figure 12.8 provides an analogous comparison of the leveraged stock/bond portfolio with a 100 percent T-bond position. In this case, the ratio of the two standard deviations is much smaller ($3.303 \div 3.056 = 1.08$). Leveraging the 30 percent S&P 500/70 percent T-bond portfolio by 1.08 equalizes its risk to the risk of the 100 percent T-bond portfolio. Here too, although the degree of improvement is smaller, once the two investments are equalized in terms of risk, it is clear that the stock/bond portfolio outperforms a pure T-bond investment.

Figure 12.8
NAV COMPARISON: LEVERAGED BEST STOCK/BOND PORTFOLIO (WITH REBALANCING) VERSUS 100 PERCENT T-BOND PORTFOLIO

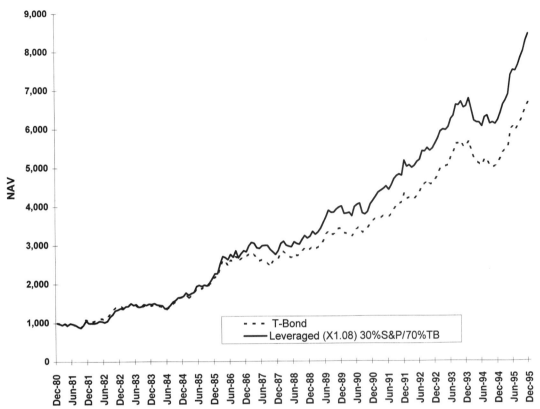

Data sources: S&P and T-bond series: Refco Information Services Inc., One World Financial Center, 200 Liberty Street, New York, NY 10281.

Definitions: S&P = S&P 500 total return; T-Bond = long-term government-bond total return.

Notes: Stock/bond portfolio leveraged by factor (1.08) to equalize standard deviation with 100 percent T-bond portfolio.

INVESTMENT IMPLICATIONS FOR THE STOCK/BOND INVESTOR

Although there may be periods when either stocks or bonds outperform the other sector to such an extent that a pure stock or bond investment might fare better than a combined portfolio, such periods are unlikely to be either predictable or sustained. Consequently, for a long-term investor, a combined stock/bond portfolio would always be preferable to a sole stock or bond investment. By increasing the leverage of the stock/bond portfolio (through the use of futures) by a factor that will equalize the risk to the considered alternative single-sector investment (e.g., 100 percent stocks), the investor can expect to achieve a *higher return* than in the single-sector investment at an *equivalent risk*.

The practical implications of the foregoing discussion for the traditional stock/bond investor is that performance can be enhanced by employing the following step-by-step procedure:

1. The investor needs to decide on the allocation of funds between stocks and bonds. The analysis of this chapter, which was based on data for the 1981–1995 period, suggests that a mix between 20 percent S&P 500/80 percent T-bond and 40 percent S&P 500/60 percent T-bond appears optimal. Future investors may wish to consider broader data periods (either beginning before 1981, extending beyond 1995, or both) to determine the preferred mix.

A long-term government T-bond fund and an S&P 500 index-based fund could be used to establish the base position for the assets available. Alternatively, futures could be used to establish a base position with a face value equal to the available assets, with the funds being invested in T-bills or money market instruments.[7] For example, assume a $3 million account, a

---

[7]Although using the futures market leaves almost all funds free to earn short-term interest income, T-bond futures positions will not earn coupon income, while S&P futures will not earn dividend income. Moreover, the participation of arbitrageurs and rational investors will assure that the spreads between nearby and forward futures contracts will eliminate any advantage in either a futures market or cash market investment. For example, since T-bill rates are invariably higher than dividend rates, forward S&P futures months always trade at a premium to nearby months. Consequently, the T-bill/dividend differential will be offset by the higher price paid for the forward contract when a futures position is rolled over.

If, for example, nearby and forward futures months traded at nearly equal prices, investors in the S&P 500 could liquidate their holdings, buy an equivalent amount of S&P futures, and invest the freed-up assets in T bills or a money market fund. These steps would maintain the same investment while increasing income by the difference between short-term interest rates and the average dividend yield. Such transactions would drive up the price of the forward S&P contract toward its theoretical level (i.e., the level that precisely offsets the T-bill/dividend differential).

If, on the other hand, the spread was significantly greater than the theoretical level, arbitrageurs could earn a risk-free profit by selling futures and buying an equivalent amount of stock. The futures and actual market positions will converge in price at expiration, with the profit on this convergence, by definition, exceeding the T-bill/dividend differential lost by holding a long actual stock/short futures position. This arbitrage activity will drive down the price of the forward futures position close to its theoretical level.

The bottom line is that there is no significant edge in an actual market position versus a futures position or vice versa. Figures 12.5 and 12.6 empirically support this theoretical conclusion.

40 percent S&P 500/60 percent T-bond allocation, an S&P futures price of 600, and a T-bond futures price of 120. In this example, a proxy stock/bond portfolio could be established by buying 4 S&P futures and 15 T-bond futures. (The contract value of S&P futures is 500 times the price, or $300,000 in our example; the contract value of T-bond futures is 1,000 times the price, or $120,000 in our example. The specified 40/60 S&P/ T-bond split would result in an allocation of $1.2 million to S&P futures and $1.8 to T-bond futures. Dividing these allocations by the contract values yields 4 S&P futures and 15 T-bond futures.)

It should be noted that commissions are not a significant factor in holding a futures position. A proxy long futures position requires only four trades a year: one at each contract rollover. Assuming a $20 round-turn commission rate, the $3.0 million portfolio described in our example would incur annual commission costs of $1,520 (4 trades × 19 contracts × $20 = $1,520), which is equal to a mere 0.05 percent of the asset base. Because commissions have such a minor impact, they are ignored in all the calculations and examples in this chapter.

2. The investor then needs to decide on a leverage factor. For example, an investor might increase leverage by a factor that equalizes the portfolio risk to the risk of a 100 percent stock position, or the risk of a 100 percent bond position, or some point in between. Risk-tolerant investors, who are willing to accept higher risk in exchange for higher return, might even choose a leverage factor that would raise the portfolio risk above the risk level of a 100 percent stock investment. On the other hand, risk-averse investors might choose not to use any leverage, effectively placing the entire benefit of diversification on the risk side. For example, if the estimated return of a 100% stock portfolio and a 30 percent S&P 500/70 percent T-bond portfolio were approximately equal, this latter approach would provide an investment with the same expected return as a 100 percent stock investment, but with a significantly lower risk level. In any event, the choice of a leverage factor, if any, depends on the individual investor's risk tolerance, which is an entirely subjective matter.

3. Once a leverage factor is determined, the investor would implement long S&P 500 and T-bond futures positions with a face value equal to the desired increase in leverage. Some specific examples were provided in the previous section.[8]

---

[8]For all but very large investors, individual futures contracts, particularly S&P futures, are too large to make exact leverage adjustments. These investors could use a stock-index-based fund and a long-term government-bond fund (as supplements or even substitutes for futures) to make fine-tuning adjustments. (An alternative that may be feasible for some investors is the use of smaller-sized futures contracts, such as the NYFE stock index contract and the MidAm T-bond contract.)

4. At the end of each month, the portfolio would be rebalanced—that is, funds would be reallocated so as to restore the original percentage breakdown of the investment between stocks and bonds (e.g., 30 percent stocks/70 percent bonds).

ADDING MANAGED FUTURES TO STOCK/BOND PORTFOLIOS

CTA Index-Based Results

In the previous sections we have established that a combined stock/bond portfolio is clearly superior to either a pure stock or pure bond investment. In this section we will examine whether adding managed futures to a stock/bond portfolio improves or hinders performance. We use the MAR equal-weighted CTA index as a proxy for managed futures.

Before proceeding, it is important to recall that, as was demonstrated in Chapter 5, a CTA index will tend to significantly understate the average risk level (or equivalently, overstate the average return/risk level) that can be expected in a single-manager investment. Therefore the conclusions of the following analysis can only be assumed to apply to an investor using a well-diversified managed futures component. Fortunately, as was shown in Chapter 11, diversification among as few as four to seven relatively uncorrelated CTAs can achieve a diversification level approximately equivalent to an investment in all the CTAs of the index. (Smaller investors can achieve equivalent diversification by investing in one or two multimanager funds that are themselves well diversified.)

Table 12.5 summarizes the modified Sharpe Ratios for various stock/bond/CTA portfolio combinations (assuming no rebalancing) in eight different survey periods. The table contains all combinations of stock/bond/CTA portfolios (at 10 percent increment levels), subject to the condition that no sector exceed 70 percent of the total portfolio. The table lists portfolios in ascending order of the percentage allocation to managed futures, beginning with no allocation, and ranging to a maximum allocation of 70 percent. Within each given level of managed futures allocation, portfolios are listed in descending order of the S&P 500 percentage of the portfolio (or equivalently, ascending order of the T-bond percentage). For example, for a managed futures allocation of 20 percent, the first listed portfolio is 70 percent S&P 500/10 percent T-bond/20 percent CTA, the next is 60 percent S&P 500/20 percent T-bond/20 percent CTA, and so on until the final portfolio of 10 percent S&P 500/70 percent T-bond/20 percent CTA.

Table 12.5
MODIFIED SHARPE RATIOS: STOCK/BOND/CTA INDEX
PORTFOLIOS, NO REBALANCING[a]

			15-Year Period	10-Year Period	5-Year Period	Other 10-Year Periods				
		Start	1981–	1986–	1991–	1981–	1982–	1983–	1984–	1985–
		End	1995	1995	1995	1990	1991	1992	1993	1994
Portfolio Relative Weights (%)										
S&P 500	T-Bonds	CTA Index								
70	30	0	1.186	1.143	**1.812**	1.019	1.262	1.163	1.181	1.087
60	40	0	1.238	1.203	1.861	1.072	1.335	1.214	1.264	1.142
50	50	0	1.280	1.262	1.893	1.117	1.406	1.263	1.345	1.196
40	60	0	1.305	1.312	1.903	1.147	1.466	1.305	1.417	1.242
30	70	0	1.309	1.344	**1.884**	1.158	1.504	1.329	1.468	1.271
70	20	10	1.363	1.231	1.808	1.251	1.443	1.277	1.298	1.185
60	30	10	1.425	1.301	**1.866**	1.318	1.534	1.340	1.391	1.251
50	40	10	1.473	1.371	**1.907**	1.372	1.622	1.403	1.483	1.316
40	50	10	1.498	1.430	**1.924**	1.406	1.694	1.457	1.561	1.373
30	60	10	1.496	1.467	**1.909**	1.413	1.738	1.488	1.613	1.409
20	70	10	**1.464**	**1.466**	**1.857**	1.391	1.740	**1.481**	**1.625**	1.411
70	10	20	**1.432**	1.281	1.781	1.378	1.534	1.343	1.357	1.245
60	20	20	**1.488**	1.352	1.845	1.442	**1.623**	1.407	**1.448**	1.314
50	30	20	**1.528**	1.421	1.894	1.491	1.705	1.469	1.534	1.380
40	40	20	**1.547**	1.478	**1.918**	1.519	1.769	1.520	1.604	1.436
30	50	20	1.539	**1.509**	1.907	**1.520**	**1.803**	**1.545**	1.646	**1.469**
20	60	20	**1.503**	**1.501**	1.854	**1.493**	1.796	1.531	**1.649**	1.467
10	70	20	**1.444**	**1.443**	**1.761**	**1.442**	**1.743**	**1.466**	**1.609**	**1.422**
70	0	30	**1.402**	**1.292**	**1.727**	**1.396**	**1.534**	**1.358**	**1.361**	**1.266**
60	10	30	**1.444**	**1.356**	**1.794**	**1.447**	**1.606**	**1.413**	**1.439**	**1.328**
50	20	30	1.472	**1.414**	**1.847**	**1.484**	**1.668**	**1.463**	**1.510**	**1.387**
40	30	30	1.481	**1.459**	1.874	**1.503**	**1.712**	**1.499**	**1.564**	1.433
30	40	30	1.471	**1.478**	1.866	1.500	1.731	1.511	1.592	1.458
20	50	30	1.440	1.461	1.814	1.477	1.718	1.488	1.589	1.451
10	60	30	1.391	1.402	1.719	1.435	1.671	1.424	1.551	1.405
0	70	30	**1.328**	**1.306**	**1.590**	**1.377**	**1.594**	**1.321**	**1.483**	**1.323**
60	0	40	1.351	**1.323**	1.709	1.388	1.528	**1.375**	**1.389**	**1.307**
50	10	40	1.368	**1.367**	1.760	1.414	1.569	1.409	**1.442**	**1.354**
40	20	40	1.372	1.397	1.787	1.427	1.596	1.428	1.480	**1.388**
30	30	40	1.362	1.404	1.779	1.425	1.604	1.427	1.498	1.403
20	40	40	1.338	1.381	1.728	1.407	1.589	1.398	1.491	1.391
10	50	40	1.301	1.326	1.635	1.376	1.552	1.339	1.458	1.349
0	60	40	1.253	1.241	1.507	1.333	1.493	1.252	1.403	1.278
50	0	50	1.260	1.301	1.637	1.330	1.457	1.332	1.359	1.299
40	10	50	1.261	1.318	1.659	1.339	1.472	1.339	1.385	1.322

TABLE 12.5 (continued)

			15-Year Period	10-Year Period	5-Year Period	Other 10-Year Periods				
		Start	1981–	1986–	1991–	1981–	1982–	1983–	1984–	1985–
		End	1995	1995	1995	1990	1991	1992	1993	1994
Portfolio Relative Weights (%)										
S&P 500	T-Bonds	CTA Index								
30	20	50	1.253	1.315	1.649	1.337	1.474	1.329	1.395	1.329
20	30	50	1.234	1.290	1.599	1.325	1.460	1.298	1.387	1.315
10	40	50	1.207	1.239	1.510	1.303	1.431	1.246	1.360	1.277
0	50	50	1.172	1.167	1.390	1.273	1.387	1.173	1.316	1.217
40	0	60	1.164	1.237	1.500	1.257	1.360	1.250	1.293	1.252
30	10	60	1.157	1.228	1.485	1.256	1.359	1.234	1.299	1.253
20	20	60	1.143	1.202	1.437	1.249	1.347	1.204	1.291	1.238
10	30	60	1.123	1.157	1.355	1.233	1.324	1.158	1.270	1.204
0	40	60	1.097	1.096	1.246	1.211	1.291	1.097	1.235	1.154
30	0	70	1.076	1.149	1.304	1.186	1.262	1.150	1.214	1.182
20	10	70	1.066	1.123	1.257	1.181	1.252	1.121	1.207	1.166
10	20	70	1.051	1.083	1.183	1.171	1.234	1.081	1.190	1.138
0	30	70	1.032	1.030	1.088	1.155	1.208	1.030	1.163	1.095

[a]Modified Sharpe Ratio defined as average annual compounded return divided by annualized standard deviation. Component returns are based on the following series: S&P 500 total return, long-term government-bond total return, and MAR equal-weighted CTA index.

For each time period, portfolios that have the highest modified Sharpe Ratio for a given S&P 500 or T-bond percentage allocation are shaded. For example, for the 1981–1995 period, the portfolio with the highest modified Sharpe Ratio among combinations containing a 60 percent allocation to the S&P 500 is the 60 percent S&P 500/20 percent T-bond/20 percent CTA portfolio. Similarly, during the same period, the portfolio with the highest modified Sharpe Ratio among combinations containing a 60 percent allocation to T-bonds is the 20 percent S&P 500/60 percent T-bond/20 percent CTA portfolio. Sometimes, a shaded portfolio can be the optimal portfolio for both a specific S&P 500 allocation and a specific T-bond allocation. For example, the 30 percent S&P 500/50 percent T-bond/20 percent CTA portfolio has the highest modified Sharpe Ratio for both a 30 percent S&P 500 allocation and a 50 percent T-bond allocation. The portfolio with the highest modified Sharpe Ratio in each period is highlighted by a bold border.

Since portfolios have been listed in ascending order of their CTA allocation, concentrations of shaded cells and the location of bordered cells indicate areas of optimal CTA allocations. The fact that all the bordered cells and the largest number of shaded cells occur in the sector corresponding to the 20 percent CTA allocation suggests that this level represents the optimal CTA allocation among the decile increments evaluated.

Table 12.6 is analogous to Table 12.5 except that the results assume monthly rebalancing of the sector allocations. With monthly rebalancing, the largest concentration of shaded cells and six out of eight of the bordered cells occur in the region corresponding to a 30 percent CTA allocation. The 20 percent CTA allocation region still has a large number of shaded cells, however, suggesting that the optimal CTA allocation may lie somewhere in between these two levels.

Table 12.7 expresses the modified Sharpe Ratios of the rebalanced portfolios as percentages of their static portfolio counterparts. Percentages greater than 100 indicate superior performance by the rebalanced portfolio. As can be seen by the predominance of values above 100, rebalancing results in an increased return/risk measure for the vast majority of portfolio/time period combinations. On average for all the portfolio/time period combinations shown, the rebalanced modified Sharpe Ratio was 6.3 percent higher. Once again, rebalancing provides a pervasive improvement in performance.

We are now ready to compare stock/bond/CTA portfolios to stock/bond portfolios. Selecting the best portfolio in each category presents a problem because it introduces hindsight into the results. Although it may seem that using hindsight for both portfolio groups might neutralize the distortion, the fact that there are many more combinations of stock/bond/CTA portfolios than stock/bond portfolios suggests that selecting the best portfolio in each group would cause a hindsight bias in favor of the former. To be conservative—that is, to minimize the chances of concluding that the addition of managed futures to a stock/bond portfolio is beneficial when this is not the case—we compare the best stock/bond portfolio (30 percent S&P 500/70 percent T-bond) with the "constrained worst" stock/bond/CTA portfolio. The "constrained worst" portfolio is defined as the portfolio with the lowest modified Sharpe Ratio subject to the following two constraints:

1. The minimum allocation to each sector is 20 percent.
2. The maximum allocation to each sector is 50 percent, except the CTA component, which is limited to 30 percent.

The rationale for these constraints is that they avoid lopsided allocations that would defeat the purpose of diversification. The lower maximum allocation specified for the CTA investment reflects the fact that it is a far more volatile component than stocks or bonds (see the standard deviation comparisons in Table 12.1).

Figure 12.9 compares the NAV of the best stock/bond portfolio with the NAV of the "constrained worst" stock/bond/CTA portfolio. Note that the

Table 12.6
MODIFIED SHARPE RATIOS: STOCK/BOND/CTA INDEX PORTFOLIOS
WITH MONTHLY REBALANCING[a]

			15-Year Period	10-Year Period	5-Year Period	Other 10-Year Periods				
		Start	1981–	1986–	1991–	1981–	1982–	1983–	1984–	1985–
		End	1995	1995	1995	1990	1991	1992	1993	1994
Portfolio Relative Weights (%)										
S&P 500	**T-Bonds**	**CTA Index**								
70	30	0	1.215	1.197	1.834	1.050	1.308	1.231	1.225	1.139
60	40	0	1.272	1.267	1.883	1.110	1.391	1.294	1.318	1.204
50	50	0	1.315	1.327	1.913	1.157	1.464	1.345	1.403	1.259
40	60	0	1.338	1.369	1.916	1.185	1.519	1.375	1.471	1.298
30	70	0	1.334	1.383	1.890	1.190	1.544	1.374	1.509	1.310
70	20	10	1.343	1.276	1.845	1.216	1.453	1.342	1.319	1.227
60	30	10	1.416	1.357	1.904	1.294	1.556	1.421	1.426	1.304
50	40	10	1.474	1.431	1.943	1.357	1.651	1.488	1.525	1.374
40	50	10	1.505	1.485	1.954	1.396	1.725	1.532	1.605	1.424
30	60	10	1.505	1.505	1.930	1.405	1.763	1.541	1.651	1.446
20	70	10	1.471	1.484	1.870	1.380	1.753	1.507	1.653	1.429
70	10	20	1.428	1.327	1.823	1.342	1.547	1.408	1.378	1.286
60	20	20	1.511	1.416	1.888	1.431	1.661	1.495	1.490	1.371
50	30	20	1.576	1.496	1.934	1.505	1.766	1.569	1.594	1.448
40	40	20	1.614	1.555	1.950	1.552	1.847	1.621	1.678	1.506
30	50	20	1.616	1.579	1.929	1.563	1.890	1.635	1.727	1.533
20	60	20	1.579	1.557	1.868	1.535	1.882	1.603	1.728	1.519
10	70	20	1.509	1.488	1.773	1.473	1.820	1.525	1.679	1.463
70	0	30	1.449	1.339	1.684	1.407	1.579	1.424	1.397	1.313
60	10	30	1.536	1.433	1.828	1.497	1.687	1.506	1.504	1.397
50	20	30	1.600	1.510	1.875	1.571	1.785	1.576	1.602	1.473
40	30	30	1.637	1.567	1.893	1.617	1.860	1.624	1.680	1.531
30	40	30	1.640	1.589	1.874	1.629	1.898	1.637	1.724	1.558
20	50	30	1.604	1.566	1.815	1.602	1.888	1.607	1.723	1.546
10	60	30	1.536	1.536	1.720	1.541	1.829	1.535	1.676	1.492
0	70	30	1.444	1.395	1.599	1.455	1.729	1.429	1.592	1.403
60	0	40	1.496	1.410	1.723	1.493	1.644	1.464	1.473	1.384
50	10	40	1.551	1.478	1.766	1.557	1.724	1.522	1.558	1.452
40	20	40	1.582	1.525	1.781	1.597	1.783	1.558	1.622	1.503
30	30	40	1.582	1.541	1.763	1.606	1.810	1.566	1.657	1.526
20	40	40	1.551	1.518	1.707	1.583	1.798	1.538	1.654	1.514
10	50	40	1.492	1.455	1.617	1.530	1.747	1.476	1.613	1.465
0	60	40	1.410	1.359	1.503	1.455	1.663	1.385	1.539	1.385
50	0	50	1.455	1.411	1.616	1.490	1.618	1.431	1.478	1.397
40	10	50	1.478	1.446	1.626	1.521	1.659	1.456	1.529	1.437

TABLE 12.6 (continued)

			15-Year Period	10-Year Period	5-Year Period	Other 10-Year Periods				
		Start	1981–	1986–	1991–	1981–	1982–	1983–	1984–	1985–
		End	1995	1995	1995	1990	1991	1992	1993	1994
Portfolio Relative Weights (%)										
S&P 500	T-Bonds	CTA Index								
30	20	50	1.477	1.454	1.607	1.528	1.675	1.457	1.554	1.454
20	30	50	1.451	1.431	1.555	1.509	1.663	1.431	1.549	1.442
10	40	50	1.402	1.375	1.474	1.467	1.620	1.378	1.514	1.400
0	50	50	1.335	1.292	1.372	1.406	1.552	1.303	1.453	1.331
40	0	60	1.356	1.350	1.446	1.422	1.524	1.342	1.421	1.353
30	10	60	1.353	1.351	1.425	1.427	1.532	1.338	1.438	1.364
20	20	60	1.332	1.327	1.378	1.412	1.519	1.313	1.432	1.351
10	30	60	1.294	1.278	1.308	1.379	1.484	1.269	1.403	1.315
0	40	60	1.240	1.207	1.219	1.331	1.430	1.208	1.354	1.257
30	0	70	1.232	1.244	1.238	1.323	1.398	1.224	1.324	1.269
20	10	70	1.214	1.221	1.195	1.312	1.384	1.201	1.318	1.256
10	20	70	1.184	1.179	1.135	1.287	1.355	1.164	1.294	1.224
0	30	70	1.142	1.119	1.060	1.249	1.312	1.114	1.254	1.176

[a]Modified Sharpe Ratio defined as average annual compounded return divided by annualized standard deviation. Component returns are based on the following series: S&P 500 total return, long-term government-bond total return, and MAR equal-weighted CTA index.

stock/bond/CTA portfolio has been leveraged by a factor that equalizes its standard deviation (a proxy for risk) to the standard deviation of the stock/bond portfolio. With risk levels equalized for the two portfolios, returns can be directly compared. It will be recalled that the same technique was used previously in this chapter to permit visual comparisons between stock/bond NAVs and single-sector NAVs. Also note that since rebalancing consistently helps performance, the comparison in Figure 12.9 assumes rebalancing for each portfolio. Figure 12.9 clearly implies that the addition of managed futures to a stock/bond portfolio aids performance.

Fund/Pool Index-Based Results

Thus far, we have used a CTA index as the representation for managed futures. We now employ a similar analysis using the MAR equal-weighted fund/pool index to represent the managed futures investment. Table 12.8 is

Table 12.7

MODIFIED SHARPE RATIOS: STOCK/BOND/CTA INDEX REBALANCED PORTFOLIOS AS % OF CORRESPONDING STATIC PORTFOLIOS[a]

			15-Year Period	10-Year Period	5-Year Period	Other 10-Year Periods				
		Start	1981–	1986–	1991–	1981–	1982–	1983–	1984–	1985–
		End	1995	1995	1995	1990	1991	1992	1993	1994
Portfolio Relative Weights (%)										
S&P 500	T-Bonds	CTA Index								
70	30	0	102.4	104.7	101.2	103.1	103.7	105.9	103.8	104.8
60	40	0	102.7	105.3	101.2	103.6	104.2	106.6	104.3	105.4
50	50	0	102.8	105.2	101.0	103.6	104.2	106.5	104.3	105.3
40	60	0	102.5	104.3	100.7	103.4	103.6	105.3	103.8	104.5
30	70	0	102.0	102.9	100.3	102.7	102.7	103.4	102.8	103.1
70	20	10	98.5	103.6	102.0	97.2	100.7	105.1	101.7	103.5
60	30	10	99.4	104.3	102.0	98.2	101.4	106.0	102.5	104.2
50	40	10	100.1	104.4	101.9	98.9	101.8	106.1	102.9	104.3
40	50	10	100.5	103.8	101.5	99.3	101.8	105.2	102.8	103.8
30	60	10	100.6	102.6	101.1	99.4	101.4	103.5	102.4	102.6
20	70	10	100.4	101.3	100.7	99.2	100.8	101.7	101.7	101.3
70	10	20	99.7	103.6	102.3	97.4	100.9	104.9	101.6	103.3
60	20	20	101.5	104.7	102.3	99.2	102.3	106.2	102.9	104.4
50	30	20	103.1	105.3	102.1	100.9	103.5	106.8	103.9	104.9
40	40	20	104.4	105.2	101.6	102.2	104.4	106.6	104.6	104.9
30	50	20	105.0	104.6	101.1	102.8	104.9	105.8	104.9	104.4
20	60	20	105.1	103.8	100.8	102.8	104.8	104.7	104.8	103.5
10	70	20	104.5	103.2	100.7	102.2	104.4	104.0	104.3	102.9
70	0	30	103.3	103.6	97.5	100.8	102.9	104.9	102.6	103.7
60	10	30	106.3	105.7	101.9	103.5	105.0	106.6	104.5	105.2
50	20	30	108.7	106.8	101.5	105.9	107.0	107.7	106.1	106.2
40	30	30	110.5	107.4	101.0	107.6	108.6	108.3	107.5	106.8
30	40	30	111.5	107.5	100.4	108.5	109.7	108.3	108.3	106.9
20	50	30	111.4	107.2	100.1	108.4	109.9	108.0	108.5	106.6
10	60	30	110.4	109.5	100.1	107.4	109.5	107.8	108.1	106.2
0	70	30	108.7	106.8	100.6	105.7	108.5	108.2	107.4	106.0
60	0	40	110.8	106.5	100.8	107.5	107.6	106.5	106.0	105.9
50	10	40	113.4	108.1	100.3	110.1	109.9	108.0	108.0	107.3
40	20	40	115.3	109.2	99.7	111.9	111.7	109.1	109.6	108.3
30	30	40	116.2	109.8	99.1	112.7	112.8	109.7	110.6	108.8
20	40	40	116.0	109.9	98.8	112.5	113.1	110.0	111.0	108.9
10	50	40	114.6	109.7	98.9	111.2	112.6	110.2	110.6	108.7
0	60	40	112.5	109.5	99.7	109.1	111.4	110.6	109.7	108.4
50	0	50	115.5	108.4	98.7	112.0	111.1	107.4	108.8	107.6

TABLE 12.7 (continued)

			15-Year Period	10-Year Period	5-Year Period	Other 10-Year Periods				
		Start	1981–	1986–	1991–	1981–	1982–	1983–	1984–	1985–
		End	1995	1995	1995	1990	1991	1992	1993	1994

Portfolio Relative Weights (%)

S&P 500	T-Bonds	CTA Index								
40	10	50	117.2	109.7	98.0	113.6	112.7	108.7	110.4	108.7
30	20	50	117.9	110.5	97.4	114.2	113.7	109.6	111.4	109.4
20	30	50	117.5	111.0	97.2	113.9	113.8	110.2	111.7	109.7
10	40	50	116.1	110.9	97.6	112.5	113.2	110.6	111.3	109.6
0	50	50	113.9	110.7	98.7	110.4	111.9	111.1	110.4	109.4
40	0	60	116.5	109.2	96.4	113.2	112.1	107.4	109.9	108.1
30	10	60	117.0	110.0	96.0	113.6	112.7	108.3	110.7	108.8
20	20	60	116.5	110.4	95.9	113.1	112.7	109.1	110.9	109.2
10	30	60	115.2	110.5	96.5	111.8	112.0	109.6	110.5	109.2
0	40	60	113.0	110.1	97.8	109.9	110.8	110.1	109.6	108.9
30	0	70	114.5	108.3	94.9	111.5	110.7	106.4	109.1	107.4
20	10	70	113.9	108.7	95.1	111.0	110.6	107.1	109.2	107.7
10	20	70	112.6	108.9	95.9	109.9	109.8	107.7	108.7	107.6
0	30	70	110.7	108.6	97.4	108.1	108.6	108.1	107.9	107.4
Average for all periods:			106.3							

[a]Rebalanced portfolios adjusted monthly to maintain indicated relative percentages. Static portfolios start at indicated relative percentages and are not subsequently adjusted.

the counterpart of Table 12.5, using the MAR equal-weighted fund/pool index instead of the MAR equal-weighted CTA index. In this instance, the shaded regions and bordered cells are most heavily concentrated in the 10 percent managed futures allocation sector, with the 20 percent sector a close second.

Table 12.9 is analogous to Table 12.8 except that the results assume monthly rebalancing of the sector allocations. The implied optimal managed futures allocation is quite similar to that indicated by Table 12.7, with the minor exception that the 10 percent and 20 percent managed futures allocations are more closely balanced in terms of being optimal performance sectors. In essence, both Tables 12.8 and 12.9 imply that the optimal futures fund/pool allocation lies somewhere between 10 percent and 20 percent. The lower managed futures allocation implied by these tables (vis-à-vis Tables 12.5 and 12.6) is no surprise, given the aforementioned subpar performance of the fund/pool index relative to the CTA index.

Figure 12.9
NAV COMPARISON: LEVERAGED "CONSTRAINED WORST" STOCK/BOND/CTA PORTFOLIO VERSUS BEST STOCK/BOND PORTFOLIO

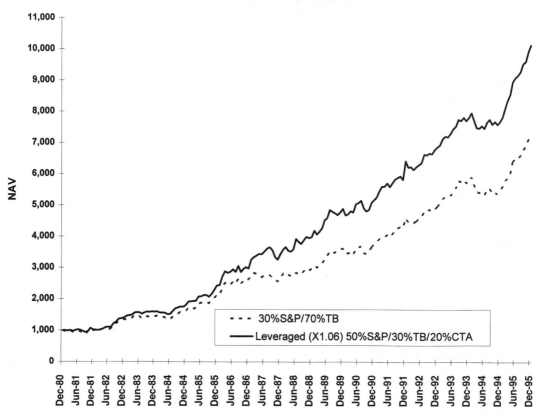

Data sources: S&P and T-bond series: Refco Information Services Inc., One World Financial Center, 200 Liberty Street, New York, NY 10281. CTA index: Managed Account Reports, 220 Fifth Avenue, New York, NY 10001.

Definitions: S&P = S&P 500 total return; TB = long-term government-bond total return; CTA Index = MAR equal-weighted CTA index.

Notes: (1) "Constrained worst" defined as stock/bond/CTA portfolio with lowest modified Sharpe Ratio subject to constraints that minimum allocation for each sector equals 20 percent and maximum allocation equals 50 percent for stock and bond sectors and 30 percent for CTA. (2) Stock/bond/CTA portfolio leveraged by factor (1.06) to equalize standard deviation with 30 percent S&P 500/70 percent T-bond portfolio. (3) Both portfolios assume monthly rebalancing.

Table 12.10 expresses the modified Sharpe Ratios of the rebalanced portfolios as percentages of their static portfolio counterparts. Percentages greater than 100 indicate superior performance by the rebalanced portfolio. As can be seen by the predominance of values above 100, rebalancing results in an increased return/risk measure for the vast majority of portfolio/time period combinations. On average for all the portfolio/time period

Table 12.8
MODIFIED SHARPE RATIOS: STOCK/BOND/FUND INDEX
PORTFOLIOS, NO REBALANCING[a]

			15-Year Period	10-Year Period	5-Year Period	Other 10-Year Periods				
		Start	1981–	1986–	1991–	1981–	1982–	1983–	1984–	1985–
		End	1995	1995	1995	1990	1991	1992	1993	1994
Portfolio Relative Weights (%)										
S&P 500	T-Bonds	Fund Index								
70	30	0	1.186	1.143	**1.812**	1.019	**1.262**	1.163	1.181	**1.087**
60	40	0	1.238	1.203	**1.861**	1.072	1.335	1.214	1.264	**1.142**
50	50	0	1.280	1.262	**1.893**	1.117	1.406	1.263	1.345	1.196
40	60	0	1.305	1.312	**1.903**	1.147	1.466	1.305	1.417	1.242
30	70	0	1.309	1.344	**1.884**	1.158	1.504	1.329	1.468	1.271
70	20	10	**1.202**	**1.139**	1.757	**1.051**	1.258	**1.169**	**1.181**	1.081
60	30	10	**1.265**	**1.203**	1.810	1.117	**1.341**	**1.226**	**1.270**	1.142
50	40	10	**1.319**	**1.268**	1.848	1.174	**1.424**	**1.284**	**1.360**	**1.202**
40	50	10	1.355	**1.327**	1.863	1.217	**1.499**	**1.337**	**1.441**	**1.258**
30	60	10	1.366	**1.368**	1.846	1.237	**1.552**	**1.373**	**1.502**	**1.297**
20	70	10	**1.349**	**1.376**	1.794	1.231	**1.570**	**1.376**	**1.528**	**1.308**
70	10	20	1.183	1.116	1.679	1.051	1.227	1.150	1.153	1.059
60	20	20	1.253	1.180	1.735	**1.124**	1.314	1.207	1.242	1.120
50	30	20	**1.315**	1.245	1.777	**1.191**	1.404	**1.267**	1.332	1.183
40	40	20	**1.360**	**1.306**	1.794	**1.244**	1.487	**1.323**	**1.415**	**1.242**
30	50	20	**1.381**	**1.350**	1.780	**1.275**	**1.552**	**1.364**	**1.481**	**1.288**
20	60	20	**1.369**	1.363	1.728	**1.276**	**1.581**	**1.374**	**1.512**	**1.306**
10	70	20	1.325	1.330	1.639	**1.246**	1.558	1.336	1.500	1.284
70	0	30	1.130	1.075	1.578	1.017	1.169	1.108	1.101	1.020
60	10	30	1.199	1.134	1.633	1.090	1.253	1.161	1.182	1.078
50	20	30	1.262	1.194	1.674	1.159	1.340	1.215	1.265	1.138
40	30	30	1.312	**1.250**	1.693	**1.218**	**1.424**	1.265	**1.343**	**1.195**
30	40	30	1.339	1.291	1.680	**1.256**	**1.492**	1.302	1.405	1.241
20	50	30	1.335	1.305	1.628	1.266	1.528	1.312	1.438	1.263
10	60	30	1.297	1.277	1.539	1.244	1.514	1.279	1.432	1.247
0	70	30	1.230	1.203	1.420	1.193	1.445	1.195	1.385	1.187
60	0	40	1.108	1.068	1.435	1.023	1.164	1.093	1.101	1.020
50	10	40	1.166	1.118	1.473	1.087	1.242	1.136	1.173	1.073
40	20	40	1.213	1.163	1.497	1.144	1.317	1.176	1.239	1.123
30	30	40	1.242	1.197	1.497	1.184	1.380	1.203	1.292	1.164
20	40	40	1.246	1.209	1.464	1.201	1.416	1.207	1.323	1.184
10	50	40	1.219	1.186	1.394	1.190	1.410	1.177	1.323	1.173
0	60	40	1.164	1.123	1.290	1.151	1.354	1.106	1.288	1.123
50	0	50	1.052	1.036	1.331	0.992	1.123	1.045	1.068	0.996

TABLE 12.8 (continued)

			15-Year Period	10-Year Period	5-Year Period	Other 10-Year Periods				
		Start	1981–	1986–	1991–	1981–	1982–	1983–	1984–	1985–
		End	1995	1995	1995	1990	1991	1992	1993	1994
Portfolio Relative Weights (%)										
S&P 500	T-Bonds	Fund Index								
40	10	50	1.093	1.071	1.347	1.042	1.185	1.072	1.121	1.037
30	20	50	1.119	1.094	1.341	1.080	1.237	1.087	1.165	1.069
20	30	50	1.125	1.099	1.304	1.100	1.267	1.085	1.191	1.085
10	40	50	1.107	1.078	1.123	1.098	1.265	1.055	1.194	1.075
0	50	50	1.064	1.022	1.134	1.073	1.224	0.995	1.170	1.035
40	0	60	0.964	0.973	1.177	0.933	1.046	0.966	1.005	0.945
30	10	60	0.985	0.987	1.163	0.966	1.085	0.971	1.038	0.968
20	20	60	0.991	0.985	1.123	0.987	1.108	0.962	1.059	0.978
10	30	60	0.979	0.962	1.054	0.991	1.108	0.934	1.063	0.969
0	40	60	0.947	0.915	0.959	0.977	1.078	0.883	1.048	0.935
30	0	70	0.856	0.883	0.975	0.857	0.941	0.864	0.922	0.870
20	10	70	0.860	0.876	0.931	0.876	0.957	0.851	0.938	0.874
10	20	70	0.851	0.852	0.863	0.883	0.956	0.823	0.942	0.864
0	30	70	0.828	0.810	0.775	0.877	0.935	0.779	0.932	0.836

[a]Modified Sharpe Ratio defined as average annual compounded return divided by annualized standard deviation. Component returns are based on the following series: S&P 500 total return, long-term government bond total return, and MAR equal-weighted fund/pool index.

combinations shown, the rebalanced modified Sharpe Ratio was 3.0 percent higher. It is worth emphasizing that rebalancing, which effectively shifts funds each month from *better to poorer* performing assets, provides a widespread improvement in performance even in this case, a situation that is characterized by one sector (fund/pool index) exhibiting significantly inferior performance (see Table 12.1 comparisons).

Figure 12.10 compares the NAV for the best stock/bond portfolio with the "constrained worst" stock/bond/fund portfolio. In this instance, the leverage factor applied to the stock/bond/fund portfolio is quite small (1.02) since the portfolio's standard deviation is only slightly lower than the stock/bond portfolio standard deviation. Once again, it is assumed that both portfolios employ monthly rebalancing. In this case, the performance of the two portfolios is virtually identical. In fact, the stock/bond portfolio actually finishes with a marginally higher NAV.

It should be recalled, however, that the stock/bond/fund NAV was based on the "constrained worst" portfolio. In Figure 12.11 we compare the best

Table 12.9
MODIFIED SHARPE RATIOS: STOCK/BOND/FUND INDEX
PORTFOLIOS WITH MONTHLY REBALANCING[a]

			15-Year Period	10-Year Period	5-Year Period	Other 10-Year Periods				
Start End			1981– 1995	1986– 1995	1991– 1995	1981– 1990	1982– 1991	1983– 1992	1984– 1993	1985– 1994

Portfolio Relative Weights (%)

S&P 500	T-Bonds	CTA Index								
70	30	0	1.215	1.197	1.834	1.050	1.308	1.231	1.225	1.139
60	40	0	1.272	1.267	1.883	1.110	1.391	1.294	1.318	1.204
50	50	0	1.315	1.327	1.913	1.157	1.464	1.345	1.403	1.259
40	60	0	1.338	1.369	1.916	1.185	1.519	1.375	1.471	1.298
30	70	0	1.334	1.383	1.890	1.190	1.544	1.374	1.509	1.310
70	20	10	1.241	1.192	1.779	1.103	1.329	1.250	1.233	1.140
60	30	10	1.311	1.269	1.833	1.176	1.424	1.324	1.334	1.213
50	40	10	1.367	1.340	1.868	1.238	1.514	1.388	1.430	1.279
40	50	10	1.401	1.393	1.876	1.280	1.585	1.432	1.510	1.330
30	60	10	1.406	1.419	1.851	1.294	1.626	1.445	1.561	1.355
20	70	10	1.379	1.405	1.794	1.278	1.626	1.419	1.571	1.346
70	10	20	1.228	1.161	1.689	1.117	1.306	1.229	1.208	1.116
60	20	20	1.304	1.240	1.745	1.199	1.405	1.305	1.310	1.191
50	30	20	1.368	1.314	1.782	1.271	1.500	1.373	1.408	1.261
40	40	20	1.411	1.374	1.792	1.324	1.579	1.425	1.492	1.319
30	50	20	1.425	1.407	1.769	1.348	1.631	1.447	1.550	1.353
20	60	20	1.404	1.403	1.712	1.338	1.641	1.430	1.568	1.354
10	70	20	1.351	1.355	1.624	1.296	1.603	1.372	1.540	1.316
70	0	30	1.174	1.108	1.566	1.092	1.244	1.172	1.154	1.068
60	10	30	1.248	1.182	1.618	1.173	1.335	1.241	1.249	1.139
50	20	30	1.313	1.253	1.652	1.246	1.423	1.305	1.340	1.208
40	30	30	1.359	1.311	1.661	1.303	1.499	1.353	1.420	1.265
30	40	30	1.378	1.347	1.639	1.334	1.551	1.377	1.477	1.303
20	50	30	1.364	1.348	1.584	1.333	1.566	1.368	1.499	1.310
10	60	30	1.320	1.309	1.500	1.299	1.539	1.321	1.480	1.282
0	70	30	1.249	1.234	1.394	1.238	1.471	1.241	1.423	1.220
60	0	40	1.155	1.102	1.458	1.107	1.230	1.148	1.162	1.066
50	10	40	1.212	1.164	1.485	1.174	1.304	1.200	1.241	1.127
40	20	40	1.254	1.216	1.490	1.227	1.367	1.239	1.310	1.179
30	30	40	1.274	1.248	1.468	1.259	1.411	1.259	1.360	1.214
20	40	40	1.267	1.251	1.416	1.264	1.426	1.253	1.382	1.225
10	50	40	1.233	1.221	1.339	1.241	1.408	1.217	1.371	1.205
0	60	40	1.175	1.158	1.242	1.193	1.356	1.153	1.327	1.155
50	0	50	1.087	1.061	1.295	1.073	1.166	1.080	1.127	1.032

TABLE 12.9 (continued)

			15-Year Period	10-Year Period	5-Year Period	Other 10-Year Periods				
		Start	1981–	1986–	1991–	1981–	1982–	1983–	1984–	1985–
		End	1995	1995	1995	1990	1991	1992	1993	1994
Portfolio Relative Weights (%)										
S&P 500	T-Bonds	CTA Index								
40	10	50	1.122	1.102	1.294	1.119	1.214	1.109	1.183	1.075
30	20	50	1.139	1.127	1.270	1.148	1.247	1.123	1.224	1.104
20	30	50	1.136	1.130	1.222	1.157	1.259	1.117	1.244	1.114
10	40	50	1.111	1.107	1.153	1.143	1.246	1.088	1.238	1.101
0	50	50	1.067	1.056	1.068	1.108	1.208	1.039	1.206	1.062
40	0	60	0.984	0.986	1.089	1.001	1.063	0.980	1.055	0.966
30	10	60	0.998	1.004	1.063	1.025	1.086	0.988	1.087	0.989
20	20	60	0.996	1.004	1.020	1.035	1.094	0.981	1.103	0.997
10	30	60	0.978	0.984	0.959	1.028	1.085	0.958	1.101	0.987
0	40	60	0.945	0.943	0.887	1.004	1.057	0.919	1.078	0.957
30	0	70	0.864	0.885	0.863	0.907	0.940	0.865	0.960	0.878
20	10	70	0.862	0.883	0.823	0.916	0.945	0.857	0.973	0.884
10	20	70	0.849	0.865	0.773	0.913	0.937	0.838	0.971	0.875
0	30	70	0.824	0.831	0.710	0.898	0.916	0.807	0.956	0.852

[a]Modified Sharpe Ratio defined as average annual compounded return divided by annualized standard deviation. Component returns are based on the following series: S&P 500 total return, long-term government-bond total return, and MAR equal-weighted CTA index.

stock/bond portfolio with the "constrained *second* worst" stock/bond/fund portfolio. In this case, the stock/bond/fund portfolio results in a modestly higher NAV. The implication is that all but the worst-performing portfolio among the portfolios meeting the constraint conditions provided some improvement over the best stock/bond portfolio.

It is interesting to note that even the inclusion of a vastly inferior sector—the fund/pool index—still seems to improve the overall portfolio performance, albeit modestly. Why? The explanation is that managed futures are almost totally uncorrelated with stocks and bonds. Table 12.11 summarizes the correlations between different sectors across 17 time periods. First, it should be emphasized that the correlation patterns are quite stable across all periods, an observation that tremendously enhances the reliability of the results. Note that both the CTA index and the fund/pool index consistently exhibit correlations near zero versus the S&P 500 and fairly low correlations (generally less than 0.20) versus T-bonds. In contrast, as might be expected, the CTA and

Table 12.10
MODIFIED SHARPE RATIOS: STOCK/BOND/FUND INDEX
REBALANCED PORTFOLIOS AS % OF CORRESPONDING
STATIC PORTFOLIOS[a]

			15-Year Period	10-Year Period	5-Year Period	Other 10-Year Periods				
		Start	1981–	1986–	1991–	1981–	1982–	1983–	1984–	1985–
		End	1995	1995	1995	1990	1991	1992	1993	1994
Portfolio Relative Weights (%)										
S&P 500	T-Bonds	CTA Index								
70	30	0	102.4	104.7	101.2	103.1	103.7	105.9	103.8	104.8
60	40	0	102.7	105.3	101.2	103.6	104.2	106.6	104.3	105.4
50	50	0	102.8	105.2	101.0	103.6	104.2	106.5	104.3	105.3
40	60	0	102.5	104.3	100.7	103.4	103.6	105.3	103.8	104.5
30	70	0	102.0	102.9	100.3	102.7	102.7	103.4	102.8	103.1
70	20	10	103.2	104.6	101.2	104.9	105.6	107.0	104.4	105.4
60	30	10	103.6	105.5	101.3	105.4	106.2	108.0	105.0	106.3
50	40	10	103.7	105.6	101.1	105.5	106.3	108.1	105.2	106.4
40	50	10	103.4	105.0	100.7	105.2	105.8	107.2	104.8	105.8
30	60	10	102.9	103.7	100.3	104.6	104.8	105.3	103.9	104.5
20	70	10	102.3	102.2	100.0	103.8	103.6	103.1	102.8	102.9
70	10	20	103.7	104.0	100.6	106.3	106.4	106.9	104.8	105.4
60	20	20	104.1	105.1	100.6	106.7	106.9	108.1	105.5	106.4
50	30	20	104.1	105.6	100.3	106.7	106.8	108.4	105.7	106.7
40	40	20	103.7	105.3	99.8	106.4	106.2	107.7	105.4	106.2
30	50	20	103.2	104.3	99.4	105.7	105.1	106.1	104.7	105.1
20	60	20	102.5	102.9	99.1	104.9	103.8	104.1	103.7	103.6
10	70	20	102.0	101.9	99.1	104.0	102.9	102.8	102.7	102.5
70	0	30	103.9	103.0	99.3	107.4	106.4	105.7	104.8	104.7
60	10	30	104.1	104.3	99.1	107.6	106.6	107.0	105.6	105.7
50	20	30	104.0	104.9	98.7	107.5	106.2	107.4	105.9	106.1
40	30	30	103.5	104.9	98.1	107.0	105.3	107.0	105.7	105.9
30	40	30	102.9	104.3	97.6	106.2	103.9	105.8	105.1	105.0
20	50	30	102.2	103.3	97.3	105.3	102.5	104.3	104.2	103.8
10	60	30	101.7	102.5	97.5	104.4	101.6	103.3	103.3	102.8
0	70	30	101.5	102.6	98.2	103.7	101.8	103.9	102.7	102.7
60	0	40	104.2	103.2	101.6	108.2	105.6	105.0	105.5	104.5
50	10	40	103.9	104.1	100.8	107.9	105.0	105.6	105.8	105.0
40	20	40	103.4	104.5	99.6	107.3	103.8	105.4	105.7	104.9
30	30	40	102.6	104.2	98.1	106.3	102.2	104.7	105.2	104.3
20	40	40	101.7	103.5	96.8	105.3	100.7	103.8	104.5	103.4
10	50	40	101.1	103.0	96.1	104.3	99.9	103.4	103.7	102.7
0	60	40	100.9	103.1	96.3	103.6	100.1	104.3	103.1	102.8

TABLE 12.10 (continued)

			15-Year Period	10-Year Period	5-Year Period	Other 10-Year Periods				
		Start	1981–	1986–	1991–	1981–	1982–	1983–	1984–	1985–
		End	1995	1995	1995	1990	1991	1992	1993	1994
Portfolio Relative Weights (%)										
S&P 500	T-Bonds	CTA Index								
50	0	50	103.3	102.4	97.3	108.1	103.8	103.4	105.5	103.6
40	10	50	102.7	102.9	96.1	107.3	102.4	103.5	105.5	103.7
30	20	50	101.8	103.0	94.7	106.3	100.8	103.3	105.1	103.3
20	30	50	101.0	102.8	93.7	105.1	99.4	103.0	104.4	102.7
10	40	50	100.4	102.7	102.7	104.1	98.5	103.1	103.7	102.4
0	50	50	100.3	103.3	94.2	103.3	98.7	104.4	103.1	102.7
40	0	60	102.1	101.3	92.5	107.2	101.6	101.5	105.0	102.3
30	10	60	101.3	101.7	91.4	106.1	100.1	101.7	104.7	102.2
20	20	60	100.5	101.9	90.8	104.9	98.7	102.0	104.2	101.9
10	30	60	99.9	102.3	91.0	103.8	97.9	102.6	103.5	101.9
0	40	60	99.8	103.1	92.5	102.8	98.0	104.1	102.9	102.4
30	0	70	100.9	100.2	88.5	105.9	99.9	100.1	104.2	101.0
20	10	70	100.2	100.8	88.4	104.6	98.7	100.8	103.7	101.1
10	20	70	99.8	101.5	89.6	103.4	98.0	101.8	103.1	101.3
0	30	70	99.5	102.6	91.6	102.4	98.0	103.6	102.5	102.0
Average for all periods:			103.0							

[a]Rebalanced portfolios adjusted monthly to maintain indicated relative percentages. Static portfolios start at indicated relative percentages and are not subsequently adjusted.

fund/pool indexes are extremely highly correlated across all time periods, while the S&P 500 and T-bonds show moderate correlation levels.

An investment that is relatively uncorrelated with other investments in a portfolio can often improve the portfolio performance even if its own performance is relatively inferior. It has been demonstrated that if a candidate asset is uncorrelated to the portfolio, its addition will increase the portfolio Sharpe Ratio as long as its return merely exceeds the risk-free return.[9] (Note that this statement is based on the Sharpe Ratio, not the modified Sharpe Ratio.)

The implied performance improvement provided by managed futures is far more muted if the fund/pool index is used as the representative invest-

---

[9]This conclusion follows directly from a formula presented by E. J. Elton, M. J. Gruber, and J. C. Rentzler in "Professionally Managed, Publicly Traded Commodity Funds," *Journal of Business*, 60(2) 1987.

Figure 12.10
NAV COMPARISON: LEVERAGED "CONSTRAINED WORST" STOCK/BOND/FUND PORTFOLIO VERSUS BEST STOCK/BOND PORTFOLIO

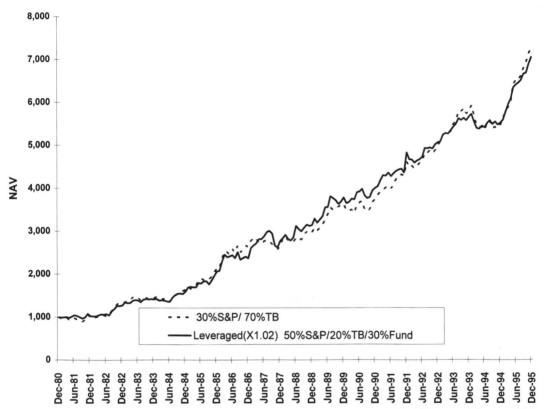

Data sources: S&P and T-bond series: Refco Information Services Inc., One World Financial Center, 200 Liberty Street, New York, NY 10281. Fund/pool index: Managed Account Reports, 220 Fifth Avenue, New York, NY 10001.

Definitions: S&P = S&P 500 total return; TB = long-term government-bond total return; Fund = MAR equal-weighted fund/pool index.

Notes: (1) "Constrained worst" defined as stock/bond/commodity fund portfolio with lowest modified Sharpe Ratio subject to constraints that minimum allocation for each sector equals 20 percent and maximum allocation equals 50 percent for stock and bond sectors and 30 percent for commodity fund/pool sector. (2) Stock/bond/commodity fund portfolio leveraged by factor (1.02) to equalize standard deviation with 30 percent S&P 500/70 percent T-bond portfolio. (3) Both portfolios assume monthly rebalancing.

ment instead of the CTA index. This observation should hardly come as a surprise in view of the inferior performance of the fund/pool index vis-à-vis the CTA index (see Table 12.1). As previously discussed, the main reason for this performance difference is cost. In this context, it should be noted that the past performance of the fund/pool index probably understates potential future performance because of the sharp decline in costs in recent years (see

Figure 12.11
NAV COMPARISON: LEVERAGED "CONSTRAINED SECOND WORST" STOCK/BOND/FUND PORTFOLIO VERSUS BEST STOCK/BOND PORTFOLIO

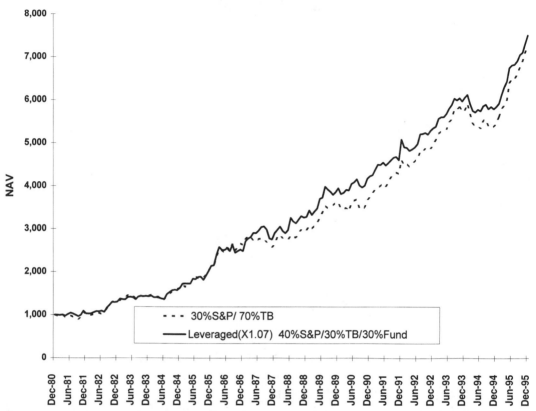

Data sources: S&P and T-bond series: Refco Information Services Inc., One World Financial Center, 200 Liberty Street, New York, NY 10281. Fund/pool indexes: Managed Account Reports, 220 Fifth Avenue, New York, NY 10001.

Definitions: S&P = S&P 500 total return; TB = long-term government-bond total return; Fund = MAR equal-weighted fund/pool index.

Notes: (1) "Constrained second worst" defined as stock/bond/commodity fund portfolio with second lowest modified Sharpe Ratio subject to constraints that minimum allocation for each sector equals 20 percent and maximum allocation equals 50 percent for stock and bond sectors and 30 percent for commodity fund/pool sector. (2) Stock/bond/commodity fund portfolio leveraged by factor (1.07) to equalize standard deviation with 30 percent S&P 500/70 percent T-bond portfolio. (3) Both portfolios assume monthly rebalancing.

Figure 12.12). Moreover, insofar as this decline in costs enhances the likelihood of above-risk-free returns, the near zero correlation of the fund/pool index with the components of a stock/bond portfolio virtually assures that its addition to the portfolio will be beneficial.

Table 12.11
CORRELATIONS BETWEEN SECTORS

	CTA Index Versus S&P 500	CTA Index Versus Long-Term T-Bond	Fund/Pool Index Versus S&P 500	Fund/Pool Index Versus Long-Term T-Bond	S&P 500 Versus Long-Term T-Bond	CTA Index Versus Fund/Pool Index
10-year periods						
1981–1990	−0.12	0.11	0.02	0.09	0.40	0.89
1982–1991	−0.10	0.08	0.05	0.08	0.37	0.89
1983–1992	−0.05	0.13	0.09	0.12	0.35	0.94
1984–1993	−0.04	0.23	0.10	0.21	0.34	0.94
1985–1994	0.00	0.21	0.17	0.20	0.37	0.93
1986–1995	−0.04	0.23	0.13	0.21	0.36	0.93
5-year periods						
1981–1985	−0.19	0.03	−0.12	0.04	0.53	0.88
1982–1986	−0.09	0.04	0.01	0.13	0.53	0.86
1983–1987	−0.14	0.09	0.06	0.08	0.25	0.93
1984–1988	−0.05	0.25	0.12	0.22	0.28	0.94
1985–1989	0.07	0.26	0.29	0.22	0.26	0.92
1986–1990	−0.06	0.23	0.15	0.18	0.30	0.91
1987–1991	−0.12	0.12	0.09	0.01	0.22	0.93
1988–1992	0.09	0.21	0.14	0.20	0.56	0.97
1989–1993	−0.02	0.16	0.06	0.17	0.50	0.96
1990–1994	−0.23	0.04	−0.18	0.10	0.59	0.98
1991–1995	0.02	0.25	0.09	0.32	0.52	0.98

STOCK/BOND/MANAGED FUTURES PORTFOLIOS VERSUS SINGLE-SECTOR PORTFOLIOS

Thus far, we have compared stock/bond/managed futures portfolios with stock/bond portfolios. It is particularly instructive to also consider comparisons with single-sector investments. In all of the following comparisons, the multisector portfolio is rebalanced monthly (a strategy that has repeatedly been demonstrated to improve performance) and leveraged to equalize its standard deviation to the single-sector investment standard deviation.

Figure 12.13 compares the "constrained worst" stock/bond/CTA portfolio with a 100 percent stock portfolio. As this chart demonstrates, the combination of diversification, leverage, and rebalancing employed by the multisector portfolio provides a tremendous improvement over a pure stock investment. Even though the two portfolios have equivalent risk levels, the

Figure 12.12
FUNDS/POOLS COSTS AS PERCENT OF EQUITY

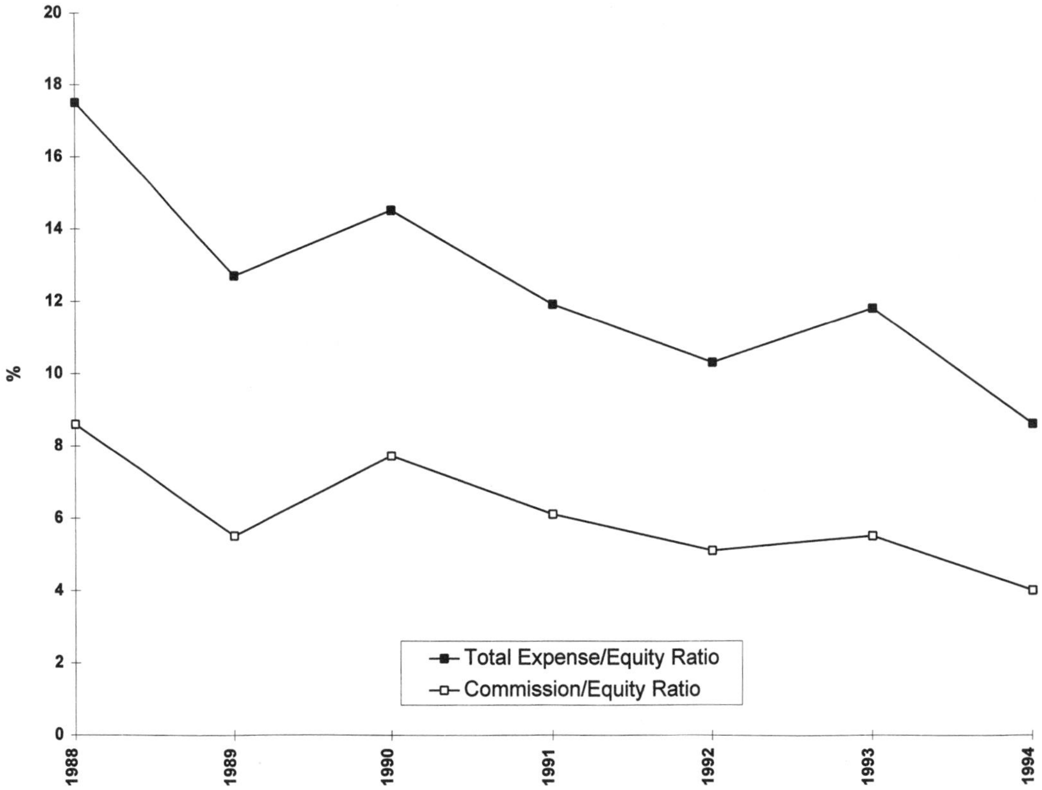

Source: Managed Accounts Reports.

ending NAV of the multisector investment including managed futures is nearly three times as high!

Figure 12.14 compares the "constrained worst" stock/bond/CTA portfolio with a 100 percent T-bond portfolio. Here too, the multisector portfolio provides a substantial improvement over the single-sector investment, although not nearly to the degree as in the case of the 100 percent stock investment. The more limited improvement is due to the much lower leverage used in this case (1.15 versus 1.46), a consequence of the much lower volatility of T-bonds.

Figures 12.15 and 12.16 are the counterparts to Figures 12.13 and 12.14 using the fund/pool index instead of the CTA index to represent managed futures. As would be expected, the performance differentials in these charts are considerably smaller than those of Figures 12.13 and

Figure 12.13
NAV COMPARISON: LEVERAGED "CONSTRAINED WORST" STOCK/BOND/CTA PORTFOLIO (WITH REBALANCING) VERSUS 100 PERCENT STOCK PORTFOLIO

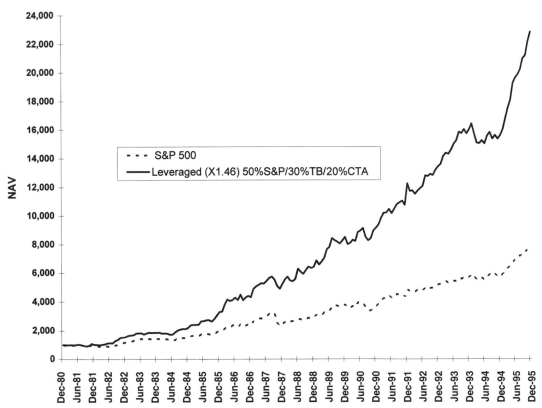

Data sources: S&P and T-bond series: Refco Information Services Inc., One World Financial Center, 200 Liberty Street, New York, NY 10281. CTA index: Managed Account Reports, 220 Fifth Avenue, New York, NY 10001.

Definitions: S&P 500 = S&P 500 total return; TB = long-term government-bond total return; CTA = MAR equal-weighted CTA index.

Notes: (1) "Constrained worst" defined as stock/bond/CTA portfolio with lowest modified Sharpe Ratio subject to constraints that minimum allocation for each sector equals 20 percent and maximum allocation equals 50 percent for stock and bond sectors and 30 percent for CTA. (2) Stock/bond/CTA portfolio leveraged by factor (1.46) to equalize standard deviation with 100 percent S&P 500 portfolio.

12.14—a result that is once again related to the inferior performance of the fund/pool index vis-à-vis the CTA index. Nevertheless, the key conclusion is that even the substantially inferior fund/pool index implies that a stock/bond/managed futures portfolio is likely to significantly outperform a 100 percent stock or 100 percent T-bond investment over the long term.

Figure 12.14
NAV COMPARISON: LEVERAGED "CONSTRAINED WORST" STOCK/BOND/CTA PORTFOLIO (WITH REBALANCING) VERSUS 100 PERCENT T-BOND PORTFOLIO

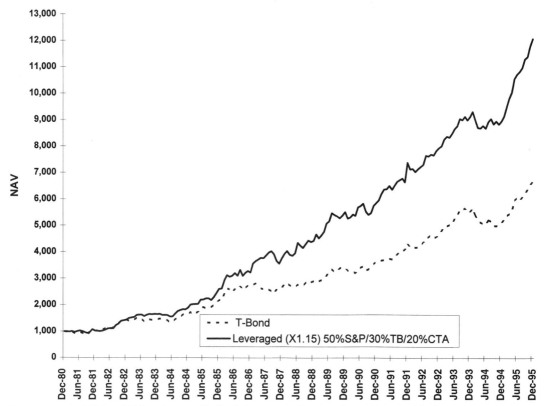

Data sources: S&P and T-bond series: Refco Information Services Inc., One World Financial Center, 200 Liberty Street, New York, NY 10281. CTA index: Managed Account Reports, 220 Fifth Avenue, New York, NY 10001.

Definitions: S&P = S&P 500 total return; T-Bond = long-term government-bond total return; CTA = MAR equal-weighted CTA index.

Notes: (1) "Constrained worst" defined as stock/bond/CTA portfolio with lowest modified Sharpe Ratio subject to constraints that minimum allocation for each sector equals 20 percent and maximum allocation equals 50 percent for stock and bond sectors and 30 percent for CTA. (2) Stock/bond/CTA portfolio leveraged by factor (1.15) to equalize standard deviation with 100 percent T-bond portfolio.

IMPLICATIONS OF OTHER STUDIES

Not surprisingly, there have been many other past studies on the efficacy of adding managed futures to conventional portfolios. As implied by the quotes at the start of this chapter, these studies have often reached completely contradictory conclusions. Fortunately, it is unnecessary to review all these articles since Edwards and Park have written a paper that, in addition to their

Figure 12.15
NAV COMPARISON: LEVERAGED "CONSTRAINED WORST" STOCK/BOND/FUND PORTFOLIO (WITH REBALANCING) VERSUS 100 PERCENT STOCK PORTFOLIO

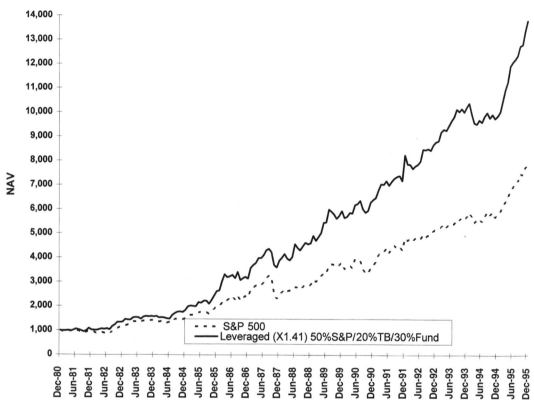

Data sources: S&P and T-bond series: Refco Information Services Inc., One World Financial Center, 200 Liberty Street, New York, NY 10281. Fund/pool index: Managed Account Reports, 220 Fifth Avenue, New York, NY 10001.

Definitions: S&P 500 = S&P 500 total return; TB = long-term government-bond total return; Fund = MAR equal-weighted fund/pool index.

Notes: (1) "Constrained worst" defined as stock/bond/commodity fund portfolio with lowest modified Sharpe Ratio subject to constraints that minimum allocation for each sector equals 20 percent and maximum allocation equals 50 percent for stock and bond sectors and 30 percent for commodity fund/pool sector. (2) Stock/bond/commodity fund portfolio leveraged by factor (1.41) to equalize standard deviation with 100 percent S&P 500 portfolio.

own research, summarizes the conclusions of other past academic studies.[10] In fact, they ultimately distill the conclusions of their own research and other past studies into a single highly informative table that is duplicated here as Table 12.12.

---

[10]Franklin R. Edwards and James M. Park, "Do Managed Futures Make Good Investments?" *The Journal of Futures Markets* 16(5) (1996).

Figure 12.16
NAV COMPARISON: LEVERAGED "CONSTRAINED WORST" STOCK/BOND/FUND
PORTFOLIO (WITH REBALANCING) VERSUS 100 PERCENT T-BOND PORTFOLIO

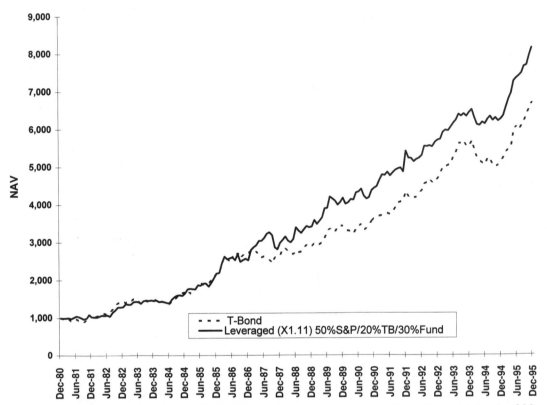

Data sources: S&P and T-bond series: Refco Information Services Inc., One World Financial Center, 200 Liberty Street, New York, NY 10281. Fund/pool index: Managed Account Reports, 220 Fifth Avenue, New York, NY 10001.

Definitions: S&P = S&P 500 total return; T-Bond and TB = long-term government-bond total return; Fund = MAR equal-weighted fund/pool index.

Notes: (1) "Constrained worst" defined as stock/bond/commodity fund portfolio with lowest modified Sharpe Ratio subject to constraints that minimum allocation for each sector equals 20 percent and maximum allocation equals 50 percent for stock and bond sectors and 30 percent for commodity fund/pool sector. (2) Stock/bond/commodity fund portfolio leveraged by factor (1.11) to equalize standard deviation with 100 percent T-bond portfolio.

An examination of Table 12.12 reveals one striking observation: *All* the past studies using CTA data found managed futures to be a beneficial portfolio asset, whereas more than half the studies using public commodity fund data reached the opposite conclusion. Thus, the apparent contradictions between the conclusions of past studies can be attributed to the type of data used: CTA or fund. In this context, it bears repeating that the historical per-

Table 12.12
SUMMARY OF ACADEMIC STUDY RESULTS

Column groups for the three performance ratings: **Performance as a Stand-Alone Investment** (Good / Mixed / Bad), **Performance as a Portfolio Asset** (Good / Mixed / Bad), **Performance as an Inflation Hedge[c]** (Good / Mixed / Bad).

CTAs	Time Period	75	76	77	78	79	80	81	82	83	84	85	86	87	88	89	90	91	92	93	SA Good	SA Mixed	SA Bad	PA Good	PA Mixed	PA Bad	IH Good	IH Mixed	IH Bad
Lintner (1983)	7/79–12/82					X	X	X	X												X			X					
Baraz & Eresian (I) (1986)	1/80–12/85						X	X	X	X	X	X									X			X					
Peters (1989)	1/80–12/88						X	X	X	X	X	X	X	X	X						X			X					
Oberuc (1990)	3/79–12/89					X	X	X	X	X	X	X	X	X	X	X					X			X					
Baraz & Eresian (II) (1990)	1/84–12/88										X	X	X	X	X						X			X					
Fischmar & Peters (1990)	1/80–12/88						X	X	X	X	X	X	X	X	X						X[a]			X					
Edwards & Park (1995)	1/83–12/92									X	X	X	X	X	X	X	X	X	X		X			X					
	1/83–12/88									X	X	X	X	X	X						X			X				X	
	1/89–12/92															X	X	X	X		X			X					
Private Commodity Pools																													
Orr (1987)	1/80–12/86						X	X	X	X	X	X	X								X			X			X		
Edwards & Park (1995)	1/83–12/92									X	X	X	X	X	X	X	X	X	X		X			X				X	
	1/83–12/88									X	X	X	X	X	X						X			X					
Public Commodity Funds																													
Lintner (1983)	7/79–12/82					X	X	X	X												X			X					
Irwin & Brorsen (1985)	1/75–12/83	X	X	X	X	X	X	X	X	X											X			X					
Brorsen & Irwin (1985)	12/78–5/83				X	X	X	X	X	X												X[b]							
Irwin & Landa (1987)	1/75–12/85	X	X	X	X	X	X	X	X	X	X	X									X			X					
Murphy (1987)	5/80–4/85						X	X	X	X	X	X										X			X				
Elton, Gruber & Rentzler (I) (1987)	7/79–6/85					X	X	X	X	X	X	X											X			X			
Elton, Gruber & Rentzler (II) (1990)	1/80–12/88						X	X	X	X	X	X	X	X	X								X			X			
Irwin, Krukmeyer & Zulaf (1992)	1/79–12/89					X	X	X	X	X	X	X	X	X	X	X						X			X				X
	1/82–12/89								X	X	X	X	X	X	X	X							X			X			X
	1/85–12/89											X	X	X	X	X							X			X			X
Edwards & Park (1995)	1/83–12/92									X	X	X	X	X	X	X	X	X	X				X			X		X	
	1/83–12/88									X	X	X	X	X	X								X			X			X
	1/89–12/92															X	X	X	X				X			X			X

Source: Franklin R. Edwards and James M. Park, "Do Managed Futures Make Good Investments?" *The Journal of Futures Markets* 16(5) (1996). Copyright © by John Wiley & Sons, Inc. Reprinted by permission of John Wiley & Sons, Inc.

[a]Fischmar and Peters use compromise stochastic dominance and find that the best compromise portfolios contain allocations to CTAs of greater than 20 percent.

[b]Borsen and Irwin apply stochastic dominance and find public futures funds to be superior for investors with higher risk tolerance, inferior for lower risk tolerance investors.

[c]All results, including this study, finding that investments with traders, pools, and funds are a good hedge against inflation, use year-to-year correlations. All results finding the contrary use month-to-month correlations.

formance difference between CTAs and funds is primarily due to the much higher costs charged by funds in the past—costs that have declined significantly in recent years. Consequently, taking into account the current lower cost structure, the weight of past studies is definitely skewed heavily in favor of adding managed futures to conventional portfolios, particularly if the investor takes care to avoid high-cost managed futures investments.

INDUSTRY CAPACITY LIMITATIONS

The research presented in this chapter, as well as the net implications of past research on the subject, strongly suggests that the addition of managed futures is likely to improve the performance of conventional stock/bond portfolios. Is there anything that could alter the validity of this conclusion in the future?

Figure 12.17
**MANAGED FUTURES: ANNUAL RETURNS VERSUS ESTIMATED
TOTAL ASSETS UNDER MANAGEMENT**

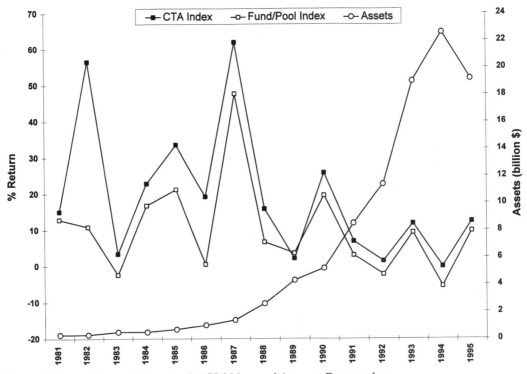

Source: Managed Account Reports; © 1996 Managed Account Reports, Inc.

Perhaps the biggest threat to continued favorable long-term performance by managed futures is excessive growth in the amount of assets under management. The capacity of the industry to manage money is not unlimited. As the percentage of assets managed by professionals becomes a larger portion of total trading, performance can be expected to deteriorate. It may not be a coincidence that the explosive expansion in assets under management during the early 1990s witnessed a simultaneous period of subpar performance (see Figure 12.17). Therefore, future excessive growth in assets under management could threaten the performance of this sector.

Over the long term, however, it is reasonable to expect an equilibrium to develop. Specifically, if excess participation of the managed trading industry as a percentage of all trading results in mediocre returns, such a lackluster performance will tend to cause some existing investors to withdraw their funds and simultaneously discourage new investors from committing funds to managed futures. The ensuing reduction of funds managed by the industry as a percentage of all trading would then allow performance to improve. Growth would thereby be contained around some theoretical equilibrium level, representing the amount of funds the industry could handle and still provide long-term performance results that are competitive with alternative investments (in terms of return/risk measures). The analogy to a natural ecological system appears appropriate. As managed futures traders overpopulate, so to speak, their numbers will exceed the level supportable by available "food" supplies. (Food, in this case, being the potential for trading profitability.)

In summary, viewed in a broad perspective, managed futures is likely to remain a viable addition to conventional stock/bond portfolios. However, periodic phases of excessive growth in assets managed should be viewed as caution signals regarding the relative performance of this sector.

BLUEPRINT FOR A SUPERIOR FUND

Using the principles suggested by the analysis of this chapter, it is possible to create a multisector fund that over the long term would have a high probability of outperforming the S&P 500, quite conceivably by a substantial margin, without any increase in risk. Since the majority of stock mutual funds underperform the S&P 500 index, the implication is that such a fund would be in the upper tier of performance within the mutual fund industry. The following step-by-step procedure could be used:

1. Decide on the percentage for the allocation of assets among the following sectors: (1) S&P 500, (2) long-term T-bonds, and (3) CTAs. The analysis of this chapter, which was based on data for the 1981–1995 period, suggests a portfolio mix of 20 percent–40 percent S&P 500, 40 percent–60 percent T-bonds, and 10 percent–30 percent CTAs (with the total obviously equaling 100 percent). The analysis of this chapter should be periodically updated to include new years of data, in order to determine whether these percentage ranges need revision.

2. Determine a leverage factor by dividing the standard deviation of the stock/bond/CTA portfolio by the standard deviation of the S&P 500 for the corresponding survey period. To avoid hindsight distortion of the analysis, it is strongly advised that the CTA index, rather than the data for CTAs actually selected, be used for the CTA component in this calculation. Risk-averse fund designers may wish to reduce the derived leverage factor by 10 to 15 percent to allow some margin for a possible increase in volatility in the stock/bond/CTA portfolio vis-à-vis the S&P 500.

3. Multiply the asset base by the leverage factor to determine the total investment size. Allocate each sector an amount equal to its percentage of the portfolio times the total investment. For example, assume a $100 million fund, using a 30 percent S&P 500/50 percent T-bond/20 percent CTA allocation and a 1.4 leverage factor. The allocations would then be: S&P 500, $42 million; T-bond, $70 million; and CTAs, $28 million.

The base stock and bond positions can be established in actual instruments or proxy futures positions. As was demonstrated earlier in this chapter, the two approaches will yield equivalent results. We will assume the use of proxy futures positions, since it simplifies the approach by using the same vehicle for both the base and leverage portions of the position.

Establish long S&P 500 and T-bond futures positions with a total contract value equal to the allocations (base plus leverage) of those sectors. As an illustration, assume the S&P 500 futures price is 600 and the T-bond futures price is 120. Using the just-cited fund example, a total of 140 S&P 500 and 583 T-bond futures contracts would be purchased. (At a price of 600, the contract value of the S&P 500 futures contract equals $300,000. Dividing the total S&P 500 allocation of $42 million by the $300,000 contract value yields 140 contracts. Similarly, at a price of 120, the contract value of the T-bond futures contract equals $120,000. Dividing the total T-bond allocation of $70 million by the $120,000 contract value yields 583 contracts.)

4. Allocate the CTA component of the investment to from four to seven CTAs that have been selected based on criteria considered important to the fund manager, as well as the criterion that they have low correlations with each other. This latter criterion, which substantially reduces the risk of the total CTA component relative to the individual CTAs chosen, should be viewed as an essential requirement as opposed to an optional condition. In fact, selecting low correlated CTAs is probably more important than any performance criteria, since correlations between past and future performance are tenuous at best (see Chapter 8), while CTA pair correlations tend to be relatively stable over time (see Chapter 11).

5. At the end of each month, rebalance the portfolio, that is, reallocate funds so as to restore the original percentage breakdown of the investment among the stock, bond, and CTA sectors (e.g., 30 percent stocks/50 percent bonds/20 percent CTAs). In addition, in line with the implications of Chapter 10, also internally rebalance the CTA component of the investment, that is, restore the original percentage allocations to each CTA at the end of each month.

STRATEGY MODIFICATIONS FOR THE INDIVIDUAL INVESTOR

An individual investor can use an analogous strategy by employing the following modifications:

1. Substitute one or two multimanager funds for the CTA component. (The large minimum account size requirements of most CTAs—often $500,000 or $1,000,000—would prohibit the use of individual CTAs by all but very wealthy individual investors.) The investor should select multimanager funds that meet the following two essential criteria:

(a) reasonable fee/commission structure;
(b) low pair correlations for the CTAs in the fund.

2. Substitute the smaller-sized NYFE futures contract for the S&P 500 futures contract and use the half-sized MidAm T-bond contract for allocation adjustments. If these smaller-sized contracts still don't allow sufficient fine-tuning of allocations, as is likely to be the case for all but very large investors, use a stock-index-based mutual fund and a long-term government T-bond fund as supplements or substitutes for S&P 500 futures and T-bond futures.

In essence, by using funds to represent all three sectors of the portfolio, even small investors can replicate the fund strategy detailed in the previous section. Of course, it would be easier to directly invest in a single fund using such a strategy, but to my knowledge none exists—at least not at this writing.

CONCLUSIONS

1. *The evidence that managed futures can boost portfolio performance is nothing short of compelling.* In the study detailed in this chapter, the addition of managed futures to a conventional stock/bond portfolio appeared to significantly improve performance *in all eight* of the periods surveyed using the CTA index as a proxy for managed futures, and in seven of the eight periods using the fund index as a proxy. In the latter case, the sole exception was the 1991–1995 period, a highly unrepresentative time frame that witnessed explosive bull markets in both stocks and bonds. Also, in view of the sharp decline in fees charged by futures funds during recent years, it is quite likely that the use of a pro forma fund index (that is, a fund index in which historical returns are adjusted to reflect current, rather than past, commission and fee levels) would show that the addition of managed futures would have improved performance even in the 1991–1995 period. (This hypothesis cannot be tested, however, because a pro forma fund index does not exist.)

The preponderance of past academic studies also concluded that the addition of managed futures improves portfolio performance. *All eight studies* listed in Table 12.12 that used either CTA or private commodity pool data found that managed futures were beneficial as a portfolio asset. The only studies that rated managed futures as a mixed or poor portfolio asset used public commodity fund data, an investment group that in the past, on average, had a very high commission rate and fee structure. In fact, some of these studies explicitly noted that the conclusion would have been different given a lower cost structure.

Thus all of the research on the merit of managed futures as a portfolio asset, both that original to this chapter as well as all the studies summarized by Edwards and Park in Table 12.12, reached the same conclusion: The addition of managed futures improved portfolio performance, except when the assumed investment vehicle was one with a high cost structure, such as public commodity funds (as a group) in past years.

2. *The improvement of a stock/bond/managed futures portfolio vis-à-vis a single-sector stock or bond investment is particularly pronounced.* For the maximum-length 15-year period, assuming monthly rebalancing, the "constrained worst"[11] stock/bond/managed futures (CTA-based) portfolio would have provided a 56 percent higher return/risk ratio than the S&P 500 total return index, and a 33 percent higher ratio than the long-term bond index. (Through the use of leverage, this performance improvement

---

[11]The assumptions implied by this term were defined earlier in this chapter.

could have been allocated entirely to higher return, entirely to lower risk, or any combination thereof.)

3. Of course, studies of the type detailed in this chapter only show which investment strategies would have been best *in the past*. The extrapolation of analogous conclusions for the future implicitly assumes similar performance patterns *in the future*. Normally, this is not a benign assumption, since the performance of different investment sectors can and does vary widely between different time periods. In this particular instance, however, this lack of performance time stability is not a problem. In fact, if anything, the variability in the relative performance of different investment sectors over time would only serve to enhance the conclusions of this chapter.

Why? Because the broad survey period (1981–1995) used in this chapter's analysis may well be the most bullish 15-year period in history for a stock/bond portfolio. Even so, the results demonstrated a pattern of pervasive improvement provided by adding managed futures to stock/bond portfolios. Consequently, in the event of more typical stock and bond market returns (viewed in terms of a broader historical perspective), the addition of managed futures to a stock/bond portfolio could be expected to boost performance even more dramatically. (An empirical test of this premise is not possible, since the managed futures industry prior to 1981 ranged from minuscule to nonexistent.) *In this context, I predict that the performance improvement provided by the addition of managed futures to stock/bond portfolios over the next 15-year period (1996–2010) will be even greater than demonstrated in this chapter for the prior 15-year period.*

4. There is a very wide range in commission rates and total fees in managed futures products. Therefore, differences in commission and fee charges alone can have a major impact on performance results (as exemplified by the wide performance difference between the CTA index and fund/pool index). The conclusions of this chapter assume that managed futures investments near the high end of the cost range are avoided. *Along this line, the substantial downtrend in commissions and fees witnessed in recent years makes it even more likely that the addition of managed futures to a portfolio will have a positive performance impact in coming years.*

5. The conclusions of this chapter assume that the managed futures investment consists of a well-diversified group of CTAs (either through direct investment or through a multimanager fund or pool). This assumption is very important because, as was demonstrated in Chapter 5, CTA indexes will tend to significantly understate the average risk level (or equivalently, overstate the average return/risk level) that can be expected in a single-manager investment. However, as was shown in Chapter 11, diversification among as few as four to seven relatively uncorrelated CTAs can achieve a diversification level approximately equivalent to an investment in all the CTAs of the index.[12] Even smaller investors should be able to fulfill this diversification assumption by investing in as few as one or two multimanager public funds that combine low-correlated CTAs.

6. *Monthly rebalancing tends to almost universally improve performance.* In fact, rebalancing even proved to have a net beneficial effect when one of the sectors (fund/pool index) exhibited significantly inferior performance to the other portfolio sectors (S&P 500 and long-term T-bonds).

7. Although the foregoing considerations provide a very strong case for the addition of managed futures to investment portfolios, one very important caveat must be cited: *If investment in managed futures grows too rapidly, the performance of this sector could be adversely affected.* Investments in the managed futures industry are absolutely minuscule compared with stock and bond investments. For example, if only 1 percent of all funds invested in mutual funds were shifted into managed futures, it would more than double the assets under management in this sector. Such an expansion, unless spread over many years, would probably have a significant negative impact on performance.

Therefore, ironically, if too many investors followed the advice of this chapter (whether influenced by this book or other sources reaching the same conclusion), the result would be self-defeating. In other words, what may be an optimal strategy for a small minority of investors is likely to be a subpar strategy if followed by a significant percentage of investors. Consequently, potential future investors are advised to monitor the growth of assets in managed futures, viewing an explosive expansion as a sign of caution.

---

[12]This is possible for two reasons: (1) As was shown in Chapter 11, most of the potential diversification benefit is achieved with the addition of the first few managers, and (2) since the index includes many CTAs that are highly correlated with other CTAs in the index, the selection of only relatively uncorrelated CTAs could yield a subset that is even more diversified than the entire index.

Epilogue

This book covers three major themes:

1. *Performance numbers are often not what they appear to be.* For a myriad of reasons detailed in Part One, it is entirely possible for one CTA to have a better trading record than another CTA, yet show inferior performance. Therefore it is important to be cognizant of these various pitfalls when evaluating and selecting CTAs. Ideally, however, in the future, a CTA reporting service will construct a pro forma CTA database that uses a common set of assumptions for all CTAs. As an example, CTA track records constructed using this method might employ the following set of assumptions:

- Monthly percent return calculations would be based only on fully funded accounts. (If none existed for the given program, notional accounts would be used, with returns based on the documented nominal account size.)
- Monthly percent return calculations would be based only on accounts without any additions/withdrawals in the given month.
- Net return calculations would be based on a common commission rate (e.g., $10–$14 per round turn) for all CTAs instead of the actual commissions paid by past investors.[1]
- A common management fee/profit incentive fee combination (e.g., 2%/20%, 1%/25%) would be used for all CTAs instead of the actual fees charged to past investors.
- A common interest income assumption would be used for all CTAs (e.g., T-bill rate, 80% T-bill rate) instead of the actual interest income received in the past.

---

[1]The performance reporting service, however, would need to know the average number of trades per $1 million for each CTA in order to translate this commission assumption into total commission figures.

Track records constructed based on the foregoing or similar guidelines would isolate differences due to trading performance as opposed to differences due to a variety of extraneous factors unrelated to trading (e.g., funding level, timing of additions/withdrawals, commissions, management fees, profit incentive fees, interest income).

2. *Past performance is far less predictive of future performance than generally believed.* Some of the specific conclusions found included:

- Prospectus results are highly biased toward overstating future potential performance—an almost inevitable consequence of the hindsight selection process used in their construction.
- Past performance *levels* are useless in predicting future performance *levels*.
- Based on the currently available data, past *relative* performance is not a statistically significant indicator of future *relative* performance. In this instance, however, it is possible that the accumulation of more data over the coming years may eventually demonstrate some correlation between past and future relative performance. In any case, at the very least, the correlation between past and future relative performance is certainly far smaller than generally believed.

3. *There are investment strategies that can be used to enhance expected portfolio performance.* Interestingly, some of these approaches are highly counterintuitive, even though the statistical evidence indicating that they provide an edge ranges from strongly suggestive to overwhelming. These investment strategies include:

- Launching investments on drawdowns rather than on upside excursions in equity will usually result in better performance outcomes.
- Diversifying among a selected group of relatively uncorrelated CTAs is likely to provide an investment with a better expected return/risk ratio than can be achieved by selecting an individual CTA. (If desired, leverage can be used to transform the reduced risk benefits into a higher return.)
- Monthly rebalancing in a multiadvisor pool is likely to significantly improve return/risk. (If desired, leverage can be used to transform the reduced risk benefits into a higher return.)
- Adding managed futures as an investment sector in a standard stock/bond portfolio is likely to improve long-term performance (in return/risk terms), provided that the selected managed futures investments have average or below-average costs. (If desired, leverage can be used to transform the reduced risk benefits into a higher return.)

Within these broad themes, this book has demonstrated many specific key fallacies and counterintuitive truths regarding managed trading. It may be useful to summarize some of these observations and conclusions:

PERFORMANCE EVALUATION

1. In the case of single-manager performance results, a properly constructed pro forma table will provide a much more realistic performance picture than a table based on so-called actual results.
2. Additions and withdrawals by investors can lead to extreme distortions in a money manager's performance statistics, *even using government-approved reporting methods.*
3. *Extracted performance*—results based on *actual* trades but limited to only a subset of markets in an existing trading program—can be as misleading as *hypothetical performance.*
4. There is a critical difference between *hypothetical* results and *simulated* results generated in real time: The former is constructed with the benefit of hindsight, whereas the latter is not.
5. *Actual* funds should never be used to measure performance in a *notionally* funded account.
6. Comparisons of performance results derived using different sets of assumptions can easily lead to wildly inaccurate conclusions. Valid performance comparisons require both similar market portfolios and common time periods. In addition, performance comparisons should also adjust for differences in management fees and commissions.
7. The Return Risk Ratio (RRR), a new measure introduced in this book series, more closely describes investors' intuitive sense of return/risk than the widely used Sharpe Ratio.
8. All conventional commodity trading advisor (CTA) indexes are misleading in that they significantly understate risk and, hence, overstate return/risk.

PREDICTABILITY OF PERFORMANCE

9. The evidence demonstrating that pool (and fund) performance routinely deteriorates dramatically below the prospectus levels is nothing short of compelling. Therefore, generally speaking, investors should not expect prospectus returns to be even remotely approached.
10. There is unanimous agreement among academic studies that past performance *levels* do not provide a reliable indication of future

performance levels (and that prepublic prospectus returns are biased as well).

11. The tenuous link between past and future performance applies not only to performance *levels* but to *relative* performance as well. Viewed across all time periods surveyed, correlations between past and future *relative* performance were remarkably close to zero for all the return and return/risk measures considered. The bottom line is that even if past and future relative performance are related, the degree of correlation is far smaller than generally assumed.

INVESTMENT AND PORTFOLIO ISSUES

12. Investors are truly their own worst enemy. The natural instincts of most investors lead them to do exactly the wrong thing with uncanny persistence.

13. A prime example of such an investor blunder is the tendency to commit to an investment right after it has done very well and to liquidate an investment right after it has done very poorly. As a corollary pertaining to managed futures, investors would be better off initiating accounts after the selected CTA has experienced a drawdown as opposed to after he or she has witnessed a winning streak. The common tendency of many people to do the exact opposite probably represents the single worst mistake made in managed futures investment.

14. The implied lesson is that investors should separate the processes of selecting and timing investments, and once having selected the investment, should wait for it to do poorly, not well, before actually initiating an account.

15. Shifting assets from traders who have just performed best in a given portfolio to those who have performed worst (i.e., rebalancing) is often an excellent investment strategy, even though it runs completely counter to natural human instincts.

16. It is questionable whether it is even possible to identify a group of managers that are likely to exhibit above-average *future* performance. Single-manager funds not only make this assumption, but make the further assumption that it is possible to identify the *single manager within this group* that is likely to have the *best future* performance. This is a highly tenuous assumption.

   Assuming that it is not possible to select a *single* manager that has a significant probability of outperforming *all* other managers in the *future*—a very realistic assumption—there would always exist a multimanager combination with a higher expected return/risk than any single manager. Therefore, *if performance is the primary criterion,* it will rarely make sense for a fund developer to use a single-manager approach.

17. The common argument cited to justify using a single-manager approach—that it increases the chances of achieving a well-above-average return (if one is willing to accept the higher risk)—is entirely fallacious. Why? Because by using leverage (through notional funding), it is always possible to add one or more managers to the original manager selected and achieve the *same expected return at a lower risk level (or an even higher return at the same risk level).*

18. In summary, the diversification debate is about as meaningful a controversy as the dispute whether the Earth is round or flat: There may be two sides to the argument, but they are hardly of equal merit. Diversification improves the odds of obtaining a more favorable return/risk outcome. Fund developers who select a single-manager as opposed to a multimanager approach are deliberately selecting a strategy with lower odds.[2]

19. Despite the overwhelming theoretical and empirical evidence supporting the benefits of diversification, as of late 1995, 57 percent of all funds and pools monitored by Managed Account Reports were single manager—a statistically inferior strategy (in return/risk terms).

20. The evidence that managed futures can boost portfolio performance is nothing short of compelling.

21. The only studies that rated managed futures as a mixed or poor portfolio asset used public commodity fund data—an investment group that in the past, on average, had a very high commission rate and fee structure. In fact, some of these studies explicitly noted that the conclusion would have been different given a lower cost structure.

22. All of the research on the merit of managed futures as a portfolio asset reached the same conclusion: The addition of managed futures improved portfolio performance, except when the assumed investment vehicle was one with a high cost structure, such as public commodity funds (as a group) in past years.

23. The performance improvement provided by a stock/bond/managed futures portfolio vis-à-vis a single sector stock or bond investment is particularly pronounced.

---

[2]Single-manager funds can be theoretically justified, however, if they are part of a group of such investments intended to be used in combination.

24. The substantial downtrend in commissions and fees witnessed in recent years makes it even more likely that the addition of managed futures to a portfolio will have a positive performance impact in coming years.

25. One important caveat to the potential benefit of adding managed futures to a portfolio is that a sudden, large investment influx into this sector could have a deleterious effect on performance.

26. Monthly rebalancing tends to almost universally improve portfolio performance. In fact, rebalancing even proved net beneficial when one of the sectors exhibited significantly inferior performance relative to the other portfolio sectors.

APPENDIXES

1 Counterpart Table to Table 1.1 with Monthly Profit Incentive Accruals Shown as per Accounting Regulations

NAV FOR CTA A

Month	Beginning Month NAV	Gross Percent Return (Expressed as a Factor of 1)	Gross Profit/Loss	Commissions[a]	Cumulative Net Profit/Loss Since Last Incentive Charge	Quarterly Profit Incentive[b]	Ending Month NAV
Jan	1,000.00	1.02	20.00	5.00	15.00	3.75	1,011.25
Feb	1,011.25	0.97	−30.34	5.06	−20.39	−3.75	979.61
Mar	979.61	0.92	−78.37	4.90	−103.66	0.00	896.34
Apr	896.34	1.09	80.67	4.48	−27.47	0.00	972.53
May	972.53	1.07	68.08	4.86	35.74	8.94	1,026.81
Jun	1,026.81	0.98	−20.54	5.13	10.07	−6.42	1,007.55
Jul	1,007.55	1.11	110.83	5.04	105.79	26.45	1,086.90
Aug	1,086.90	1.13	141.30	5.43	241.66	33.97	1,188.80
Sep	1,188.80	0.88	−142.66	5.94	93.06	−37.15	1,077.35
Oct	1,077.35	1.04	43.09	5.39	37.71	9.43	1,105.63
Nov	1,105.63	0.99	−11.06	5.53	21.12	−4.15	1,093.19
Dec	1,093.19	0.94	−65.59	5.47	−49.93	−5.28	1,027.41
Jan	1,027.41	1.07	71.92	5.14	16.85	4.21	1,089.98
Feb	1,089.98	1.06	65.40	5.45	76.80	14.99	1,134.94
Mar	1,134.94	1.02	22.70	5.67	93.82	4.26	1,147.71
Apr	1,147.71	0.95	−57.39	5.74	−63.12	0.00	1,084.59
May	1,084.59	1.07	75.92	5.42	7.37	1.84	1,153.24
Jun	1,153.24	1.08	92.26	5.77	93.87	21.62	1,218.11
Jul	1,218.11	0.93	−85.27	6.09	−91.36	0.00	1,126.75
Aug	1,126.75	0.98	−22.54	5.63	−119.53	0.00	1,098.59
Sep	1,098.59	1.12	131.83	5.49	6.81	1.70	1,223.22
Oct	1,223.22	1.06	73.39	6.12	67.28	16.82	1,273.68
Nov	1,273.68	1.02	25.47	6.37	86.38	4.78	1,288.01
Dec	1,288.01	0.98	−25.76	6.44	54.18	−8.05	1,263.86

[a]Commissions are assumed to equal 0.0005 of beginning month NAV (1,000 trades per month, per $1 million, at $5 round turn).

[b]Profit incentive fee paid quarterly and assumed to equal 25 percent of cumulative net new profits since payment of last incentive fee. Fee, however, is shown accrued monthly in conformance with CFTC accounting regulations.

2 Sample EXCEL Worksheet Calculation of Return Retracement Ratio

	A	B	C	D	E	F	G	H
1		MONTH-END EQUITY (E)	MONTHLY RETURN	DECIMAL RETURN	PEAK EQUITY (PE)	MAXIMUM RETRACEMENT FROM PRIOR PEAK (MRPP)	MAXIMUM RETRACEMENT TO SUBSEQUENT LOW (MRSL)	MAXIMUM RETRACEMENT (MR)
2	Dec 92	1,000.0			1,000.0			
3	Jan 93	1,007.2	0.72	1.0072	1,007.2	0.00	0.39	0.39
4	Feb 93	1,007.0	-0.02	0.9998	1,007.2	0.02	1.10	1.10
5	Mar 93	996.1	-1.08	0.9892	1,007.2	1.10	1.08	1.10
6	Apr 93	1,059.2	6.33	1.0633	1,059.2	0.00	0.00	0.00
7	May 93	1,105.0	4.33	1.0433	1,105.0	0.00	0.00	0.00
8	Jun 93	1,180.1	6.79	1.0679	1,180.1	0.00	0.00	0.00
9	Jul 93	1,244.3	5.44	1.0544	1,244.3	0.00	2.78	2.78
10	Aug 93	1,241.8	-0.20	0.9980	1,244.3	0.20	7.80	7.80
11	Sep 93	1,252.3	0.85	1.0085	1,252.3	0.00	7.61	7.61
12	Oct 93	1,147.3	-8.39	0.9161	1,252.3	8.39	8.39	8.39
13	Nov 93	1,185.1	3.30	1.0330	1,252.3	5.37	0.00	5.37
14	Dec 93	1,259.5	6.28	1.0628	1,259.5	0.00	0.00	0.00
15	Jan 94	1,299.9	3.20	1.0320	1,299.9	0.00	4.57	4.57
16	Feb 94	1,202.0	-7.53	0.9247	1,299.9	7.53	7.53	7.53
17	Mar 94	1,274.5	6.03	1.0603	1,299.9	1.95	0.00	1.95
18	Apr 94	1,268.8	-0.44	0.9956	1,299.9	2.39	0.44	2.39
19	May 94	1,300.9	2.53	1.0253	1,300.9	0.00	0.00	0.00
20	Jun 94	1,330.3	2.26	1.0226	1,330.3	0.00	0.00	0.00
21	Jul 94	1,362.8	2.44	1.0244	1,362.8	0.00	0.00	0.00
22	Aug 94	1,342.0	-1.53	0.9847	1,362.8	1.53	1.53	1.53
23	Sep 94	1,386.0	3.28	1.0328	1,386.0	0.00	0.00	0.00
24	Oct 94	1,431.2	3.26	1.0326	1,431.2	0.00	0.00	0.00
25	Nov 94	1,531.1	6.98	1.0698	1,531.1	0.00	0.34	0.34
26	Dec 94	1,475.9	-3.60	0.9640	1,531.1	3.60	6.84	6.84

27	Jan 95	1,426.3	-3.36	0.9664	1,531.1	6.84	3.36	6.84
28	Feb 95	1,505.1	5.52	1.0552	1,531.1	1.70	0.00	1.70
29	Mar 95	1,635.1	8.64	1.0864	1,635.1	0.00	4.73	4.73
30	Apr 95	1,691.7	3.46	1.0346	1,691.7	0.00	12.31	12.31
31	May 95	1,759.7	4.02	1.0402	1,759.7	0.00	15.24	15.24
32	Jun 95	1,794.7	1.99	1.0199	1,794.7	0.00	18.52	18.52
33	Jul 95	1,676.1	-6.61	0.9339	1,794.7	6.61	20.11	20.11
34	Aug 95	1,572.8	-6.16	0.9384	1,794.7	12.36	14.45	14.45
35	Sep 95	1,470.6	-6.5	0.9350	1,794.7	18.06	8.84	18.06
36	Oct 95	1,433.8	-2.5	0.9750	1,794.7	20.11	2.50	20.11
37	Nov 95	1,559.3	8.75	1.0875	1,794.7	13.12	0.00	13.12
38	Dec 95	1,703.5	9.25	1.0925	1,794.7	5.08	0.00	5.08
39		**R =**	**19.43**				**AMR =**	**5.83**
40							**RRR =**	**3.3320**

40 Instructions:

41 Note: The following instructions assume first data line is row 2 and first monthly return is entered in row 3:

42 1. Set both Equity (E) [cell B2] and Peak Equity (PE) [cell E2] equal to 1,000 for month prior to first month of return data.

43 2. Enter months [cell A2 down], and insert monthly returns in column C [cell C3 down].

44 3. Enter following formula in cell B3: **=B2*(1+(C3/100))**

45 4. Enter following formula in cell D3: **=(1+C3/100)**

46 5. Enter following formula in cell E3: **=MAX(B3,E2)**

47 6. Enter following formula in cell F3: **=100*(E3-B3)/E3**

48 7. Enter following formula in cell G3: **=100*(B2-MIN(B2:B$38))/B2**   (Note:This formula and steps 10 and 11 below use "38"

49 because 38 is last data row. In practice, substitute number of actual last row for 38.)

50 8. Enter following formula in cell H3: **=MAX(F3,G3)**

51 9. Drag and fill entries for B3,D3,E3,F3,G3, and H3 through row containing last month of return data.

52 10. Enter following formula in cell for average annualized compounded return (R): **=100*(POWER(GEOMEAN(D3:D38),12)-1)**

53 11. Enter following formula in cell for average maximum retracement (AMR): **=AVERAGE(H3:H38)**

54 12. The return retracement ratio (RRR) is equal to R/AMR. In this sample sheet formula for R: **= D39/H39**

55

3 CTA Lists Used for Performance Ranking Tests for Past Periods

CTA LIST USED FOR PERFORMANCE RANKING TESTS FOR PAST PERIODS BEGINNING IN 1987

Advisor Name	Program Name
Anglo Dutch Investments Limited	CP Energy
AZF Commodity Management	General
Beacon Management Corporation	Beacon System
Campbell & Company	Global Diversified Portfolio
Commodity Capital, Inc.	Agricultural
Cristo Commodities Inc.	Primarily Energy
Dunn Capital Management, Inc.	World Monetary Assets Program
EMC Capital Management, Inc.	Diversified
Fairfield Financial Group, Inc.	Composite
Fundamental Futures, Inc.	Grains & Meats
ICSC, Inc.	Diversified
JPD Enterprises, Inc.	Global Diversified
Knilo International Trading Limited	Diversified
LaSalle Portfolio Management, Inc.	Financial Instruments Program
Little Brook Corporation of New Jersey	CRAFT
MC Futures Inc.	Diversified
Millburn Ridgefield Corporation	Composite
Mississippi River Investments, Inc.	Managed Account Program
Prospective Commodities Inc.	Strategic Diversified
Rabar Market Research Inc.	Diversified
RXR Inc.	Diversified Trading Program
Sunrise Capital Partners, LLC (Sunrise)	Diversified
Tactical Investment Management Corp.	Flagship Program
Visioneering R & D Co.	V-100 Model
Waldner Financial Corporation	Diversified

CTA LIST USED FOR PERFORMANCE RANKING TESTS FOR PAST PERIODS BEGINNING IN 1988

Advisor Name	Program Name
Anglo Dutch Investments Limited	CP Energy
AZF Commodity Management	General
Beacon Management Corporation	Beacon System
Campbell & Company	Global Diversified Portfolio
Commodity Capital, Inc.	Agricultural
Cristo Commodities Inc.	Primarily Energy
Dunn Capital Management, Inc.	World Monetary Assets Program
EMC Capital Management, Inc.	Diversified
Fairfield Financial Group, Inc.	Composite
Fundamental Futures, Inc.	Grains & Meats
ICSC, Inc.	Diversified
JPD Enterprises, Inc.	Global Diversified
Knilo International Trading Limited	Diversified
LaSalle Portfolio Management, Inc.	Financial Instruments Program
Little Brook Corporation of New Jersey	CRAFT
MC Futures Inc.	Diversified
Millburn Ridgefield Corporation	Composite
Mississippi River Investments, Inc.	Managed Account Program
Prospective Commodities Inc.	Strategic Diversified
Rabar Market Research Inc.	Diversified
RXR Inc.	Diversified Trading Program
Sunrise Capital Partners, LLC (Sunrise)	Diversified
Tactical Investment Management Corp.	Flagship Program
Visioneering R & D Co.	V-100 Model
Waldner Financial Corporation	Diversified
Chesapeake Capital Corporation	Diversified
Crow Trading, Inc.	Agricultural
Gaiacorp Ireland Limited	GAIA Hedge II
Gateway Investment Advisers Inc.	Index/RA
Hyman Beck & Company, Inc.	Composite
PRAGMA, Inc.	Beta
Trendlogic Associates, Inc.	Diversified
Willowbridge Associates Inc.	Rex
Willowbridge Associates Inc.	Vulcan

CTA LIST USED FOR PERFORMANCE RANKING TESTS FOR PAST PERIODS BEGINNING IN 1989

Advisor Name	Program Name
AZF Commodity Management	General
Beacon Management Corporation	Beacon System
Campbell & Company	Global Diversified Portfolio
Commodity Capital, Inc.	Agricultural
Cristo Commodities Inc.	Primarily Energy
Dunn Capital Management, Inc.	World Monetary Assets Program
EMC Capital Management, Inc.	Diversified
Fairfield Financial Group, Inc.	Composite
Fundamental Futures, Inc.	Grains & Meats
ICSC, Inc.	Diversified
JPD Enterprises, Inc.	Global Diversified
Knilo International Trading Limited	Diversified
LaSalle Portfolio Management, Inc.	Financial Instruments Program
Little Brook Corporation of New Jersey	CRAFT
Millburn Ridgefield Corporation	Composite
Mississippi River Investments, Inc.	Managed Account Program
Prospective Commodities Inc.	Strategic Diversified
Rabar Market Research Inc.	Diversified
RXR Inc.	Diversified Trading Program
Sunrise Capital Partners, LLC (Sunrise)	Diversified
Tactical Investment Management Corp.	Flagship Program
Visioneering R & D Co.	V-100 Model
Waldner Financial Corporation	Diversified
Chesapeake Capital Corporation	Diversified
Crow Trading, Inc.	Agricultural
D.F. Advisors, Inc.	Composite
Dallas Commodity Co., Inc.	Computek
Gaiacorp Ireland Limited	GAIA Hedge II
Gandon Fund Management Ltd.	Global Financial
Gateway Investment Advisers Inc.	Index/RA
Hawksbill Capital Management	Global Diversified
Hyman Beck & Company, Inc.	Diversified
Northfield Trading L.P.	Diversified
PRAGMA, Inc.	Beta
Saxon Investment Corporation	Diversified Program
SJO, Inc.	Foreign Financials
Strategic Investments	Strategic Timing Program
Trendlogic Associates, Inc.	Diversified
Trendstat Capital Management, Inc.	Multi-Trend
Willowbridge Associates Inc.	Rex
Willowbridge Associates Inc.	Vulcan

CTA LIST USED FOR PERFORMANCE RANKING TESTS FOR PAST PERIODS BEGINNING IN 1990

Advisor Name	Program Name
A. Gary Shilling & Co., Inc.	Thematic Investment Partners
Abacus Trading Corporation	Diversified
Abraham Trading Co.	Diversified
Advanced Trading Strategies Ltd.	Alert Currency Trading Program
Andre Dudek	Composite
Anglo Dutch Investments Limited	CP Energy
AZF Commodity Management	General
Beacon Management Corporation	Composite
Beacon Management Corporation	Beacon System
Bishop Enderby Corporation	Composite
Campbell & Company	Global Diversified Portfolio
Capital Futures Management S.A.	Financial
Charles C. Curran	Harvest Futures Fund
Chesapeake Capital Corporation	Diversified
Colorado Commodities Management Corporation	Currency/Financial Program
Commodity Capital, Inc.	Agricultural
Cristo Commodities Inc.	Primarily Energy
Crow Trading, Inc.	Agricultural
D.F. Advisors, Inc.	Composite
Denant Pty. Limited	Australian Program
DGM Investments Inc.	Cotton Trading Partners, L.P.
Dominion Futures Limited	Composite
Duich Investment Company, Inc.	Diversified
Dunn Capital Management, Inc.	World Monetary Assets Program
EMC Capital Management, Inc.	Diversified
Fairfield Financial Group, Inc.	Composite
Friedberg Commodity Management Inc.	Currency Only Trading Program
Fundamental Futures, Inc.	Grains & Meats
FX Concepts, Inc.	7X Leverage CAAC
FX500 Ltd.	Speculative Account
Gaiacorp Ireland Limited	GAIA Hedge II
Gallagher Investment Limited	Currency
Gandon Fund Management Ltd.	Global Financial
Gateway Investment Advisers Inc.	Index/RA
GK Capital Management Inc.	International Currency Program
GNI Fund Management	The Spread Programme
groupVERITAS	Diversified
Hanseatic Corporation	S&P 500 Futures
Hawksbill Capital Management	Global Diversified
Hyman Beck & Company, Inc.	Diversified

CTA LIST USED FOR PERFORMANCE RANKING TESTS FOR PAST PERIODS BEGINNING IN 1990 (continued)

Advisor Name	Program Name
ICSC, Inc.	Diversified
III Associates, Inc.	III Limited Partnership
JPD Enterprises, Inc.	Global Diversified
KMJ Capital Management, Inc.	Diversified
Knilo International Trading Limited	Diversified
LaSalle Portfolio Management, Inc.	Financial Instruments Program
Little Brook Corporation of New Jersey	CRAFT
Lyon Investment Corporation	Composite
Marathon Capital Growth Partners, L.L.C.	System Diversified
Mark J. Walsh & Company	Diversified
Michael J. Frischmeyer	Iowa Commodities Fee Schedule
Millburn Ridgefield Corporation	Composite
Mississippi River Investments, Inc.	Managed Account Program
Namath-Hanger Investment Corporation	Diversified
Niederhoffer Investments, Inc.	Composite
Norshield Asset Management Ltd.	Intermediate Term
Northfield Trading L.P.	Diversified
PRAGMA, Inc.	Beta
Prospective Commodities Inc.	Strategic Diversified
Qualchan Investments, Inc.	Financial
Quantitative Financial Strategies, Inc.	IPS Financial Futures
Quicksilver Trading, Inc.	Original Program
Rabar Market Research Inc.	Diversified
Red Oak Commodities Advisors, Inc.	Diversified
Regal Asset Management Corporation	Composite
RXR Inc.	Diversified Trading Program
Sabre Fund Management, Ltd.	Diversified
Saxon Investment Corporation	Diversified Program
SCI Capital Management	Domestic Asset Allocation
SJO, Inc.	Foreign Financials
Star-Tex Asset Management, Inc.	Diversified
Strategic Investments	Strategic Timing Program
Sunrise Capital Partners, LLC (Sunrise)	Diversified
Tactical Investment Management Corp.	Flagship Program
Tamiso & Company	Lexford Partners
Telesis Management, Inc.	Institutional Program
TimeTech Management, Inc.	TimeTech Managed Account
Trendlogic Associates, Inc.	Diversified
Trendstat Capital Management, Inc.	Multi-Trend
Visioneering R & D Co.	V-100 Model
Visioneering R & D Co.	V-50 Model

CTA LIST USED FOR PERFORMANCE RANKING TESTS FOR PAST PERIODS BEGINNING IN 1990 (continued)

Advisor Name	Program Name
Waldner Financial Corporation	Diversified
Willowbridge Associates Inc.	Rex
Willowbridge Associates Inc.	Vulcan
Witter & Lester, Inc.	Stock Index Futures Trading
Zack H. Bacon III	Bacon Fund

4 Formula for Calculating Profit Incentive Fees for 2-CTA Fund

CRITERIA

The formula provided meets the following criteria:

1. The fund is only charged an incentive feel when the fund reaches a new high quarterly net asset value (NAV), and the fee is paid only on the new high profits *of the fund*.
2. When condition 1 is met and both commodity trading advisors (CTAs) reach a new high quarterly NAV, each CTA will receive an incentive fee equal to the difference between the cumulative incentive they would have received on their own minus the cumulative incentive fee they had received as of the prior quarter.
3. When condition 1 is met and only one CTA makes a new high, the incentive fee is distributed in such a way so that the cumulative incentive fees received by each CTA will be proportional to their performance.

LIST OF SYMBOLS

$$PIFCTA1 = \text{Quarterly profit incentive fee due CTA1}$$
$$ACUMCTA1 = \text{Actual cumulative profit incentive fee of CTA1}$$
$$ACUMCTA1PQ = \text{Actual cumulative profit incentive fee of CTA1 in prior quarter}$$
$$ACUMFUND = \text{Actual cumulative profit incentive fee of fund}$$

ACUMFUNDPQ =   Actual cumulative profit incentive fee of fund in
                prior quarter
TCUMCTA1 =   Theoretical cumulative profit incentive fee of CTA1
                (i.e., fee CTA would have received in a single
                CTA fund)
TCUMCTA2 =   Theoretical cumulative profit incentive fee of CTA2

FORMULA FOR QUARTERLY PROFIT INCENTIVE FEE PAYMENT

Case 1. Fund NAV Is Not a New High.   No incentive fee is paid.

Case 2. Fund NAV Is a New High and Both CTA NAVs Are New Highs.   Each CTA will receive the amount necessary to bring their cumulative incentive fee up to the amount they would have received in a single CTA fund with the same profit incentive fee rate. Or in formula terms (for CTA1; CTA2 analogous):

$$PIFCTA1 = TCUMCTA1 - ACUMCTA1PQ$$

Case 3. Fund NAV Is a New High and Only One CTA NAV Is a New High.   The following formula will result in the ratio of the cumulative incentive fees paid to the CTAs being equal to the ratio of their theoretical profit incentive fees (*to the extent possible without having any CTA return any previously received incentive fees*). (The formula is stated in terms of CTA1; CTA2 analogous):

$$PIFCTA1 = ACUMCTA1 - ACUMCTA1PQ$$
$$\text{where } ACUMCTA1 = \text{Minimum of:}$$

1. Maximum of:
   (a) ACUMCTA1PQ, and
   (b) $(TCUMCTA1/ (TCUMCTA1 + TCUMCTA2))^*$ ACUMFUND
2. ACUMCTA1PQ + ACUMFUND – ACUMFUNDPQ

Once the actual cumulative profit incentive fee is calculated, the derivation of the quarterly profit incentive fee payment is a matter of simple subtraction. The following EXCEL worksheet example and formulas illustrate a spreadsheet methodology for calculating the actual cumulative profit incentive fee.

SAMPLE EXCEL WORKSHEET: CUMULATIVE PROFIT INCENTIVE FEE CALCULATION FOR 2-CTA CASE

	A	B	C	D	E	F	G	H	I	J	K
1	NAV1	NAV2	PEAK NAV1	PEAK NAV2	THEOR. CUM. PIF CTA1	THEOR. CUM. PIF CTA2	POOL NAV	PEAK NAV POOL	CUM. PIF POOL	ACTUAL CUM. PIF CTA1	ACTUAL CUM. PIF CTA2
2	1000	1000	1000	1000			2000	2000			
3	900	1100	1000	1100	0	20	2000	2000	0	0	0
4	1100	800	1100	1100	20	20	1900	2000	0	0	0
5	1400	1100	1400	1100	80	20	2500	2500	100	80	20
6	1200	1200	1400	1200	80	40	2400	2500	100	80	20
7	1400	1000	1400	1200	80	40	2400	2500	100	80	20
8	800	900	1400	1200	80	40	1700	2500	100	80	20
9	1600	1300	1600	1300	120	60	2900	2900	180	120	60
10	1500	1200	1600	1300	120	60	2700	2900	180	120	60
11	1800	1500	1800	1500	160	100	3300	3300	260	160	100
12	1600	1800	1800	1800	160	160	3400	3400	280	160	120
13	1800	2200	1800	2200	160	240	4000	4000	400	160	240
14	2200	1800	2200	2200	240	240	4000	4000	400	160	240
15	2600	2200	2600	2200	320	240	4800	4800	560	320	240
16	3000	2500	3000	2500	400	300	5500	5500	700	400	300
17	3200	2200	3200	2500	440	300	5400	5500	700	400	300
18	2800	2600	3200	2600	440	320	5400	5500	700	400	300
19	2600	3000	3200	3000	440	400	5600	5600	720	400	320
20	3200	2900	3200	3000	440	400	6100	6100	820	429.524	390.47619
21											
22	The fixed entries for row 2 and the EXCEL formulas for row 3 are as follows (drag and fill columns C through										
23	K for entries in other rows):										
24											
25											

	A	B	C	D	E
1	NAV1	NAV2	Peak NAV1	Peak NAV2	Theor. Cum. PIF CTA1
2	1000	1000	1000	1000	
3	900	1100	=MAX(A3,C2)	=MAX(B3,D2)	=0.2*(C3-1000)

	F	G	H	I
1	Theor. Cum. PIF CTA2	Pool NAV	Peak NAV Pool	Cum. PIF Pool
2		2000	2000	
3	=0.2*(D3-1000)	=(A3+B3)	=MAX(G3,H2)	=0.2*(H3-2000)

	J
1	**Actual Cumulative Profit Incentive Fees CTA1**
2	
3	=IF(I3=E3+F3,E3,IF(I3>I2,MIN(MAX(J2,(E3/(E3+F3))*I3),J2+I3-I2),J2))

	K
1	**Actual Cumulative Profit Incentive Fees CTA2**
2	
3	=IF(I3=E3+F3,F3,IF(I3>I2,MIN(MAX(K2,(F3/(E3+F3))*I3),K2+I3-I2),K2))

5 Sample EXCEL Worksheet: Cumulative Profit Incentive Fee Calculation for 3-CTA Case

The calculation for the profit incentive fee distribution in a multimanager fund becomes considerably more complex when there are more than two CTAs. In essence, in this instance, it is necessary to introduce an intermediate calculation for "conditional" actual profit incentive fees (conditional on sufficient available funds). If funds are not sufficient, a second-stage calculation is made to derive the actual profit incentive fees. The following EXCEL worksheet example and formulas illustrate a spreadsheet methodology for calculating the actual cumulative profit incentive fees in a 3-CTA case. An analogous approach would apply to the case of four or more CTAs.

SAMPLE EXCEL WORKSHEET: CUMULATIVE PROFIT
INCENTIVE FEE CALCULATION FOR 3-CTA CASE

	A	B	C	D	E	F	G	H	I	J	K	L
1	NAV1	NAV2	NAV3	PEAK NAV1	PEAK NAV2	PEAK NAV3	THEO. CUM. PIF CTA1	THEO. CUM. PIF CTA2	THEO. CUM. PIF CTA3	POOL NAV	PEAK NAV POOL	CUM. PIF POOL
2	1000	1000	1000	1000	1000	1000				3000	3000	
3	900	1100	800	1000	1100	1000	0	20	0	2800	3000	0
4	1100	800	1200	1100	1100	1200	20	20	40	3100	3100	20
5	1400	1100	1000	1400	1100	1200	80	20	40	3500	3500	100
6	1200	1200	1400	1400	1200	1400	80	40	80	3800	3800	160
7	1400	1000	1600	1400	1200	1600	80	40	120	4000	4000	200
8	800	900	1800	1400	1200	1800	80	40	160	3500	4000	200
9	1600	1300	1400	1600	1300	1800	120	60	160	4300	4300	260
10	1500	1200	1200	1600	1300	1800	120	60	160	3900	4300	260
11	1800	1500	900	1800	1500	1800	160	100	160	4200	4300	260
12	1600	1800	1100	1800	1800	1800	160	160	160	4500	4500	300
13	1800	2200	1600	1800	2200	1800	160	240	160	5600	5600	520
14	2200	1800	2000	2200	2200	2000	240	240	200	6000	6000	600
15	2600	2200	1800	2600	2200	2000	320	240	200	6600	6600	720
16	3000	2500	1800	3000	2500	2000	400	300	200	7300	7300	860
17	3200	2200	2200	3200	2500	2200	440	300	240	7600	7600	920
18	2800	2600	1800	3200	2600	2200	440	320	240	7200	7600	920
19	2600	3000	1400	3200	3000	2200	440	400	240	7000	7600	920
20	3200	2900	1200	3200	3000	2200	440	400	240	7300	7600	920
21												
22												
23												
24												
25												
26												
27												

	M	N	O	P	Q	R	S	T	U
1	COND. ACTUAL CUM. PIF CTA1	COND. ACTUAL CUM. PIF CTA2	COND. ACTUAL CUM. PIF CTA3	SUM OF COND. ACTUALS	SUM OF COND. ACTUALS WITH AN INCREASE	CUM. PIF AVAIL. FOR DISTRIB.	ACTUAL CUM. PIF CTA1	ACTUAL CUM. PIF CTA2	ACTUAL CUM. PIF CTA3
2	0.00	0.00	0.00						
3	0.00	0.00	0.00	0.00	0.00	0.00	0.00	0.00	0.00
4	5.00	5.00	10.00	20.00	20.00	20.00	5.00	5.00	10.00
5	57.14	14.29	28.57	100.00	100.00	100.00	57.14	14.29	28.57
6	64.00	32.00	64.00	160.00	160.00	160.00	64.00	32.00	64.00
7	66.67	33.33	100.00	200.00	200.00	200.00	66.67	33.33	100.00
8	66.67	33.33	100.00	200.00	0.00	0.00	66.67	33.33	100.00
9	91.76	45.88	122.35	260.00	260.00	260.00	91.76	45.88	122.35
10	91.76	45.88	122.35	260.00	0.00	0.00	91.76	45.88	122.35
11	91.76	45.88	122.35	260.00	0.00	0.00	91.76	45.88	122.35
12	100.00	85.88	122.35	308.24	185.88	177.65	95.57	82.08	122.35
13	148.57	222.86	148.57	520.00	520.00	520.00	148.57	222.86	148.57
14	211.76	222.86	176.47	611.09	388.24	377.14	205.71	222.86	171.43
15	303.16	227.37	189.47	720.00	720.00	720.00	303.16	227.37	189.47
16	382.22	286.67	191.11	860.00	860.00	860.00	382.22	286.67	191.11
17	413.06	286.67	225.31	925.03	638.37	633.33	409.80	286.67	223.53
18	413.06	286.67	225.31	925.03	0.00	−5.03	409.80	286.67	223.53
19	413.06	286.67	225.31	925.03	0.00	−5.03	409.80	286.67	223.53
20	413.06	286.67	225.31	925.03	0.00	−5.03	409.80	286.67	223.53
21									
22	The fixed entries for row 2 and the EXCEL formulas for row 3 are as follows (drag and fill columns D through U for								
23	entries in other rows):								
24									
25									
26									
27									

	A	B	C	D	E	F
1	NAV1	NAV2	NAV3	PEAK NAV1	PEAK NAV2	PEAK NAV3
2	1000	1000	1000	1000	1000	1000
3	900	1100	800	=MAX(A3,D2)	=MAX(B3,E2)	=MAX(C3,F2)

	G	H	I	J	K
1	THEOR. CUM. PIF CTA1	THEOR. CUM. PIF CTA2	PIF CTA3	PEAK NAV POOL NAV	POOL
2				3000	3000
3	=0.2*(D3-1000)	=0.2*(E3-1000)	=0.2*(F3-1000)	=(A3+B3+C3)	=MAX(J3,K2)

	L
1	CUM. PIF POOL
2	
3	=0.2*(K3-3000)

	M
1	COND. ACTUAL CUM. PIF CTA1
2	0
3	=IF(L3=G3+H3+I3,G3,IF(L3>L2,MIN(MAX(M2,(G3/(G3+H3+I3))*L3),M2+L3-L2),M2))

	N
1	COND. ACTUAL CUM. PIF CTA2
2	0
3	=IF(L3=G3+H3+I3,H3,IF(L3>L2,MIN(MAX(N2,(H3/(G3+H3+I3))*L3),N2+L3-L2),N2))

	O
1	COND. ACTUAL CUM. PIF CTA3
2	0
3	=IF(L3=G3+H3+I3,I3,IF(L3>L2,MIN(MAX(O2,(I3/(G3+H3+I3))*L3),O2+L3-L2),O2))

	P	Q
1	SUM OF COND. ACTUALS	SUM OF COND. ACTUALS WITH AN INCREASE
2 3	=SUM(M3:O3)	=SUM(IF(M3-M2>0,M3,0)+IF(N3-N2>0,N3,0)+IF(O3-O2>0,O3,0))

	R
1	CUM. PIF AVAILABLE FOR DISTRIB.
2 3	=L3-SUM(IF(M3-M2=0,M3,0)+IF(N3-N2=0,N3,0)+IF(O3-O2=0,O3,0))

	S
1	ACTUAL CUM. PIF CTA1
2 3	=IF($P3=$L3,M3,MAX(S2,IF($Q3>0,M3*($R3/$Q3),S2)))

	T
1	ACTUAL CUM. PIF CTA2
2 3	=IF($P3=$L3,N3,MAX(T2,IF($Q3>0,N3*($R3/$Q3),T2)))

	U
1	ACTUAL CUM. PIF CTA3
2 3	=IF($P3=$L3,O3,MAX(U2,IF($Q3>0,O3*($R3/$Q3),U2)))

Index